AMC'S MOUNTAIN SKILLS MANUAL

THE ESSENTIAL HIKING AND BACKPACKING GUIDE

BY CHRISTIAN BISSON AND JAMIE HANNON

AMC SKILLS SERIES

Appalachian Mountain Club Books
Boston, Massachusetts

AMC is a nonprofit organization, and sales of AMC Books fund our mission of protecting the Northeast outdoors. If you appreciate our efforts and would like to become a member or make a donation to AMC, visit outdoors.org, call 800-372-1758, or contact us at Appalachian Mountain Club, 5 Joy Street, Boston, MA 02108.

outdoors.org/publications/books

Distributed by National Book Network.

Front cover photograph © Dennis Welsh
Back cover photographs (top to bottom) © Maury Eldridge; Jerry Monkman; Herb Swanson; Nathanael Callon; Diana, Creative Commons on Flickr.
Cover design by Joe Morris, Joem Design
Interior design by Abigail Coyle
Illustrations by Deb Eccleston

Library of Congress Cataloging-in-Publication Data

Names: Bisson, Christian A., 1964– author. | Hannon, Jamie, author.
Title: AMC's mountain skills manual : a comprehensive desk reference for
   backpackers of all skill levels / by Christian Bisson and Jamie Hannon.
Description: Boston, Massachusetts : Appalachian Mountain Club, 2017. |
   Includes index.
Identifiers: LCCN 2016046564 (print) | LCCN 2016054164 (ebook) | ISBN
   9781628420258 (pbk. : alk. paper) | ISBN 9781628420265 (epub) | ISBN
   9781628420272 (mobi) | ISBN 9781628420265 (ePub) | ISBN 9781628420272
   (Mobi)
Subjects: LCSH: Backpacking–Handbooks, manuals, etc.
Classification: LCC GV199.6 .B57 2017 (print) | LCC GV199.6 (ebook) | DDC
   796.522–dc23
LC record available at https://lccn.loc.gov/2016046564

The paper used in this publication meets the minimum requirements of the American National Standard for Information Sciences-Permanence of Paper for Printed Library Materials, ANSI Z39.48-1984. ∞

Interior pages contain 30 percent post-consumer recycled fiber.
Cover contains 10 percent post-consumer recycled fiber.
Printed in the United States of America,
using vegetable-based inks.

21 20 19 18 17   1 2 3 4

CONTENTS

❄ 10: WINTER SKILLS

💬 11: GROUPS

🚶 12: ULTRALIGHT BACKPACKING

ACKNOWLEDGMENTS

Many people helped in creating this book. The editors would like to thank Kevin Breunig, Larry Garland, Lisa Gilbert, Aaron Gorban, Ryan Smith, and Jennifer Wehunt at Appalachian Mountain Club for their guidance in helping to shape the quality of this book's content. Shannon Smith was irreplaceable in picking up this project, running with it, and victoriously carrying it over the editing finish line. The AMC volunteers Charles Arsenault, Nathan Baker, Michael Blair, Bill Brook, Stephen Cohen, William Curley, Roger David, Paul Fofonoff, Dale Geslien, Pat Grimm, Michael Henry, Ann Hudnall, Doron Kalir, David Lloyd, Debbie Melita, Sage Narbonne, Michael Nelson, Peg Peterson, David Phillips, Renee Pittelli, Karen Rosencrans, Rich Rosencrans, Rick Silverberg, Ingrid Strauch, Mark Warren, Rick Whitney, and Phil Wilsey offered their time in reading early drafts of the manuscript and provided essential feedback. The editors would like to especially thank Colby Meehan and Lindsey Mersereau of AMC for the hours they spent looking over each chapter and for their incredible knowledge and expertise throughout. Deb Eccleston provided top-notch illustrations on very tight deadlines, and we are grateful for her quick turnaround and professional services. Abigail Coyle designed a practical interior layout that makes for an effortless reading experience. This book was a collaborative effort throughout the Appalachian Mountain Club, and we appreciate everyone who helped in its creation. Any errors of commission or omission are the responsibility of the editors.

INTRODUCTION
TAKING TO THE WOODS

Why go to the woods? Why go to the mountains?

You can make a compelling case that we are at our happiest in our amenity-rich cities or on our cozy couches watching television. For those among us fortunate enough to be comfortable, there is little that causes us real physical discomfort. We control the temperature in our houses. We choose the freshest food at grocery stores and farmers markets. We can even find entertainment in the palms of our hands. We are almost never more than a few moments away from talking with a friend or a family member. But being in the woods and mountains can mean that we get damp or cold, that we must eat unusual food, that we risk injury and illness, and that we must endure periods of intense quiet, stillness, and solitude. Yet almost 35 million people per year turn to the woods and mountains of North America to hike and backpack. So what draws us there?

Henry David Thoreau once wrote, "In Wildness is the preservation of the world." At first one might think he meant *wilderness:* craggy, misty peaks or deep, thick forests. But Thoreau was not talking about an actual place or landscape. He meant the wild, internal landscape within. Thoreau knew that inside each of us is the same boundless, untamed nature that can be found in a field of wildflowers, the call of a bull moose, and a swirling alpine storm. This internal, primal wildness is what first calls us to the woods and mountains then draws us there time and again.

Thoreau's idea, conceived in the mid-1800s, is even more resonant today. The pace of our lives is ever accelerating, with pressures to communicate, produce, consume, and achieve more than at any other time in human history. In fact, psychologists and biologists tell us our bodies and minds are challenged by these contemporary demands. Millions of years of evolution have not fully prepared us for the past hundred years of technological development. Thoreau saw this effect in his own time, and it has only hastened. Heading into the forests and mountains helps us simplify, return to ourselves, repair our frazzled nerves, and hear, once again, the wildness within. We return to our modern lives with clearer perspective, renewed attention, greater confidence, closer relationships, and more vitality.

We find and nourish our wildness in many ways. Maybe it is in the sublime adventure of summiting a 4,000-foot peak or in the deep satisfaction of successfully navigating untracked forests. Maybe the wildness is found in the joyous camaraderie of a group of friends sharing a delicious meal or in the intense solitude of a late-autumn alpine bog. Perhaps it is found in the majesty of a mountain range, alight in alpenglow, or in the delicate song of a hermit thrush deep in the understory of the forest. In all of this, wildness is finding and restoring feelings of connectedness—with the natural world, with each other, with ourselves. Whatever form it takes, heeding this call is both the reason and the reward for traveling into the wilderness. Whether we go for a day, a week, or a month, going out truly is going home.

HOW TO USE THIS BOOK

Heading into the backcountry, whether for a brief excursion or a major expedition, should be joyful and as simple as possible. This book is intended to facilitate exactly that. If you are a first-time hiker, this book is full of the basics, ready to prepare you for your first mile, first day, or first weekend. Maybe you have had a taste of the backcountry and are yearning for a deeper experience. This book can help you refine your techniques and give you ideas for improving, be it by traveling faster, finding a more comfortable way to camp, exploring more safely, or just sharing the experience with others. And if you are an experienced explorer and trip leader, this book offers numerous new ideas and ways to professionalize your practices. Look for the "Pro Tips" throughout the text.

Different readers may use this book in different ways. We recommend that back-country novices start at the very beginning and read chapter by chapter. To facilitate this front-to-back approach, we've begun with the most elemental aspects—trip planning, land ethics, and weather—that you must consider before so much as choosing your outdoor destination. From there, we delve into progressively advanced material, saving the most complex skills for last. (You don't need to know how to tie a trucker's hitch knot on your very first day hike, but you do need to know how much water to carry to avoid dehydration.)

Intermediate readers may also choose to read front to back. You might be surprised by how many considerations you've unwittingly glossed over—or even lucked out on—on previous trips. Advanced readers may pick and choose as needed, treating the book as a quick reference guide when a specific question arises or for gaining deeper insight into certain skills, such as ultralight hiking. We've also saved some of our leadership tips for last, when the onetime novice has become a seasoned backpacker. But then again, even pros might choose to read front to back, treating this book as an opportunity to reinstill best practices. Each chapter has been vetted by members of AMC's Outdoor Learning and Leadership team, and therefore the information presented coincides with AMC's best practices.

We are both National Outdoor Leadership School (NOLS) instructors and seasoned leaders in the field of outdoor education. Christian, who has a doctorate in education, has taught backpacking at the higher-education level for 20 years and has been an outdoor instructor for 30 years. He now teaches Adventure Education at New Hampshire's Plymouth State University and has taught at Wyoming's NOLS since 1990, specializing in wilderness backpacking for outdoor educators. In other words, when it comes to training the pros, he's a pro. Same goes for Jamie, who, as an associate professor of Adventure Education at Plymouth State, teaches courses in both practical skills and theory. Jamie has been leading outdoor programming since 1981. Both of us live in New Hampshire and hike regularly with our families—so you know if we trust the information and guidance in this book to keep our own kids safe, you can rely on it for yourself.

Throughout this book, we will refer to our experiences in the field guiding students as they learn the basics of outdoor travel. Gendered pronouns will be used when such language requires correct subject-verb agreement; however, all examples used throughout apply to any gender.

We hope you take the skills you learn in this book and apply them to your own adventures outdoors so that you can not merely survive in the wilderness—you can thrive.

CHAPTER 1
BEFORE YOU GO

Walking out the door is easy. Grab your coat and keys, and you're ready for a stroll around the neighborhood. You can enjoy the accessibility and exercise of city life on a whim, but enjoying the great outdoors will require some planning.

As with a walk around the block, the most basic thing you need to go hiking is something you carry everywhere: your body. Easy to overlook, our most basic biological needs become something we must plan for when venturing outside the comfort of our normal routines. The wilderness is so remote that taking care of these needs requires thinking of them in a new light.

This chapter covers serving those needs, and others, through three topics you should study before you go: trip planning; the environment and how to properly care for it while hiking; and backcountry weather. These are all subjects that should be considered and planned for before even leaving your house.

→ TRIP PLANNING

Many beginner hikers (and even some veteran backpackers) believe that planning involves getting some gear together, throwing some food and water into a backpack, grabbing a map, and driving to the trailhead. The reality is that planning a successful day hike or an overnight backpacking trip requires careful preparation to ensure comfort, enjoyment, and safety. This is why we would like to offer a new axiom: "Proper Prior Planning Promotes Preferred Expedition." Of course, here the emphasis is on "proper" planning—meaning not only is it important to plan ahead, but that it is most important to properly plan before heading out to a trailhead.

The White Mountain National Forest and New Hampshire Fish and Game Department has issued and promotes a hiker responsibility code called "hikeSafe" that reinforces many elements of the Proper Prior Planning adage. It's a great place for us to start.

1

As a hiker, you are responsible for:

1. **Knowledge and gear.** Become self-reliant by learning about the terrain, conditions, local weather, and your equipment before you start.

2. **Leaving your plans.** Tell someone where you are going, the trails you are hiking, when you'll return, and your emergency plans.

3. **Staying together.** When you start as a group, hike as a group and end as a group. Pace your hike to the slowest person.

4. **Turning back.** Weather changes quickly in the mountains. Fatigue and unexpected conditions can also affect your hike. Know your limitations and when to postpone your hike. The mountains will be there another day.

5. **Dealing with emergencies.** Even if you are headed out for just an hour, an unexpected hurdle such as an injury, severe weather, or a wrong turn could become life-threatening. Don't assume you will be rescued; know how to rescue yourself.

6. **Sharing the hiker code with others.**

Beyond knowing the code, proper planning means that most elements of a hiking experience have been addressed beforehand—that many details have been thought over. In the book *AMC's Guide to Outdoor Leadership*, author Alex Kosseff proposes a set of prompts to achieve proper planning. These questions are:

Why?
Who?
Where?
When?
What?
What if?

These questions are an excellent place to start because when they are carefully answered, they help us cover many of the elements of an outing. But to be more thorough, let us add three more prompting questions to Kosseff's planning system:

How?
How much?
Then what?

With these additional questions, we will be able to make decisions and plan for all of the essential components of a day hike, a weekend trip, or even a long wilderness expedition. Let's begin by addressing these essential questions.

WHY?

This is perhaps the most essential question of them all, but it is too often overshadowed by other questions, such as *where* should we go and *what* food should we bring. Yet these other questions cannot be truly answered if you cannot clearly identify your reasons for wanting to leave the comfort of your home. Asking yourself (and all other participants) *why* you want to go on a specific outdoor excursion will help clarify your personal goals and desired outcomes.

Too many hiking and backpacking trips end in frustration simply because the participants—sometimes friends, significant others, or family members—have differing goals for a shared outdoor experience. Embarking on a three-day backpacking trip with someone committed to bagging a peak via a difficult route while the rest of the expedition members are going along to relax, take pictures, and enjoy the wildflowers is bound to create tension, resentment, and even conflict among the expedition members.

It is essential for expedition members to discuss and agree upon common goals for the outing. If you are making a solo trip, it is still important to keep in mind *why* you are setting off alone and to set goals and put limits on how far you are willing to push yourself (or your good fortune) to achieve these goals.

Once shared goals and personal outcomes have been identified and discussed among group members, it is appropriate to continue planning your trip. Make sure that these goals remain flexible, however. Kosseff advises us not to engrave these goals in stone but to mark them in clay—and rightly so. If environmental or terrain conditions change or are not what you expected, or if a group member's physical condition worsens, be ready to adjust your trip goals. There is one goal that should be the core of all outdoor outings and shared by all members of an outdoor trip: to come back alive and uninjured. Safety and care for self and others, plus learning, enjoyment, and caring for the environment, should always be at the top of your list of goals for hiking and backpacking trips.

WHO?

Knowing who is coming on an outdoor trip can greatly affect your goals. If children are joining your excursion, the goals for your trip will change, and so will your route, the gear you bring, and your trail rations; it might mean more gummy bears as trail rewards. (See page 248 in Chapter 11, Groups, for more tips on how to plan an outdoor excursion with children.) It is important to know how many people are coming, as well as the participants' ages, levels of outdoor experience, physical abilities, and pertinent medical information, such as allergies and medications. It is also important to know how many people are coming due to limitations on permits, Leave No Trace ethics, and land management agency restrictions.

Another very important but too often overlooked element of trip planning is identifying and agreeing on leaders. It might be hard to imagine that a hiking trip among friends or family members needs a leader, but thanks to the "groupthink" effect and the often-unconscious tendency to shift or drop responsibilities, leaderless groups can make poor decisions when presented with unexpected challenges.

1

When faced with a serious and risky situation, the following situations can occur:

1.   No one speaks up to voice his or her concerns or doubts, and the group keeps on doing something that is increasingly risky—with no decision made. Or,

2.   The most vocal member of the group, who may not be the one with the most outdoor experience, makes wrong decisions.

In either case, the result could be devastating for the entire group. Of course, we are not advising that all backpacking trips be run by a self-appointed or elected leader who dictates every decision, from how much salt should go in the soup to where the shelter should be set up. But group members should agree on who will make the final decision if a serious, risk-related circumstance arises. This role should go to the member with the most outdoor experience, regardless of gender or age.

THE OUTDOORS IS FOR EVERYONE

One thing to consider in planning the *who* of your trip is whether anyone in your group has an impairment of any kind. If someone does, then accessibility becomes an issue for the whole group. This does not mean you should assume the individual cannot accomplish the goals of the group, just that his or her ability to do so must be accommodated. Many trails have been updated for accessibility and more are added or modified every year. The outdoors should be enjoyed by all, and an inclusive hike involves some planning. For more information and resources on how to plan an inclusive outing, see page 266 in Chapter 11, Groups.

WHERE?

Where should we go? This is commonly the leading question for a backpacking expedition or a day hike. Even so, we've already learned that this question should not be the first one considered, not before we know *why* we are going and *who* is coming with us. Once these two questions have been carefully answered, *where* to go becomes one of the most exciting parts of trip planning. You might even feel that time has been suspended while you pore over maps, browse through guidebooks, or listen attentively to fellow hikers describing the places they've visited.

Deciding where to go will also help you identify some very important details for your trip, such as:

1.   How many miles will be covered in the allotted time?

2.   What will be the distance covered each day?

3.   What activities or interesting features will the route provide? These could include swimming holes, fishing streams, geocaches, spring flowers, alpine zones, signs of human heritage, vistas, etc.

4. Will the route be a loop? Or will you retrace your path so you can return to the same trailhead you started from? Will the route be a linear trip, requiring you to place a second vehicle at another trailhead, or will you need to plan for a shuttle service (for example, AMC's White Mountain shuttle, in New Hampshire)?

5. Will the hike be mostly on trails or mainly off-trail?

6. Will the route be on public or private land?

7. Will the route traverse designated wilderness areas?

8. Which camping or traveling regulations should be followed while traveling in these areas, especially if they are designated wilderness areas? Regulations could include group size, fires, bear-proofing food, and pets, to name a few.

9. Do you need to make reservations for specific camping sites, tent platforms, shelters, or huts? And is your chosen site open for the season during the dates you want to visit?

10. Which natural hazards might you encounter on your route? These could include major river crossings, steep slopes, scree terrain, boulder fields, areas above treeline, slick bedrock, and difficult off-trail sections.

FIGURE 1. Collaboration is key to trip planning. Be sure to include the whole group when discussing common goals for your outing.

11. Does the trailhead(s) provide ample parking space, especially popular locations during holiday weekends? Note that carpooling is always encouraged for group trips.

12. Do you need to pay to park your vehicle at the trailhead?

13. Are there exit points along the route that can be used in case of an emergency? Determine bailout routes before your trip.

As you see, there are many questions to be answered when choosing a route, so take the time to look at maps, read guidebooks, and ask public land managers and friends who have experience in the places you're thinking of hiking or backpacking. Blog posts and trip reports also provide valuable and updated information before you set out, but never rely solely on a map or trip details you glean from a blog.

WHEN?

Deciding when to go is not only about determining when you can spend time away from your daily life and work schedule to explore wild places, but also about figuring out when the best time is to visit these places. You might need to take into consideration a few time-related factors. For instance, which season is best to visit this area according to your goals? Will snow or ice still be on the trails at certain altitudes or on the north side of some mountains? Will water supplies be readily available during that season? Will you be going during hunting season? If so, what precautions should be taken? What about insects? Are you ready to deal with swarms of blackflies, mosquitoes, horse flies, and ticks, or should you avoid their prime hatching periods? Camping during the buggy season has its obvious disadvantages, but also some advantages: You might have to deal with bloodthirsty pests, but you likely won't have to deal with overcrowded trails and campsites. The same can be said for the weather. Some seasons will bring more rain and foul weather in certain areas, but you might find more solitude during the rainy season. Again, it is all about your trip goals.

Once you've selected a season, you still have to choose a specific set of days. Here, it is all about the crowding effect of holidays and long weekends. Make sure you're aware of your route's popularity before choosing when to go. If you, like so many of us, are going to the mountains and forests to seek solitude and quiet experiences in nature, it would be inadvisable to plan your trip at the peak of the outdoor tourist season for your trail of choice. Whenever possible, fill out trip reports for the land management agency where you are recreating so that they can track trail and campsite usage during specific times. Be prepared to adapt your route and campsite accordingly—especially for sites where the rule is first come, first served.

WHAT?

The *what* of trip planning will be covered in great detail in the following chapters, but in a few words, it refers to the personal and group gear you should bring on a trip, as well as what type of food to pack for your excursion. Here again, answers to questions of *why*, *who*, *where*, and *when* will have a direct effect on the gear you select for your trip. For instance, traveling to the White Mountains of New Hampshire to climb a 4,000-foot peak with a group of experienced friends in mid-April would lead you to include microspikes and hiking poles on your list of personal gear. For the same trip, you'd also need a certain amount of high-caloric food.

To help with this phase of trip planning, we've included personal and group gear checklists for various seasons in the appendices of this book. Take the time to read through these checklists and modify them to your own needs. Trip leaders should send out gear lists to all participants prior to a trip. Even experienced and professional outdoor leaders use checklists to plan their expeditions. Be like them and avoid the classic "Oh, no!"—often uttered over an open backpack followed by an angry, "I can't believe I forgot to bring . . ."

What to bring also means having the ten essential pieces of gear, a list developed by The Mountaineers. Regardless of the length of your trip, from a three-hour hike to a three-day or three-week expedition, carrying the ten essentials is a must. They are:

1. **Map**

2. **Compass—and the knowledge to use one**

3. **Warm clothing:**
   - Warm upper-body layer
   - Warm lower-body layer
   - Warm hat

4. **Extra food and water**

5. **Flashlight or headlamp**

6. **Matches/fire starter**

7. **First-aid kit and repair kit**

8. **Whistle**

9. **Waterproof/windproof upper- and lower-body layers**

10. **Pocket knife**

Of course, some of the ten essentials are only as good as your ability to use them.

1

A compass, a whistle, and a first-aid kit are often carried by hikers who have very little knowledge of how to properly use them. Make sure you know how to use your navigation and emergency equipment before going out. See Chapter 4, Navigation (page 79), for more on navigation and Chapter 7, Prevention and Safety (page 144), for more on basic first-aid skills. In Chapter 3, Gear (page 41), you'll find more on the Ten Essentials.

A few additional questions to consider during Proper Prior Planning: What should I know before going on this outdoor adventure? *Which* outdoor technical skills should I refresh, practice, or learn before I go? *Which* newly acquired piece of equipment should I test before using it on an outing? Wouldn't it be safer and less frustrating to test this new stove at home rather than try to learn how to use it in the field? Would it not be better to really learn how to orient a map with a compass at home before trying to guess how they work together during an off-trail hike? At home you can always consult the Internet, but you can't assume you'll have a great Wi-Fi connection on a remote mountainside.

NEW HAMPSHIRE HIKESAFE CARD

In 2015, the New Hampshire Fish and Game Department, which is in charge of the great majority of seach-and-rescue missions in the state, began to issue what's called a hikeSafe card. This voluntary card insures its owner for any expenses relating to a search and evacuation. This "free rescue" insurance card is a good way to plan for the financial ramifications of a "What if?" situation. The card, which in 2016 cost $25 per person and $35 per family, is valid for one year (January 1 to December 31) and can be purchased online at hikesafe.com. You do not need to carry the card with you while hiking or backpacking. **Important note:** This card is not like a Monopoly "Get Out of Jail Free" card. New Hampshire Fish and Game clearly explains that "if you or anyone in your hiking group acts recklessly—or fails to practice proper preparation as outlined by the hiker responsibility code—resulting in Search and Rescue, you could be liable to pay the costs of your search and rescue mission."

HOW?

The question of *how* refers to how you get to the trailhead. This might seem obvious, but there are a few planning details to consider. The first concerns your route: If your hike is linear, you may need to plan for two vehicles, leaving one at your entrance trailhead and another at your exit trailhead. This system is obviously the most complicated in terms of time, mileage, and cost.

Or you could choose a route with a single trailhead, of which there are a couple of types: a loop or circular route in which you leave from one trailhead and use various trails or off-trail navigation to return to the same trailhead; and a backtrack route, where you follow a trail to your destination, then use that same trail to return

1

to your original trailhead. With a single trailhead, you obviously save on time, mileage, gas, and parking permit expenses. In addition, you reduce your carbon footprint for the trip by using only one vehicle. You can also look into the possibility of using a shuttle service, or carpooling, to reach or to return from a trailhead. One note of caution: Don't leave valuables in your car at the trailhead.

How to get there is also about determining the highways, roads, and secondary roads you will take to reach your trailhead. Don't forget that most car GPS systems are designed for urban and highway environments. Entrusting a vehicle or smartphone GPS to get you to a remote trailhead might force you to have your first adventure before you even park your car. Use a good road map; it will condition your mind to pay attention to your surroundings before your boots hit the trail.

WHAT IF?

"What if?" is your risk-management plan, and you should always answer it before leaving home. This plan should include the emergency exits along your route, also known as evacuation points. Knowing where these trailheads are, as well as any roads you can reach along your route, will allow you to bail out from your hiking adventure or to evacuate a hiking member or yourself, if needed. Some routes will have many possible exit points, while others will have only one or two. The worst-case scenario is a hiking route that provides no emergency-exit point, other than the trailhead back at the start or at your destination. Once you have identified your possible evacuation points, make sure to indicate them on your map.

Knowing where to quickly get out of the field is important, but what if you cannot get out? What if you are unable to continue due to injury, illness, or environmental conditions? It is critical to your risk-management plan to write down on an actual piece of paper—no digital devices, which can lose power in the event of an emergency!—the phone numbers of the local or regional agencies responsible for conducting search and rescues in the area of your trip. Always have this list with you and keep it in a zipper-closure bag to protect it from getting wet. This obviously implies you have a way to communicate with the agencies. Thus, your "What if?" plan should consider the likelihood of being able to use a cell phone, a satellite phone, or a personal locator beacon (PLB). We'll cover more on these devices and the options they provide on pages 97–100 in Chapter 3, Gear.

Finally, leave a detailed travel plan with someone responsible whom you trust and who will be expecting your return. This plan should include information such as the day and time of your departure and your return, the details of the route you plan to follow, information about the campsites you expect to use, evacuation points you have identified, where you will park your car/s, contact information for any coleaders, and, finally, the names and phone numbers of all party members. For an example, see Appendix B, page 290.

OTHER FACTORS

1

How Much?

Although hiking and backpacking are two of the more affordable outdoor activities, there are still some costs to consider. In your planning, you'll want to look at the expenses your trip will incur. These might include travel, permits, camping fees, shelter and lodge fees, specialized maps, any gear that you don't already own or can't borrow or rent, and consumables such as food and camping fuel.

It might be appropriate to divide some of the costs among you and your fellow group members. Of course, if you are going out on a hike as a family or by yourself, you will need to absorb all expenses and make sure the trip you are planning is within your budget. Don't forget that, more often than not, club membership will provide you certain discounts for camping or lodging. For more information on AMC's lodge and hut discounts, visit outdoors.org/membership.

Then What?

It might seem strange to think about the end of your hike before it even begins, but good trip planning should include next steps for after the hike. Returning from the field happy and rejuvenated with sore muscles and a strong desire for a shower might lead you to think that once you're back at home you can afford to drop your pack on the floor and forget about it for a few days. The reality is you should plan for an after-trip clean-up right from the beginning. Returning home sometimes involves as much work as preparing your pack for the trail.

Here are a few of the tasks that need to be completed and prioritized upon your return:

1. First and foremost, make sure to contact the person you entrusted to keep an eye out for your return. Consider calling or texting this person as soon as you are out of the field, ideally at the trailhead. It would be unfortunate if you didn't contact them at the trailhead then experienced a problem on your drive home. Any later-than-planned return home could result in a friend or family member activating an unnecessary search for you on the trail. Be proactive and keep them posted.

2. To prevent mold or mildew, all nylon material should be thoroughly dry before storing—especially your shelter and sleeping bag.

3. All cookware and personal eating utensils and dishware should be cleaned and sterilized. Using a dishwasher or hand washing in hot water will do the trick.

4. Leftover food and garbage needs to be properly disposed of.

5. For any electronic devices used only on the trip, remove batteries before storing to preserve battery life and to avoid accidental acid leaks.

1

6.   If you are using a down sleeping bag, check the bag's cleaning instructions. It might be appropriate to gently dry it in a dryer with a tennis ball to restore its loft.

7.   If you are using an open-cell camping mattress, remember that it should be stored with the valve open, allowing any moisture to escape.

8.   Remember, sleeping bags should not be stored in compression stuff sacks. Use the storage bag your sleeping bag came with or simply hang it. By doing so, you will protect your bag's insulation and help keep its original volume.

9.   Hiking boots should be thoroughly dry before storing. Place them in an area with a warm and gentle air flow. If you wear leather hiking boots, consider cleaning them, drying them, and waxing them to protect the suppleness of the leather.

10. Finally, wash your personal clothing. Trust us: It will smell.

How to Plan?

Any experienced hiker and backpacker will tell you trip planning is an art as well as a science. It is an art because good planning is intuitive: It requires you to imagine your future needs while drawing from your past experiences. And it's a science because it requires you to be systematic. As explained in this chapter, the best way to do so is to use checklists. Airplane pilots still use checklists before departure because they know that, despite their training and experience, they are still human and can make common mistakes and forget things. We have seen seasoned outdoor leaders planning 30-day wilderness expeditions for groups of twelve people still forget to pack their own sleeping bags. So, please, consider using a checklist when planning your next expedition. The various checklists we have included in Appendix A on page 287 will help you get organized. Don't forget: These lists are only starting points; the best checklist will be the one you create for your own needs.

→ LAND ETHICS

Before you set so much as a boot outside, consider how doing so will impact the environment—and that includes your home turf and the frontcountry, as well as the backcountry. Taking steps to minimize your footprint is a crucial part of trip planning and should inform your decision-making from the very beginning. Below, we'll cover land ethics for three distinct areas: the backcountry, the frontcountry, and "urbancountry" (at home).

BACKCOUNTRY LAND ETHIC

When we discuss the merits of practicing Leave No Trace (LNT) camping with our students, we often play devil's advocate and argue that the best "leave no trace" practice would be to stay at home. Of course, this argument is designed to make our students understand that going camping or even hiking will have some form of impact on the land, and that truly leaving no trace while enjoying the great outdoors is simply impossible. What we have to understand is that outdoor enthusiasts can learn to protect and conserve the beauty of the places they love by taking a few actions that will minimize their impacts on the environment.

The LNT program in the United States was created in the 1980s as a cooperative effort between the U.S. Forest Service, the National Park Service, and the Bureau of Land Management. Its purpose was to develop hiking and camping principles that promoted a new wilderness land ethic. In the early '90s, the U.S. Forest Service partnered with the National Outdoor Leadership School to develop a science-based curriculum for training public land managers, outdoor professionals, and outdoor recreationists. Today, the seven LNT principles are widely accepted as the seven commandments of any serious and educated hiker or backpacker. They are easy to understand and, with some guidance, quite simple to put in practice.

It is important to note that in many locations, public land agencies have used some of the seven LNT principles to establish rules and regulations for outdoor users. This means that not practicing some of these principles results in infractions with concrete consequences, such as a fine or expulsion from a public land area. There are some pristine natural areas in the United States you cannot enter without demonstrating you have received basic LNT training.

LNT trainings are available to all recreationists and/or professionals in the United States and Canada. The training structure includes three levels: (1) the LNT Master Educator certification, a five-day course designed for professionals in the outdoor industry who intend to instruct LNT Trainer or Awareness Workshops; (2) the LNT Trainer certification, a two-day course designed for educators, guides, agency employees, and other outdoor professionals that allows LNT Trainers to provide LNT Awareness Workshops to the general public and outdoor recreationists; and (3) the LNT Awareness Workshop certification, a short training that can last from 30 minutes to a few hours, intended to bring awareness to various groups, such as educators, children, college students, outdoor camp counselors, Girl Scouts, Boy Scouts, trail crews, hiking club members, and others interested in Leave No Trace skills and ethics. AMC provides LNT training courses throughout the year, and it might be wise to take one of these formal training workshops if you are an avid hiker or backpacker, or if you intend to lead others into the backcountry.

LNT principles also must be included in a common-sense approach to risk management. We often remind our students that in a critical incident, any actions taken to mitigate the situation should prioritize the following elements, in this order:

- Safety of the individual (i.e., yourself and others)
- Safety of the equipment
- Safety of the environment

1

If you keep this in mind, you will be able to respond to an emergency without feeling bad about the impact your action might have on the environment. For instance, in a situation where someone in your party has broken through ice and is soaked, with wet clothing, it would be appropriate to set up camp near the site of the incident, even if it is near a water source, and to build a large fire to dry the wet clothing while you are actively warming the person. You might be breaking a few LNT principles, but this situation calls for you to prioritize the unfortunate companion.

THE SEVEN LNT PRINCIPLES

Below you will find the seven LNT principles adopted by the Center for Outdoor Ethics, which manages and promotes LNT in North America. Read carefully both the principles and the examples of concrete actions you can take to meet them. Note that these are only a few samples and that throughout the book we will highlight more specific strategies to minimize your environmental and social impact during your outdoor excursions. Look for the round symbol with the "Leave No Trace" label, shown below, to quickly find examples. The numbers correspond to the seven LNT principles.

 Plan Ahead and Prepare

- Know the regulations and special concerns for the area you'll visit.
- Prepare for extreme weather, hazards, and emergencies.
- Schedule your trip to avoid times of high use.
- Visit in small groups when possible. Consider splitting larger groups into smaller groups.
- Repackage food to minimize waste.
- Use a map and compass to eliminate the use of marking paint, rock cairns, or flagging.

1

2 Travel and Camp on Durable Surfaces

- Durable surfaces include established trails and campsites, rock, gravel, dry grasses, or snow.
- Protect riparian areas by camping at least 200 feet from lakes and streams.
- Good campsites are found, not made. Altering a site is not necessary.
- In popular areas, concentrate use on existing trails and campsites; walk single file in the middle of the trail, even when wet or muddy; and keep campsites small. Focus activity in areas where vegetation is absent.
- In pristine areas, disperse use to prevent the creation of campsites and trails, and avoid places where impacts are just beginning.

3 Dispose of Waste Properly

- Pack it in, pack it out. Inspect your campsite and rest areas for trash or spilled foods. Pack out all trash, leftover food, and litter.
- Deposit solid human waste in cat holes dug 6 to 8 inches deep, at least 200 feet from water, camp, and trails. Cover and disguise the cat hole when finished.
- Pack out toilet paper and hygiene products.
- To wash yourself or your dishes, carry water 200 feet away from streams or lakes, and use small amounts of biodegradable soap. Scatter strained dishwater.

4 Leave What You Find

- Preserve the past: Examine, but do not touch, cultural or historic structures and artifacts.
- Leave rocks, plants, and other natural objects as you find them.
- Avoid introducing or transporting nonnative species.
- Do not build structures or furniture and do not dig trenches.

5 Minimize Campfire Impacts

- Campfires can leave a lasting impact on the backcountry. Use a lightweight stove for cooking and enjoy a candle lantern for light.
- Where fires are permitted, use established fire rings, fire pans, or mound fires.

- Keep fires small. Use only sticks from the ground that can be broken by hand.
- Burn all wood and coals to ash, put out campfires completely, and then scatter the cooled ashes.

1

6 Respect Wildlife

- Observe wildlife from a distance. Do not follow or approach animals.
- Never feed animals. Feeding wildlife damages their health, alters natural behaviors, and exposes them to predators and other dangers.
- Protect wildlife and your food by storing rations and trash securely.
- Learn the area's regulations on pets and obey those rules. If you cannot control your dog, leave him at home.
- Avoid wildlife during sensitive times, such as when animals are mating, nesting, raising young, or during winter.

7 Be Considerate of Other Visitors

- Respect other visitors and protect the quality of their experience.
- Be courteous. Yield to other users on the trail.
- Step to the downhill side of the trail when encountering horses and other pack stock.
- Take breaks and camp away from trails and other visitors.
- Let nature's sounds prevail. Avoid loud voices and noises.

The above is taken from the official Leave No Trace website, lnt.org.

ADAPTING LNT PRACTICES TO THE ECOSYSTEM

Although this book focuses on hiking and backpacking skills related to forest and mountain regions, the LNT practices presented here are relevant for other ecosystems as well. The LNT principles were created with wide application in mind and can be adapted to various environments.

For instance, the third LNT principle, "Dispose of Waste Properly," instructs you to dig a cat hole away from water sources, campsites, and official trails to properly dispose of human waste when traveling in forest or mountain regions. Along certain seashores, however, it would be more appropriate to use a portable latrine that would allow you to carry out your waste. Be aware of any regulations that might apply to the areas you visit.

Another example of ecosystem adaptation, this time associated with the second LNT principle, "Travel and Camp on Durable Surfaces," states that in forest re-

1

gions, it is appropriate to disperse a group of hikers when traveling off-trail to minimize the chance of creating a new trail. That practice would not be appropriate for the desert regions of the American Southwest, however. When traveling in very fragile terrain, such as cryptogamic or cryptobiotic soil (a biological soil crust that hosts a rich and delicate community of living organisms), it might be better to walk single file, matching the leader's steps. There are many other LNT adaptations for various ecosystems and outdoor activities.

Although this book is not the proper forum to identify and explain all of these variations, we recommend you review the *Outdoor Skills & Ethics* booklets published by the LNT Center for Outdoor Ethics. These focus on LNT principles and techniques for specific areas or activities. The collection includes the titles *Alaska Wildlands, Northeast Mountains, Pacific Northwest, Rocky Mountains, Sierra Nevada*, and more. These booklets also cover various outdoor activities: *Fishing, Mountain Biking, Rock Climbing*, and more. All of these can be purchased from the LNT website (lnt.org).

FRONTCOUNTRY LAND ETHIC

Traveling or camping in the backcountry will bring you to pristine areas untouched by human beings, perhaps even wilderness or primitive regions. But many of us also enjoy camping and traveling in the frontcountry. For the purpose of this book, the frontcountry could be defined as the area within one hour of a trailhead or where camping is done in established campsites adjacent to a road—in other words, car camping.

In this environment the LNT principles are still applicable, but their practices are modified significantly. Most often these locations provide services, such as latrines, outhouses or bathrooms; fire pits; trash cans, bear-proof trash cans, bear-proof boxes, or bear-proof poles. In these locations, it is best practice to use the provided facilities and to follow all of the rules and regulations specific to these areas.

Practicing LNT skills in the frontcountry can be more important than you'd think. These areas often receive more visitors and thus face a greater potential impact than many backcountry areas. It is imperative to practice good LNT skills when using or visiting these locations.

"URBANCOUNTRY" LAND ETHIC

When discussing LNT principles and ethics with our students, we invite them to consider the idea that practicing LNT skills in the back- or frontcountry is important to the conservation of wild and natural areas, but it's not enough. Minimizing one's impact during a hike or a backpacking trip is the right thing to do, but minimizing one's daily effect on the environment back at home will have an even greater positive footprint on the planet. This is true for all of us. Minimizing our

1

footprint on the environment by carefully looking at how we shelter, transport, and feed ourselves on a daily basis will have a greater conservation impact over a single year than all of the wilderness expeditions one experiences in a lifetime. With climate change a stark reality, reducing our own carbon footprints will be better for the planet than all the "light steps" we can take on our outdoor travels.

How you can reduce your ecological footprint on the planet is a whole other book, but nevertheless, adopting backcountry LNT principles should be only one component of your overall land ethic.

➔ WEATHER

Similar to land ethics, weather should be in the forefront of your mind at all times, from the moment you conceive a backpacking trip. If you first think about weather when a drop of rain hits you, you're way too late—not by minutes or hours but by months. Mastering backcountry weather wisdom is a big step on the path to becoming an expert mountain traveler, and it's something you can practice in your daily life. Although mountain weather can differ greatly from that at ground level, much less in the middle of cities, you can and should practice identifying common signs—such as those heralding cold and warm fronts—anywhere. (Not only is it safer to recognize certain weather signs, it is satisfying to be sipping a hot drink under a tarp in your tidy camp as the first afternoon shower rolls through.)

Most people head into the backcountry to heighten their sensitivity to the world around them, and learning weather's signs is a perfect focus for this increased

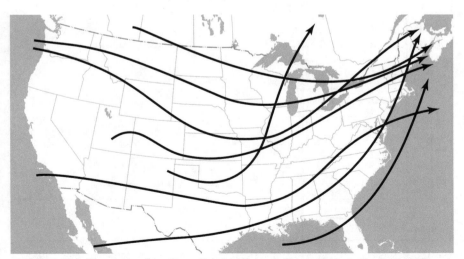

FIGURE 2. This illustration from Peter Marchand's book *Nature Guide to the Northern Forest* (AMC Books, 2010) illustrates how weather patterns across North America converge in the mountainous regions of the Northeast.

1

awareness. That said, you can never completely master Mother Nature. One of the great variables of any trip into the mountains of the Northeast is the weather. In every season, weather conditions can change quickly, and stormy weather is possible any time of the year. As air masses cross the North American continent, typical high-altitude wind patterns drive them toward New England, where they all tend to converge: Cold, dry air from the polar regions of Canada; wet weather moving across the Midwest; and hot air masses sweeping up from the Southwest all mix with the humid ocean air masses of the Atlantic. It is the interaction of these different air masses that creates weather events, such as rain, snow, lightning, high winds, heat waves, cold spells, and more. Add to this mixing of air masses the potent influence of mountain topography, and weather becomes one of the most dynamic elements of mountain travel.

The speed and range of weather changes in this region are legendary. With all this variability, however, there are still many regular patterns you can learn to recognize and, to a certain degree, predict with an educated guess. There are also long-term climatic trends averaging 30 years or more that are fairly reliable for each season of the year, as well as for given regions and topographies. Knowing these patterns will help any mountain traveler make reasonably accurate weather predictions, sometimes stretching up to three days into the future. A little weather knowledge is an essential foundation for staying safe and enjoying your trip.

HEAT INDEX
TEMPERATURE (°F)

RELATIVE HUMIDITY (percent)	80	82	84	86	88	90	92	94	96	98	100	102	104	106	108	110
40	80	81	83	85	88	91	94	97	101	105	109	114	119	124	130	136
45	80	82	84	87	89	93	96	100	104	109	114	119	124	130	137	
50	81	83	85	88	91	95	99	103	108	113	118	124	131	137		
55	81	84	86	89	93	97	101	106	112	117	124	130	137			
60	82	84	88	91	95	100	105	110	116	123	129	137				
65	82	85	89	93	98	103	108	114	121	128	136					
70	83	86	90	95	100	105	112	119	126	136						
75	84	88	92	97	103	109	116	124	132							
80	84	89	94	100	106	113	121	129								
85	85	90	96	102	110	117	126	136								
90	86	91	98	105	113	122	131									
95	86	93	100	108	117	127										
100	87	95	103	112	121	132										

Likelihood of Heat Disorders with Prolonged Exposure or Strenuous Activity:

☐ Caution   ☐ Extreme Caution   ▨ Danger   ■ Extreme Danger

FIGURE 3. This chart from the National Oceanic and Atmospheric Administration (NOAA) shows the impact relative humidity has on the heat index, or how hot the air temperature actually feels.

THE WEATHER MACHINE

What we experience as weather—heat and cold, sun and clouds, precipitation and drying—is powered by two cosmic generators: the sun's heating of air masses and the rotation of Earth toward the east. Heated air becomes less dense, absorbs moisture, and rises in the atmosphere. Because heated air is less dense, it usually has a lower barometric pressure than cool air. Cooled air becomes denser, tends to release moisture, and sinks toward the earth. Because it is dense, it usually has a higher barometric pressure than heated air. Earth's rotation powers a prevailing movement of wind from west to east and directs the spinning air masses as they rise and fall from heating and cooling.

The contact zone between two or more air masses is a mixing zone, and where this zone contacts Earth's surface it is called a "front." Usually this front is described by the temperature of the air mass that is overtaking from the west, so a warm air mass riding over relatively cooler air is called a "warm front," while a cold air mass pushing against and under a relatively warm one is called a "cold front." (The terms "warm" and "cold" are only relative to each other, and each type of front occurs in every season.) Due to their relative densities, their interactions are fairly predictable. Warm air masses ride up over the backs of cold air masses, and cold air masses push against and under the backs of warm air masses. Clouds and "weather" occur where the two air masses contact each other. Fortunately, the two types of fronts produce very different weather patterns, and recognizing these patterns is the way to understand what will happen to the weather in the near term.

WARM FRONTS

Warm fronts are relatively moist and slow-moving, traveling across the land at roughly 5 to 10 MPH. The contact between the warm and cool air is an upward-sloping mixing zone sometimes 1,000 miles long, with different types of clouds forming all along this boundary. Long before warm, humid air arrives at ground level, a layer of warm and moist air has formed high above. This slow march of upper-level

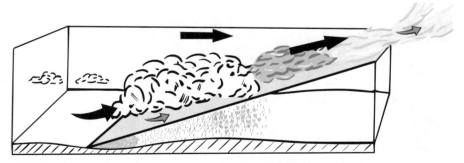

FIGURE 4. Warm, less dense air moves up and away from Earth, rising over the cold air.

warm air usually announces the front's arrival many hours, or even days, ahead of time. The first indication that there is more humid air aloft is often the persistence of jet contrails in the sky. Passenger jets typically cruise at about 30,000 feet, and their engines release water vapor as they fly. If the air is dry, this water vapor is absorbed, remaining invisible. But if the air aloft is humid, the water vapor will immediately form the recognizable linear cloud of a contrail. When high-flying jets leave thick contrails as they travel, this indicates a wedge of warm air high above. This weather sign is quite reliable, and it is a good early indication that the weather could shift warmer and wetter in the next 36 to 48 hours.

If you are lucky enough not to notice any jets overhead, the sloping boundary layer of the warm front still produces a very recognizable sequence of clouds. The first clouds, called cirrus, are high, wispy clouds resembling horses' tails or sometimes fish scales. These "mare's tails and mackerel scales" often appear high in an otherwise clear and sunny sky. They indicate a warmer, wetter turn of the weather coming in 24 to 36 hours. After these first indications, the cloud layer progressively thickens, darkens, and lowers, and may eventually produce fog at ground level. Usually during this time, the prevailing winds will begin to blow from the south or southeast. If the air mass has enough latent moisture, varied precipitation will occur over a broad swath of time and space, perhaps 12 to 24 hours, as the front approaches then passes. Recognizing an approaching warm front is one of the easiest weather patterns to master, but telling when it will leave is more difficult. The precipitation will end and clouds will clear gradually, signaled by a rising barometer (see "Barometric Pressure," page 26) and wind shifting from the south or east toward the west.

FIGURE 5. A cold front occurs when a cold air mass pushes against a warm air mass. Cold fronts can produce dramatic changes in the weather, such as high wind, heavy rain, hail, and thunderstorms.

WIND CHILL																		
TEMPERATURE (°F)																		
calm	40	35	30	25	20	15	10	5	0	-5	-10	-15	-20	-25	-30	-35	-40	-45
5	36	31	25	19	13	7	1	-5	-11	-16	-22	-28	-34	-40	-46	-52	-57	-63
10	34	27	21	15	9	3	-4	-10	-16	-22	-28	-35	-41	-47	-53	-59	-66	-72
15	32	25	19	13	6	0	-7	-13	-19	-26	-32	-39	-45	-51	-58	-64	-71	-77
20	30	24	17	11	4	-2	-9	-15	-22	-29	-35	-42	-48	-55	-61	-68	-74	-81
25	29	23	16	9	3	-4	-11	-17	-24	-31	-37	-44	-51	-58	-64	-71	-78	-84
30	28	22	15	8	1	-5	-12	-19	-26	-33	-39	-46	-53	-60	-67	-73	-80	-87
35	28	21	14	7	0	-7	-14	-21	-27	-34	-41	-48	-55	-62	-69	-76	-82	-89
40	27	20	13	6	-1	-8	-15	-22	-29	-36	-43	-50	-57	-64	-71	-78	-84	-91
45	26	19	12	5	-2	-9	-16	-23	-30	-37	-44	-51	-58	-65	-72	-79	-86	-93
50	26	19	12	4	-3	-10	-17	-24	-31	-38	-45	-52	-60	-67	-74	-81	-88	-95
55	25	18	11	4	-3	-11	-18	-25	-32	-39	-46	-54	-61	-68	-75	-82	-89	-97
60	25	17	10	3	-4	-11	-19	-26	-33	-40	-48	-55	-62	-69	-76	-84	-91	-98

WIND (MPH)

Frostbite Times: [ ] 30 minutes [ ] 10 minutes [ ] 5 minutes

Wind Chill (°F) = $35.74 + 0.6215T - 35.75(V^{0.16}) + 0.4275T(V^{0.16})$ where T = Air Temperature (°F), V = Wind Speed (MPH)

FIGURE 6. This wind chill chart, used by NOAA and the National Weather Service, illustrates how wind speed impacts wind chill, or how cold the air temperature actually feels.

COLD FRONTS

Cold fronts move at about twice the speed of warm fronts, sometimes as fast as 30 MPH. Instead of having a long, sloping contact zone, they are vertical and abrupt, as the denser, faster-moving cold air lifts the warm air aloft. This zone of rapid mixing is characterized by turbulent convection currents, with warm air rising and cold air sinking in close proximity to each other. This process produces characteristic vertical, puffy clouds, called cumulus. If the warm air mass does not have much moisture, the front will not produce much precipitation at all. If, however, there is a lot of latent moisture present in the system, the convection is likely to produce dramatic (and sometimes severe) thunderstorms. The hiker's sense of the air humidity is a good indication of the air mass's moisture level, so this is a valid weather sign to note.

Even though a cold front's approach is more rapid than a warm front's, it still provides a few reliable weather signs. First, the vertical mixing zone produces a rapid buildup of vertically piled cumulus clouds. In open country these clouds often appear as a long line across the western horizon, although the mountains can obscure them from view. Second, this abrupt zone of turbulent mixing produces strong, gusty winds from the south and southeast. If precipitation occurs, it will be heavier, more variable, and more localized than with a warm front. Fortunately, most cold fronts pass quickly, and the period of rain should persist for less than six hours. When the barometer begins to rise and the wind shifts from a southerly direction to a more westerly direction, the front has passed and clearing will follow.

OCCLUDED FRONTS AND STATIONARY FRONTS

Occluded fronts are a special three-way collision in which a cold front catches up with a warm front. In an occluded front, a warm air mass rides up over a cooler air mass; then an even colder air mass pushes under the warm air, lifting it into the upper atmosphere. Backcountry travelers can detect occluded fronts when a weather system that starts out like a warm front (progressive cloud thickening and lowering; steady rain) ends like a cold front (strong, gusty winds; intense rain showers). Upon clearing, the weather will go from cool to cold rather than from cool to warm. Additionally, during the transition to the cold air mass, thunderstorms may form within the existing cloud layers ("embedded" thunderstorms). These storms can be difficult to predict.

A stationary front occurs when two air masses abut each other, and neither has the ability to move the other. Their zone of mixing does not move across the land. To the hiker, the weather feels like a warm front but less severe, and it lasts for a longer time. These stable weather systems are less common in mountainous terrain and tend to dissipate over a period of several days.

OROGRAPHIC LIFTING

Orographic lifting is another powerful influence on localized weather in mountain terrain. Prevailing winds lift air masses up the windward sides of mountains, and as an air mass is lifted, it cools. A hiker climbing a mountain will notice the temperature dropping about 3.5 degrees for every 1,000 feet of elevation gain. As the air cools, any moisture it contains may begin to condense and precipitate. For this reason, mountain summits will be colder, wetter, and cloudier on average than the valleys below. As air descends, the opposite occurs, with the air becoming drier, warmer, and clearer. (Local mountain topography in the Northeast encourages this effect, since the majority of mountain ranges in this region trend north–south, perpendicular to the prevailing westerly winds.) As the winds push air masses up against and over the summits and ridges, hikers often will notice a stationary cloud cap over the mountain, a wetter western slope, and a drier eastern slope. These predictable patterns shape the unique vegetation of mountain summits and can help inform the backcountry traveler's summit expectations, as well as the choice of route and campsite.

AFTERNOON THUNDERSTORMS

Another common weather phenomenon in the summer backcountry is an afternoon thunderstorm. Afternoon thunderstorms differ from cold-front storms because they do not signal a weather change. On clear, warm days the sun heats the air close to the ground, causing it to rise into the upper atmosphere. There it cools and sinks back to the surface, where it is heated again, creating a convection cell. If the original air mass contains a lot of moisture (i.e., it feels humid), this convection process will produce dark, towering cumulonimbus clouds. When the rising

1

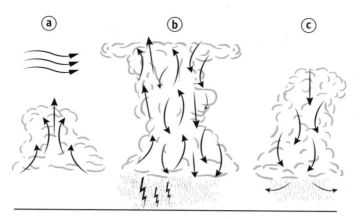

FIGURE 7. The life cycle of a thunderstorm. (a) In the cumulus stage, warm air rises in an updraft. The moisture in this warm air condenses into a large cloud as it hits the cooler atmosphere. (b) Once the cloud reaches the warmer winds of the stratosphere, it cannot rise any higher, causing it to spread out at the top and take on an anvil-like appearance. The moisture in the cloud then grows heavy and sinks back through the warm air, forming a downdraft. Rain, thunder, and lightning will occur. (c) In the dissipating stage, the downdrafts within the cloud overtake the updrafts. The warm air no longer rises, rain stops, and the storm dies out. In a normal thunderstorm cell, it takes about half an hour from the start of a storm until dissipation.

air cools in the upper atmosphere, the water vapor it contains condenses into rain droplets and ice crystals. As these fall, they rub against other rain and ice pellets that are being lifted by the powerful updrafts, and this friction generates static electricity charges. When the electric potential between the cloud and the ground is great enough, lightning will form to equalize these charges. (See the lightning safety section below.) Even without lightning, these storm cells can produce gusty winds and strong rain showers, enough to soak an unprepared camper and to create hazards in camp and on the trail.

Powered by daily warming and evaporation, this cycle can repeat itself each afternoon in any warm and humid air mass or where there is a ready source of humidity from bodies of water, vegetation, or the land itself. This kind of storm is also encouraged by the orographic lifting described above. Summer backcountry travelers should expect that any humid air mass will eventually produce afternoon thunderstorms, especially near mountain summits. This is very rare after September 15 or before May 15 and is totally dependent on having a sustained period of heat and humidity; in other words, afternoon thunderstorms are unique to the summer months. For this reason, it is wise to avoid an afternoon summit time and to set up camp by middle or late afternoon.

Staying out of the way of these storms is not difficult with a little awareness. First, notice the heat and humidity of the air through which you are hiking. If it is hot and humid, assume afternoon thunderstorms are likely and plan accordingly.

Try to stay off the summits after lunch and to set up your camp securely as soon as you arrive. Each storm cloud generally will travel across the land in a southwest-to-northeast direction. Storms that are forming or visible to the south and west are direct threats and need to be monitored closely. Storms that can be seen to the north and east might still generate hazardous lightning, but their general trajectory will usually be away from the observer. Remember that these are general rules, and that mountain and valley topography can greatly influence these paths. A storm cell can get funneled along a valley by the mountains on either side, and it can get stalled against a major ridge or peak. Being aware of your surrounding topography will help you assess these situations.

LIGHTNING

Encountering lightning is quite common in the summer, and its power is so immense that it must be taken very seriously. Lightning strikes cannot be prevented completely, but hikers can still follow good practices to reduce the likelihood of a strike. Fortunately, thunderstorms usually communicate their approach, giving the hiker plenty of opportunity to prepare.

The most effective lightning safety practices involve choosing a safer location during a storm. The best place to be in a lightning storm is in a building (with four walls, not a lean-to) or a car. If these options are available, choose them. In the backcountry, these two options won't always be available, but you can still make good location choices. As noted above, lightning-producing storms are usually part of an approaching cold front or a convective cell developing in warm, humid air, and can be more common near mountain summits. Keeping your eye on the sky throughout the day will allow you to notice a cold front approaching or the buildup of cumulonimbus clouds. Stay off mountain summits on summer afternoons, especially when clouds are building above and to the west. If you must be in these places at these times, have a bail-out plan ready in case the weather turns for the worse. Make good campsite choices, avoiding exposed knobs and wide-open sites that sit in drainages or atop the roots of major trees. The best situation is to be in a forest on rolling, lowland terrain, away from any trees that tower above those around it.

Current research in wilderness medicine and lightning safety suggests that traditional lightning safety practices—assuming the lightning position (described below), sitting on a ground pad, wearing rain clothing—do not reduce the likelihood of a lightning injury for the backcountry traveler. The only reliable, proven practices are maintaining an awareness of weather changes and staying out of the wrong place at the wrong time. Many organizations still maintain other traditional lightning practices as part of their required operating procedures. Because of this, and because there is a hypothetical chance some of these traditional practices might be protective in some small way, it is worth knowing them and putting them to use when possible, as long as you prioritize choosing the safest location possible.

Thunder indicates the presence of lightning, even if lightning is not visible. As soon as you hear thunder, it is time to retreat to the safest terrain possible; again, choosing a good location is the only reliable risk-mitigation strategy. In the forested landscape of the Northeast, once a storm with thunder approaches within 2 to 3 miles, it is time to take additional steps to protect yourself. A somewhat reliable method for estimating your distance from a storm utilizes the different rates of speed at which light and sound travel. For every five seconds between the flash of lightning and the crash of thunder ("flash to crash"), the storm is roughly a mile away. If the flash-to-crash time is fifteen seconds or less, the storm is less than 3 miles away. At this point, everyone in camp should implement the following lightning procedures:

1

- Spread the group out in all directions at least 20 feet apart so that if there is a lightning strike, it is more likely some people will be unaffected and able to respond to the injured.

- Stay away from the bases of tall trees; large metal objects, such as fire towers; drainages, where water will conduct electricity; shallow caves; rock overhangs; and the front openings of lean-tos.

- Don your rain gear, as the water film on its surface may redirect some surface current around the body. For this same reason, crouching under a tarp may have some protective effects.

- Assume the lightning position: Crouch as low as possible on a foam pad or another insulating item, allowing only the bases of your feet to touch the pad, and attempt to keep your heels touching at all times.

- Maintain this lightning drill until the storm passes, and flash to crash is greater than 15 seconds.

OTHER HAZARDOUS WEATHER

Armed with all of this weather knowledge, a backcountry traveler can make better decisions about when and where to hike and camp, and how to prepare for the day's likely weather. Sometimes, though, hazardous weather just finds us, and it is important to know how to handle such emergencies. Weather hazards for summer mountain hikers include extreme rain events, extreme wind events, and lightning. Extreme rain can lead to flash flooding, dangerous river crossings, and mud-slicked trails. If the rain soaks all of your gear, it can lead to hypothermia. Extreme wind events can cause trees to uproot or snap, falling across trails and in campsites. Extreme wind can even blow a person off a ridge or over a cliff. Fortunately, these wind and rain hazards can be mitigated with good preventative practices. Avoid campsites that contain runoff streams and potential widowmakers (leaning or weakened branches or trees that can fall on a hiker or camper). Be aware of deteriorating weather conditions and take a break to consider your options if these conditions occur. Pushing ahead regardless of the weather leads to many unfortunate scenarios, so it is often wise to

1

stay put and tap into your weather sense. Most intense rain and wind events will not last more than 2 to 3 hours, so staying dry and warm in camp is a reasonable option. And if you are in the woods during a long-lasting, historic event, sheltering in camp makes even more sense.

MORE USEFUL WEATHER INDICATORS

In addition to cloud progressions and wind changes, there are a handful of other useful backcountry weather indicators and principles that give some reliable insight into what to expect during the coming hours.

Barometric Pressure

Barometric pressure can be measured with many small, portable weather devices and can be interpreted using the altimeter of many sports watches. In brief, falling atmospheric pressure indicates incoming clouds and possibly rain, while rising pressure suggests a clearing period ahead. The more rapid the barometric change, the more sudden and turbulent the weather event will be. Barometers are especially useful for giving the first (encouraging) indication that a persistent rain event may be about to end.

Wind Direction and Speed

As noted above, direction and speed tell us a great deal about what is happening or going to happen in the weather. While many old weather sayings have little merit, one we have found quite reliable goes:

> *Wind from the west brings weather that's best.*
> *Wind from the north brings cold weather forth.*
> *Wind from the south brings rain in its mouth.*
> *Wind from the east brings weather not fit for man nor beast.*

In the temperate latitudes of the Northeast, this simple rhyme captures the regular wind dynamics of most typical storm cells and major weather systems. Another reliable indicator is based on the strength and duration of the wind. An approaching weather system marked by strong and prolonged winds ultimately will be stronger and last longer.

Halos

Halos around the moon and sun are caused by a high, thin layer of ice-crystal clouds. Along with the "mare's tails and mackerel scales," they are early indicators of an approaching warm front, perhaps 24 hours away.

Remember, noticing weather signs is a natural and satisfying element of backcountry travel, and weather systems usually provide numerous clues as to what is coming next. Keeping your eye on the sky throughout the day will lead you to a safer and more enjoyable mountain trip.

CHAPTER 2
CLOTHING

Legend has it that the famed naturalist John Muir took to the mountains in an old overcoat, with just a crust of bread in his pocket. Maybe that's why he had so many daring adventures, such as surviving a spring mountain blizzard by spending the night baking in the mud of a bubbling, geothermal hot pot. While escapades like that are memorable, they aren't the best way for most people to enjoy the mountains. With the forethought described in the previous chapter and the right equipment, you can do more than just survive in the mountains. You can thrive.

Early mountaineers and backcountry travelers wore clothes not too different from those they sported around town: wool pants and shirts, stout shoes, and a waxed cotton or woolen overcoat. Even in the 1980s, hardy outdoorfolk could satisfy most of their needs at the thrift store, with getups surprisingly similar to those worn by early mountaineers: a pair of wool dress pants, a wool sweater, a nylon anorak, and an old rubber raincoat for when the rain got heavy. These worked—and by "worked," they could keep you warm and dry enough to explore the woods and waterways of New England for days at a time.

But that simplicity seems to have slipped away. Going into a gear store now or looking for clothes online can be bewildering—even overwhelming. With constant changes in manufacturing and fabric technology, there are hundreds of new choices for today's backcountry traveler. Which are necessary? What fabric is best? Is that high-tech jacket really worth its price tag? Well, take heart: It doesn't need to be this complex.

Our bodies work well only when kept in a very narrow temperature range. Clothing is the tool we use to help keep us in that range. The key to finding your way out of the spruce trap of choices is to focus on function. Even with the explosion of options, outdoor clothing's sole purpose remains quite simple: Keep us warm when we want to be warm, cool when we want to be cool, and dry when the weather changes for the worse.

2

A layering approach is the best way to ensure that outdoor clothes are comfortable and ready for anything. By wearing several thinner layers (each with its own purpose) rather than a single thick layer (such as a heavy down parka), we can make sure our clothing system will adapt to almost any weather condition. Clothing needs to wick moisture from the skin as we sweat. It needs to insulate us from the cold or heat of the ambient air. It needs to provide a shelter against precipitation, wind, and sun. Finally, we need to have just enough extra clothing to accommodate changes in the environment. The Wilderness Education Association calls this the WISE system: **Wicking, Insulating, Sheltering, Extra.**

➔ WISE SYSTEM

WICKING

Wicking layers are worn directly against the skin. Their purpose is to bring the sweat from our bodies away from our skin, preventing that moisture from making us feel cold and clammy. The moisture actually travels up the fabric fibers to the surface, where it can evaporate or at least be isolated from our skin. On a cold or wintry hike, when perspiration could lead to chills and then to hypothermia, this function is literally lifesaving, but even in other times of the year it offers a real improvement in comfort. Effective wicking layers are made of wool or synthetic fabrics, such as polyester, spandex, and polypropylene. For most day hikes and backpacking trips, it's a good idea to bring two inner layers, so that if one gets soaked from sweat (or from falling in a stream) you can quickly switch into the other.

INSULATING

Insulating clothes create an air space between our wicking layers and the outside environment. This air keeps body heat from escaping with the breeze or simply radiating away from us. Examples of insulating clothing are fleece, wool shirts and sweaters, and down or fiberfill jackets. Each of these types of insulation traps warm air and holds it in place. The loftier the layer, the more insulation you have. Some insulation, such as fleece or wool, works well in damp environments. Others, particularly down, lose their loft when wet and are a good choice only when you can ensure the insulation will stay dry.

SHELTERING

Sheltering clothes are worn on the outside of our clothing system. They are the shell that keeps rain and wind away from our skin and other clothes while also allowing any body moisture we generate to escape into the atmosphere. They must fit over all of our other layers. (In the Northeast, we almost always face some chance of precipitation, so shell layers must be able to handle an extended rainfall.) At the same time, since we generate some excess heat and moisture just from the work of walking on the trail, the shell layer needs to be able to release this extra heat and maximize the wicking of moisture into the atmosphere. There are two ways shells get this job done. First, a shell can have vents, usually zippered, that allow air to circulate inside. Second, a shell can be made of a fabric that is waterproof but still allows water vapor to pass right through. This is called a waterproof-breathable fabric. GORE-TEX is the iconic example of waterproof breathability, but there are many different kinds of these fabrics now. If possible, choose a shell layer that offers a combination of waterproof-breathable fabric and mechanical venting options. This approach will allow you to stay active in the widest possible range of weather conditions.

2

EXTRA

Having extra clothes with us allows us to adapt to changing weather conditions and activity levels. It is colder in the morning than at noon, and it could be colder still at night. You might fall into a stream. You will definitely not generate as much heat while in camp as you will when hiking on the trail. On a longer trip you will need to have something to wear while your laundry dries. You may be leading a trip and your group members have not packed adequately. For these reasons, we add some extra clothes to our packs—just enough for comfort and safety, but no more!

FIGURE 8. The WISE system calls for layering clothes in the following order, working from nearest to skin outward: wicking, insulating, shell, extra.

2

FABRIC CHOICES

One of the most basic choices we face in clothing is whether to buy clothes made from synthetic or natural fibers. Since the 1970s, synthetic fabrics, such as nylon or polypropylene, have been the material of choice for most outdoor recreational clothing. Such fabrics are light for their warmth, dry quickly, and have become very affordable. Recent years have seen a strong resurgence of fine wool from the merino sheep as a very functional layer, both for wicking and insulation, and even woven into certain kinds of cold-weather shells. The choice between these two options is not clear, and there are advantages to both.

Both wool and synthetic fabrics will keep you warm when they are wet, an important property. The synthetics have a slight advantage over wool in wicking and cost, and they are likely to dry more quickly when completely soaked. Synthetics do have disadvantages, however. They are more flammable around fires or the camp stove, and they are likely to accumulate odors over the course of even a two- to three-day trip. Wool is usually a bit more expensive, but it has a wider comfort range and is much more resistant to picking up odors. When you're in the store, this might not seem like a good trade-off, but after a few days on the trail your perspective might be different. If you ever share a tent with someone whose synthetic clothing is smelly, you will agree the extra cost would have been worth it. Sometimes, synthetic clothing becomes too smelly to keep using, even if it's still in excellent physical shape. Wool does not have this problem, and you'll need to retire it only when it becomes threadbare. Finally, many of us take to the woods to connect with nature, so considering the environmental impacts of our clothing choices makes sense. Synthetic clothes are petroleum products, whereas wool is a renewable resource. Looking into the ecological footprint of your fabrics will help you decide which of these choices is right for you.

The other natural fabric is cotton, and it is a poor choice for the backcountry traveler. Cotton fibers are hydrophilic, meaning they cling to water. Instead of wicking moisture to the outside, cotton becomes soaked, and in cold environments, this wet cloth against your skin can be deadly. In extreme heat, a loose-fitting cotton shirt can help keep you cool, and some hikers like to bring a cotton T-shirt for luxurious camp wear. This means your beloved blue jeans will have to stay home. Cotton clothes just don't work well in the backcountry.

MULTIPURPOSE LAYERS

One of the most interesting developments in backcountry clothing in recent years is the design of clothing that serves multiple purposes and functions within the widest range of conditions and temperatures. An example might be a windproof softshell jacket with a layer of fleece laminated inside. Such a jacket would provide wind protection and insulation at the same time. While these work all right for a wider range of purposes than the heaviest parkas, there is still a compromise with versatility. A midweight fleece shirt combined with a breathable shell will be only a few ounces heavier than the multipurpose jacket, and together they can handle a much wider range of environmental conditions.

RAIN GEAR

2

Rain gear has a hard job. It needs to keep you dry while allowing heat and moisture from your sweat to escape. Even with all of the technical advances in waterproof-breathable materials, these conflicting goals are hard to achieve simultaneously. Understanding how rain gear accomplishes both tasks is essential to selecting—and having realistic expectations for—your rain gear.

Barrier

Rain gear must feature a barrier that is impenetrable to water. These barriers come in two primary forms: laminates and coatings. A laminate is a thin sheet of material glued to the inside of the jacket's outer layer. Laminates are more durable and also about twice as expensive as coatings. A coating is a thin layer that is essentially painted on the inside of the jacket. Coatings are typically lighter in weight and more affordable. Coatings, however, will wear quickly with regular use, especially in areas that are flexed frequently, such as the elbows or the joint of the hood.

DWR

Durable water repellency, or DWR, is a chemical treatment applied to rain gear that causes water to bead up and roll off without penetrating the fabric. Keeping the fabric from "wetting out" prolongs its breathability. DWR always wears off with use and can be reapplied using after-market products.

Breathability

Rain gear must allow heat and water vapor to escape from the inside. As discussed above, most modern hiking shells use a laminate or coating that allows water vapor to pass through. These high-tech fabrics pass this vapor especially well in the cold, dry air of winter. But in rainy, humid weather, when the exterior of the jacket is already wet from rain, fabric breathability will always be limited (or eliminated). Heat, a separate problem from water vapor, is not vented through the fabric, and must be released through convection, or air movement. In other words, the jacket is breathable, unless it rains. If you are prioritizing rain protection when choosing your sheltering layer, focus on the waterproofness not the breathability. Ultimately, in those humid conditions, the only breathability will come from good mechanical venting features such as zippers under the armpits ("pit zips") or mesh-lined venting pockets. In you are a very warm-natured hiker, or in warm weather, it may be most comfortable and effective to simply accept wet skin as you travel in the rain, and save your shell layer for comfort once you change in camp.

2

Proper Fit

For maximum protection and comfort, a good rain jacket should fit easily over multiple layers without constricting motion. The sleeves should not pull away from your wrists when you extend your arms, and the cuffs should seal tightly to prevent water from leaking in. The waist should extend below your lower back, and the hood should tighten snugly and move with you as you turn your head. For rain pants, look for zippers that extend above the knee, enabling you to easily slip them on and off while wearing bulky footwear.

→ PUTTING IT ALL TOGETHER

By using the WISE system, it is easy to compose a simple outfit that will work in any season. Let's look at what WISE means in summer, followed by the shoulder seasons of spring and fall. (For information on how to dress for nature's most challenging season, see Chapter 10, Winter Skills, on page 232.)

SUMMER

Summer is obviously a warm time to take to the woods, but the weather can be unpredictable. Since a hiker can see anything from 90-degree sunshine to 50-degree sideways rain and high winds, particularly above treeline, the backcountry traveler's clothing will be light but still able to meet these challenges.

Wicking

For wicking clothes, a summer hiker might bring only a T-shirt and shorts made from synthetic fabric. Ultra-thin liner shorts can increase comfort and prevent chafing. Some hikers also like the wicking effect of thin liner socks, keeping their feet a bit drier and less prone to blisters.

Insulating

Even in the hottest weather, hikers often want an extra layer to buffer a chill. A simple, lightweight fleece can do the job (and double as a camp pillow, too). If it has a hood, it becomes even more versatile. Another option is a lightweight synthetic puffy jacket. These layers feel good when the sun dips low or when you are sitting in damp clothes on a breezy summit.

Sheltering

This layer provides the shell that keeps the wind and rain on the outside, away from skin. A summer hiker will want a waterproof-breathable jacket and pants. Unless you are headed off-trail for some bushwhacking, a lightweight fabric should be enough. Since getting rid of heat in a humid environment is a challenge, the best choice for jackets will have extra zippers for maximum ventilation. Sheltering also means keeping us protected from the sun, so this layer should include a hat with a brim. Our feet need shelter from the trail's mud and water as well, so for longer hikes and overnights, everyone will benefit from using some kind of gaiter that will keep the dirt out of your boots.

Extra

Even in summer, bringing a little extra clothing is a smart choice, especially if heading above treeline. The amount you need depends on the weather forecast and the time of year. For a multiday trip, carrying at least an extra T-shirt and a pair of shorts and socks is a good idea. We usually also include a light-colored, long-sleeved wicking shirt, for bug and sun protection. It also offers extra insulation on unexpectedly cool or rainy days. You might add a pair of lightweight wicking bottoms for the same reason. The other item that belongs in your pack is a light-weight warm hat for those cool mornings, sitting around camp, or relaxing under the stars. Once you've packed these items, you can choose to add luxury items, such as a cotton T-shirt for sleeping. Don't load up too much on luxury, though; keeping it light will let you travel more easily, carry more food, and enjoy your time on the trail more.

With this light but versatile setup, a hiker can handle many days of variable summer weather, from roasting hot to rainy and cool. You'll have enough clothing to stay warm, dry, and protected from the sun, with enough versatility to remain cool on long distances, and you'll have something to wear while washing dirty layers.

FALL AND SPRING: THE SHOULDER SEASONS

For some hikers, the shoulder seasons are the best time to be in the woods and mountains. It's joyful to return to the forests without winter's challenges. In spring the forest is just awakening, with wildflowers and spring peepers appearing, while snowfields remain above in the peaks. Fall offers a respite from summer's heat, humidity, and insects, with glorious foliage filling the valleys. Each autumn hike is a treasure because it won't be long before the world is transformed by winter again. In both spring and fall, the crowds dissipate and it feels like the woods belong only to you.

The price of heading into the woods in these seasons is that we have to accept greater variability of weather and generally cooler temperatures with more rain. With the WISE system, we can handle this challenge easily and enjoy hikes in every condition.

Wicking

Wicking long underwear forms the base for the shoulder-season outfit. These layers can be light or midweight, and if you bring an extra set, you can double them up for extra insulation.

Insulating

At least one warmer insulating layer for top and bottom is necessary. A midweight fleece or wool sweater works great on top, as does a layer of similar weight on the bottom. Due to the chance of near-freezing weather, it is also a good idea to bring a jacket with some kind of puffy insulation. A synthetic fiberfill insulation is a good choice because it can handle getting damp in the rain. A midweight wool or fleece hat is also necessary, as is a pair of similar gloves or mittens.

Sheltering

This layer is not very different in the shoulder seasons. If you purchased your shell jacket and pants with the idea that you could fit them over extra insulation, then they should work fine in spring and fall, too.

Extra

To be safe and comfortable, it is always a good idea to have an extra layer of wicking long underwear (for a total of two layers) and an extra warm top layer (also for a total of two). In these seasons we usually add an additional pair of socks over what we would have brought in summer (for a total of three). At the extreme end of fall, getting toward winter, we will bring extra hats and a pair of mittens, too, just to be sure we are covered for the unexpected snowstorm or frosty night.

Imagine arriving at camp after hiking in 50-degree Fahrenheit (10-degree Celsius) drizzle for an hour or two. Your base layer will be wet, and you will get chilled quickly when you stop hiking. But right away you change into your extra wicking base layers, put on a fleece or wool sweater, put on your hat, change your socks, and put your shell clothes back on over all of it. If you are especially chilled, you can wear your fiberfill jacket under your raincoat while you make the hot cocoa. In a matter of five minutes you can go from soggy and cool to dry and warm with the aid of the few extra items you brought.

Bringing just the right amount of extra clothing for spring and fall hiking is a matter of skill and careful planning, but it also helps to have a bit of luck. It is far better to bring a bit more than you thought you'd need than to sit huddled in the cold, wishing you had carried that one extra pound of warm clothing. The shoulder seasons are full of wonder and solitude, and they are worth the small price of a few extra pieces of clothing.

→ **PRO TIP** Wear your rain pants over your gaiters, not inside your gaiters, in wet weather. This creates a watershed effect that keeps your feet drier.

OTHER CLOTHING ITEMS

Well-dressed backpackers will assemble their own preferred system using the WISE approach and the footwear recommendations above. In addition to these selections, there are a few other pieces of clothing that should be in all backpacks or on every body.

- **Gaiters** cover the top of your boots, preventing water, stones, and dirt from getting inside. Keeping feet and socks clean and dry prevents blisters and other foot ailments. Also, this extra level of protection allows a hiker to tromp right through those trail puddles, avoiding the adjacent vegetation. For more on gaiters, see page 40 later in this chapter.

- **Brimmed hats** are necessary for keeping sun off the face, but they also shield the hiker from rain and wind, and are useful for holding a bug head net away from the face.

- **Gloves** are useful in all seasons, for cold mornings, sun protection, and for some heat resistance in the kitchen. (Choose gloves with leather palms if their primary purpose is kitchen use.)

- **Sunglasses** can be vital to your enjoyment of a hike and also protect your eyes from the sun's damaging rays. Be sure to select a pair that offers UV protection.

2

→ SOCKS

Your feet are one of the sweatiest parts of your body after your armpits. Each foot can generate between half a cup and a cup of perspiration per day! This moisture can lead to soggy, soft skin that is easily blistered. Managing this moisture is your socks' most important job, followed closely by padding the foot, limiting friction, and keeping your skin at the desired temperature.

PROPER FIT

A properly fitting sock will be snug on your foot, and it won't bunch up, move around while you're active, or slump down around your ankles. Choose styles with elastic in strategic positions to prevent slumping. Also be sure to choose socks that truly fit your length and width. Too large will promote bagging and blisters; too small will cause the socks to wear out quickly.

MATERIAL

- **Merino wool** is the preferred fabric for socks, with good reason. It manages moisture well and sucks both liquid and vapor sweat away from your feet. Wool provides good padding and warmth, and can absorb up to a third of its weight in water without feeling damp or losing much of its insulating ability. Socks need

2

some elastic material for an optimum fit, however, and those with nylon will have higher durability.

- **Cotton** appears in a lot of inexpensive socks but should be avoided, as with all the other WISE layers. It absorbs more moisture than wool, loses all of its insulating ability when saturated, takes forever to dry, and will sag and bunch when wet.

- **Nylon** and **polyester** are extremely durable and often provide the base fabric through which wool is woven. These synthetic, nonporous materials absorb very little water, dry quickly, and help give socks form and structure. Another option is to wear a very thin sock of wicking, synthetic material against the skin, under a second layer of a merino wool blend. Proponents of this layering system report that it reduces friction and manages moisture better. If you want to experiment with this system, you must be sure that your boots have enough extra space to accommodate the two layers. The most common cause of blisters is too-tight boots.

➜ BOOTS

On a day hike or a backpacking trip, our most important outfitting choice is what to wear on our feet. Having a comfortable and functional pair of boots or shoes is one of the key differences between surviving and thriving, and it can mean the difference between completing your trip or not. In recent years, there have been many positive developments in footwear, and hikers rarely need to wear the trail-crushing wafflestompers of the stereotypical backpacker. Your choice will depend on three variables: how much weight you are carrying, what type of terrain you are traveling, and how often you will be hiking. Note that for women, it's important to try to wear women's hiking boots, as they are narrower in the heel cup. This can help prevent Achilles tendinitis, a condition common when hikers with narrower feet wear wider hiking boots.

Hiking footwear can be separated into three categories, primarily based on the weight of the boots. There is some truth to the old saying, "A pound on your feet is like five on your back." It's worth finding boots that meet your needs and are as light as they are practical.

LIGHTWEIGHT

Lightweight hiking boots look an awful lot like trail-running shoes. In fact, experienced long-distance hikers often use trail-running shoes as their hiking shoe of choice. This category of boot weighs 1.5 to 2 pounds per pair or less. Often a lightweight boot reaches no higher on the ankle than a pair of running shoes, although many lightweights do rise up (often called a midrise). They are made mostly of nylon fabric, without much (if any) leather, and feel broken-in right out of the box. An important difference between a trail-running shoe and a lightweight hiking boot is the amount of support on the arch. A hiking boot will be supportive enough to provide comfort with a pack weighing up to 20 pounds. Lightweight boots are often surprisingly competent, and ongoing innovation by boot manufacturers continues to extend their usefulness.

HEAVYWEIGHT

2

These boots are at the other end of the spectrum, often weighing 4 pounds or more. For all of this weight, you get several features that increase durability and waterproofing. The most common are a full-grain leather upper, extra ankle support, and a multilayer midsole with enough arch support to help carry the heaviest expedition packs. Heavyweight boots are also frequently built with a wraparound rubber section at the base of the upper (called a rand), adding durability and waterproofing. Another common feature is a gusseted tongue, which is connected to the boot all the way up each side. These gussets prevent trail debris from sifting through the boot laces, increasing comfort and decreasing the likelihood of blisters. To provide the greatest accessibility to terrain, the outsoles are deeply lugged and are often crampon-compatible for snow hiking. When well made, these boots will last seemingly forever. Unfortunately, that's also how long it can feel like it takes to break then in. It is not unusual for you to walk 20 to 50 miles before your feet come to a truce with these boots. A heavyweight pair of boots is not multipurpose. They shine amid the rough terrain, wet conditions, and heavy loads of a true expedition, but not much of anywhere else.

MIDWEIGHT

Midweight boots are the middle ground, and few hikers will ever need more than this kind of footwear. A midweight boot weighs between 2 and 4 pounds per pair. Hiking-boot design is a game of compromises, and midweight boots are the best example of this. In trying to resolve conflicting demands, such as being waterproof *and* breathable, lightweight *and* supportive, durable *and* good-looking, midweight boot manufacturers have come up with a diversity of solutions. Some midweights are all leather. Others are a hybrid of leather and fabric. They will have a rugged-enough sole to handle any terrain in the Northeast, and all should be supportive enough to help you carry a pack with up to a week's supplies.

Looking at these three categories should help you decide which option is right for you. A lightweight boot is probably right if you expect to primarily take day hikes and trips of less than three days, for a total of twenty days a year or less. You might also choose a lightweight boot if you consider yourself a fastpacker or an ultralight hiker (see Chapter 12, Ultralight Backpacking, on page 275 for more information). The versatile midweight boot is probably the best choice for trips longer than three days or for people who spend more than twenty days a year hiking in their boots. (Midweight boots are the standard choice for the backcountry traveler in the Northeast.) And what about those impressive heavyweights, the wafflestompers of yore? Those are best saved for expeditions of more than two weeks in wet or cold conditions, or on very rough terrain.

FITTING YOUR BOOTS

Once you decide which category of boot will work for you, it's time to try some on. In this age of internet shopping, it is tempting to order a pair of well-reviewed boots online. Finding a boot that matches your foot's idiosyncrasies, however, is an experiential process. While certain items of outdoor gear are fine to buy online, there is no substitute for spending some time in potential boots. Once you have done your internet research, a trip to an outdoor footwear retailer is worth the time and effort.

Be sure to wear the same socks in which you'll hike, and try on several different sizes and brands. Walk all over the store and try to find places to climb and descend sloping surfaces. (Most good stores will have a ramp of some sort where you can do this.) Load up a pack with the amount of weight you intend to carry on your heaviest trip. Our feet change shape when we add weight to our bodies, so this will affect how your boots fit. When laced up snugly, your boot should have even pressure across all of the laces. There should be enough room in the toe box for all toes to wiggle, and your toes should never touch the end of the boot—even when descending a slope. As you walk and ascend a slope, your heel should stay in the heel cup without moving at all. Pay particular attention to possible pressure points on the back of the heel, the top of the toes, and the top of the instep. While a heavyweight boot will not be as comfortable in the store as a lightweight, the basic fit will not change as it breaks in. A painful boot in the store will be a painful boot forever. A few boot manufacturers have a fit guarantee, meriting those brands special consideration. Once you have found your perfect fit, celebrate and imagine all the wonderful places these shoes will take you.

FABRIC HYBRID VERSUS FULL LEATHER

Modern boots are often light and comfortable right out of the box, well ventilated and fast drying, and still supportive enough to carry a full pack on a multiday trip. The easiest way for boot manufacturers to accomplish these ends is to make the boots out of a hybrid of nylon fabric and split-grain leather instead of full-grain leather only. The results are impressive, with a comfortable, functional, waterproof-breathable hiking boot weighing barely more than 2 pounds a pair. Well fitted, they are a joy on your feet. But before you completely discount the old-school leather boot, there are two trade-offs you should consider.

First, hybrid-fabric boots are waterproof because they have some kind of membrane (such as GORE-TEX) on the fabric. Whatever the brand name, all of these

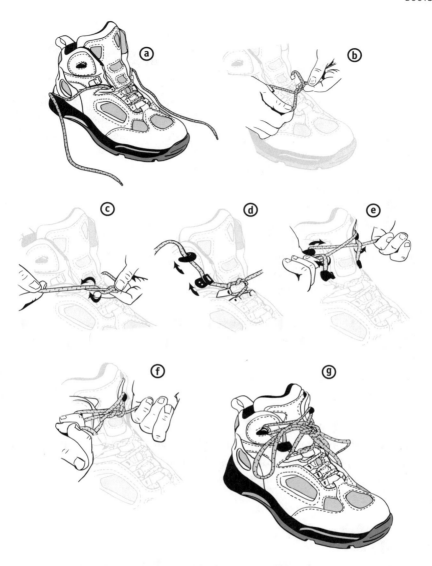

FIGURE 9. To properly lace hiking boots, begin by securing your ankle at the back of your boot. (a) Lace as usual through the regular eyelets, stopping before you reach the hooks up top known as "speed laces." These are the open-ended holders nearest the ankle; typical boots have two per side, with the lower speed laces often different in shape from the uppers. (b) Tie a double overhand knot, meaning (c) over, under, and over again. This locks off tension in the lower part of the boot, nearest the toe. (d) Take the right lace and pass it through both speed laces on the right side. Do the same with the left lace on the left side. (e) Now take the right lace and weave it underneath the length of lace stretched between the two left speed laces. Do the same on the other side. This looks a bit like a cat's cradle, and when you pull it taut, the laces create tension at the top and bottom. (f) Make another double overhand knot to hold the tension. (g) Then tie a bow like you usually would and double-knot it.

membranes will fail to function as designed before the boot wears out. The repetitive flexing of walking creates leak spots in the fabric after a fairly short distance. And the sweaty, dirty environment of a hiking boot leads to eventual clogging of the fabric's breathable pores. You can end up with a boot that does not breathe nor keep water out. While a full-leather boot never breathes as well as a fabric hybrid, its waterproofness can always be restored with boot wax or some other type of waterproofing treatment—even during a long expedition. This benefit is particularly important in the woods and mountains of the Northeast, where we almost always encounter wet conditions at some point in a hike.

The other trade-off is in durability. A full-leather boot can last for thousands of miles and will need to be retired only when the sole is too worn to be repaired. We each have had full-leather boots that served hundreds of days in the field. Fabric hybrid boots, on the other hand, have a shorter lifespan, based on the durability of the stitching that holds together the various panels. At high-abrasion areas, such as at the flex points next to the big and little toes, fabric hybrid boots often begin to pull apart or unravel when the rest of the boot is still in excellent shape.

So what to do? Think about the type of hiking you are likely to pursue and how often you are likely to do it. For day hikes and trips shorter than three days, with a total of fewer than twenty days a year, choose a hybrid fabric boot. This is especially true if you expect to hike mostly in dry summer conditions and stick mostly to marked forest trails. Once home, you can help sustain the breathability of your boots by rinsing them in cool, clean water and allowing them to dry. Also, look for boots that are constructed with very durable materials and thread, such as Kevlar, for enhanced longevity. If you are hiking more often, will be heading out in wet shoulder-season conditions, or will be spending a lot of time with a heavy pack in rough, rocky terrain, go with a full-leather boot or at least a boot that has minimal stitching and fabric. The small increase in weight will be worth the substantial increase in longevity.

→ GAITERS

Keeping your feet and socks clean and dry is the most important thing you can do to prevent foot blisters. A good pair of gaiters will shed a lot of water and mud, and will keep dust and pebbles from finding their way into your shoes. Full-height versions can also save your ankles and shins from scree, rocks, and brush.

Gaiters should fit flush against your boots and lower pant layers without being constrictive, but they must be tight enough to prevent your boot from filling with mud and water. The more of your footwear that's covered by gaiters, the warmer and drier (but less breathable) your boots will be. Finally, recognize that it's rough out there in gaiter country. Look for the most durable models that will fit your needs but accept that you inevitably will repair them at some point.

CHAPTER 3
GEAR

While we all share John Muir's passion for the wilderness, most of us differ in our approach to equipment. Leaving for the mountains with the right gear on your back, and on your body, is critical to enjoying your time there. As you get ready for your trip, you will consider the questions of "why," "who," "where," and "when."

Depending on your answers to these questions, you'll make different decisions about what to wear, what to sleep in and on, what you need to cook, which safety essentials to bring, which extras to bring for comfort, and finally, what you are going to carry all of this in! We'll look at these seven categories of gear that are important to consider:

- Safety essentials
- Clothing and footwear
- Cooking and kitchen supplies
- Shelter
- Sleeping systems
- Other essential and nonessential items
- Backpacks

→ SAFETY ESSENTIALS

All of us aspire to travel through the mountains unencumbered, but experienced backcountry travelers and outdoor professionals have identified a list of ten essential items that should be carried anytime a person treks into the mountains, whether for a day or a month. Versions of this list are endorsed by all major land management agencies and respected outdoor organizations. The ten essential items are:

1. **Map**
2. **Compass—and the knowledge to use one**
3. **Warm clothing**
   - Warm upper-body layer
   - Warm lower-body layer
   - Warm hat
4. **Extra food and water**
5. **Flashlight or headlamp**
6. **Matches/fire starter**
7. **First-aid kit and repair kit**
8. **Whistle**
9. **Waterproof and windproof upper- and lower-body layers**
10. **Pocket knife**

This traditional ten is simple, time-tested, and still utilized by some land management agencies. For experienced backcountry travelers, though, it has been refined to describe a more systematic set of needs every backcountry traveler should be prepared to meet. This approach gives hikers more flexibility and judgment regarding what gear they carry while still meeting their fundamental safety requirements:

1. **Navigation**
2. **Sun protection**
3. **Insulation**
4. **Illumination**
5. **First-aid supplies**
6. **Fire starting**
7. **Repair kit and tools**
8. **Nutrition**

9.   **Hydration**

10.   **Emergency shelter**

Regardless of which of these two lists you use, all discussions of gear and equipment must start and end here. Consider the ten essentials the underlying foundation of all gear choices discussed below, and always be sure you have the gear serving these functions before you hit the trail.

➜ OTHER ESSENTIALS AND NONESSENTIALS

3

In addition to the items noted above, there are a few more items most backpackers would consider essential, plus many optional items for comfort and enjoyment.

ESSENTIAL ITEMS

Our truly essential list is not long, and some of these items can be shared by the entire group:

- **Maps.** We prefer to always carry United States Geological Survey (USGS) topographic maps of our travel routes, in addition to detailed trail maps for the area where you will be traveling. One-gallon zippered freezer bags make excellent map cases with enough durability for a week or more on the trail.

- **Trail guide.** Unless you are intimately familiar with your route, bring a photocopy of the trail guide description. It will come in handy if you need to adjust your route or when trying to sort out the confusion at that backcountry trail junction.

- **Headlamp.** Choose an LED model with adjustable brightness and a lens that can be pointed downward. A spare set of batteries is a small weight penalty for big insurance that your headlamp will continue to work.

- **Water containers.** Either bottles or bladders, they should be big enough to carry 2 quarts of water for personal use.

- **Toiletries.** These items are guided by personal preference, but good hygiene in the backcountry is considerate of your travel partners and an important part of preventing illness. Weight savers can get away with a toilet kit weighing less than 2 ounces: sunscreen, nail clippers, a shortened toothbrush, travel-size toothpaste, and a comb.

- **Personal prescription medications.** Don't end your trip early because these were left at home!

- **Sunglasses.** Protect the eyes from sunburn, especially if traveling above treeline or along bodies of water.

3

- **Camp shoes.** A light pair of sneakers or rubber sandals perhaps isn't required, but they are strongly recommended. Camp shoes allow your feet time to breathe and expand, sometimes preventing blisters and other foot ailments. The smaller tread of camp shoes will do a lot less damage to the ground in campsites, reducing a hiker's overall impact. In situations where a boot is damaged, lost, or a foot is badly blistered, a hiker can continue on in certain conditions.

- **Pocket knife or multitool.** A basic blade is necessary for all kinds of chores in camp. Choose a folding model that locks open, with a blade no longer than 3 inches. A larger, fixed-blade sheath knife is less useful and adds unnecessary weight. Some backpackers like to bring a multitool instead of a plain knife, but be sure that the model you choose has only tools you are likely to use.

- **Lighter.** This is necessary to start the stove, useful for sealing the ends of fraying cord and webbing, and helpful for emergency fire-starting. Bringing at least two is a good idea.

- **First-aid kit.** This is a group item. It usually is helpful to have both a very small foot-care kit and a slightly larger full first-aid kit. See Chapter 6, Health and Hygiene, for a full discussion of this essential item.

- **Repair kit.** Another essential group item. See "Repair Kit Essentials and Options," below, for more.

REPAIR KIT ESSENTIALS AND OPTIONS

A repair kit is one of the ten safety essentials. With some key items on hand, a backcountry traveler can prevent a gear or clothing malfunction from ruining a trip—or worse. There are a handful of absolute must-haves and a few other items that depend on your other gear selections.

For us, these items have proven extremely useful over decades of backcountry travel:

- **Duct tape.** Ten feet will be more than enough for a week or two. Wrapping it around water bottles and trekking poles is a popular method, but be careful that it doesn't become permanently attached (likely, if you put hot water in your bottles).

- **Needle and thread.** With a small and large needle and regular and heavy-duty thread, there is no fabric that can't be repaired, from long johns to packs.

- **Safety pins.** Four or five of these are unnoticeable in a pack, but will find a thousand uses, such as replacing broken zipper pulls or holding fabric together while you sew it.

(continued)

- **Small scissors.** The careful cutting action of scissors is hard to improvise when slicing tape or making other repairs. One reasonable ultralight alternative is a razor blade, which is capable of fine cuts in fabric, similar to scissors.

- **Seam adhesive.** There are many different brands of this gooey product, which can be used for an endless number of tasks, from stopping leaks to fixing blown-out boot soles.

- **Clear repair tape or patches.** This stretchy tape matches any fabric color and will instantly repair raincoats, tent flies, and tarps. If you are camping with equipment made from silicone-nylon fabric, be sure the brand you purchase will adhere to it.

3

- **Spare pack belt buckle and shoulder-strap slider buckle.** When broken, these two pack parts can lead to a very difficult hike. While it is possible to improvise solutions, they are rarely satisfactory. Some models will need to be sewn on, and others are designed to slip right onto the existing webbing strap.

- **Hot glue stick.** Manufactured for use in hot glue guns, these glue sticks can be melted with a lighter and applied to any fabric or hard plastic (such as food bowls, sunglasses frames, or kitchen utensils). They can also be used to patch small punctures in self-inflating mattresses. One is enough for a weeklong trip.

- **Small cordage.** About 10 feet of 1/8-inch nylon cord packs to about the size of a golf ball but can be used for numerous functions, such as replacing a tarp tie-out cord, hanging up the laundry, or attaching an item to a pack. Don't bring too much; 10 feet will do it.

- **Extra batteries.** Not exactly a repair item, but still required to keep your headlamp and other electronics functioning.

Other items to consider, depending on the group's size, your equipment selections, and the length of the trip:

- **Sleeping pad repair kit.** If you have an inflatable mattress, you should know which materials are required to repair tears and punctures, and how to do so. Sometimes a tiny pinhole can be filled with glue alone, but larger damage usually requires fabric and glue designed specifically for sleeping pads.

- **Stove maintenance and repair kit.** Testing your stove at home beforehand will prevent many field-repair situations, but the need for maintenance can come up. A couple of O-rings weigh almost nothing, and they can't be improvised.

(continued)

- **Tent pole repair sleeve.** This 2- to 3-inch sleeve of aluminum slides over a broken tent pole, splinting it. These are hard to improvise in the field, so carrying one can solve a trip-ending problem.

- **Speedy-stitcher sewing awl.** These devices combine the functions of an awl and a sewing machine into one portable tool, great for extended expeditions and groups. A wooden handle and large-diameter needle penetrate heavy fabrics with ease, and the heavy waxed thread is extremely strong and durable. They are priceless for major repairs to packs, camp chairs, food duffel bags, and webbing, and a well done speedy-stitcher repair will be permanent and effective.

- **Zipper repair kit.** Most zippers have sliders that can be replaced if broken. If the slider can't be coaxed to work better, replace it with a new one. The other option is to sew or safety-pin the zipper shut, which may work for a day but will be a hassle for an entire trip.

The most important resources in field repair are not physical; they are ingenuity and know-how. Rather than overfill your repair kit, get to know your equipment well. Take it apart and reassemble it at home. Read the repair and maintenance instructions that come with complex equipment such as water filters and liquid-fuel stoves. There are also a few excellent gear-repair books that really boost a hiker's knowledge and creativity. *Complete Guide to Outdoor Gear Maintenance and Repair* by Kristin Hostetter (Falcon, 2012) is one such reference book. A well-done repair will save a lot of discomfort and possibly an entire trip. Skillful, elegant field repairs become a matter of pride for experienced backpackers, demonstrating the kind of resourcefulness and mastery that are the hallmark of the true wilderness traveler.

OPTIONAL ITEMS

The list of optional items to consider for comfort is much longer. If you brought everything on this list, your pack would balloon in size and weight. Choosing judiciously and sharing items among group members can add a lot of comfort and enjoyment to a backcountry trip.

- **Biting-insect protection.** In many regions from mid-May to mid-September, biting flies can impact a backcountry trip. A simple head net weighs less than an ounce and provides a lot of relief. (In the heart of blackfly season, May and June, a head net belongs on the required list.) For maximum relief, consider bringing a repellent pump or lotion made with 25 to 30 percent picaridin (no need for a greater concentration). The same concentration of DEET is considered safe and also works, but DEET can dissolve certain plastics and ruin waterproofing. Picaridin is a better choice for the backcountry.

- **Bandanas.** A couple of these are incredibly useful for first aid, for straining debris from water, as clothing items, or as patching material.

- **Waterproof backpack cover.** Depending on your personal system, this can add extra security to your pack's contents.

- **Vacuum bottle.** A 0.5- or 0.75-liter bottle allows a hiker to "cook" quick foods on the trail and store hot water in the camp kitchen, saving fuel. At the end of a cool, damp day, it can be great to not have to wait for that first hot drink.

3

- **Coffee maker.** If you are an obligatory coffee drinker who isn't willing to use instant coffee, there are many dedicated backcountry devices that can brew an excellent cup.

- **Cookbook or other recipes.** Depending on your kitchen plans, it might be helpful to have some inspiration for creative cooking creations.

- **Trekking poles.** Many hikers report that trekking poles alleviate knee pain (especially on long descents) and allow them to travel over uneven terrain more quickly and efficiently.

- **Camp chair.** Some models integrate with a sleeping pad, and others are independent. Many backcountry travelers enjoy the experience of lounging in a camp chair at the end of the day while eating dinner or taking in a vista. Look for ways to make the chair multipurpose, such as utilizing it as extra structure for a light pack or sliding it under your sleeping pad for extra comfort and protection.

- **Pillow.** Most hikers can make a comfortable pillow by filling a stuff sack with a fleece jacket, but if you really like the perfect pillow, there are inflatable camping versions that have foamy padding and soft flannel exteriors.

- **Notebook and writing utensils.** Great for keeping track of trip events, sketching, writing letters to friends, or sending out emergency messages.

- **Pack towel.** Some people prefer to not have to drip dry.

- **Hanging lantern.** Either candle- or battery-powered, a lantern adds nice ambiance in a tent, tarp, or lean-to and can provide enough shared light for cooking, reading, or playing cards.

- **Fishing gear.** Be sure to check the local fishing regulations before you head out, and use fish only as a supplemental part of your trip menu.

- **Books.** Some hikers really enjoy having a novel or some nonfiction to read in camp. Others bring backcountry-skills reference books or carry their favorite field guides for birds, mammals, amphibians, trees, or wildflowers. The weight of all of these can add up quickly, so look for one general-purpose guide that provides adequate information or consider bringing a phone, e-reader, or small tablet. (Be sure to read the note about electronics, below.)

- **Games and toys.** Some hikers enjoy having games to play in camp. There are lightweight versions of playing cards and trivia cards, and travel sets of chess, cribbage, backgammon, and checkers. Other hikers like foldable flying discs or juggling sacks. Items like this can be especially helpful for families with children who find themselves camping in wet weather.

OPTIONAL ELECTRONICS

Before setting out on your trip, remember that technology use should be a point of discussion with your group beforehand. Many people use hiking/backpacking as an opportunity to unplug and may be bothered by glowing screens. Electronics also mean extra logistical considerations that everyone might not be on board with.

- **GPS unit.** Many hikers are happy to navigate with only a map and compass, but others find a GPS unit helpful. These units can provide a source of fun for geocaching adventures.

- **Communication devices.** Perhaps forgotten except in an emergency, most hikers will want to bring a cell phone. International travelers may carry satellite-based technologies, such as phones or texting devices. Other groups might bring two-way radios for short-distance communication on the trail.

- **Personal emergency location devices.** There are a few satellite-based devices that can convey your location to people in the frontcountry, activating a search-and-response team, if necessary (e.g., SPOT Personal Trackers and emergency position indicating radio beacons, or EPIRBs). These are not completely fail-safe, however, and should only be used in case of emergency.

- **Camera.** If you want to unplug from your phone, a dedicated digital camera will have much more storage capacity and much longer battery life, usually with higher resolution for both videos and still shots.

- **External power source.** All these electronics need power! Backcountry travelers replenishing their devices can choose between batteries and a generator. There are many models of supplemental batteries that can be charged at home then used to recharge devices in the backcountry. These have a direct relation between power and weight. Generators are cutting-edge backcountry technology and can be mechanical, solar, or even thermal. Mechanical models use some kind of winding crank and are best used for emergency purposes. Solar panels are relatively expensive, and usually need more surface area and time than a backpacker can dedicate to the process. One innovative company (BioLite) is producing a biomass-burning stove that uses its excess heat to produce electricity. For the gadget-oriented hiker, this might be an ideal power-source solution.

→ SHELTER

We all dream of sleeping out beneath starry skies, warm and comfortable. And occasionally, everything aligns for one of these magical experiences. When hiking, though, it is always wise to bring something in which to shelter you and your sleeping bag from the elements as you sleep. Depending on your goals, travel location, and the weather forecast, you might choose to bring any combination of a bivouac sac, a tarp, or a tent.

BIVOUAC SAC (BIVY)

3

A bivouac sac (or "bivy") is the simplest form of protection for you and your sleeping bag. It is a roomy cover that encases the sleeping bag and pad, protecting them from dirt, rain, and dew. It will have a durable, waterproof lower half (against the ground) and an upper half made from a waterproof-breathable fabric. Usually a bivy will also include some form of bug screen and the option to zip up in wet weather. Fancier versions begin to resemble tiny solo tents with one or two small poles that lift the fabric off the face and the feet. Sleeping in a zipped-up bivy is not particularly pleasant, though, so most people prefer the simpler version. If the weather is wet or the bugs are bad, it's time to get under a tarp or in a tent. A bivy is essential gear for anyone hoping to sleep out under the stars or under a tarp. It's also useful for hikers sleeping

in a lean-to for protection from driving rain—or even in a tent, in especially cold conditions. A bivy must be roomy enough to allow your sleeping bag's insulation to fully expand, and it will add 5 to 10 degrees (Fahrenheit or Celsius) of warmth to a bag's rating.

FIGURE 10. A bivouac sac, or bivy, provides protection from the elements and insects while allowing you to sleep without a tent or other shelter in moderate weather.

TARPS   6×8,   8×10,   10×10,   10×12   •Best sizes

Tarps are arguably the most important piece of equipment in your pack. Their versatility is unparalleled. Tarps can provide a nighttime sleeping shelter, a roof for your camp kitchen, shade from the summer sun, or protection from powerful winds. They can be pitched low in storms, high in good weather, or with a lean-to shape for a porchlike feel. Expert campers will pitch their tarps in all kinds of configurations, depending on their needs. In seasons where biting insects are not a concern, a tarp is often all the shelter you need, especially when paired with a bivy for a little extra protection. A 10-by-12-foot tarp made from silicon-coated nylon

• Highly affordable
• Easy to repair

will weigh less than a pound but can easily serve four people's needs for sleeping and kitchen shelter. We outfit our tarps of this size with eight to ten 20-foot tie-out lines made from lightweight, reflective cord, and the total package compresses to half the size of a loaf of bread. Even when a tent is the best choice due to insects or weather, most hikers will want some kind of tarp for a kitchen shelter. A small 6-by-8-foot tarp provides adequate cooking coverage for two to three people if you're not also using it for sleeping.

TENTS

The tent is the iconic representation of camping life. A truly great tent becomes a trusted companion on many backcountry adventures and a welcome haven at the end of a long or stormy day. Tents provide the maximum possible shelter from weather, as well as increased privacy over a tarp. Even so, their greatest feature might be their protection from biting insects. There are three basic categories of tent construction from which a hiker can choose, depending on goals and budget.

→ THREE-SEASON BACKPACKING TENT

This is the typical choice for the summer backcountry traveler. A three-season backpacking tent has an inner body made mostly of mesh, which keeps the bugs away while releasing body heat and humidity. A network of poles typically supports the mesh body, making the tent free-standing. A waterproof nylon fly, designed to keep rain out, fits over the poles and the mesh body. The lower the fly reaches toward the base of the tent, the better it will protect against rain, but a longer fly will encourage condensation from breath and sweat. In clear but buggy weather, it's a good idea to roll up the fly as high as possible or to leave it off. Other tent amenities a hiker might find helpful are interior pockets, an external fly extension (called a "vestibule") for covering shoes and packs, and multiple doors. Each amenity adds some heft, and the weight range for this class of tent is broad. A three-season backpacking tent for two people usually weighs between 3.5 and 6 pounds, and costs between $150 and $450. The same class of tent for four people could weigh as much as 9 pounds and cost $250 to $650.

MOUNTAINEERING TENTS

Mountaineering tents are built similarly to three-season backpacking tents, but they are designed to handle the extreme winds, rain, and cold weather of all seasons, as well as to provide a spacious shelter for stormbound mountaineers. They are sturdy, with hardier fabric on the inner tent body, heavier-gauge aluminum poles, and a fly that reaches all the way to the ground. The trade-offs for this durability are a 25 to 50 percent weight increase and a substantial decrease in breathability. Most mountaineering tents require mechanical ventilation—zippers and vents—to release condensation, again adding more weight. A good mountaineering tent can

FIGURE 11. A three-season backpacking tent (shown, from left, without and with a fly) provides more protection than a bivy but adds considerable weight.

withstand heavy snow loads and 60 MPH winds. If you plan on camping in these conditions and you can afford only one tent, then a true mountaineering tent is for you. If not, you will be completely satisfied with a three-season tent. Expect to pay as much as $600 for an 11-pound, three-person tent or $850 for the lightest options (about 7.5 pounds) with high-tech fabrics and carbon-fiber poles.

LEAN-TOS AND OTHER STRUCTURES

Lean-tos, or three-sided semipermanent to permanent shelters typically constructed from logs, and other structures, such as huts, are also shelter options in many parts of the Northeast. Their locations are publicly available and close to popular hiking areas. It is possible to plan a hiking itinerary that takes you from one to the next, never requiring a night in a tent. Most lean-tos don't provide much protection from biting insects, though, so summer hikers may want to carry at least a bivy with bug netting. A hiker planning to sleep in lean-tos should also carry some form of tarp in case of an unexpected delay resulting in the need to shelter from a storm. (This tarp will also allow you to cook away from the lean-to in damp weather, which is good practice for bear-conscious camping and is considerate of other lean-to visitors.)

Staying in lean-tos involves extra planning and social considerations. Some lean-tos require a fee, while others do not. Most have a first-come, first-served policy, so you could arrive and find there is no more room. Be aware that lean-tos and other buildings inside federally designated wilderness areas are considered nonconforming structures, meaning they no longer comply with federal wilderness regulations. As these lean-tos age and need replacement, they are usually removed. Be sure that your information is up-to-date by checking with local agencies or organizations. If you have planned effectively, you will not be surprised.

FIGURE 12. A typical backcountry lean-to, or three-sided shelter, offers additional protection from the weather for backpackers who choose to use a bivy. Call ahead to ensure all lean-tos on your itinerary are in good condition.

There are also some rules of etiquette when staying in any shared backcountry shelter, be it a lean-to or a hut. In these heavy-use areas, the seven Leave No Trace (LNT) principles are more necessary than ever. Plan to arrive in daylight and keep your group's noise and visual impact as minor as possible. As night falls, be aware of others' desire to sleep. Many backpackers prefer an early to bed, early to rise pattern in the backcountry, so that late-night poker game should happen elsewhere. The lean-to is primarily for sleeping, so don't hang dirty laundry there or dump out your backpack on the floor. For safety and courtesy, cooking should occur 200 feet from the structure. As hubs of human activity, lean-tos are also very attractive to nuisance animals, from mice to bears, so be especially vigilant about protecting food and garbage. While some lean-to areas may have a big fire pit, the wood supply likely will have been exhausted. If you must have a fire and regulations allow it, gather firewood a 15- to 20-minute walk away. Long-distance hikers (such as those thru-hiking the Appalachian Trail) often rely on lean-tos, so they are typically given a space, even if they arrive late. If your group is larger than three or four people, it is better to use a tent or another shelter option. By attentively practicing the LNT principles and maintaining a basic level of courtesy and thoughtfulness, you will help these backcountry shelters remain places of enjoyment and positive social connection.

• Mouse city! Beware of rodents

➔ SLEEPING GEAR

Once you know what you are sleeping under, it is time to create your sleep system. Sleeping gear choices are very personal, so it's no surprise there is a great diversity of options. Any sleep system should help you maintain the right temperature, protect you from the lumpy ground, stay functional in a wide range of weather conditions for the duration of your trip, and be durable enough to last for many backcountry excursions. Along with the bivy, mentioned above, a standard sleeping setup involves a sleeping pad and a sleeping bag.

SLEEPING PADS

3

Sleeping pads can be as simple as a half-inch-thick foam mat that you roll out each night or as sophisticated as a 3-inch-thick inflatable air mattress with a layer of memory-foam padding. In between these two ends of the spectrum are more moderately padded self-inflating mattresses that combine air and foam. All three of these options have advantages and disadvantages.

The simple foam pad is enough comfort for many hikers, providing adequate cushioning and lots of insulation. The pad cannot pop or deflate unexpectedly at night, and it is inexpensive (about $15) to purchase and replace. A full-length model weighs only about half a pound. That said, the only models worth considering are made from closed-cell foam that does not absorb water. The iconic model is simply flat foam, but there are versions that use waffle or egg-crate shapes to increase padding and insulation without adding extra weight. Because these types of pads don't compress well, hikers often want to store them outside their packs. Unfortunately, the closed-cell foam is not particularly durable, and branches regularly tear bits off, littering the trail. If you are hiking on wide-open trails this might not be a problem, but otherwise, it will be necessary to pack the mattress inside your pack.

Self-inflating air mattresses have open-cell foam laminated inside a

> ➔ **PRO TIP** If you are a foam pad aficionado, try the "cinnamon roll" method to protect your pad and still maximize room in your pack: Roll up the pad then insert it vertically into your pack. Encourage the roll to unwind partway, pressing against the inside walls of the pack. This will leave a large open space in the center. Fill this space with your gear. This method gives extra structure to lightweight backpacks and leaves a tight, smooth-looking pack. The foam is useful material for a variety of camp projects (e.g., insulating a bowl, building a splint, or padding an inadequate or oversize hip belt), so it often gets cannibalized bit by bit over the course of several trips. Since these pads are so inexpensive, nobody seems to mind! Choose the foam pad if you are a no-fuss camper looking for an inexpensive, classic, and lightweight option.

waterproof, inflatable, coated-nylon container. The open-cell foam compresses further and is more easily packable than a closed-cell foam pad, which makes it softer and cushier, too. The thinnest, lightest models are about 1 inch thick and weigh about 1.1 pounds, providing excellent comfort at a reasonable addition to pack weight. At the other end of the spectrum are pads that are 2.5 inches thick and weigh almost 3 pounds. These are for the hiker who prioritizes sleep comfort and who does not want to spend much time looking for a flat piece of ground. A pad this thick can smooth out most roots and bumps. One of the challenges of the self-inflating air mattress is that the open-cell foam requires greater thickness to produce the same level of insulation as much thinner closed-cell foam. If you expect to be sleeping on frozen ground or snow, choose a self-inflating pad that is at least 1.5 inches thick, with an insulation rating (called the "R-value") of at least four. (Another option for frequent winter campers is to bring both, placing a closed-cell foam pad against the ground and a self-inflating air mattress on top of that. Luxury!) Another important consideration is that self-inflating mattresses require some care to prevent punctures, and you should know how to repair one in case yours gets a leak. Prices for self-inflating mattresses range from $80 to $150. A sleeping pad in this category is the standard choice for most hikers, providing reliability, relative ease of use, and multiseason versatility.

The relative newcomers to the sleeping pad game are the true air mattresses. These options resemble a classic floating pool mattress, and they usually don't contain any foam inside their nylon or vinyl covers. With only air inside, these mattresses can pack down extremely small (about the size of a 1-quart water bottle) and very light (about 3 ounces more than a closed-cell foam pad), while providing 3 inches or more (one model offers 6 inches) of comfort padding. These are revered by many backpackers for their ability to smooth the roughest campsite ground. There are a few downsides to this design, though. The bouncy, pool-mattress feel may take some getting used to, and if it gets punctured, absolutely no padding remains. It is also difficult to achieve the same level of insulation as with the other two categories of sleeping pad, so most air mattresses are confined to trips that do not involve sleeping on very cold ground or snow. (A few models do provide limited insulation, at a cost to both weight and compressibility.)

Most people will find the greatest drawback to be the effort required to inflate these mattresses. Because there is no internal foam to assist the inflation process, each night requires serious lung power—enough to cause you to hyperventilate and get dizzy if you don't pace yourself. Many companies are incorporating innovative inflation technologies into their mattresses that alleviate this drawback, but none is time-proven yet. Air mattress prices are in the $120 to $200 range. Choose this kind of air mattress if the price doesn't bother you, you want the cushiest sleeping platform for three-season use, you prioritize a small and light pack, and you don't mind a little extra setup each night in camp.

SLEEPING BAGS

Once you decide what you will use for a shelter and how you will protect yourself from the ground, it's time for some backcountry bedding. The main choices in sleeping bags revolve around temperature rating, shape, and insulation type. Once you have settled on these parameters, there are several other features and options to consider as well.

Temperature Rating

How warm of a bag you need is a personal decision, depending on the seasons in which you expect to hike as well as your own thermostat. It is common for experienced hikers to own two or more sleeping bags that meet specific needs and conditions, perhaps a warm bag (+/- 15 degrees Fahrenheit; +/- -9 degrees Celsius) for early and late season, and a very light bag (45F, 7C) for midsummer. The bag with the greatest versatility is a bag rated comfortable down to 20 to 25F (-7 to -4C), because it will withstand any normal three-season conditions and can always be opened up to vent extra heat. The opposite choice is a 40 to 45F bag (4 to 7C), which is just warm enough to let a hiker sleep in confidence on midsummer mountain nights. Many manufacturers make a bag in the 32F (0C) range as well, which may be the best solution if you need just one bag for the full range of conditions, May to September. If you are a normal to warm sleeper, you can accept most manufacturers' temperature ratings as roughly accurate. If you are a cold sleeper, consider adding 10 to 15 degrees to the suggested temperature ratings. Research confirms that women and smaller people both have a tendency to sleep colder than the average male, so look for bags designed specifically for you or buy a warmer unisex bag. Remember that warmer bags have more lofting insulation, so they will take up more space and add more weight to your pack. Some people stretch the temperature rating of cooler sleeping bags by wearing extra clothes to bed. This strategy can work, but too many clothes will compress the loft of the bag, actually making you colder.

Insulation Material

Once you settle on the best temperature rating for your needs, you can consider the insulation options. Sleeping bags maintain their insulating air space with lofting material made from either synthetic polyester filament or natural goose down. Sleeping bags insulated with synthetic fiber have disadvantages and advantages. Even when stuffed into a compression stuff sack, a 20F synthetic bag (-7C) rarely gets smaller than a small beach ball. It will take up a significant amount of real estate in a hiker's pack. Another drawback is that the synthetic fibers eventually get crimped and broken from repeatedly being forced into their stuff sacks, losing some loft over a multiyear period. (A well-cared-for synthetic bag, even when used for 20 to 30 nights a year, will still have enough loft to retain most of its temperature rating after many years of use.) Offsetting these disadvantages are the clear cost advantage of synthetic bags, sometimes found on sale for less than $100, and their ability to retain most of their loft when your tent leaks, your backpack accidentally gets dunked, or rain clouds hang around for days.

Down-insulated bags use feathers to maintain air space. The loftiness, or fluffiness, of down can vary and is reported by a measure called fill power. Fill power represents the number of cubic inches that 1 ounce of down will expand to fill. The higher the number, the loftier the down, meaning that less of it will provide the same amount of insulation. Reasonable-quality down sleeping bags begin at 600 fill power. Avoid bags that have 550 fill power or lower, as these will perform similarly to much less expensive synthetic bags. The high end of the range is 900 fill power, which is extremely warm, with a noticeable advantage in weight and compressibility. Since high-fill-power down is rarer and more sought after, it is also more expensive. Bags in the 700 to 800 fill power range often strike the best compromise between performance and price. All down bags compress well, with a good-quality 20F down bag (-7C) easily compressing to the size of a loaf of bread or smaller. Down also retains more of its ability to fluff back up, even after hundreds of stuffing cycles. Plus, as a natural product, down has a much lower carbon footprint than any of the synthetic-fill options. (You may wish to look for manufacturers who intentionally purchase their down from ethical sources.) A down bag will cost at least 20 percent more than a comparable synthetic bag, with high-fill-power 20F (-7C) bags reaching $500.

The problem with these bags is down's inability to maintain loft in wet conditions. Unprotected down exposed to persistent rain or an accidental dunking always ends up soggy and worthless. In recent years, technological developments have allowed manufacturers to apply durable water-repellent treatments directly to the down feathers. Nearly all sleeping bag companies offer a version of this "hydrophobic" down, promising better performance in wet conditions. Field-testing supports these claims to a point. Hydrophobic down bags (and garments) still do not perform as well as synthetics when saturated, but they do resist clumping and compression when exposed to moderate wetness. While not perfect, even this amount of water resistance is a tremendous improvement over untreated down. Expect to add another $30 to $50 to the cost of a sleeping bag filled with hydrophobic down.

Shape

For backcountry hiking, a mummy-shaped bag is the most versatile choice. Compared with a mummy bag's sleek, tapered shape, a rectangular bag is heavy and bulky, and is best saved for car camping. The ideal bag allows for some movement and is not snug on any part of the body. A good mummy bag's contoured shape includes a foot box with enough room for a little movement. A contoured hood adds a small amount of weight but may provide greater comfort in cool or cold conditions. A good test of fit is if you get in wearing fleece layers on top and bottom, and you don't feel like the bag is tight. Hikers of all shapes and sizes can find a good fit, with most manufacturers producing bags in a few widths and at least two lengths. Be sure your choice has no more than 6 inches of extra space in the foot box, as more airspace there will lead to cold feet. Sleepers who curl up in a ball or roll around a lot might look at bags with an hourglass shape or those that have baffles stitched with elastic thread, allowing for greater freedom of movement.

Other Options

Once you settle on a temperature rating, insulation type, and shape, you can get creative with lots of other options. Some bags have elastic straps that hold the bag and pad together. Zippers can be placed on the left or right side of the body or can go right down the center of the bag. Hikers looking to shave weight may choose a bag with a zipper that reaches only to the hip, although most prefer to have the option of venting their feet on warmer nights. Since they will be compressed by body weight anyway, a few bags have no insulation on the underside. These weight-savers have a sleeve that holds an insulated sleeping pad in place—a good strategy in warmer seasons. A few bags carry this design to the extreme, removing the zipper altogether and functioning more like a quilt. Another consideration is shell material. Some hikers prefer to shave weight here, too, with the lightest microfiber fabrics. Others choose to emphasize weatherproofing, selecting bags with waterproof-breathable outers. If you travel in the backcountry with your intimate partner, most manufacturers create bags (and sleeping pads) that attach together, creating one cozy sleep space for a couple.

Balancing all the different choices of sleeping bag design can feel daunting, especially when taking cost into consideration. But sleeping bags deserve careful thought, perhaps more than almost any other piece of equipment. Hikers will spend a third or more of their backcountry time in their sleep system, and the sleeping bag is one of the single largest and heaviest items in the backpack. It's worth the effort to find the best possible solutions.

To summarize, synthetic bags are excellent for backpackers on a budget, for novices, for anyone who does not want to fuss with equipment, and for anyone who holds water resistance as a key priority. With a little smart shopping, highly functional, comfortable, three-season bags in this category can be found for as little as $100. A down bag is a good choice for more experienced hikers or those who don't mind putting effort into keeping their bags dry in rainy weather. A good three-season down bag can be found for $150, and versions with hydrophobic down can be found for about $200. Enjoy this selection process and envision the cozy cocoon you'll have soon. With just a little time and effort, you'll select a bag that becomes a cherished companion on backcountry travels for years to come.

3

• Challenging to set properly

HAMMOCKS   *• Heavier than most options*

Hammocks turn a lot of the preceding discussion about shelter and sleeping systems upside down. Hammock camping has become more popular in recent years, especially among hikers interested in going lighter. Several companies now make durable, well-designed products in this vein. Dedicated hammock sleepers are quite passionate about their approach to backcountry sleeping. First they will tell you about the unparalleled comfort, "like sleeping on a cloud." They will tell you they are liberated from worry about rocky, sloping, or muddy ground. They will tell you hammocks do less damage to backcountry campsites, since campers do not compress the ground and vegetation where they sleep. They might tell you they can sleep anywhere there are two trees near each other. All of this is true, but hammock sleepers still have to solve the same three basic challenges of sleeping in the backcountry: rain, bugs, and cold.

Rain is the easiest challenge to meet. A well-sized tarp over the hammock, pitched correctly, will shed nearly any storm, and some hammock users use a bivy to add a little more protection to their sleeping bag. Biting insects can be defeated with some kind of personal bug net, maybe a head net over a brimmed hat or a bug net integrated into the bivy. Cold is the most difficult problem to solve. The sleeper compresses the loft of the sleeping bag against the hammock, but there is no sleeping pad as there would be on the ground. One solution is to purchase a special insulated quilt that encases the underside of the hammock, but most hammock users simply avoid them or choose another option in very cold conditions.

By the time hikers put a separate hammock, tarp, bug net, and bivy together, they are approaching the weight of a light tent, and they have a lot of individual pieces to work with when pitching camp. A simpler solution many hammock campers prefer is an integrated hammock sleep system. These "tents in the sky" combine the hammock with an over-tarp and bug net, and they pitch with one simple process. Zippered walls and low-hanging tarp ends make them weather-tight, so most users will not bring a bivy. There are sizes for one or two people. With all of the required gear for suspension in the trees, a one-person integrated hammock system will weigh about 4 pounds and cost about $200. If you are an adventurous person looking to break the mold of the typical backpacker while lightening your pack a bit, hammock camping might be for you.

• Sleep diagonally to lay flat

→ CAMP KITCHEN

When our groups head into the backcountry, we want them to really live in the woods, to thrive there and not merely survive. Good food and shared meals support this outcome, so we have a basic kitchen setup that balances weight with functionality. A kitchen outfit does not need to be heavy or bulky to be capable of producing delicious meals for a group of two to four people. Like all outdoor gear, cooking equipment is lighter and more functional now than ever before. With the gear described below, we can eat very well and still have more than enough room in our pack for weeks on the trail. You can use a small collection of pots, stove, utensils, and accessories, along with some way to protect your food from animals, to prepare a nearly limitless diversity of satisfying meals. Let's look at each of these elements.

POTS

3

Our basic pot set consists of one or two nesting pots with at least one lid and a multipurpose fry-bake pan that also has a lid. Depending on your group size, go with a 1- and a 2-liter pot, or a 2- and a 3-liter pot. With this setup you can produce lots of hot water—an important kitchen commodity—and still cook nearly any recipe imaginable, even ones that technically call for a double boiler or a pizza oven. Stainless steel pots are durable and fairly inexpensive, and they distribute the heat from a cookstove quite well. They also work well when used over an open fire. Titanium pots cost about three times as much as stainless for a few ounces of weight savings. If you are trying to go ultralight, a simple, economical approach is to leave one stainless pot behind. Nonstick coatings don't hold up well for extended use, so give a little more attention to keeping the heat low on the stove, when possible. Using a lid on pots minimizes fuel usage, so always bring at least one that can work on either pot. A pot lid also doubles as a serving tray and a cutting platform. The Alpine or Base pot set from Mountain Safety Research (MSR) works well. In our experience, it never wears out, even after thousands of meals.

A frying pan might seem luxurious, but it is incredibly useful in our camp kitchen. Sautéing vegetables or small portions of meat helps release their flavors and lets you combine these ingredients with pasta, rice, or other grains. Sauces are easier to make in a frying pan. And you can turn simple ingredients into interesting dishes, such as lasagna. Choose a frying pan with a lid, as this doubles its utility. One of our most important pieces of kitchen gear is the Banks Fry-Bake pan (frybake.com). Designed for backcountry travel, this frying pan comes with a cover and doubles as a baking oven. It is made of anodized aluminum that distributes heat well and is resistant to scorching and sticking while frying. The snug-fitting lid seals in heat and even holds burning twigs or coals, enabling it to bake as well as fry. The 10.5-inch pan weighs 1.75 pounds, as compared to 6 pounds for an aluminum Dutch oven or 13 pounds for a cast iron version. There's also a smaller model that works well for solo or lightweight trips.

STOVES

The stove is the workhorse of the kitchen, and it must operate reliably. For the kind of cooking we do, the ideal stove has many qualities. It is light, packable, and easy to use. It is powerful and uses fuel efficiently. It is both durable and field-repairable. It can produce a range of temperatures, from jet engine to gentle simmer. It will boil water quickly but still allow for interesting cooking. There are several types of stoves to consider, but first you should revisit your goals for the trip and for your camp kitchen.

3

For some backpackers, camp cooking means rapidly boiling water for a ramen packet or a freeze-dried meal in a bag. For others, it means preparing homemade spicy Thai peanut sauce over noodles, with brownies for dessert. For those who are especially interested in preparing healthy, delicious meals in the backcountry, check out *AMC's Real Trail Meals* by Ethan and Sarah Hipple (April 2017; amcstore.outdoors.org). Determining where you and the other travelers in your group fall on this spectrum will help you make your stove choice, as will answers to a few other questions: Do you want a stove that operates as quickly and simply as your kitchen range at home, or is it OK for your stove to require a bit of technique? Do you mind if your stove makes a roaring noise as it works? Can you live with the occasional smell of gasoline? Will your trips be mostly a day or two, or will you be out for more than three or four days? Will you be hiking in very cold environments or on winter trips? How many people will you be cooking for? Do you ever expect to take your stove on international trips? Your answer to each of these questions will inform your decision to go with a canister stove, an integrated pot-stove system, a liquid-fuel stove, or another option.

The first choice is between canister and liquid-fuel stoves. Canister stoves use pre-pressurized cans of highly refined, liquefied natural gas (usually a blend of isobutane and propane). One can of fuel is enough to cook for two people for about two or three days in warm weather. Integrated pot-stove systems, such as Jetboil stoves or the MSR Reactor, are a subset of this category. Canister stoves are incredibly easy to operate, especially for the novice hiker, with setup times of a minute and instant lighting without preheating. There is no chance to spill fuel on your gear, food, or hands. The lightest versions are true featherweights, weighing only a couple of ounces and fitting in the palm of your hand (without the fuel canister attached).

As with all equipment choices, the canister stove's ease of use comes with some trade-offs. Once the temperature drops below freezing, pressure in the canister decreases to the point that fuel will not come out. The stove will not work unless you have purchased a model that can invert the canister to burn the liquid fuel (much less efficiently). Windy conditions steal the heat from the stove, and you can't use a windscreen with most models since the fuel can overheat to the point of explosion.

STOVE ECONOMICS

A 4-ounce canister of fuel costs roughly $5 and can boil about 20 liters of water in the most efficient pot-stove systems. A 20-ounce bottle of white gas costs about $2 to fill with high-quality camping gas and can boil at least 36 liters of water. Doing the math, that means that every liter of water boiled with canister fuel costs about 25 cents, whereas every liter boiled with white gas costs about a nickel. On a short solo trip, this difference might not matter, but on longer trips or with more than one person, the cost of canisters adds up quickly.

If you can't decide between canister and liquid fuel, a hybrid fuel stove (such as the MSR Whisperlite Universal or the Primus Omnifuel) might be for you. These stoves use interchangeable fuel jets, among other parts, that are compatible with both canister fuel and white gas. These stoves provide maximum versatility but there's a trade-off, of course. The hybrid-fuel stoves are the same size as the liquid-fuel options, and they cost about 20 percent more than the other choices. A hybrid-fuel stove may be the right choice if you expect to take very short trips with small groups and longer trips with larger groups, or if you expect to be traveling in a region where fuel availability is unpredictable.

3

The fuel cans are typically only available at camping retailers and are nonrefillable, so the cost per meal is substantially higher than for camping gas. Also, the empty metal canisters must be recycled by using a special tool to puncture the can and release the remnants of the fuel into the atmosphere.

Integrated Pot-Stove Systems

Integrated pot-stove systems also use a canister. They address some of the above problems but have trade-offs of their own. These cooking systems combine the canister, stove, small pot, windscreen, and heat exchanger into one unit that weighs about 1.25 to 1.5 pounds. They often cost three times what a comparable canister or liquid-fuel stove does, and with less functionality. An integrated system is awesomely efficient at boiling a liter of water—but not much else. There is little capacity to simmer and no ability to use a different pot or pan. If you think a canister stove might be for you, consider an integrated system if you expect to travel with one or two people in above-freezing weather, and if you want to prepare meals in the backcountry by heating water and adding instant food.

Liquid-Fuel Stoves

These stoves burn some variant of petroleum, typically white gas, a generic term for camp stove and lantern fuel, usually naphtha. Some models can burn unleaded automotive gas, or even kerosene or diesel fuel, which is a real advantage if you expect to travel internationally. Instead of a prepressurized, prefilled canister, liquid-fuel stoves use refillable bottles connected to the stove body with a flexible fuel

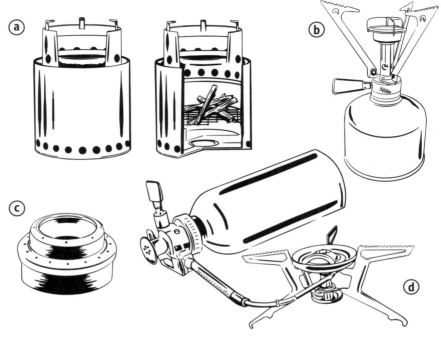

FIGURE 13. Pictured above: (a) a biomass burner, which uses organic material as tinder; (b) a canister stove; (c) an alcohol stove (see Chapter 12, Ultralight Backpacking, for more on alcohol stoves); (d) a typical liquid-fuel stove, with the burner attached directly to the fuel source.

line. This bottle is pressurized with a small, integrated pump, and the stove must be preheated (called "priming") with a small amount of fuel before it will work.

At first glance, liquid-fuel stoves don't seem to rival canister stoves. They are certainly not as quick or brainless to operate. Instead of the instant-on experience of a canister stove, that initial assembly, pumping, and priming could add a couple of minutes before your liquid-fuel stove is humming along under your pot. By the time you add the various parts—pump, stove body, fuel line—a liquid-fuel stove is likely to be at least 6 to 10 ounces heavier than a typical canister stove. So, if they are heavier and require more setup and fussing, why does anyone choose a liquid-fuel stove? There are many reasons. These stoves operate in any weather condition, regardless of wind or temperature. They boil water very rapidly and simmer well, too, so they are versatile enough to cook complex meals forwgenerating metallic waste that must be recycled or disposed of in a landfill.

COOKING OVER CAMPFIRES

LEAVE NO TRACE **5**   What about the no-fuel (and no-stove) cooking solution? Cooking around a campfire is one of the most time-honored camping experiences, and in some ways, the ultimate cooking solution. In many environments the fuel is plentiful, and you don't have to carry it in your pack. With a little practice, it's not difficult or time-consuming to start a small fire just large enough to cook over—only two or three minutes in dry weather, which can give a great feeling of accomplishment, too. And instead of the roar of a gas burner and the smell of fumes, you get crackling twigs and wood-smoke ambiance. For some hikers, these benefits are a fair trade-off for blackened pots and smoky eyes.

3

That said, there are many good reasons why camp stoves have become the dominant choice over campfires throughout the Northeast. In very wet or snowy weather, cooking over fires can become a burden or a near impossibility. What's more, preventing substantial impacts from your campfire requires real attention, effort, and skill. There are many locations where fires are not appropriate due to fuel unavailability and the likelihood of leaving a fire scar. Nor are they appropriate in the many locations where fires are not allowed at all or during the frequent fire bans put in place due to elevated fire danger. Unless you know you are camping only at sites with existing fire grates, campfires are not a weightless cooking option. You still need to carry something that will allow you to hold your pots and pans over the flames, such as a tripod system or portable burner. Even the lightest of these will weigh roughly the same as a stove system.

There is no denying the great ambiance and primitive satisfaction that comes with cooking over fires. But in contemporary times it is no longer appropriate to rely exclusively on campfires for cooking in the backcountry. With much greater user pressure on the backcountry than in decades past, and with large areas of the Northeast's recreation lands off-limits to campfires, stoves are the better choice for the backcountry hiker. Campfires are best kept to established, designated sites—or even better, frontcountry campfire rings.

BIOMASS BURNERS

One possible cooking system that is a hybrid of stove and campfire is a biomass-burning stove. Usually these involve a battery-powered fan that drives a draft into small woodchips, pinecones, and other small, woody debris. The stove weight is about the same as that of a canister stove, and you do not have to carry fuel from place to place. These biomass burners, however, are still vulnerable to the same constraints as a campfire: wet weather, regulations, fuel-gathering impact, and fire hazard. They are only functional for one to two people and have a lower temperature adjustability

3

EFFICACY OF STOVE TYPES			
Fuel/Stove Type	**Advantages**	**Disadvantages**	**Best Choice For**
Liquid Gas	• Works in all conditions • Inexpensive fuel • Easy to find fuel • Fast boil times • Can handle large or small groups • No disposable canisters	• Bulkier and heavier • Requires assembly, priming, and pumping • Fuel can spill on gear, hands, or food • Generally louder when lit • Needs occasional cleaning of fuel line and burner	• Maximum versatility • You don't mind having to perform occasional stove maintenance • Winter camping, long expeditions, international travel • You want to save money on fuel
Canister	• Easy to light and run • Quieter operation • Smaller and lighter • No fuel spillage	• Canisters less commonly available than liquid fuel • Much costlier than liquid fuel • Disposable canisters create waste problems • Must carry canister, even when empty • Quickly loses efficiency below freezing	• Trips shorter than two days, or with fewer than four days between resupplies • Groups of three or fewer • Weather above freezing • Ease of use is your priority
Hybrid-fuel	• Versatility	• Same bulk and weight as a liquid-fuel stove • Must change stove jet to switch between fuels	• Switching between fuel sources • Good for both very short trips and longer trips • Traveling internationally, where fuel flexibility is important • You don't mind having to perform occasional stove maintenance

EFFICACY OF STOVE TYPES (CONTINUED)			
Fuel/Stove Type	Advantages	Disadvantages	Best Choice For
Pot-stove canister systems	▪ Greatest efficiency for canister stoves ▪ Shortest boil times ▪ No maintenance ▪ Can eliminate one eating bowl	▪ No choice of pots ▪ No frying or baking ▪ Limited capacity for creativity ▪ Most expensive category	▪ Fast and light ▪ Traveling solo or in a group of two ▪ "Cooking" means boiling water
Biomass	▪ Fuel source is free and readily available ▪ Campfire ambiance	▪ Need fire-lighting skills ▪ Requires constant tending/feeding of fuel ▪ Can't use where fires are banned (or in alpine or desert areas) ▪ Challenging after very wet periods ▪ Blackens pots	▪ Travel in forested environments ▪ Travel in good weather ▪ You have strong fire-lighting skills ▪ Traveling solo or in pairs ▪ You like tending a fire in camp
Campfire	▪ Ambiance ▪ Connection with nature and human history	▪ Prone to leaving a big impact ▪ Blackened pots ▪ Not appropriate in alpine environments or high-fire-danger times	▪ Semiprimitive experience ▪ Don't mind blackened pots

3

than either canister or liquid-fuel stoves. If you do choose to use fires or a biomass burner for part of your hike, be sure that you consult the camping regulations for the specific location and overseeing agency where you are headed, and check the overall fire danger rating as well.

UTENSILS

You need only a few kitchen utensils to cook anything, so utensil choice is a great opportunity to keep it simple. With a small spatula and a spoon for stirring and perhaps serving, you have what you need to cook it all. While plastic utensils are the lightest, we often choose metal ones for their durability and their ability to scrape food from pots, a frying pan, and bowls.

All hikers also need their own bowl, cup, and spoon. Having lids for the bowl and the cup helps keep food warm, allows for the storage of leftovers, prevents spills, and can facilitate hydrating or slow-cooking. A durable, resealable leftover container (holding 12 to 16 fluid ounces) from the grocery store is our choice for a

> ➜ **PRO TIP** Use a small amount of closed-cell foam from an old sleeping pad to make a "bowl-cozy" for your covered eating bowl. This will keep your food warm for a long time and will make it easier to use your bowl for rehydrating and slow-cooking.

very effective and low-cost option. There are also numerous designs available from outdoor companies that nest within a pot set. Some ultralighters choose to have only one personal container: a large cup/bowl, for example. This does shave some weight, but we usually prefer to have the option to drink and eat at the same time.

Like all things in our pack, we do our best to make our kitchen utensils as multifunctional as possible. For example, our kitchen knife is just our everyday pocket knife. Pot-grips are the best example of the multifunction principle. We don't bring a dedicated pot-gripper. Instead we bring a pair of small (4.5 inches long) tongue-and-groove pliers (often known as Channellock pliers). This tool can grip any pot from a variety of angles and can be used to crimp rivets, tighten zippers, remove fish hooks, and repair stoves, in addition to a huge range of other purposes. The added weight is worth the extra function, but a gram saver might experiment with using a small multitool (such as those from Gerber or Leatherman) for even more functionality.

NECESSARY ACCESSORIES

- **Windscreen.** If you are using a stove with liquid fuel or a remote butane canister, a windscreen will keep your cooking fire's heat from blowing away. By increasing your stove's efficiency, you save on fuel costs, fuel weight, and environmental impact. Safety note: Using a windscreen with a conventional canister stove is never safe, as it overheats the canister, potentially causing it to explode.

- **Ground shield (metal).** Stoves that do not sit right on top of a canister benefit from resting on top of a simple piece of lightweight aluminum. Many manufacturers include this item with their stoves. The ground shield reflects some radiant heat upward, increasing the stove's efficiency, and protects the ground from scorching.

- **Cleaning supplies.** Through careful cooking, kitchen cleanup can be a minimal process. For example, when we make a pasta-and-cheese dish, we usually avoid mixing the cheese directly into the pot, which makes the pot hard to clean. Instead we usually choose to refry the pasta with some cheese in the frying pan (toasty cheese is delicious!), or mix some cheese into the pasta in our personal bowls. Then, before our pots and bowls ever get near soap and water, we do our best to dry-scrape them until they are nearly clean. By following this process we minimize both the need for hot cleaning water and the introduction of soap into the environment. Still, cleaning needs to happen, so we bring a small kit that consists simply of a nylon scrubbing pad (cut down to about a 2-by-2-inch size) and a bottle of biodegradable camp soap (1 to 2 ounces is enough for multiple weeks of travel). If our pots are going to get blackened by fire, we might also bring a small piece of coarse steel wool, although scrubbing with fine sand will remove the black, too. Putting all of this into a little mesh bag helps it to dry quickly.

3

- **Sanitation.** Again, we like to thrive in the backcountry, not just survive. An upset stomach can really ruin a trip and is usually avoidable. Keeping our food free from bacterial contaminants is no harder in the backcountry than it is at home. Nearly all gastrointestinal illnesses in the backcountry come from our own hands, so we always wash our hands before cooking and after using the bathroom. This practice also slows the spread of colds or other illnesses among groups. For this reason, always bring some solid antibacterial soap in a small resealable container and keep it near the top of the kitchen supplies. A 1-inch cube is enough for a week or more on the trail.

- **Sump screen.** A small screen is essential to strain the very last bits of gray water after you've cleaned your dishes. By pouring the gray water through the screen into a small hole in the soil, any bits of food are removed, preventing them from contaminating the water or attracting wildlife.

  LEAVE NO TRACE **3**   LEAVE NO TRACE **6**

- **Water reservoir (dromedary).** One of the best features about backpacking in the Northeast is our relative abundance of water. Nearly all designated campsites are within easy walking distance of a reliable water source, and even when camping in remote or pristine places, water is usually not far away. No matter your campsite's proximity to water, though, we recommend bringing some kind of durable, collapsible water reservoir that can be used to transport water from the source and store it in camp. Using a container like this decreases the need to camp on the banks of streams and creeks, and reduces the number of walking trips you must make between kitchen and water source. Not only is a water reservoir convenient, it prevents streamside trampling of fragile plants and foot-trail development. There are many good options from which to choose, with sizes ranging from 2 liters (acceptable for a solo trip) to 10 liters (good for groups up to four or five). If you are concerned about weight, consider using the reservoir during the day as one of your containers for carrying water as you hike, eliminating a water bottle.

> ➔ **PRO TIP** One of the best features of a water reservoir is that on longer trips you can fill it with warm water and use it as a backcountry shower!

OPTIONAL EXTRAS

3

- **Rubber spatula.** A rubber spatula can be very useful in the kitchen. Convenient for scraping out food containers before washing them, and for getting the most out of your bread and brownie batters, these little tools come in handy. Choosing a narrow model and trimming a bit of its handle helps make the weight trade-off worth it.

- **Measuring cup.** A 1-cup measurer can be very helpful for novice outdoor cooks trying out new recipes. A measuring cup with a handle doubles as an effective dipper for serving food and hot water.

- **Baking accessories.** We have already mentioned the value of a covered frying pan for baking, and this is probably all you will need. (Skillful technique is your best ally in the quest for the perfect cinnamon bun!) The truly avid back-country baker might also consider bringing a couple of other small accessories. A diffuser plate sits between your stove's flame and the bottom of your baking pan and helps to prevent scorching. A fireproof pot-cozy is made from fiber-glass and usually has a reflective aluminum interior. It creates a hot microen-vironment for your baking pan, decreasing fuel usage and baking times while also increasing the uniformity of heat. The Pot Parka from Backpacker's Pantry is the best-known example of this tool.

- **Extra stove.** For groups larger than five or six, a single stove starts to feel a bit cramped. You might decide to split into two smaller cooking groups or stay in one group with one stove for food and another for hot water. Either way, a second stove will be a welcome addition in groups this size or larger.

➜ BACKPACK

Eventually you have all of your backcountry gear collected and ready to go. You have made good choices, removed the unnecessary, and pared down as much weight as you can. You have also made some delicious food decisions and have just the right amount of sustenance, too. Now you need something to carry it in—a backpack!

All backpacks are basically a combination of a big fabric bag and a harness that attaches that bag to your body. The harness, usually consisting of shoulder straps and a hip belt, is called the suspension. Pack volume comes from the dimensions of the bag (and any pockets), and pack size comes from the dimensions of the suspension. Selecting a pack involves choosing the optimal volume for your purposes, the right size for your body, and the optional features that meet your needs.

Backpack volume is measured in liters or cubic inches, and you will see either or both, depending on the manufacturer. It might help to remember that 1,000 cubic inches equals about 16 liters. Pack volume categories are roughly based on the number of nights a backcountry traveler expects to be out on the trail and usually correlate with intended pack weight, as well. This system makes sense, as there will be a 1.5- to 2.25-pound increase in food weight for each person, each day on the trail. (See Chapter 9, Cooking Skills, for more details about food planning.)

The smallest packs are meant for a single night out. Packs in this category will be between 40 and 50 liters (2,500 to 3,000 cubic inches) and are designed to carry loads of less than 25 pounds. Even for one night out, these packs will require efficient packing and a minimal amount of compact equipment. Some experienced hikers consider them fair-weather or summer packs, since there isn't much room for extra layers or a tent. In cold, wet conditions, it will be challenging to fit all of the required gear into a pack of this volume.

3

The next tier of packs is between 50 and 75 liters (3,000 to 4,500 cubic inches), designed to carry loads up to about 40 pounds. These versatile "weekender" packs are very functional for two to four days on the trail, or even a couple more if you are an extremely efficient packer.

For trips of a week or longer, look for a pack between 75 and 90 liters (4,500 to 5,500 cubic inches), designed to hold big loads up to 50 or 60 pounds. The biggest packs are 100 liters or more (more than 6,000 cubic inches). These monster load-haulers are designed for multiweek expeditions with bulky gear or for parents carrying supplies for the whole family. Densely packed with food and equipment, an expedition megapack can easily top 70 pounds or more.

Pick the pack volume that fits your most typical outdoor experiences. If the majority of your trips are two or three nights, choose a weekender pack. If you know you'll regularly head out for a week or more, choose from the 75- to 90-liter class. Take comfort in knowing that most packs will be able to stretch up and down, into the adjacent category. A 65-liter weekender can be cinched down for the occasional overnight or expanded to handle the load of a five-day trip. One poor strategy is to buy the largest pack you might ever need, thinking you can just use its straps to cinch it down. In an emergency, this is certainly workable, but it is not a wise choice. An oversize pack will not feel comfortable or carry its load well if it is not sufficiently filled. And beware: An empty-seeming cavernous pack is very easy to fill up with unnecessary items. Finally, remember that as the pack volume increases, the weight of the pack itself will also increase. If you buy a giant pack, you will always be toting around a few extra pounds of suspension and heavy-duty fabric—weight that will never get used, could simply be left behind, or could be dedicated to more food or luxury items. Choose a pack with the volume that is right for you.

PACK SIZE AND SUSPENSION

Choosing a pack with the appropriate size and suspension is one of the most important factors in a comfortable, injury-free trip to the mountains. Padding on the

3

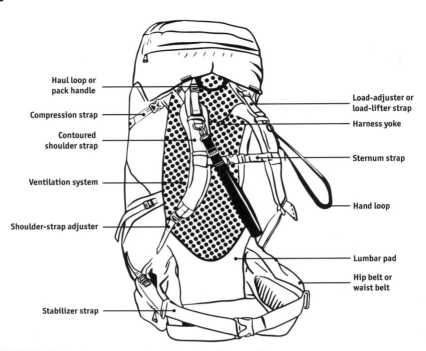

Haul loop or pack handle

Compression strap

Contoured shoulder strap

Ventilation system

Shoulder-strap adjuster

Stabilizer strap

Load-adjuster or load-lifter strap

Harness yoke

Sternum strap

Hand loop

Lumbar pad

Hip belt or waist belt

FIGURE 14. The basic components of a backpacking pack.

shoulder straps and hip belt add a little comfort, but the way these pieces fit your body is most important. Correct torso and hip sizing will optimize weight distribution across the widest range of the body. This is the secret to minimizing pressure points and feeling like your pack is floating on your body.

The most important dimension is the length of your torso (not your height), followed by the circumference of your hips (not your waist). Torso length is measured between two points on your spine, and you will probably need a friend to help you measure it. The top point is the seventh cervical vertebra (C7), the bony bump right at the base of the neck. If you look downward, it pokes outward and becomes obvious. The bottom point is the center of the line that connects the two bony tops of your hips (the iliac crests). If you rest your hands on top of your hips, fingers forward and thumbs backward, the line connecting your thumbs is the bottom point. Standing with good posture, the measurement between C7 and the line connecting the iliac crests is your torso length.

Hip belt comfort is extremely important. The hips should carry 75 to 80 percent of the pack weight, and it is the hip belt, in contact with the iliac crests, that transfers this load. An accurate measurement of hip circumference is less important than torso length because it's easier to adjust the size of a hip belt. Since some packs offer different sizes of hip belt, though, it's good to know your own dimensions. Hip circumference is measured right at the top of the hip crests described above, all the way around the body. It is a good idea to take this measurement wearing all of the different combinations of clothing you will wear on the trail, from lightweight hiking shorts to a fleece jacket and rain shell. You will then have a range with lower and upper limits, which your pack's hip belt should be able to accommodate.

Once you know your torso and hip sizes, you can choose your pack size. Manufacturers address pack sizing in two ways. One way is to offer sizes similar to clothing (e.g., XS, S, M, L, XL). Packs with this approach have a fixed torso length, so it is important to choose correctly. As with any clothing selection, a person can be between sizes, where it's difficult to get a perfect fit. The other method for pack sizing is to create an adjustable suspension, with a system of buckles and webbing that allows for substantial changes in torso length. Packs with this approach usually come in two overlapping size ranges. The adjustability makes it possible to get a custom fit, but the extra material will add some weight. Again, spend the time to make sure that your pack fits you perfectly, and prioritize fit over all other pack features. It is far more important that your pack fits you right than to have a desired configuration of pockets or zippers.

PACK FEATURES AND OPTIONS

After you find a pack with the appropriate volume and get it to fit your body like a glove, the rest will seem easy. There are a few standard features that all desirable packs will have: load-adjuster straps above the shoulders, a sternum strap, stabilizers connecting the hip belt to the main bag, side compression straps, and small pockets at the base of each side. If the pack you are considering is missing any of these features, it's not likely to work for real mountain travel. Once you've got all of those, a few personal preferences remain. These variables primarily are related to gender specificity, access methods, and compartments and external pockets. Let's consider the options.

Some gender-specific pack-design features have an anatomical root, while others have more of a cultural root. In general, anatomical considerations lead to additional customization for a woman's body. Compared with men, women tend to have shorter torsos, narrower shoulders, and broader, more flared hips. To respond to these anatomical features, some packs are offered in size ranges better suited to female averages. These packs may have shoulder straps that are attached more closely to each other, with a more pronounced "S" shape to accommodate breasts, and a hip belt that has a more conical shape. These design features can help women find packs that fit comfortably. The other elements of gender-specific design are more culturally driven, such as different colors and extra organizing pockets. Each hiker will have to decide if these design features are desirable or not.

Pack manufacturers generally offer two choices for accessing a pack's main well: a drawstring or roll-top closure, or a zipper closure. The drawstring and roll-top methods create a giant central space, with most access through the top. They also

60° (max.)   **45° (ideal)**   **30° (min.)**

FIGURE 15. When fitting a backpack, a 45-degree angle between the pack's load-adjuster strap and the wearer's neck is ideal. Make sure you have no less than a 30-degree angle and no more than a 60-degree angle to avoid the risk of injury. See "Adjusting Your Pack for Comfort and Efficiency" on page 107.

3

allow for a long collar of lightweight material that can be expanded to swallow oversize loads. These designs promote a bottom-up packing approach that has to be reversed whenever an item on the bottom is needed.

The zipper closure (also called "panel access") design provides access differently. These packs are usually packed while laid flat on the ground, on top of their shoulder straps. A large zipper, sometimes horseshoe-shaped, opens the pack for full access to the interior, something like a traditional suitcase. Panel-access packs eliminate the problem of getting to an item at the bottom of the pack, but they do not allow for much volume expansion. Also, when they're fully packed, the zipper takes a great deal of strain. It will be the first part of the pack to wear out, and sometimes this failure happens during the trip—a major hassle. Most packs try to combine the drawstring's durability and expandability with some zipper access. Often a drawstring or roll-top bag will have a horizontal zipper for bottom access and/or a vertical zipper down one side. Some combination similar to this is the best choice for a majority of backpackers.

There are other pack features designed to promote organization and easy access to essentials. The most common is a separate bottom compartment for a sleeping bag, usually with a zipper. The zipper itself, if it's durable, can be a helpful feature for reaching items in the bottom of the pack. But nearly all contemporary, three-season sleeping bags compress much smaller than the compartment itself. If the pack has a divider that separates the upper section from the sleeping bag compartment, this divider will lead to a lumpy pack, with pockets of unused space in the bottom. Usually the divider can be detached, but if not, consider cutting it right out or choosing a pack without this feature. It is extra fabric weight that may never be used.

Packs can also promote organization and accessibility via external pockets. Most drawstring-closure packs have a useful "lid" with a pocket. The most useful lids can expand upward as the pack is loaded (a "floating" lid), and can be detached for use as a small fanny pack for day hikes. Another common location for external pockets is high on the center of the back, opposite the hiker's spine. These "kangaroo" pockets are quite useful and where we often stash a first-aid kit, a fuel bottle, and a field notebook. Beware of filling these pockets too heavily. Because they are far from the hiker's back, they move the pack's center of gravity backward, forcing the hiker to lean farther forward to maintain balance. Only fairly light items should be placed in this pocket. The final location for external pockets is on the pack's sides, a design feature that was much more common twenty years ago. Pockets in this location tend to be tall and narrow, and they can be useful for isolating fuel bottles from the rest of the load. But most contemporary backpackers find that the sides of the pack are better used for strapping on trekking poles or other long and slim items.

3

When considering the quantity and the location of external pockets, remember that every pocket adds fabric and zipper weight to your pack. In our experience, an abundance of external pockets often seems to discourage good organization; there's always a pocket in which to stuff something that isn't really necessary to keep handy. With a little experience, backcountry travelers will quickly develop organizational strategies that prioritize the main pack compartment, with a lid and perhaps a kangaroo pocket for holding truly essential trail items.

There is an almost endless list of potential pack features to consider, and pack manufacturers offer new ones each year. Remember that the bells and whistles of pack design have as much to do with attracting a customer's attention as they do with on-trail functionality, so focus on the essentials. Once you have a pack of the correct volume that fits you well, all other features are less important.

PACK WEIGHT

The weight of all of this gear, from clothes to kitchen goods to the pack itself, begins to add up, which leads to two questions. How much can a person carry, and how much should a person expect to carry on a trip? Historically, wilderness-leadership organizations have used percentage of body weight as a sliding scale to find maximum pack weight. With a well-fitted pack, healthy adult hikers typically should be able to carry 35 to 40 percent of their body weight, while experienced and seasoned hikers can carry 40 to 50 percent of their body weight, if required. These maximum percentages should not be seen as targets. Rather, these upper limits have been defined by wilderness-education institutions to prevent the risk of injury from overloading and to promote equitable distribution of a group's gear among its members.

Of course, maximum is not optimum, and as modern backpacking equipment gets smaller and lighter, pack weights have also dropped. Without food and water, a reasonable and affordable kit for three-season travel will weigh roughly 20 pounds, which assumes the following:

- Sleeping bag (2.5 pounds)
- Sleeping pad (1 pound)
- Sheltering items such as a tent, hammock, or tarp and bivy (4 pounds)
- Stove, fuel, and other cooking items (5 pounds)
- Remaining clothing and safety essentials (4 pounds)
- The pack itself (3.5 pounds)

3

On top of this, add two quarts of water (4 pounds total) and food (let's say 6 pounds for a three-day trip). These bring the pack's total weight to about 30 pounds without any luxury items. Most contemporary backpackers would consider a 30-pound pack to be quite manageable and comfortable, especially if it allows them to travel for two or three nights in the backcountry. For a week on the trail, add another 8 pounds for food and perhaps an additional 2 pounds for clothing or luxury items. These bring the pack weight to about 40 pounds at the trailhead, getting a bit lighter with each meal. If the trip includes activities that require specialized gear (such as snow and ice travel, or backcountry rock climbing), the weight estimates will increase, but even so, there is no need to shoulder a monster load for a week of backcountry travel.

➜ PACKING YOUR PACK

To reduce shoulder and hip discomfort, as well as to better organize and care for your equipment, it is best to load your pack by following some basic packing principles. We call these principles the ABCDs of packing. In this mnemonic, "A" stands for **accessibility**, "B" for **balance**, "C" for **compactness**, and "D" for **dryness**.

ACCESSIBILITY

When packing your gear for a day on the trail, it's important to think about what you will (or might) need to quickly retrieve during the hike. Some gear and items of clothing should be kept easily accessible so that no one in your group will have to wait for you in the rain because you stuck your raincoat at the very bottom of your pack. The items that are most often identified as "accessible" include: water bottle, trail food, sunglasses, sunscreen and lip balm, map, first-aid kit, headlamp, camp trowel, personal hygiene kit, compass, GPS, camera, and cell phone or other communication device. The "A" items should also include extra layers of clothing, such as a rain jacket and rain pants, a medium-weight upper layer, a warm hat and/or a sun hat, and gloves or mittens. Items that do not need to be readily accessible include your sleeping equipment, shelter, kitchen equipment, and the rest of your clothing and camp shoes.

Depending on your pack, the location for these "A" items can vary, but often it's effective to use the top lid pocket (a.k.a. brain) of the pack, followed by side or rear pockets, if your pack has them. Compress your supplementary warm and rain layers between the top of the pack's main pack and the bottom of the lid pocket. Many modern packs come with a hydration system, giving you easy access via a hydration tube to water in a hydration bladder worn inside the pack. Other packs include water-bottle-sized side pockets specifically designed to be easily reachable without having to put down the pack or asking someone else to hand you your water.

Note that accessibility does not mean packing your pack like a Christmas tree. Forget about hanging many items on the exterior of your pack. These most likely will throw you off balance if they're heavy or get caught on branches. Keep your gear inside and safe.

3

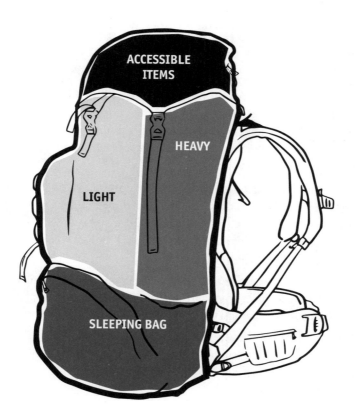

FIGURE 16. When packing a backpack, distributing weight as illustrated above reduces the risk of hip and back injury, transferring much of the work to the legs.

BALANCE

When it comes to balance, we're now talking about your pack's center of mass. Here, the word "balance" refers to three types of weight distribution that settle most of your pack weight on your hips, which in turn transfer most of the work of carrying your pack to your legs—the strongest set of muscles in your body.

Your pack weight needs to be balanced on its vertical axis, its horizontal axis, and its medial axis (i.e., depth). Your goal when packing the main compartment is to place the heaviest items closest to the pack harness, centered between the shoulder straps where the yoke is. Dense and heavy items, such as food, cooking gear, and your hydration system (if your pack has one), should be about two-thirds of the height of your main compartment on the vertical axis, mostly center on the horizontal axis, and anterior (or at the back) on the medial axis. If you place these items in this location, your pack's mass will be located between your shoulder blades and close to your back. Remember, when the center of your pack's mass is placed in this location, you will be able to transfer most of your pack weight onto your legs.

COMPACTNESS

Every pack has limited carrying capacity, but with a few tips and techniques, you can stretch this capacity much further. In other words, you can always put more in a pack than you think. Now, we are not advocating that you bring unnecessary equipment or clothing, but by using the right technique, you easily will be able to bring all of the gear you really need. Here are a few tips and techniques for compacting all of your gear in your pack.

1. If your pack has an internal divider between its bottom and middle parts, consider removing it. Most dividers can be unzipped or detached easily. Dividers have a tendency to create empty spaces above and below them, and it's easier to compact your equipment without them. Think of your pack as a big tube that is filled from the top.

2. Start filling the bottom part of your pack with as many camp items as possible, such as your sleeping gear, warm clothing, and camp shoes. Use your fist to push down these soft items.

3. Shrink your sleeping bag by using either a compression stuff sack or a garbage bag. Using a garbage bag will allow you not only to compress your sleeping bag but also to waterproof it. Read the time-tested technique described below, under "Dryness."

4. Warm and bulky clothing, such as jackets and pants, also can be placed in stuff sacks, but smaller clothing items—socks, shirts, upper and lower base layers—should be stuffed into empty spaces at the bottom of your pack.

5. Containers such as pots, fry pans, cups, and bowls should be filled with smaller objects or food.

6. Finally, once all of your equipment, clothing, and food are inside your pack, use the external compression straps to further cinch and shrink your pack, stabilizing your load.

DRYNESS

There are many ways to keep a pack dry. For more information on the methods behind each of these, see "Keeping Dry" on page 109. Here is a quick list of different ways to keep dry when the weather turns for the worst.

3

                                –Contributed by Matt Heid; see outdoors.org/dryness

- **Garbage bags.** The ultimate in lightweight, inexpensive, stay-dry versatility, garbage bags can be used in two primary ways: as a waterproof liner inside your backpack or as inside-the-stuff-sack protection for your clothes, sleeping bag, and other gear.

    For a pack liner, you'll need a large, heavy-duty trash bag ample enough to accommodate all of your gear and durable enough to handle repeated use and abuse. Look for heavy-duty trash bags designed for outdoor cleanup with a thickness of at least 3 mil. Contractor bags work well; the best are orange or another bright color, which improves your visibility in the event of a survival situation. A heavy-duty trash bag can also serve double duty as an emergency shelter.

- **Pack covers.** Although you can use a garbage bag to cover the outside of your pack, it's a poor substitute for an actual pack cover. Garbage bags flap wildly in the wind, don't hold up well to brush and branches, and must be cut to allow shoulder straps to pass through. Pack covers, on the other hand, are typically made of lightweight coated nylon or ultralight silnylon, and feature an elastic cord that tightens around the pack, securing it in place. A cover protects most of your pack, as well as items lashed to the outside, from the elements.

    Pack covers do have weaknesses, however. Most notably, they don't fully cover the area around your shoulder straps and hip belts. The area immediately above and around your shoulders is particularly vulnerable. In a daylong rain, water will often find its way in. And while they're considerably more durable than garbage bags, pack covers can still snag and tear on brush and branches in densely forested terrain.

    Various sizes and materials are available. For a secure fit and maximum protection, select one that is just large enough for your needs. Oversized versions dangle loosely, making them more susceptible to snags and moisture. Pack covers run roughly $20 to $40, depending on the style and material.

- **Zipper-closure bags.** To protect smaller water-sensitive items (maps, electronics, etc.), a durable zipper-closure bag is hard to beat. Freezer-style versions are the best. They feature thicker and more durable plastic than lighter-weight sandwich bags. Avoid sliding closures, which are prone to failure after repeated use and often don't provide a complete seal at the corners.

  To minimize air inside the zipper-closure bag, seal the bag nearly closed but leave a small opening at one end. After pushing as much air as possible out of the opening, use your mouth or a straw to suck out the remaining air and then quickly seal the bag closed. See Figure 50 on page 230 in Chapter 9, Cooking Skills, for an example of the technique.

- **Waterproof stuff sacks and bags.** In order for a stuff sack or dry bag to be completely waterproof, it must feature a waterproof material and a fully watertight closure system, typically a roll-top closure that seals with a clip. For hiking, light-weight coated nylon and polyester are common materials.

  For paddling, heavy-duty waterproof dry bags made from vinyl offer the extreme durability necessary to withstand repeated crammings into tight boat hatches. Dry bags with a clear window, or ones made entirely from see-through material, are a plus for quickly finding the right item of gear. A range of sizes and shapes are available, so you should be able to find options that work for the shape and capacity of your boat compartments. Paddling dry bags range from roughly $20 to $60, depending on size and features.

  One of the great challenges of a waterproof bag is getting excess air out so that you aren't left with a puffy, hard-to-pack balloon. To avoid this, look for stuff sacks made with eVent, a fully waterproof material that keeps water out but lets air through, and dry bags that feature a one-way purge valve, which allows you to force air out while blocking outside air from entering.

CHAPTER 4
NAVIGATION

Co-author Christian shares the following: Many years ago, I was scouting a forested area for a winter survival course I was scheduled to teach in Québec's Eastern Township, near Sherbrooke. I was traveling an old logging road when I noticed a silhouette slowly coming toward me on the trail. As we got closer to each other, I realized the silhouette was a young man with a long rifle held across his chest—a hunter. I was readying myself to say, "Bonjour," when I was caught off guard by the young man's exhausted, sweaty appearance. His coat was open and sliding off one of his shoulders; his hat was crooked; and, because his body heat had fogged his lenses, he had to tilt his head slightly backward to look below his glasses to see me.

After a short greeting, he asked me where this logging road was leading. Once I told him where he was, he pulled a sighting compass out of his coat pocket, opened it, looked at it briefly—in a vertical position—and proudly exclaimed, "This makes sense. I know where we are."

As I watched him walk away toward the trailhead from which I had come, I knew this poor young man had been lost for hours and also had been a victim of "outdoor gear checklist syndrome." I can imagine him planning his hunting outing by collecting all of the gear he had listed as essential or that someone else had told him to bring. Unfortunately, too many outdoor recreationists carry outdoor-related equipment in their packs that they have no idea how to use. The classic symptoms of this syndrome are the "outdoor first-aid kit," the "multitool pocket knife with a can opener," and, of course, "the compass."

If you are like this young man and carry a compass with you but don't know how to use it with a map, or how to safely follow a field bearing, then your chances of properly using it when you really need it are very low. Make sure you do not carry equipment with you that gives you a false sense of security. Learn to read topographic maps and to use a compass and a GPS.

This chapter will help you develop your understanding of basic navigation skills on- and off-trail using various tools and strategies. Like we often say to our students, "Learn the skills to navigate in the outdoors or get lost!"

➜ MAPS

Together, a map and compass are part of the ten essentials discussed in Chapter 1. Although both are essential to have in your pack when backpacking, a map is far more useful than a compass—especially if you intend to travel only on trails. If you intend to leave the beaten path and travel off-trail, a compass is the tool to have, unless you have a GPS—but remember, the odds of a compass failing are much less than that of a GPS. Compass versus GPS is part of the classic argument between traditional and modern technologies. Compasses are simple and reliable if used properly. They have no batteries or software issues and no spotty reception (Earth's magnetic field is always reliable), while GPS reception can be affected by thick forest canopy or limited open-sky access. Later in this chapter, we will explore in further depth the advantages and disadvantages of handheld GPS systems, but for now let us focus on maps and compasses.

When these two navigation tools are combined, they will allow you to properly read your map on- and off-trail, as well as to navigate through wild places, making your own path when necessary. They can also help you find your way if you are disoriented or lost. Again, we will learn more about the latter in this chapter, but first let us discuss the various types of maps we use to hike and backpack.

TYPES OF MAPS

If you remember your middle school social studies class, you will know there are many types of maps: political, climatic, economic, and physical, just to name a few. For hikers, the two types that are most useful are topographic and recreational. Topographic maps, especially the ones produced by the United States Geological Survey (USGS), are useful for navigating in wilderness areas. Their 7.5 minute quadrangle series (1:24,000 scale) is by far the most popular topographic map for outdoor lovers. The 7.5-minute series represents an area measuring 7.5 minutes of latitude and 7.5 minutes of longitude, and in the U.S. represent an area of 49 to 70 square miles. This series provides great detail in terms of terrain, watershed, and vegetation density. Although these

> ➜ **PRO TIP** If you are inclined to bring electronic devices on your hikes, you might consider uploading the apps Topo Maps for Apple devices and US Topo Maps for Android devices. Both apps give access to all USGS 1:24,000 topographic maps for the cost of the app ($8 for Apple, $11.15 for Android). When used with a tablet, these apps are excellent for navigation on- and off-trail.

maps' size, and lack of waterproofing and durability, are disadvantages, the topographic information they provide far outweighs their shortcomings. Putting a USGS quad or other paper map in a zipper-closure bag may offset some of these disadvantages on the trail, but they are downsides to consider when using a map outdoors. The other type of map that is quite useful is what we often call outdoor recreational maps, more commonly known as "trail maps." These maps combine the landscape information found on topographic maps but also include updated details about hiking trails, campsites, shelters, and lodges. AMC maps are a great resource for outdoor recreational maps along the East Coast. For more information on AMC maps, visit amcstore.outdoors.org/books-maps/maps.

MAP COLORS

The different colors in USGS topographic maps impart information that can be used to help with navigation.

4

- **Brown** lines represent elevation change. The contour interval, or distance between each line, can vary depending on the terrain. Most maps in the 7.5 series have 40-foot contour intervals, but others can have as low as 10-foot or as high as 100-foot contour lines. Always make sure to check how much change in elevation each contour line represents when using a new map. In addition, know that a bump or a small ridge of 30 feet will not show up on a map with 40-foot contour intervals. Keep the contour interval in mind when interpreting your map and the land it represents.

- **Blue** represents water features: brooks, streams, rivers, springs, ponds, lakes, glaciers, snowfields, and even marshy areas. Some of these hydrologic features are permanent, so they will be represented by solid blue lines, while intermittent or seasonal water features, such as a small brook, will show up as a blue dashed line.

- **Green and white** are interdependent colors representing the density of vegetation on the land. Green sections of the map indicate vegetation dense enough to hide an Army platoon (between 15 and 30 troops) in 1 acre (about 208 feet by 208 feet, or 25 percent less area than a football field). White represents an area with no dense overhead vegetation, but that doesn't mean this area is without some scattered trees, bushes, or grass.

- **Black** always represents human-made features. Hiking trails are represented by black dashed lines, but a well-traveled game trail will not appear on your topographic map. Unimproved forest roads will be shown as double dashed lines. Black is also used for buildings, cabins, shelters, and bridges. (Some non-USGS-produced maps, such as those from AMC, use red for trails, campgrounds, cabins, and shelters.)

- **Red** also represents human-made features, generally larger roads. Light red is used to represent boundaries, such as those for wilderness areas, so pay attention to where you are.

- **Purple** was used in the past to represent field corrections and revisions on maps, but the USGS has abandoned this practice.

For more details and information about colors and symbols found on USGS topographic maps, please see the online PDF at pubs.usgs.gov/gip/Topographic MapSymbols/topomapsymbols.pdf.

A TRICK FOR REMEMBERING MAP COLORS

Not all colors are created equal on a topographic map. There's a scale of trust-worthiness, given that some features, such as trails or even water, can change over time, while others, such as elevation, are less likely to change. To help re-member the order of trustworthiness—brown, blue, green, white, and black—we tell our students the following rhyme: "Brown is sound, blue is mostly true, green and white are sometimes right, and black is wack." We find this helps them remember to confirm a confusing trail junction or section by examining the sur-rounding landscape (brown), nearby water features (blue), or forest density (green and white). We look to features in this order because land forms rarely get modified during our lifetime, and although a stream can dry out, the signs of its bed remain. Vegetation density, on the other hand, can gradually or rapidly change from year to year. And we say that black is wack because trails often ap-pear and disappear from the landscape—they get rerouted, lose their signage, or can be misrepresented on a map.

USING A MAP

The art of reading a map comes from practice, so take the time to compare what is shown on the map to what you see around you. As you practice, some fundamental strategies will improve your map-reading skills.

- **Always orient the map with the field.** This means that, when you pull out your map, whether it be topographic or recreational, take the time to orient it so that the features on the map match the features you see in the surrounding terrain. In other words, make sure that north on the map (i.e., the top of the map, by convention) points approximately north in real life. Your map does not need to be perfectly oriented to the north, but it should match the landscape. This way, if you are facing north, what you see to your own right (i.e., east) should be to the right of where you are on the map. This does not mean you always need to face north when reading a map; you can face any direction in the field, as long as you orient the map so it's facing the same direction.

- **Always use obvious landmarks to confirm where you are.** If you think you know where you are on a map, don't look at the trail only but confirm your location by making sure the topography of the area matches the contour lines on the map. Remember, brown is sound! You can also use other reliable landmarks, such as streams, ponds, and lakes.

- **Know how to differentiate between ridges and drainages.** This is perhaps one of the most difficult skills to acquire, as the two land features can look similar on a topographic map. Contour lines forming a "V" represent either a ridge (a line of high ground, usually connecting mountaintops) or a drainage (a moving body of water). When the lines represent a ridge, the apexes of the "V" point toward lower elevations. When they represent drainages, the apexes of the "V" point toward higher elevations. When a V-shaped contour line nests a blue line, it obviously represents a drainage, where the blue line represents flowing water.

- **See the third dimension.** This skill requires more time to acquire, but it's the only way to use a topographic map to its full potential. The best way to begin to see contour lines from the third dimension is to look for summits (i.e., small circles) and study them in reference to the valley floors and drainages (i.e., open flat space and blue lines). Once you see the third dimension, you can better understand the surrounding landscape, anticipate what's coming up on a hike, judge whether a potential camping area might be suitable, and anticipate what to avoid when traveling off-trail.

- **Estimate distance.** Using the distance scale at the bottom of a topographic map, measure the length of 1 mile with your fingers. We often demonstrate this by extending the index and pinky fingers while holding the middle and ring finger with your thumb. Not only are you indicating that you're ready to rock 'n' roll; you also are measuring the approximate distance of 1 mile on a classic 1:24,000 topographic map. Depending on the size of your hand, you might need to adjust the width between your fingers but in general, you'll be able to quickly estimate the distance you're planning to travel. For a more accurate measurement, use a string (shoelace, necklace, whistle cord, etc.) to carefully measure your anticipated traveling distance by placing your improvised measuring string along the curves of the trail or off-trail route on the map. Mark the two ends of the distance with your fingers or a pen. Then, working in sections as needed, compare your string distance to the distance scale on the map. Note that you can use more precise map-distance measuring tools, such as a digital or mechanical map wheel calculator.

  If you are using a recreational map, such as an AMC trail guide map, you will notice the distance on trails has already been measured for your convenience. Distance usually is measured between trail junctions or from a trailhead. By convention, distances are shown in red along the trail between two red dots that indicate the length. Note that the measurements are presented in increments of one-tenth of a mile.

4

- **Count the contour lines.** When appropriate, take the time to calculate the elevation gain or loss by counting every contour line your route will have you cross. Make sure to verify the contour interval on the map you are using. USGS topographic maps use different contour-line heights depending on the type of terrain they represent. Flat land might have a contour interval of 10 feet, accentuating the minimal changes in the landscape, while mountain areas might be shown with 100-foot contour lines. Most 1:24,000-scale maps, though, have 40-foot contour lines. Note that at every five contour intervals, you will find a darker/bolder brown contour line. We call these "index contour lines." They can be used to quickly count continuous elevation gain or loss since their value is five times the contour line interval. For instance, on a map with a 40-foot contour line interval, every index contour line represents 200 feet.

  When calculating elevation gain, which is often more important information than elevation loss, make sure you "see the third dimension" so that you count only the contour lines you'll cross while traveling upward. Avoid calculating any downhill contour lines. Most important, avoid the temptation to subtract the lowest point of your journey from the highest point, since your route might require you to gain much more elevation than you'd get from that simple equation if it includes many ups and downs.

- **Keep your map handy.** This seems obvious, but too often laziness creeps up behind you on the trail. Then, when it would be essential to pull out a map, you might decide it's tucked too far away to reach with ease. So, don't keep your map inside your pack—not even inside the brain. Instead, consider carrying your map in a pants pocket or attaching a map pocket to your backpack shoulder strap. Some people also like to tuck the map under their backpack sternum strap. Note that it is a good idea to place your map in a waterproof plastic bag to protect it from rain, an accidental spill, or sweat.

- **Know how to fold your map.** If you are using USGS topographic maps, you'll quickly realize they don't come prefolded but as large, flat pieces of paper—not an easy format for hikers to carry. There is a simple way to fold these maps, though, that will simplify their transport and identification. If you look at a 1:24,000 scale USGS topographic map, you will notice that the name of the map, also known as a "quadrangle," is located on the upper-right and lower-right corners. Obviously, when the map is folded, it's useful to have these names visible for quick identification of the map you want. Following the steps below will allow you to properly fold these maps.

  1. Fold the map in half along its longer axis. Make sure you fold the map inward, meaning that the printed side is folded against itself. In other words, make the names of the map disappear.

2.   Fold each half of the long axis outward in a one-quarter fold. This will make the names of the map reappear.

3.   Fold the map in half on the horizontal axis by matching the names of the map, meaning the upper- and lower-right corners. The names of the map will disappear again.

4.   Fold the map in a one-quarter fold along the horizontal axis, which will once again make the names of the map appear on each side of the folded map.

MAP FEATURES

Learning to read a topographic map also means being able to identify and interpret some classic land formations and how they are represented on a two-dimensional map. Take the time to look at the sample land features represented below. Again, the trick here is to "see the third dimension" through the contour lines. Before looking at these samples, remember the basic principle that contour lines are equidistant, meaning they remain at the same altitude above sea level throughout their course along the landscape. Therefore, the closer they are to each other, the steeper the terrain will be, while the opposite is also true: The more distance between the contour lines, the gentler the slope in the terrain will be.

Summits

Summits can be recognized by the concentric circles formed by the contour lines, as represented in Figure 17.

Saddles

Saddles are lower points found on a ridge between two higher adjacent summits. Figure 18 is an excellent representation of a saddle. Notice how the contour lines interact to represent two opposite uphill slopes positioned perpendicularly to two opposite downhill slopes.

Drainages

Drainages are often easy to identify when they include a blue line representing a river, stream, creek, brook, or spring. When they don't include a water feature, remember that drainages are represented by V- or U-shaped contour lines, with the open end of these letters representing lower terrain, or the downhill portion of the drainage, while their points face uphill. We often tell our students to think of a river delta, which fans out when it reaches the ocean. The wider part of the delta always indicates the lower part of the river, and the same is true with a drainage represented on a topographic map. See the Figure 19 to see drainages with and without a water feature.

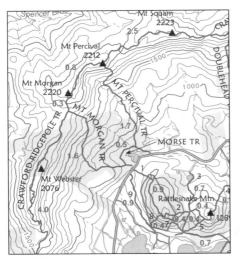

LEFT: **FIGURE 17.** An example of summits (Squam, Percival, etc.) from AMC's White Mountains Trail Map 3: Crawford Notch–Sandwich Range.

BELOW, LEFT TO RIGHT: **FIGURE 18.** An example of a saddle from AMC's White Mountains Trail Map 2: Franconia–Pemigewasset. **FIGURE 19.** An example of a drainage from AMC's White Mountains Trail Map 3: Crawford Notch–Sandwich Range.

BOTTOM, LEFT TO RIGHT: **FIGURE 20.** An example of a ridge from AMC's White Mountains Trail Map 1: Presidential Range. **FIGURE 21.** An example of slopes and cliffs from AMC's White Mountains Trail Map 3: Crawford Notch–Sandwich Range.

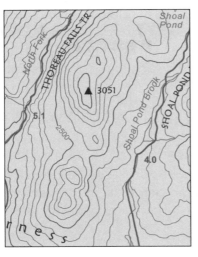
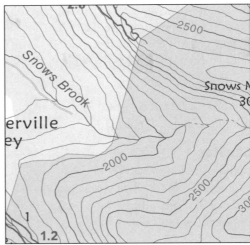
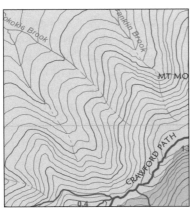
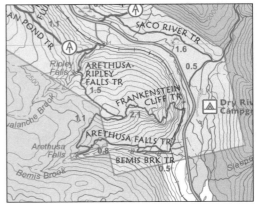

Ridges

Ridges are also represented by V- or U-shaped contour lines. Be careful not to con-fuse them with drainages. For one thing, never expect a ridge to have a blue line in the middle of its contour lines. Because they are the opposite of drainages, ridges are represented by their widest part of the V or U pointing uphill. Note that when the ridge is narrow and has steep slopes on each side, the contour lines look more like a V, but when the ridge has a broad crest with gentle slopes on each side, the contour lines look more like a U. See Figure 20 to compare these two types of ridges.

Slopes and Cliffs

Slopes are represented by parallel contour lines. When a slope turns into a cliff, you will see the contours get much closer to each other. If they seem to disappear under each other, it means the cliff is vertical or even overhanging. These are places to avoid hiking unless you are a climber or a mountain goat, but they often provide a beautiful vista if you can reach their summit via a gentler slope. Figure 21 represents a gentle slope becoming steeper and culminating in an overhanging cliff.

4

ON-TRAIL NAVIGATION

Navigating on trails seems easy, but this assumption can get people in trouble. The mindless pounding of boots on the trail under an often too-heavy backpack leads hikers and backpackers to misinterpret where they are, miss a trail junction, or leave the proper trail while following an abandoned trail or a well-used game trail. What's more, hikers can place too much faith in trail signage, such as blazes (swaths of a specific color of paint or a small plaque on a tree), cairns (intentional rock piles indicating a trail), and the classic wooden sign at a trail junction. The reality is trail signage can be wrong, hidden, or sometimes absent.

Therefore, trail hiking also means map reading. Carefully study the map prior to beginning your hike and memorize obvious features that will be easy to recognize along the trail. Think of them as mental waypoints you'll be seeking. You can even mark these waypoints on your map to help you. We use numerous mental waypoints. They may include obvious features: stream crossings, bridges, trail junctions, and major changes in direction of travel, such as a 90-degree turn on a trail. They may also include types of terrain: swampy areas, ridges and drainages, and steep ascents or descents.

It's good to memorize two or three of these features in the order they should appear along the trail. Hike while enjoying the scenery, have a conversation, but also keep an eye out for these features. If you are heading in the right direction, they should come in the right order, one after the other. Once you have confirmed your last mental waypoint, pull out the map and memorize the next few obvious features you should encounter. This technique not only will allow you to keep track of where you are, but it will also stop you from needing to take too many map breaks because you haven't kept an eye, or your mind, on the trail.

OFF-TRAIL NAVIGATION

As a rule, you should walk off the trail only in appropriate contexts, such as bush-whacking and orienteering in stable ecosystems. Venturing off-trail increases both your risk of personal injury and your impact on the natural environment. In keeping with LNT principles, AMC recommends that hikers stay on the trail whenever possible. When you do need to navigate the wilderness, the following methods will help you do so with marginal impact. To prepare you for your journey, we have put together a few strategies that will help you navigate your route without the use of a compass or a GPS. Be smart but do not be afraid. Once practiced, these are good tools to use when going off-trail and navigating forests, meadows, and lakes using only a topographic map.

And remember: Study your route before starting your hike and memorize obvious waypoints based on terrain, water features, and anticipated vegetation. The more you know about your route from the map, the better honed your route-finding will be. Here are a few of our most trusted strategies for traveling off-trail.

Handrail

Handrails are natural features that one can follow when traveling the land, such as rivers, creeks, brooks, lake and pond shores, edges of a meadow, ridges, and drainages. You can also turn manufactured features, such as power lines, a gas line, or even a railroad, into handrails. The idea is, first, to know where you are; to identify the appropriate handrail along a desired route; and to keep that handrail on your right or your left as you travel. You can be close to or far away from the handrail as long as you can see it or hear it, such as when you are following a noisy mountain stream. Sometimes you even walk on the handrail, as when you are traversing a ridge or a drainage. If you cross your handrail, make sure to remember on which side, your right or left, it is now located.

Backstop

Similar to handrails, backstops are natural or manufactured features that you can use to keep from getting lost. They are often long features, such as a waterway, lake-shore, trail, road, railroad, or power line. Contrary to handrails, which are parallel to your traveling route, backstops are perpendicular to your route. The strategy here is to hike in one general direction, which is easy enough to do for a quarter-mile or a half-mile, until you come across the backstop you had identified on the map. Once you have reached the backstop, you turn right or left and use it as a handrail until you reach your desired location. For a longer distance, it's safer to use a compass to help you reach your backstop. If you do not have a compass with you, you can use the shadow compass strategy described below, if the conditions are right.

Shadow Compass

This strategy works best at midday when the sun is near or at its zenith. If the sky is clear and you are traveling between 10 A.M. and 2 P.M., you can use your shadow as a compass to hike in a relatively straight line for 20 to 30 minutes at a time. So, if you need to hike a quarter- to a half-mile off-trail without a compass, pick the direction you need to travel by orienting the map with the surrounding landscape, notice where your body is casting a shadow, and walk by keeping your shadow at the same angle. For instance, if it is noon and you want to travel northwest for a quarter-mile, your shadow will be on your right at about 2 P.M. Note that this is not an actual time reference but the location of the hour hand on an imaginary clock, with you at the center of the clock and your nose pointed toward 12 o'clock. You can travel only a short distance using this shadow compass. As the sun continues its course across the sky, it will affect the location of your shadow.

4

Macro and Micro Route

When traveling off-trail, you'll need to keep in mind two types of route findings. First, there's your general direction of travel. We call this the "macro route," or the big picture. Second, you will have to negotiate the numerous obstacles along your journey, such as steep terrain, trees, boulders, wet areas, and thick vegetation. At these points, you will have to decide whether it is easier to walk on the right or the left of, or over or under, an obstacle. This is known as the "micro route," or the re-fined picture. The micro route will keep you busy, but don't forget the macro route or you risk getting lost. Similarly, do not travel over difficult or dangerous terrain just because you want to stick to the macro route. The micro route should allow you to follow the macro route by using the most effective and safe line of travel.

Elastic Route Finding

If you are traveling off-trail in a small group, consider using this technique, which will help you in your micro-route finding. The principle is simple. In a small group, identify a micro-route finder. Then assign to that hiker a second group member whose job is to keep an eye on the route finder and to adjust the route for the other hikers based on the difficulty or ease of travel experienced by the route finder. Obviously, it is easier to do this if the second hiker keeps a certain distance from the route finder. That way, the second hiker can correct any mistakes made by the route finder by choosing a better micro route. When travel is easy, the hikers can be close to each other, but when the terrain becomes more difficult, the distance between the route finder and the second hiker can increase—hence the idea of elasticity between the route finder and the rest of the hikers. Rotate the roles among the group to give your route finder(s) a break.

LNT Off-Trail Hiking

 Hiking off-trail will bring you to some very scenic and pristine areas. You might see forested areas with green moss carpets, birch groves filled with ferns, or the edges of wetlands with precious and rare aquatic plants. The problem with hiking off-trail is that a group of four hikers can cause more impact on the land than 1,000 hikers on an established trail. For that reason, it is important to consider this LNT technique: On durable surfaces such as bedrock, sand, grassy fields, leafy forest floor, and snow, hike in a single file. On fragile terrain, such as moss, fern patches, wetlands, and flowering meadows, it is less impactful to spread out the members of your group, reducing the concentration of boot trampling.

→ COMPASSES

As you may know, the first magnetic compass was invented in ancient China, about 200 BCE. But what most outdoor gear enthusiasts do not know is that, for many centuries, the magnetic compass was not used for navigation but for divination. It's too bad that some of today's hikers and backpackers still carry this tool more as a good luck charm than as an essential navigation tool. As mentioned previously, do not carry a compass unless you truly know how to use it, since misusing it could turn a situation in which you are simply confused into one where you are totally lost. If you really want to use a compass, learn how it works and how to use it properly.

COMPASS TYPES AND COMPONENTS

There are many kinds of compasses on the market for outdoor recreationists, but the two primary types are the lensatic compass, often referred to as a military compass, and the baseplate compass (see Figure 22 on page 91). By far the most popular, useful, and easy to use type of compass for navigating with or without a map is the baseplate compass, which can also be used as a protractor. Because of its rectangular baseplate, this type of compass will allow you to calculate a bearing (i.e., direction of travel) on a map and transfer it to a field bearing that you can follow to reach a desired destination; more on this below.

The baseplate compass was invented in Sweden in 1928 by Gunnar Tillander, who cofounded the Silva compass company in 1932. In terms of practicality, the baseplate compass far surpassed the plateless lensatic compass.

A baseplate compass includes three important parts:

1. The baseplate, which features the "direction-of-travel" arrow, or DOT, and the index pointer.

2. The compass housing, which includes the orienteering arrow (a.k.a. the shed), the orienteering lines, and the dial with degrees.

3. The magnetic needle, with its red and white sections.

PARTS OF A COMPASS

- **Baseplate.** This is the hard and transparent, flat surface on which the rest of the compass is mounted. It often has rulers and scales on its edges for measuring distances on maps. Its edges are straight and useful for laying (i.e., protracting) lines on a map.

- **Direction-of-travel arrow (DOT).** Marked at the midpoint on the baseplate, this is used to point at an object, to take a bearing, or to follow when traveling.

- **Index pointer.** Located at the end of the DOT, right at the edge of the dial, this is used to read the degree on the dial.

- **Compass housing.** This transparent plastic capsule houses the magnetic needle. It is filled with an alcohol-based liquid or purified kerosene to dampen the movement of the needle when the housing rotates. Alcohol or kerosene is used in liquid-compass housings to avoid the liquid freezing at low temperatures.

4

- **Orienteering arrow (shed).** Marked on the bottom of the housing, the orienteering arrow rotates with the housing when the dial is turned. It is used to orient a

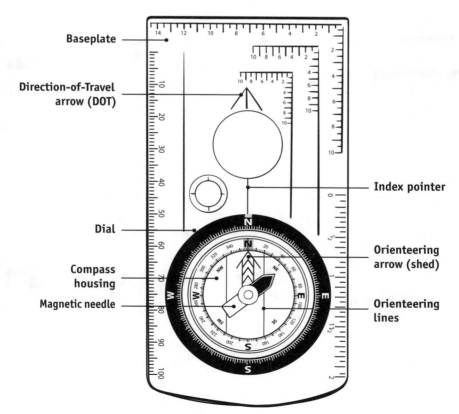

FIGURE 22. The parts of a baseplate compass.

compass to a certain bearing (i.e., degree) in one of two ways: either by rotating the entire compass until the "red" is in the "shed"; or by rotating the compass housing until the "shed" captures the "red."

- **Orienteering lines.** This series of parallel lines is marked on the bottom of the housing. Orienteering lines are used to help calculate a bearing or to adjust for a magnetic declination.

- **Dial.** This ring around the housing has engraved degree markings, which often come in 2- or 5-degree increments. Note that a compass dial is sometimes referred to as a "bezel."

- **Magnetic needle.** This magnetized piece of metal has one end painted red to indicate north. It sits on a fine point that is nearly frictionless so it rotates freely when the compass is held fairly level and steady. Magnetic needles are balanced for use in either the northern or the southern hemisphere due to the differences in the magnetic dip. The "magnetic dip" is the horizontal angle of the magnetic field along the surface of the planet. Do not expect a compass made for the United States to work in Australia, and vice versa.

HOW A COMPASS WORKS

A compass works by pointing north. This is the simple explanation, but in reality, a compass does not point anywhere in particular. It simply aligns itself with Earth's magnetic field. "Pointing north" is something we have arbitrarily decided to say when using a compass. The truth is that the red, or magnetic, north end on a compass needle has been magnetized with a positive charge and is attracted by its opposite: Earth's south magnetic pole, which is located near the geographic North Pole. Yes, you read that right: The red end of the needle on your compass actually points to the South Pole (i.e., negative pole) of Earth's magnetic field. But by convention, and to avoid confusion, we say that a compass needle always points north. Again, this is true only if no other metallic or magnetic object interferes with the needle. Beware of large belt buckles, eyeglass frames, garments with sewn-in magnets (a substitute for Velcro), or even a bra with a metallic underwire.

Magnetic Declination

Magnetic declination refers to the angle created between the geographic north and the magnetic north at your current location. Yes, we know now that what we call the magnetic North Pole is actually the South Pole, but let's not make things more complicated. Let's go along with the agreed-upon name of the North Pole when talking about the magnetic pole located in the Arctic Ocean.

You will discover that good hiking and topographic maps always indicate the local magnetic declination via a declination diagram, which includes an arrow pointing to the geographic north (labeled as True North, "TN") or with a star symbol (✶) representing Polaris, the North Star, and another arrow indicating the Magnetic North, labeled as "MN." The degree of declination is recorded between these two arrows. Remember, though, that magnetic poles are wanderers. They keep on moving each year, so if you are using an old edition of a map, you might want to visit the NOAA Declination Calculator website, which will calculate the current declination for your location (ngdc.noaa.gov/geomag-web/#declination). (In provisional 7.5-minute topo maps, the declination is given in the text box at the lower-left corner of the map.)

It is also important to note that Earth's magnetic field is not composed of straight lines; rather, the magnetic field is created by curved lines of magnetism. Figure 23, below, shows the current magnetic field, with its corresponding degree of declination. Notice that in some parts of the United States, such as in Rochester, Minnesota, the declination is zero. If you are located on the East Coast, however, you will have to deal with a western declination, because magnetic north is west of geographic north. Consequently, if you are on the West Coast, you will have an eastern declination, because magnetic north is east of geographic north.

4

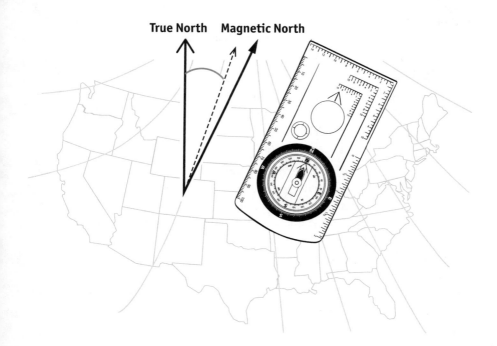

FIGURE 23. "True North" points to geographic north, a fixed point, while "Magnetic North" points to the North Pole, which changes over time.

→ USING A COMPASS WITH A MAP

ORIENTING A MAP WITH A COMPASS

This is perhaps the most important skill to master when navigating via map and compass or when determining where you are. Remember how we explained earlier that the first thing to do when using a map is to orient it with the surrounding landscape? Doing so helps you read your map: What is north on the map will be north for you in the field. Although it is often sufficient to approximately orient the map with the field, in some situations it is essential to precisely orient the map with the field. This is when a compass becomes so useful. But to combine a map and a compass, you will need to calculate for the declination error of your location unless you are at or near the 0-degree declination line.

Many of you might have heard or tried to learn confusing rhymes and acronyms, such as, "From map to field, the proper yield is east is least and west is best," or, "LARS: Left-Add, Right-Subtract." The reality is much simpler. All you need to do is follow these steps:

1. On your compass, rotate the dial until the "N" (for north) is on the index pointer.

2. Place your compass on any map near the declination diagram, with the edge of the baseplate along the True North arrow on the diagram. Make sure the DOT on your compass points north, or toward the top of the map.

3. Turn the dial in the same direction as the Magnetic North arrow on the declination diagram. Make sure you move the dial the same amount of degrees as is indicated on the declination diagram. For instance, if the diagram says 16 degrees and the MN arrow is right of the TN arrow, your dial should now indicate 344 degrees. Conversely, if the diagram says 16 degrees and the MN arrow is left of the TN arrow, your dial should now indicate 16 degrees.

4. Now that you have compensated for your local magnetic declination, place your compass baseplate along the edge of the map, and rotate the map and compass until the *red* is in the *shed*. In other words, rotate until the red part of the magnetic needle overlays the orienteering arrow. Voilà: Your map is now accurately oriented with your surroundings.

The beauty of this method is that you do not need to remember whether you should add or subtract, turn right or turn left, or rotate the compass dial clockwise or counterclockwise. All you need to remember is to match the direction of the MN arrow on your map. This will be true whether you are in California, Maine, or somewhere in between. (One note: This only works for a declination diagram, not for the text declination, as given on a provisional 7.5-minute topo map.)

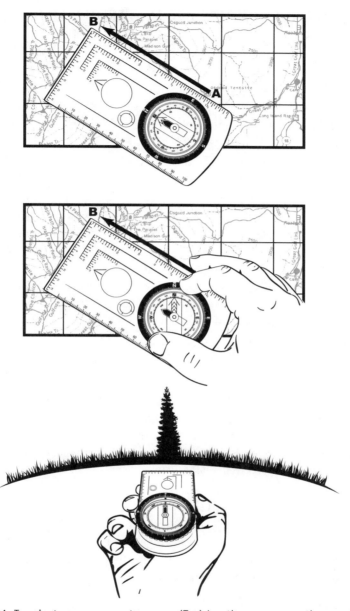

FIGURE 24. To orient your compass to a map: (Top) Lay the compass on the map, aligning the baseplate edge from A (your starting point) to point B (your destination). Make sure the orienteering arrow is at 0 degrees. (Middle) Now align the orienteering arrow with the meridian lines on your map to get an accurate reading without moving the baseplate. (Bottom) When you are sure you have the compass housing pointing north, remove the compass from the map and, holding the compass, turn your body until the red end of the magnetic needle moves inside the orienteering arrow. Follow this direction to get from point A to point B.

TRANSFERRING A COMPASS BEARING FROM MAP TO FIELD

Once you have mastered the skill described above and can easily orient a map to the field using a compass, you can now use a map to reach a location that is out of your sight. For instance, let's say you are standing at a junction of two trails that is clearly marked on the map. You want to reach a secret waterfall half a mile away, and there is no trail leading to the waterfall. You can use your compass to reach this location by taking a bearing on the map then following that bearing in the field. The steps to accomplish this are as follows.

1.   Orient the map with the terrain by using the technique previously described. Then identify your current location and the location you want to reach on the map.

2.   Without moving the map *(Note: This is very important; keep your map as still as possible after having accurately oriented it with the terrain)*, place the right (it could also be the left) lower corner of the baseplate at your current location on the map. Then place the upper-right corner (DOT arrow end) of the baseplate on the location you want to reach. If the location on the map you want to reach is farther than the length of the baseplate, extend the baseplate's right edge with a piece of paper or anything that creates a straight line between your location and the location you want to reach.

3.   Without moving the map or the compass baseplate, turn the compass dial until the *shed* is placed under the *red*. In other words, turn the dial until the orienting arrow boxes the red part of the magnetic needle.

4.   Pick up your compass and read the degree (i.e., the bearing) at the compass index pointer. You now have a field bearing that will allow you to hike in a straight line between where you stand and the location you want to reach. Well, that's true if you know how to read a field bearing and how to follow it without drifting. More on the latter below.

FOLLOWING A FIELD BEARING

Following a bearing is not as easy as it seems. Many outdoor recreationists make mistakes when trying to follow a field bearing. Some keep looking at their compasses, thinking if they can keep *red* in the *shed* they will hike in a straight line. This leads them to drift from the intended bearing to parallel bearings, slowly moving away from the straight line established between the starting location and the ending location. Some people also take vague intermediate landmarks and end up drifting away from their original bearing, and other zealous hikers stubbornly try to travel in a straight line between landmarks, forcing them to walk through thick vegetation, puddles, and over boulders or fallen trees. To avoid these mistakes, learn and practice the following skills.

1. Once you have your field bearing, hold the compass properly. This means that, if the compass has a lanyard, place the lanyard around your neck and place the compass on your chest or belly (depending on the length of the lanyard) so that the DOT faces away from your body. Keep the compass DOT perpendicular to your body, at the midline of your body. Try to keep the compass perfectly flat (horizontal) while doing this. Hold the compass firmly with both hands, placing your index fingers on either side of the baseplate. Your elbows should be held firmly against your sides.

2. While looking down at your compass, turn your body and the compass as one unit until the *red* is in the *shed*.

3. Carefully look up in a straight line, extending the DOT in front of you, and look for a faraway but distinctive landmark along this line of sight. A good landmark can be a tree, a boulder, a stump, or even a fellow hiker you directed to walk ahead of you and asked to stand still on your bearing. We call this technique "leap-frogging."

4. Memorize this landmark, drop your compass, and find the easiest and safest way to reach the chosen landmark. Once you have reached the landmark, stand behind it and repeat the above steps.

4

Now, you can hike in a straight line on a desired bearing without drifting, to the right or to the left of your objective. Plus, you can safely and effectively hike off-trail without getting lost. Note that you can apply the same technique when taking a field bearing. For instance, imagine that you are standing on a ridge, and perpendicular to the ridge you see a nearby lake. You want to reach the lake, but there are no trails from the ridge to the lake, and you know that as you descend from the ridge you will lose sight of the lake. All you have to do is take a field bearing by holding the compass properly, turning the dial until the *shed* is boxing the *red*. Now read the bearing, find a landmark on that bearing, and travel safely to the landmark. Repeat these last steps until your reach the lake. To return to the ridge, reverse the bearing by boxing the *white* part of the magnetic needle in the *shed*. By doing this, you will travel a 180-degree reverse course from the lake to the ridge. Or just turn the compass around so the DOT arrow is pointing toward you and put the *red* in the *shed*.

→ GPS DEVICES

GPS devices are now omnipresent in our daily lives. They are in our cars, cell phones, tablets, computers—even in our watches. So it's not surprising to see them in our backpacks. GPS handheld devices are wonderful when traveling on- or off-trail. On trails, they can provide us with useful information about our current and average speed of travel, our distance hiked so far, our current elevation, our location coordinates, and even when the sun will rise and set. But as with any technology, it only works if you know how to use it. You also need to know what to do if it doesn't work.

HOW A GPS WORKS

The Global Positioning System (GPS) was initially created for the U.S. Department of Defense. When it was made available for civilian use in the mid-1990s, the GPS satellite signal was purposely degraded for civilian users. At that point, outdoor GPS devices were not so accurate or popular with hikers. But in 2000, the intentional degradation of civilian GPS was lifted, and GPS soon became a popular way to navigate and hike in wild places.

The Global Positioning System includes three segments: the user segment, or devices such as a handheld GPS, a cell phone, or a dash-mounted or integrated car device; the ground-control segment, or stations; and the space segment, or orbital satellite network.

User Segment

GPS handheld devices are a bit like an AM radio, as they passively receive data from a satellite. This is one reason why, if they don't have many bells and whistles, most handheld devices can be used for long periods of time without taxing their batteries. A few of the GPS devices on the market also serve as two-way text devices or as personal locator beacons (PLBs), but these devices require more battery power and therefore might call for lithium-based batteries. When selecting a handheld GPS device, remember that it might be more important to purchase a device with a good antenna than one with a camera, a two-way radio, an internal barometric altimeter, or an electronic compass. If you can afford the price, avoid purchasing a device with a flat-patch antenna, which gets its best reception only when held horizontally. In contrast, a GPS receiver with a spiraling "quad helix" antenna gets the same reception, regardless of whether it's held horizontally, sits upright in your pocket, or is stuffed into your pack lid.

Although satellite signals are not affected by atmospheric conditions, the system requires a direct line of sight between your handheld device and the satellites. So, be more concerned about thick forest canopy, steep mountain walls, or deep canyons providing limited sky coverage than with the weather.

Finally, your GPS needs to receive strong signals from at least four satellites for its internal algorithm to calculate your location through a process called "trilateration." This may sound like "triangulation," but it's actually quite different. Don't worry: There are 32 satellites in various orbits around the planet, so your GPS receiver will have plenty of choices. Actually, the more satellites your GPS receiver captures, the more precise it will be. In addition, most modern handheld devices will give you the option to activate the Wide Area Augmentation System (WAAS), which will use signals from air-navigation ground control to improve or correct any errors from the GPS signals. You can activate the WAAS mode by going into the device's settings. Just remember this mode will use more battery power to determine your location. The accuracy of a good outdoor recreation GPS receiver is only to within 9 feet; with the WAAS mode, this accuracy can drop to within 3 feet.

Ground-Control Segment

The ground-control segment monitors satellite operation and provides correction when needed. Ground-control stations are located around the globe along the equator. The master control station is located in Colorado, at the Schriever Air Force Base in Colorado Springs.

Space Satellite Segment

4

Composed of 32 satellites in various orbits around the planet, the system needs at least 24 functioning satellites to operate properly. Orbits are arranged so that at least six satellites are always within line of sight of almost any location on Earth's surface.

WHAT CAN YOU DO WITH A GPS?

GPS receivers are quite versatile if they are used properly. Most of them have interfaces that are easy to navigate. Although many offer lots of bells and whistles, the essential functions of a GPS receiver are to navigate a route, track where you have been, and tell you where you are. Let's look at a few of the essential functions of a GPS receiver.

Preload a Route or Waypoints

Your GPS device can be preloaded with a series of specific waypoints that will allow you to follow a planned route—even on a network of confusing trails or when you're away from trails or roads. There are many topographic map software programs that will allow you to plan a desired route, then transfer those waypoints to your GPS receiver. This map software will calculate your route distance and total elevation gain and loss; it will give you an elevation-change profile; and some will even allow you to view a 3-D flight of your route. The GPS will continuously update the bearing to the waypoint.

If you are into geocaching (an outdoor recreational activity in which participants use GPS devices to find "caches," or little containers filled with trinkets), you can also download the locations of thousands of geocache waypoints from geocaching websites.

Create Waypoints in the Field

Once in the field, you can create waypoints for various reasons. You can waypoint a remote campsite that you want to find again on your next outing. You can waypoint your campsite to make sure you're able to return to it at the end of the day. Most

GPS devices also have a tracking function that will keep track of your movement, thereby creating a route you can transfer to a map once you have returned home. And if you are geocaching, you can waypoint a new cache you have created yourself.

Know Where You Are

Perhaps the most essential information a GPS receiver can give you is your exact location on the planet. The GPS will do this by indicating your geographical coordinates, which can be preselected to appear either as longitude and latitude (i.e., Degree–Minutes–Seconds or Degree–Minutes–Decimal) or UTM (Universal Transverse Mercator). For instance, if you stand in front of the Statute of Liberty in New York Harbor, your GPS could give you these various coordinates while representing the exact same location: 40° 41′ 21″ N, 74° 2′ 40″ W (Degree–Minutes–Seconds); 40° 41.35′ N, 74° 2.67′ W (Degree–Minutes–Decimal); or Zone 18T 580741E 4504692N (UTM). Whichever format you select, make sure you are able to translate it to your map, especially if your GPS receiver does not include detailed map software.

UTM COORDINATES

The easiest coordinate system, by far, is the UTM system, which is a metric system of measurement. Actually, UTM numbers are a distance in meters from where you are to a known Cartesian point on the UTM grid system, where "easting" refers to the X-coordinate and "northing" to the Y-coordinate. For instance, if you are standing on the summit of Mount Washington in New Hampshire, your northing UTM coordinate would be 4904496, which means you are 4,904,496 meters from the equator (or about 4,900 kilometers). Easting corresponds to the distance in meters from your location to the eastern border of the UTM zone in which you're located. Easting is the distance in meters from the reference line, which is always west and outside of the zone you are in. The farther east you are in the zone, the larger the numbers get.

The whole UTM coordinate for New Hampshire's Mount Washington is 19T 0316179E 4904496N, which means that the mountain is in the 19T zone of the UTM grid, and that it is at 0316179 of easting and 4904496 of northing. By convention, the easting coordinate is always given before the northing coordinate.

If you use a UTM grid finder, you will see it is easy to transfer the information from your GPS to your map. If your topographic map is already pregridded with the UTM system, you can use the UTM immediately. If the grid is absent, you will have to draw the UTM grid you need to find your location.

The edge of a USGS topographic map always displays the UTM grid markers. They are marked with blue tics and identified by the first number of the coordinate, such as 316 for the easting and 4904 for the northing. Note that the last three digits of the coordinates are missing on these tics. They would typically be written as follows: 316000m Easting and 4904000m Northing. The last three digits will be found using your UTM grid reader.

Now, to find a location on a map after reading the GPS UTM coordinates, simply follow these steps:

1. Read the first four numbers of the easting coordinate, disregarding the zero at the beginning, and find the corresponding three remaining digits for the easting coordinate on your map, which will be located at the bottom and top margins of the map. (About that missing digit, just remember your GPS will always give seven digits of easting starting with a zero, while your map will have UTM grid tics with three-digit numbers for the easting; the map omits the first zero and the last three digits.)

2. Read the first four numbers of the northing coordinate and find the corresponding four digits on your map, which will be located on the left and the right margins of the map for the northing coordinate.

3. Place the bottom left corner of your UTM grid reader where the two UTM lines you have just found meet on the map.

4. Read the last three digits of the easting coordinate from your GPS. Your grid represents 1,000 meters by 1,000 meters, so reading from left to right, find the column corresponding to the first digit of that three-digit number.

5. Read the last three digits of the northing coordinate from your GPS and find the row corresponding to the first digit of that three-digit number.

6. Find the intersection of the column and row you have just identified. You are somewhere within this 100-square-meter area.

UTM SAMPLE READING

Let's say you are hiking along a ridge in the White Mountains of New Hampshire and, due to dense fog, you lose track of exactly where you are on the ridge. It's already 3 P.M., and you are starting to wonder if you will have enough time to get back to your car or if you'll have to bivy somewhere along your route. Since you cannot use your map alone to figure out where you are, you decide to use your GPS receiver, knowing it will work in any weather condition. After you verify that your GPS setting has the corresponding datum as your topographic map (see "North American Datum (NAD)," on page 102), your GPS receiver gives your current location as follows: 19T 0304238E 4869815N.

You look at the first four digits of the easting and note they correspond to 304 on the bottom margin of your map. Then you note that the first digits of the northing are 4869, which you easily find on the right side of your map. You then find the point on the map where these two UTM lines meet. Luckily for you, the map edition you have includes the UTM grid system. So you place the bottom left corner

4

of your UTM grid reader and look for the easting column 4. You then look for the northing row 8. You find where column 4 and row 8 meet in the grid, and now you know quite precisely where you are. You are still half a mile from the south summit on the Tripyramid Ridge.

As a final note, remember that if you do not have your GPS or if it isn't working, you can still use your UTM grid reader to identify the UTM coordinate of your current location. With good map-reading skills, you can locate where you are on a map then use the UTM grid reader to find your coordinates.

NORTH AMERICAN DATUM (NAD)

Over the past decades, the UTM grid was corrected twice, in 1927 and in 1983. We identify these as NAD27 and NAD83/WGS84, where NAD means North American Datum and WGS means World Geodetic System. A datum is the technical name for a coordinate system. What is important to know is that the NAD27 is not exactly the same as the NAD83/WGS84, and that some maps will have grids with either the NAD27 or the NAD83/WGS84. Luckily for us, GPS receivers can be set for either datum. So, make sure you always identify the datum on the map you are using and adjust your GPS settings to the same datum. You will find the datum information on the bottom left side of a typical USGS map. In the UTM grid reader example, the location given was for NAD27. The corresponding location in the NAD83/WGS84 would have been 19T 0304287E 4870029N.

→ CELESTIAL NAVIGATION

Navigating by the stars is one of the oldest traditional outdoor skills, but it has been largely forgotten over the ages. We can easily imagine shepherds, herders, trappers, and sailors using basic star navigation to identify the four cardinal directions: north, east, south, and west.

Once you know where north is, you can travel in your desired direction for some time. There are two basic forms of celestial navigation, one that uses the star Polaris (the North Star) for night navigation and one that uses the sun for daytime navigation. Remember, our sun is a star as well.

HOW TO USE POLARIS

At night, the best way to find your four cardinal directions is to find Polaris. To find this star in the northern hemisphere, first find the Big Dipper, which is part of the Ursa Major constellation. The Big Dipper is perhaps the most easily recognizable constellation in the northern sky. Once you have found this collection of seven distinctive stars that looks like a pot with a long handle or a ladle (dipper), you can easily find Polaris.

To do so, draw an imaginary line between the two pointer stars of the dipper (i.e., the two stars farthest from the handle) and extend that line out of the dipper for five times the distance between the pointers. At the end of this imaginary line, you will find a dim little star—not so bright—at the center of a dark patch of the night sky. This is Polaris, the North Star.

Why is it named the North Star? The main reason is that if you were to stand at the geographic north of our planet and look up at your zenith, meaning straight above your head, you would see a single, fixed, little star in the night sky. If you have ever seen a photo lapse of the northern hemisphere night sky, you've seen that all of the stars and constellations are rotating around a single point. That celestial pivot point is Polaris. Wherever you are in the northern hemisphere, if you can face Polaris, you know you are also facing geographic north, which means that east is on your right, south is behind you, and west is on your left. From here you can hike at night in a desired direction while keeping an eye on Polaris.

4

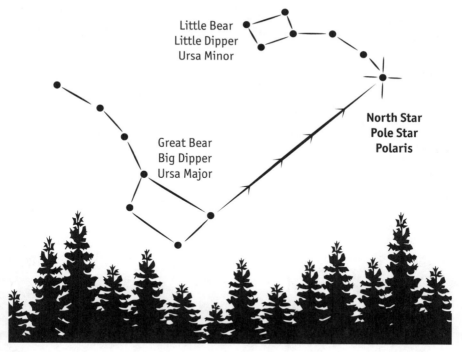

FIGURE 25. To find Polaris, or the North Star, look for the constellation commonly known as the Big Dipper. Locate the star that serves as the Big Dipper's top-right pot corner then trace a line from it to the last star in the Little Dipper's pot handle. This dim star in a dark patch of sky is Polaris.

HOW TO USE THE SUN

During the day, you can use an analog watch to find the southern cardinal direction by pointing the hour hand toward the sun. Then find the midpoint between the hour hand and noon (without daylight-saving time) or 1 o'clock (with daylight-saving time). That midpoint on your watch indicates south. From there, you can choose to travel in a desired direction without the need of a compass or a GPS.

Knowing how to travel using either Polaris or the sun can be useful, but it won't take you to a specific location. It will allow you only to travel in a desired general direction, perhaps toward a backstop, such as a road, trail, railroad, power line, river, or large lake. Do not use these techniques as a way to navigate to a precise location, such as an off-trail campsite or a trailhead via bushwhacking. Exact locations are much easier to reach using a compass or a GPS receiver.

4

CHAPTER 5
TRAIL SKILLS AND ETIQUETTE

While walking through a serene forest is often much easier than slogging up endless elevation gain, many are surprised to learn there are various techniques and skills that can make hiking safer and more efficient on mountain trails.

Let's be honest: Carrying moderate to heavy loads on our backs is not natural. The human skeleton was not meant to support a load that mostly falls a few inches away from our own centers of gravity. This is why backpacking often leads to shoulder pain and sore hips, and it's especially true when a hiker does not know how to properly load weight in a backpack or how to adjust the backpack support system to the body—or simply hikes using improper technique.

This chapter will look at how to improve your hiking skills and will educate you on the trail etiquette commonly practiced in American outdoors recreation areas.

→ CARRYING YOUR PACK
LIFTING YOUR PACK ON YOUR BACK
A fully loaded backpack is not an item you can easily pick up with one arm and throw on your back. Recklessly lifting a pack is the perfect recipe for a painful back injury. Instead of using your back muscles incorrectly, use any of these three techniques.

Technique 1: Backpack Lift with a Partner
With this technique, you will avoid any back torsion (spinal twisting), so it's a safe method to use for very heavy packs. The steps for this assisted lift are as follows:

1. Face your backpack's harness and grip it by the shoulder straps. Your partner should be on the other side of your pack, facing you while holding the base of your backpack. Your partner should be squatting down so that he or she can help you lift your pack by using only the legs while keeping the spine straight.

2. In coordination with your partner, lift the backpack to the proper height for your back.

3. Before turning yourself to slide your arms into the backpack harness, confirm that your partner is ready to hold the load of your pack.

4. Once your pack is on your shoulders, begin your backpack adjustment (see below).

Technique 2: Backpack Lift Solo

If you are alone or feel you can handle the weight of your backpack by yourself, follow these steps to get it easily from the ground to your back without hurting yourself:

1. Facing your backpack harness while your pack is sitting upright on the ground, use your nondominant hand to hold the pack's haul loop: the loop on top of the pack, also known as the "pack handle." Use your dominant hand to help lift the pack by holding one of the shoulder straps.

2. Taking a wide stance with knees bent, place the leg corresponding to your dominant hand against the back of your pack. Lift and slide the pack up to your thigh and let it rest in an upright position on your thigh.

3. Steady the pack with your nondominant hand by holding the haul loop.

4. Slip your dominant arm and shoulder through one of the shoulder straps and grab the bottom of your pack with that hand.

5. In a smooth motion, swing the pack onto your back and slip your arm through the other shoulder strap.

6. Once your pack in on your shoulders, stand up straight and begin your backpack adjustment (see below).

Technique 3: Backpack Lift from a Shelf

If you can find a boulder, a fallen tree along the trail, a picnic table, or the elevated floor of a shelter in camp, use these waist-high "shelves" to put on your backpack by yourself. Here are the steps for this easy technique:

1. Find the appropriate natural or humanmade shelf and lift your backpack onto it by using your pack haul loop and one of the shoulder straps.

2. While keeping the backpack upright on the shelf, turn your back toward the harness of your backpack and slide your arms through the shoulder straps.

3. Carefully transfer the pack from the shelf to your back by standing up or leaning forward.

4. Once your pack is on your shoulders, begin your backpack adjustment (see Figure 26 on page 108).

When removing your pack, don't be lazy or careless; take the time to reverse the process of any one of the above techniques. Throwing off your pack or falling backward onto your pack at the end of a hike is a sure way to injure yourself or damage gear.

➜ ADJUSTING YOUR PACK FOR COMFORT AND EFFICIENCY

Fine-tuning your backpack harness and load-adjustment straps is as essential as proper packing technique to ensure comfort on long hikes. Most modern internal frame packs now come with comfortable harnesses and well-designed load-adjustment straps.

First, it is important to understand there are two types of adjustment-strap systems on your backpack. One set is there to adjust and conform your backpack harness to your body, and a second set properly distributes the pack weight on your harness. The straps used to fit your harness to your body are called the hip belt (a.k.a. waist belt), the shoulder straps, and the sternum strap. The straps used to adjust the weight of your pack are known as the load-adjuster straps (a.k.a. load lifter straps) and the lower stabilizer straps. By following the steps described below, you can properly adjust your pack for comfort and efficiency.

5

1. Make sure your harness yoke, or the point where both shoulder straps meet, is properly placed for the length of your torso. For proper fitting, the midline of your hip belt should fall on your iliac crest (the upper tip of your hip bone); see Figure 26 on page 108 for more on fit. The harness yoke should fall at the center point between your shoulder blades. Most modern backpacks have adjustable harness yokes, and fit is crucial.

2. Before you place your pack on your back, loosen all of the straps on your harness. It will be easier to adjust and fit your harness if all straps are loose.

3. Place the center line of your hip belt over your iliac crest, clip the hip belt buckle, and pull the hip belt straps evenly on both sides. Make the hip belt very tight, as you want to transfer most of your pack weight to your hips. Make sure your hip belt perfectly conforms to the shape of your waist. There should be no gap(s) between your pack hip belt and your waist.

4. Slowly tighten your shoulder straps by pulling both straps—right and left—at the same time. Do not overtighten these straps. You should feel only a light pressure on your shoulders. See these straps as a way to keep your pack upright and not as a way to carry your load. Again, make sure that your shoulder straps

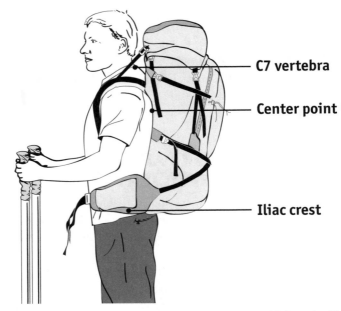

C7 vertebra

Center point

Iliac crest

FIGURE 26. For proper backpack fit, the midline of the hip belt should fall on the iliac crest (the upper tip of the hip bone), and the harness yoke should fall at the center point between the shoulder blades. To tighten the shoulder straps, pull both at the same time. There should be no gaps between the pack and your body.

perfectly conform to your shoulders' natural shape. There should be no gap(s) between your pack shoulder straps and your body.

Now that your pack harness properly fits your body shape, it is time to transfer and stabilize your pack weight on your pack harness. Follow these steps to complete the adjustment of your pack.

1. Pull the stabilizer straps located on either side of your hip belt. You should feel the pack weight shifting your hips forward.

2. Gently pull on the load-adjuster straps, located at the top of your shoulder straps. Do not pull too much on these straps—just enough to feel the load shifting toward the top of your pack harness. If your harness is properly adjusted for the length of your torso, your load-adjuster straps should form a 30- to 60-degree angle from the bottom of your earlobes. The ideal angle for the load-adjuster straps is 45 degrees.

3. Last, clip your sternum-strap buckle and tighten it lightly. This strap keeps your shoulder straps in place and prevents them from slipping off your shoulders. Note that most sternum straps can be moved up or down along the shoulder straps. Place your sternum strap in a position that is most comfortable for you but be careful not to bring it too close to your neck. For women, it is best for the sternum strap to be positioned above the breasts.

KEEPING DRY

Although you can use a pack rain cover (or garbage bag) to protect your equipment from getting wet, there are two items that you should keep completely waterproofed inside your pack, particularly if the weather forecast calls for heavy rain or if your route includes a potentially deep river crossing. These two items are your sleeping bag and your warmest clothing layers.

To waterproof your sleeping bag, you can use a lightweight, waterproof stuff sack, which are now becoming quite popular in backpacking. These stuff sacks are not your common paddling stuff sacks. They are made of lightweight, waterproof nylon with tape-sealed seams and an easy-to-use, waterproof closing buckle system. If you do not have a lightweight dry sack, you can use this simple but effective alternative:

1. Place a plastic bag—trash compactor bags are best for this task—inside your sleeping bag stuff sack. Make sure that one-third to one-half of the opening side of the plastic bag spills out of your stuff sack.

2. Place your sleeping bag inside the plastic bag/stuff sack contraption by stuffing the foot of your sleeping bag first. Carefully make a fist with your dominant hand and stuff the bottom of your plastic bag/stuff sack while holding the lips of the plastic bag and stuff sack with your other hand.

3. Once the entire sleeping bag is inside the layered stuff sack, pull the plastic bag neck while pushing the sleeping bag inside. Then hold the neck of the plastic bag in one hand to create a valve with your fingers around the neck of the plastic bag.

4. Open your grip and push the air out of the stuff sack by pushing down on the stuff sack. This technique is best performed while the bottom of the stuff sack is on the ground.

5. Use your body weight to compress your sleeping bag until most of the air has been expelled through your finger valve.

6. Once this is accomplished, close your finger valve to seal the plastic bag.

7. Spin the sleeping bag stuff sack a few times, then tie an overhand knot (see Figure 37 on page 184) in the neck of the plastic bag.

And there you have it. Your sleeping bag is now compressed and waterproofed; plus, if you completed this technique properly, your sleeping bag stuff sack is one-third or one-half of its original size. (You can also look online for helpful videos to show you how to do this.)

If you are using a compression stuff sack, use the same technique described above, with the following adaptation:

1. Layer the inside of the compression stuff sack with a plastic bag and stuff your sleeping bag the same way as described above.

2.   Once the entire sleeping bag is inside the plastic bag/compression stuff sack, cinch the cord of the stuff sack to partially close the sack while letting the neck of the plastic bag emerge through the compression stuff sack opening.

3.   Create a finger valve around the neck of the plastic bag and compress the stuff sack by cinching the compression straps.

4.   Once most of the air in the stuff sack is out, close your finger valve, spin the neck of the plastic bag, and tie an overhand knot in the plastic bag.

By using either of these techniques, you will be able to compress and waterproof your sleeping bag, which, it's good to remember, is the warmest layer you will carry.

The same technique can be used to compress and waterproof your warmest clothing. Although you might not be able to as drastically reduce the volume of your warmest items, unless they are filled with goose down, you will be able to waterproof them.

Note that this technique is far more effective than putting your sleeping bag or clothing into a stuff sack, which you then put in a plastic bag. When you place a plastic bag inside a stuff sack, you're using the plastic bag to vacuum the air out of the stuff sack while also waterproofing your equipment and clothing. The stuff sack, then, is used to protect your plastic bag, as the nylon will protect the plastic bag from scratches, rips, and tears.

Finally, if you are expecting a lot of rain on the trail, it's appropriate to line the interior of your entire backpack with a commercially made backpack liner or a heavy-duty plastic bag, such as a contractor garbage bag. This waterproofing technique, combined with the sleeping bag stuff sack and a pack rain cover, will keep your gear dry even in the worst monsoonlike conditions.

HAND STRAPS

Have you noticed that hikers often have a tendency to place their thumbs under their pack shoulder straps while hiking? Well, there is a more convenient way to shift your pack weight from your shoulders or your hips. Place webbing loops (a loop-shaped removable cord or strap), about 12 to 14 inches long, on each of your shoulder straps' accessory loops (often used to clip on a camera or other small items) or between your pack's shoulder straps and shoulder pads.

While hiking, place your hands in these webbing loops and shift your pack's weight from your shoulders or your hips by pulling the webbings forward, sideways, or upward. Using your triceps to hold the weight of your pack while freeing your hips is an amazing feeling, especially when hiking uphill. But be careful with these hand loops. Do not place both hands in the webbings when navigating difficult terrain, such as a boulder field, or when hopping over wet rocks. In these situations, it is best to hold the hand straps only by inserting your thumbs into them. This way, it will be easy to remove your hands from the webbing to protect yourself from a sudden fall.

→ CONSERVING ENERGY

Now that you've got your pack fitted properly, it's time to look for other ways to conserve that most precious natural resource: your body. When backpacking, energy conservation is the name of the game. Remember that reaching a mountain summit is often the halfway point in your route. Always think of ways to conserve and maintain your energy while hiking. Here are some trail-tested techniques to avoid fatigue.

DRESSING FOR HIKING

Overheating will make you uncomfortable and will tire you quickly on the trail. Instead of starting your hike and then having to stop to rest after eight or ten minutes, it is best to start your day feeling a bit cold for the weather. Unless it's raining hard or is very chilly, hiking in shorts (with gaiters) is best because your legs will generate a lot of heat from muscle contraction. For your upper layer, it is best to wear a light synthetic or wool T-shirt with a lightweight long-sleeve and zippered base layer. This way you can easily adjust your temperature while hiking by unzipping your shirt or rolling up your sleeves. If it's windy, wear a lightweight wind jacket or pullover. Whatever you're wearing, if you feel yourself becoming fatigued because your body is too hot, stop and adjust your layers.

FOOT PLACEMENT

For safety and energy conservation, it is always best to hike flatfooted, even when the trail gets very steep. Walking on your toes will cause your calf muscles to contract, which will eventually lead to muscle fatigue, soreness, and even cramps. Be conscious of each foot placement and seek ways to always walk flatfooted.

Good foot placement also means avoiding taking big steps, especially when climbing a steep section of trail. Big steps require a lot of muscle power from your quadriceps. On the other hand, taking small, vertical steps will allow you to conserve energy. Sometimes raising your foot only a few inches on a steep trail is enough to make your climb easier and will allow you to avoid taking a large step. This is especially true when you encounter water bars or manufactured rock steps on the trail. In these situations, take the time to look for small raises near these obstacles so you can take a small step and avoid bending your leg at the knee in order to get up.

REST-STEP TECHNIQUE

Many students in our backpacking courses do not believe us when we tell them they will need to relearn how to walk when hiking. For many of us, hiking seems like a simple activity, but hiking with a heavy pack on your back for six to eight hours a day is not as simple as you might think. This is especially true when you

5

are gaining altitude on steep trails. One technique that can save you from muscle pain, energy loss, and the sinking feeling that hiking is a miserable endeavor is known as the rest step.

The rest step is not natural, so it takes some practice. Beginners will need to be conscious of performing it properly. It is most effective on very steep terrain and is done as follows:

1. With your right leg, take a short step uphill using a flatfoot placement.

2. Explosively, or at least rapidly, contract your quadriceps muscle and extend your right leg to a vertical position.

3. Lock your right knee in a straight position, taking care not to overextend your knee.

4. Bring your left (lower) leg up past your extended right leg and take another short, uphill, flatfoot step.

5. Repeat the explosive extension with the upper leg and continue the process until the terrain is more moderate.

The way the rest step works is twofold. First, by quickly contracting your muscles you will save energy, a bit like the way an Olympic weight lifter quickly explodes to perform a "clean and jerk" lift. Second, by extending your leg to a vertical position you will allow the contracted leg to take a moment of muscular rest by placing most of your body and pack weight on your leg bones. This microrest will ease tension in your muscles and allow them to save energy while recuperating with each rest step.

When this is done properly, a hiker can get into a good rhythm, combining a rest step with each breath and moving from one balanced foot position to another. There are many online videos in which you can watch this technique.

TREKKING POLES

A good way to save energy while hiking, especially on a steep uphill or downhill section of the trail, is to use one or two trekking poles (a.k.a. hiking poles). When used properly, trekking poles can help transfer some weight to your arms and there-fore reduce the strain on your legs. Poles are also effective at reducing the stress put on your knees when descending steep terrain.

To properly use your poles, it is essential you hold them correctly. Contrary to using alpine ski poles, you should take advantage of your trekking poles' handle straps. To hold the strap properly, enter it from below by following the shaft of the pole. Once your hand has fully passed the strap, lower your hand and grip the pole handle by inserting the strap between your thumb and index finger. This way you will not only keep track of your pole if you release your grip on the handle, but you will also be able to use the strap to push down on the pole.

When hiking on flat and uphill terrain, adjust your trekking poles' length so that your elbows form 90-degree angles when you are holding the grip of the

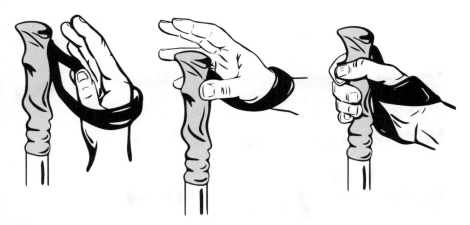

FIGURE 27. To hold a trekking pole correctly, insert your hand from the bottom of the loop then grip the pole so the strap forms a yoke across your palm. Wrap your fingers around the pole, thumb on top.

5

pole and the pole tip is touching the ground. When descending a trail, extend the length of your poles so you can rest on them sooner and avoid having to lean forward to reach the ground. Note that during a steep downhill descent, it is appropriate to place your hands on top of the pole handles and push down on the poles when taking a big step down.

When hiking on flat terrain or uphill, always make sure to plant your forward pole a few inches behind your front foot for maximum efficiency. Never plant your pole in front of your forward foot on flat, easy terrain, as doing so won't give you much mechanical advantage until your foot passes your pole.

Your pole action should be asymmetrical to your leg action: When your right foot moves forward, your left pole moves forward. Conversely, when your left foot moves forward, your right pole moves forward. This is the way your arms and legs naturally move, so there's no need to change your motion simply because you have poles in your hands.

When the terrain is easy and mostly flat, you can collapse your trekking poles and secure them to the side of your pack. With the help of a partner, you can retrieve them easily when the terrain requires their usage.

TRAIL HAZARDS TO AVOID

With every step you take on a trail, you have to make a conscious, and sometimes unconscious, decision as to where your foot will fall. When the terrain is flat and rocks and roots are absent, it's easy to place your foot on the ground and enjoy the hike by looking around or talking with a fellow hiker. But when the terrain presents a more uneven surface with small or large obstacles, you should focus on your foot placement and trying to avoid stepping on (or off) hazardous trail features. The classic features on a trail that will throw you to the ground or potentially injure one of your joints, such as an ankle or a knee, are wet logs and rocks, narrow gaps between rocks, muddy sections, and low branches. You can avoid injury from these common trail hazards by following these safety precautions:

- On wet trails, always avoid placing your foot on a log stripped of its bark, such as the kind used to direct water runoff. In wet conditions, these logs are as slippery as a plate of butter.

- On wet trails, be very careful when hiking on split logs—the kind cut in half lengthwise and laid over wetlands or low spots, also called trunk trails. These logs get very slippery when wet and should not be trusted.

- On cold mornings or days, be very cautious of wet rocks in a creek or brook. These rocks can hide an invisible layer of ice that will send you to the ground in no time.

- On steep terrain, while going uphill or downhill, avoid placing your foot between two narrow rocks. If your boot gets wedged, you risk injuring your ankle or knee when your body moves forward but your foot stays anchored.

- On exposed bedrock, do not trust wet sections of rock; they can be very slippery due to polishing (erosion) or microalgae colonies growing on them.

- When traveling a muddy trail, avoid jumping from foot placement to foot placement. Muddy sections of a trail can hide deep holes that can suck in your entire boot or leg. Instead, carefully place each foot on a section that seems firm, then transfer your weight gradually form footstep to footstep.

- Low branches across the trail can be a great hazard, especially if someone directly in front of you pushes them aside then lets them go. Make sure you leave some distance between you and your fellow hikers, or stay close to one another and pass your hold on the potential wipeout branch to the hiker behind you.

PACING

Of the techniques for conserving energy on the trail, pacing is perhaps the most important. In simple terms, pacing refers to your average speed of travel while hiking. A typical speed for walking is around 2 MPH. It is possible to hike up to 4 MPH, but beyond that you are entering the realm of jogging. When the terrain is steep or technical, don't be surprised to see your speed reduce to 1 or even 0.5 MPH.

If you can average a typical hiking speed of 2 MPH, you can plan to cover 2 miles in about 60 minutes or 1 mile in about 30 minutes. This is why having a watch on the trail can be so useful. If you are using a GPS, these devices can give detailed information about your current speed as well as your average traveling speed, which can help you gauge your trail fitness level.

What is most important while hiking, however, is to not hike faster than your body or the conditions will allow—hence the importance of knowing your own pace.

Learn Your Hiking Pace

Your hiking pace is a speed of travel that keeps your body in an aerobic state, allowing you to hike for long periods of time without fatigue or exhaustion. A good rule of thumb for finding your appropriate hiking pace is to monitor your ability to carry on a conversation. If you can talk while hiking without being out of breath, it means you are not overexerting your cardiovascular system, which is perfect. If you can sing at the top of your lungs while hiking, perhaps you are hiking at a pace that is too slow for you. Finally, if you cannot carry on a simple conversation, you are hiking too fast for your body.

Beginner hikers have a tendency to go too fast at the start of a hike. Start off slow and let your muscles warm up before hitting your appropriate stride. Get into a routine of pushing for about 60 minutes of low-grade exercise before stepping off the trail and putting down your pack. A 10-minute break for water and a snack while gently moving your legs will help you avoid building lactic acid in your muscles. Breaking too often will discourage you, as you will not progress far along the trail. If needed, you can stop after 30 minutes for quick hydration without putting down your pack.

Remember, once you have found your ideal trail pace you will be able to hike for a large portion of the day, cover multiple miles, and arrive in camp with enough energy in reserve to perform your camp chores and enjoy your well-earned relaxation.

5

NO BREAKS ON HILLS

To keep your motivation high and your hiking pace effective, avoid taking a break on a long uphill slope. Breaking along a long climbing trail can be demoralizing and can interrupt your pace. Lactic acid might build up in your muscles, and restarting the hike will be more painful and depressing. Instead, make it a goal to take a break at the top of a steep section. This way you will have a feeling of accomplishment, as well as an easier restart on flatter terrain.

➜ BUSHWHACKING

Off-trail travel—bushwhacking—increases both your risk of injury and your impact on the natural environment. AMC generally recommends hikers stay on the trail whenever possible. Bushwhacking can be very challenging. Vegetation often appears to be a barrier to your route. Rhododendron, hobble-bush, and other shrubs can create thickets of woody stems, as can close-growing hardwood saplings or subalpine fir and spruce. In other spots, great fields of wind-thrown trunks will create a three-dimensional blowdown maze, often in a sea of young, densely packed saplings. In part due to these challenges, if you arrive at a destination that was unreachable any other way, you may feel the rewards of solitude and personal accomplishment even greater. A little off-trail travel also gives the wilderness enthusiast some extra insight about what hiking must have been like in these mountains and forests during the time of exploration, before the great trail-building era.

It takes skill to make forward progress in off-trail environments. In addition to the off-trail navigation techniques recommended in Chapter 4, pages 88–90, following these basic principles will help:

- Maintain your commitment to LNT principles. Remember, hiking off-trail is a choice, and if you cannot minimize your impact, your party belongs on the trail.

- Look for durable surfaces on which to place your feet. Choose rocks, gravel, and needle duff rather than moss, bog, or meadow. One of our favorite "invisible" options is to walk right up or down a streambed. If this path offers reasonably safe footing, a hiker will leave behind no footprints at all. Wet boots are a small price to pay for protecting the integrity of pristine areas.

- Be stealthy as you slide between tree trunks and branches, breaking as few twigs as possible. Broken twigs will remain noticeable for a long time and could attract enough off-trail hikers to create yet another new trail.

- Groups should choose whichever approach will leave less impact: a single-file line or a horizontal line. Usually our groups choose the horizontal line method, in which group members "filter" through the woods in a general direction, staying within sight of one another but are not stepping in each other's footpaths.

- Pack a smooth, streamlined backpack, putting as much inside your pack as possible—especially any closed-cell foam pads. Anything you have to strap to the outside of your pack should be securely fastened. Off-trail vegetation has a way of unzipping pockets and puncturing sleeping pads, as well as stripping off fuel bottles, water bottles, tent poles, electronic technology items, and more. Not only will these losses be a huge inconvenience, they will create an unwanted discovery for other off-trail hikers and could harm wildlife.

- Expect to cut your hiking pace in half (double your travel time) when off-trail. While a skilled hiker can move at 3 MPH on a level trail, that same person will slow to 1 MPH or less when swimming through spruce or walking up a streambed.

- Look for the paths of least resistance. Skilled hikers develop an eye for animal trails and will exploit these gaps in vegetation when possible. Streambeds can also provide these gaps.

- Accept a high degree of flexibility in your route. As long as you know where you are and can arrive at your intended destination, let your route drift substantially to avoid particularly impenetrable areas.

- Remember that sudden drops smaller than your map's contour interval will not appear on your topographic map. Depending on your map, this could be as high as 49 feet! These hazards will be unmarked and can appear in your path at any time.

- In extreme blowdown mazes (numerous trees felled by storms), you will find yourself crawling under trunks, climbing over them, and walking atop them. It could be much faster to just skirt the entire maze, but if you can't, be very careful, especially if the ground is obscured by young growth. While walking along a trunk, you might suddenly realize you are 15 feet in the air. Mazes are also easy places to twist a knee or take a high fall. In very difficult places, look for ways to spot other group members or perhaps to pass packs.

- When bushwhacking through tight fir and spruce forests, it may be worth the extra heat to wear a jacket or a shirt that has a hood. A snug-fitting hood will keep tree debris from going down the back of your shirt, where it will cause a lot of irritation as it works its way downward.

- Even in the heat, consider wearing pants when bushwhacking to prevent scratches and abrasions. For the same purpose as the hood, wear those pants on the outside of your gaiters, sloughing the needles over your boots, not into them.

- Carefully lift branches out of your way rather than taking a "bull of the woods" approach. This will protect the vegetation, as well as your clothing, pack, and skin.

- Be wary of eye injuries from branches or conifer needles. Keep enough spacing between group members that branches can swing back in place without hitting anyone, and consider wearing sunglasses as protective gear.

- Maintain your sense of humor—and wonder. You are seeing a part of the mountains reserved only for those who are willing to work hard for it.

ROCKY TERRAIN

Sometimes hikers both on- and off-trail encounter slick rock, nearly vertical routes, and fields of fractured, unstable rock. Short sections of this type of terrain are common, and it is important to have some strategies ready to deploy when needed.

When hiking up bare, sloping rock, it's usually best to try to place your entire boot sole on the rock. This technique requires you to have ankle and calf flexibility, but it pays off with better traction and less overall strain on your legs. Hiking down bare rock is similar in that you should place your entire foot on the rock. When descending, try to emphasize the downward pressure of your toes in your boots, rather than your heels. A common tendency of timid hikers is to lean back, putting their weight on their heels, but this weighting will lead to a fall as soon as they encounter slippery terrain. A hiker who slips while pressing on his or her forefoot may slide a bit but is much more likely to remain upright. Hiking groups moving up or down bare rock should consider how members might help one another by spotting or passing packs. Group members should also make decisions about spacing so that they can assist a sliding member or stay out of each other's way.

Talus, or fractured rock slabs, can range in size from a foot to many feet in diameter. Sloping fields of talus slabs are found at the bases of cliffs—the accumulated debris of eons of ice fracturing and rock fall. Talus slabs are often unstable with deep, foot-size gaps and holes between them. Mindful footing is the most important strategy for traversing talus; know where each foot is going to land. The slabs will be less likely to shift or slide if you step high on their uphill side and keep a balanced, upright stance rather than leaning into the hill. If the slope is steep and there is a possibility of slabs tumbling downhill, hikers must be very vigilant. The first hiker of the group should test each foot placement and refrain from stepping on talus that seems likely to fall. If a rock is kicked loose, the hiker should immediately yell, "Rock!" Hikers below must also be aware. In any steep talus field, avoid hiking directly below another hiker. Alternative options are to hike off to one side of the person above or to use a zigzag route, in which all members of the party collect at each switchback. If neither of these options will work, it is best to travel one at a time, with each hiker stopping at a stable resting spot and waiting for the other members to catch up.

Boulder fields are also common in the mountains of the Northeast. Boulders can vary from a few feet in height to the size of a small house. Sometimes the best route will involve a lot of up, down, and around, which will add a lot of time to your travel. When possible, most hikers will try to hop from boulder top to boulder top. Plan each move carefully and only make hops you are sure you will land. Unweighted, this approach can be fun. Remember, though, that a pack (especially a heavy one) will add a lot of force to your dynamic movements. Knees can buckle and calf muscles can tear, so be realistic about what you are asking of your body. Search-and-rescue evacuations in boulder fields are some of the slowest and trickiest.

For all difficult, unstable terrain, it will help to have your pack fit closely to your body, and to tighten any stabilizing straps to eliminate swaying and wobbling. Try to lower the height of the pack, if possible. If you know that a significant part of the day will involve scrambling or vertical terrain, consider modifying the weight distribution inside your pack. Moving heavier items closer to your lumbar (just above the sleeping bag, closest to your back) will lower your center of gravity. A pack filled correctly for on-trail travel may sway and feel top-heavy when going vertical.

For hikers with partners or in groups, you can also try spotting one another, passing packs through difficult terrain, or even using roped protection. If the group is carrying ropes for protecting food from animals, these ropes may be of sufficient strength and length to use as fixed lines (think of a rope handrail) or for short-roping (connecting two or more people by tying a length of rope around them). These methods are especially helpful if there is a wide range of skill level in the group, but they require effort to learn and implement safely.

➜ RIVER AND STREAM CROSSINGS

A specialized terrain feature common in the Northeast is the river and stream crossing. Some hikers might find it refreshing to splash across an ankle-deep stream in mid-August, but when the water deepens, the current speeds up, or the riverbed widens, river crossings test a backpacker's skills of risk assessment and management. River crossings expose hikers to the hazards of cold-water immersion, foot entrapments, log strainers (logs over and around which water can flow but solid objects cannot), and keeper holes (a sort of river whirlpool). These require extra focus and special skills to navigate safely.

Occasionally a crossing can be accomplished with dry feet by finding a log bridge or the perfect series of boulders. When this works, it is brilliant, but be careful. Hopping across slippery rocks with a pack often ends in a wet and painful fall. It's worse to find yourself in the water unexpectedly than it is to have planned to cross the water all along. Once you decide that a wet crossing is necessary, the keys to accomplishing it safely are choosing a suitable location and using a stable, proven technique.

5

CHOOSING A LOCATION

Spend the time to scout up and down a river looking for the best spot to cross. The ideal spot will be shallow and have slow-moving water, with a gravel bottom and banks on both sides that are easily ascended and descended. As you scout, consider looking upstream first, rather than down. As the river forks higher up in the drainage, you may find that it is easier to cross multiple smaller tributaries, one at a time, rather than the main branch all at once. Diligent scouting is worth the effort. For truly hazardous crossings, a good location will mitigate many of the hazards the crossing will pose. Be sure to consider:

- Depth, speed, and temperature of the water

- Substrate of the bottom

- Ease of entry and exit from the river channel

- Hazards to a swimmer downstream

- Swimming abilities and general skill level of the group

In general, choose wide, straight sections, as they will be shallower and more consistent than narrow and curvier sections. Don't be fooled by the shallow slip-off slope inside a river curve. Sandbars found there will rapidly become a deep, fast channel against the steep-cut bank on the other side. As you scout, you should eliminate any options that involve the following:

- Extremely cold water, especially when combined with cold air temperature

- A waterfall, rapid, or other major water feature just downstream of your crossing site

- A river in flood or near flood, indicated by water level in the riverside vegetation, floating debris in the water, or muddy and turbulent water

- A river bottom composed of very large boulders or a bottom that isn't visible

- A river that is deeper than the knee and moving faster than 3 to 4 MPH

Sometimes, such as during spring melt or after heavy rains, it is impossible to find a location where the risks are reasonable and mitigatable. You must accept that you may need to divert a significant distance from your route—or abandon your intended route altogether—to make a safe crossing.

CROSSING METHODS

If you find a reasonable location, you can practice a proven crossing technique. There are several good strategies, depending on the river conditions and the group profile. All of the strategies share the same core principles of movement:

- Maintain a wide stance

5

- Take small, shuffling steps

- Move one foot at a time

- Do not use a crossover step

If you are hiking solo, you will be limited to shuffling sideways while facing upstream. Use a trekking pole or a stout branch as a third leg of support. Pairs of hikers should use a similar approach but with the hikers facing each other, one upstream and one down. For groups, you have four basic options: the rolling wheel, the horizontal line, the upstream line, and the upstream wedge.

1. **Rolling wheel.** This technique involves three to four people facing inward with their arms around one another's shoulders. Their hands grip the clothing or pack straps of those beside them. The downstream-most person (facing upstream) stands still, and the others rotate around that person toward the opposite shore. This movement creates a new downstream person, and the rotation continues until the group completes the crossing. Since this technique involves at least one person at a time facing downstream, it is best used for crossings in light to moderate current.

2. **Horizontal line.** This crossing can involve four to six people, sometimes more. It is quite simple in concept. Everyone assembles in a line facing the opposite shore, firmly grasps the clothing or shoulders of the person in front of them, and then methodically shuffles across the river. Because each hiker must handle the impact of the current individually, this method is also best used for light to moderate current.

Best Method

3. **Upstream line.** This technique has three to five people, all facing upstream, stacked one behind the other. The upstream person (leaning on a pole or a

branch) is supported from behind. That person breaks the current and all the others stand in the eddy this creates. The group can all shuffle together or, in more challenging conditions, can have each person take one shuffle step at a time, starting with the downstream-most person. Because the group benefits from the eddy behind the upstream leader, this method is especially useful for faster current and deeper channels.

4. **Upstream wedge.** This crossing requires at least five people in a pyramid formation facing upstream. Movement is similar to the upstream line, with all members shuffling simultaneously as a single unit. With enough people, the upstream wedge is the most stable and reliable method for the most challenging crossings.

No matter which of the methods you choose, you should follow these guidelines:

- Have a plan and practice the group techniques on dry land.
- Look upstream and ahead as you cross, as looking down at the river can be disorienting.
- Move methodically, feeling for potholes or unstable rocks before shifting your weight.
- Keep packs on, but completely unbuckle the hip belts and sternum straps so they can be easily removed.
- Wear footwear. We usually prefer to get our boots wet and save our dry camp shoes for camp. If you have only one crossing on your day's route, consider removing your boot insoles and socks so they will be dry later.
- Wear shorts, not pants. Shorts will cause less drag on your legs from the current.
- Depending on water depth, a river that is moving much faster than you can walk (more than 3 MPH) will feel very powerful and may be too strong to cross.
- In fast water, do not stand up until the water is shallower than your knees.
- Always place a safety person downstream of the crossing site. Use a long branch or a length of food-protection rope with a water bottle tied to the end as a lifesaving device.

JUDGMENT

Interesting terrain features, such as talus fields and rapid rivers, will be some of the most memorable events of a mountain journey. They increase the sense of adventure and self-reliance as they test a hiker's range of skills. It is important to remember that, while skills such as foot placement and river scouting are very important, your greatest asset will be your mountain sense and hiking judgment. In unusual terrain, an experienced hiker constantly will be engaged in a process of comparative risk analysis. In this process, the hiker honestly assesses the likelihood and the severity of potential accidents. When traversing bare rock or choosing a river crossing, consider the likelihood of a mishap, as well as the consequences if that mishap were to happen. If a fall is very unlikely and the consequences of that fall are minimal, go for it. If the fall is very likely but the consequences are still minimal, it is probably safe to proceed with elevated safety practices, such as group spotting or a safety rope. Things get much more serious if a mishap is very likely and the consequences would be serious or fatal. In these circumstances, the obvious choice is to find a new route.

The situation that truly tests a backcountry traveler arises when a mishap is unlikely but the consequences would be dire. Our judgment is often skewed by desire: to complete our route; not to disappoint other group members; an irrational belief that accidents happen to other people. Be very wary of rationalizations that are really just disguises for gambling. The measure of a skillful hiker is not the number of near-misses survived but the number of mountain miles enjoyed without incident.

WHAT TO DO IF YOU ARE SWEPT OFF YOUR FEET

- Slip out of your shoulder straps and allow your pack to float away.

- Roll your body so your feet are downstream and you are floating on your back.

- If there are no imminent downstream hazards, backstroke your way to the desired shore.

- If downstream hazards are present, aggressively swim away from them. If they cannot be avoided, attempt to climb on top of them.

Finally, in this era of pack rafting and other creative travel methods, some hikers might consider swimming with their packs. It is possible to float a watertight pack with the help of an inflatable sleeping pad, although this approach is not suitable for moving water. Like an upset canoeist in a rapid, the swimmer will not be able to simultaneously control the pack and make progress toward the other shore. Consider a swimming crossing only in the calmest of water.

→ TRAIL ETIQUETTE

Encountering strangers on a hiking trail differs from crossing paths on a busy sidewalk in a large city. In the former, you are pretty sure to receive a polite greeting, a quick conversation, or at the very least, eye contact and a genuine smile. The unwritten rule of the trail is that fellow hikers have something in common and therefore are friendly. So, it's important to share the trail in friendly ways. Here is some common trail etiquette to practice when encountering other nature lovers.

PASSING OTHER HIKERS

If you are hiking a busy trail, especially near the trailhead, you are bound to catch up to slower hikers. In these situations, it's appropriate to let them know you are behind them and would like to pass them. Coming up from behind them and simply asking politely, "May we pass?" is a more polite and less aggressive way of making this clear than by saying, "Coming through," or, "On your right." If the trail is narrow, wet, or technical, the unwritten rule is that on flat terrain, larger groups should yield to smaller groups, since it's more inconvenient for a small group or a solo hiker to wait for a large group to pass. On steep inclines, common courtesy is to have the party traveling downhill yield to the party or hiker traveling uphill. This is appropriate since it takes more effort for a hiker going uphill to stop and restart a climbing pace than someone descending downhill. But as these are unwritten rules, don't be surprised to see uphill hikers stepping off the trail to let you pass.

RESTING ALONG THE TRAIL

When taking a "pack-off" break along the trail, it is better LNT practice to seek a durable surface away from the trail. This way, no one will need to hike through your group, stepping over your pack or picnic, to continue on the trail. When resting is done properly, you will see hikers passing by you without them even noticing your presence.

5

ENCOUNTERING PACK ANIMALS

  For safety reasons, hikers always yield to horseback riders and pack animals. The simple reason is that horses and pack animals can be spooked by your large pack or trekking poles. Before they get close to you, step aside and wait to see what the horse or pack animal handler tells you to do. If the handler knows his or her four-legged friend needs more space, he or she will tell you that and also where to stand. In all cases, avoid moving your arms (such as in a polite hand wave), since a stressed animal could perceive this as a threat. With horses, in particular, do not reach your hand out with fingers extended—as in reaching out to pet them. Human fingers may resemble claws or talons to horses and may trigger them to spook if they're not expecting to see you and don't know you. Horses are natural prey animals, meaning their first reaction to startling new encounters is almost always flight.

If you encounter a horseback rider on steep slopeside trails, move off the trail on the downhill side of the slope. It's easier for a rider to handle a spooked horse moving uphill than downhill. If the animal handler invites you to greet his or her trail companion, follow that recommendation. The handler knows best.

HIKING IN SMALLER GROUPS

If you are part of a group larger than five people, you might consider hiking in smaller groups of two or three. It will be easier for your travel—fewer bladders always means better hiking time—and will be less impactful of others' hiking.

TECHNOLOGY ON THE TRAIL

Even if you are an avid consumer of technology, you might consider putting away your cell phone while hiking or listening to music via earbuds rather than out loud. Remember: Many people go to the woods or the mountains for quiet and solitude. Loud cell phone conversations and music are not part of that experience—nor part of nature.

HIKING IN GROUPS OF VARYING ABILITY LEVEL

If you are in a group with some very experienced backpackers and some novices or those not in the best physical shape, a good rule is to match the pace of the group to the slowest hikers. Even if you have summit fever and really want to reach the top of the peak, be mindful of all participants in your group and keep them company on their way up. This keeps the outing enjoyable for all and is the best hiking etiquette for groups of varying abilities. We were all beginners once, and if you had been in a group where the fittest took off and left you alone on the trail, how might that have colored your experience of the great outdoors? Keep in mind: You are stewards of the trail, and one of your goals should be ensuring that your group enjoys the outing and is motivated to return to and care about the places you visit—now and in the years to come. For more information on hiking in groups, see Chapter 11, Groups, on page 248.

DOG ETIQUETTE

If you are bringing your dog on a hike or a backpacking trip, remember to be a responsible human. Read the dogs section on pages 262–264 in Chapter 11 for proper trail etiquette.

→ IF YOU'RE LOST

Whether you're an avid hiker or a newbie, you have to admit to yourself that getting lost in the woods or a wilderness area is a possibility. There are different levels of "lost," of course. Sometimes you may be a bit disoriented for a few minutes before you suddenly see a landmark that hints at where you are. Sometimes, though, you have to admit that you have no clue where you are and are simply lost. In these cases, it is essential to do a few things.

1. **Admit that you are lost.** Realize that you might need to take rational actions to help yourself.

2. **Adopt an English attitude toward the situation at hand: Keep calm and carry on.** It is not the time to panic or to start running around in the hope of finding a person or a trail you recognize. The best thing to do is to sit and take a break, look calmly at your situation, and evaluate your options.

3. **Take appropriate actions.** This means you might need to prepare yourself for a night away from camp or your planned destination. It might also mean taking action to be more visible, if someone might be looking for you sooner or later. Taking proper action could also mean using a rational way to find your way back to a known area.

TAKING PROPER ACTION

Carefully read the following strategies, memorize them, and watch videos on how to apply these strategies. Better yet, take the time to practice them in a controlled environment. If ever you get truly lost, your training will help you stay calm and deal with the situation more effectively. Here are a few steps to help you weather an unfortunate situation in the woods.

5

- **Prepare for the night or a change in weather.** Night is usually colder, and rain often comes at night in summertime, so be prepared. If you got lost on your way to a location and you have a fully equipped backpack, make camp in the best spot you can find. If you are away from camp and your gear, you will need to improvise for the night. There are many great books on outdoor survival skills, so make sure you take the time to read one of those before your next outing. Because that topic is a book of its own, we're focusing here on how to survive a night alone without equipment. First, shelter and a fire should be your top priority. Use natural shelter areas, such as the base of a large and dense conifer tree or an overhanging boulder or rock formation. Insulate your clothing and the ground you will sit or sleep on. Use raw materials from the environment around you: Are there dry leaves nearby? Grasses and moss? The thicker the insulation, the better, so stuff dry foliage in your upper garments—between your body and your jacket, for instance. Your torso holds vital organs, so you want to keep them warm with extra insulation. The same can be said about the ground you intend to sleep or sit on, since the soil is colder than your body. Due to the laws of thermodynamics, you will lose heat through the ground, so never sleep on bare earth.

  If you have a fire source, make a fire. It will help you stay warmer and will give you emotional comfort. Read more about how to make a fire in Chapter 8, Camping Skills, on page 201–207.

- **Make yourself more visible.** If you know your only hope is to stay put and wait for others to come to your rescue then you want to take actions to attract them. Marking your area with visible flags—stuff sacks attached to tree branches, bandanas, or any other piece of clothing you can spare—could attract a rescue team. Building cairns around your location could also catch the eye of a search party. Obviously, making a fire and using a whistle will help. If you have a whistle, remember that sound does not travel far in a forested area, so do not put all of your energy into screaming or whistling. When whistling, use the internationally known rescue code of three repeated, distinctive whistle blasts.

- **Find your own way back.** There is a not-so-well-known approach to finding your way back to a more familiar area without getting yourself more lost in the process. We call this strategy the find-me cross. This technique is quite effective if used with discipline. It's most appropriate when you're near a known area, such as your campsite or cabin, or near a prominent feature, such as a trail, river, or lake.

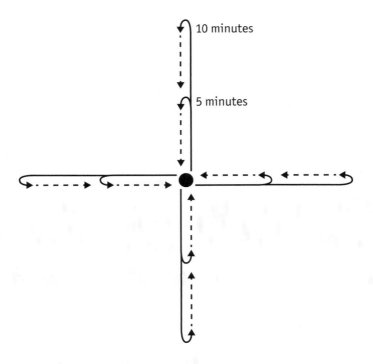

10 minutes

5 minutes

FIGURE 28. To use the find-me cross, build an impossible-to-miss home base out of available material, such as downed branches. From there, walk five minutes in one direction then return to your home base. Repeat in the remaining three directions. If you don't recognize your surroundings, repeat again, extending your walks to ten minutes each. Repeat until you recognize a trail or a landmark.

After admitting that you are lost, mark your known location by building an obvious landmark with rocks, branches, plants—anything will do, as long as you build a large, sculpturelike object that you can easily recognize from any direction. This is your safe spot, the place you know. From this location, choose four directions opposite one another, forming a cross. They could be cardinal directions, but this isn't necessary. Then do the following:

1. Hike in a straight line away from the center of your cross in the most promising direction. Mark your path along the way by breaking branches or building small cairns. Hike on this path for five minutes while looking around to see if you recognize any familiar landmarks. After five minutes, follow your marked path to return to the center of the cross, the site of your large sculpture.

2. From the center of the cross, now hike in the direction opposite the one you just explored. Again, mark your way along this path while looking for familiar areas. Hike on this path for five minutes only, then return to the center of your cross.

3. Repeat the same five-minute hikes in the two remaining directions, which will be perpendicular to your first two walks.

4. If the first set of five-minute walks did not reveal any known or familiar terrain then proceed to hike again in the first path of the cross, this time for ten minutes. Again, take your time to walk slowly, looking for hints as to where you are, listening for familiar sounds, and marking your path. At the end of the allotted time, return to the center of the cross and continue your search in the three other directions.

5. Repeat this exercise, adding five minutes to each direction until you find your way back to your camp, your vehicle, or a known location.

Remember, use the find-me cross only when necessary and be disciplined. Always return to your center until you find a truly familiar landmark. If not used properly, this strategy could get you more lost than found.

CHAPTER 6
HEALTH AND HYGIENE

Being in the woods for an extended period can really feel like an adventure exempt from the everyday hassles we have back home. Out in the backcountry, it's easy to forsake your normal routines, such as brushing your teeth, washing your clothes, and staying clean. But when it comes to your body, you should strive to maintain your normal hygiene standards in the wilderness. Central to all human health and hygiene is the most abundant resource on our planet: water. This chapter will advise you on the various means of backcountry water treatment, or how you can make water found in the backcountry safe to drink or use for cleaning. It's important to remain healthy on your trip, and taking care of yourself is paramount to an enjoyable experience.

➜ STAYING HYDRATED

If aliens were to visit us, they would describe our biology as "ugly bags containing mostly water." (If you recognize this as a *Star Trek* reference, you are right.) Indeed, our bodies contain a significant amount of water—on average, 60 percent of our body weight. Why so much water? Because, quite simply, water is life. A watery environment is essential to the complex chemistry orchestrating the multiple biological functions in our physiology. In other words, keeping our bodies hydrated is a lifelong endeavor, especially when exercising in the open air. Perhaps this is why one of the best water bottles we have ever seen on the trail was inscribed with the motto: "Hydrate or Die!"

The outdoor environment increases our rate of dehydration through wind and fluctuating temperatures. Exercising for long periods of time, as we do when hiking, also contributes to dehydration through forced respiration and sweating. Dehydration on the trail is often the source of common symptoms such as headaches, muscle aches, fatigue, and lack of appetite. It's often said that, in survival situations, one can live without food for three weeks but without water for only three days. Consequently, hydration should always be a big part of your daily routine—but especially while backpacking.

These days you can easily stay hydrated by carrying a dromedary-style hydration system in your pack. These systems allow you to sip on a water tube anytime you want, without even pausing your hike. With it this simple, there is no excuse for you not to stay hydrated. All you have to do is make sure to start the day with a full bag of water in your pack and hydrate as you go.

If you are carrying water bottles, you will need to be more disciplined and stop every 30 minutes to hydrate. Hydration can be done while keeping your pack on by stashing your water bottle in an accessible side pocket or by asking for a fellow hiker's assistance. A good hydration routine during a long hike should include a quick pack-on water break after 30 minutes, followed by a pack-off 10-minute break with more hydration and quick food intake after one hour.

Daily recommended water intake depends on your body weight. Larger people need more water, while smaller people need less. The table below gives you the approximate recommended water intake by body weight.

| RECOMMENDED DAILY WATER INTAKE ACCORDING TO BODY WEIGHT ||
Body Weight in Pounds	Water Intake in Liters (34 oz.)
100	3
120	3.6
140	4.2
160	4.8
180	5.4
200	6

Source: *The National Outdoor Leadership School's Wilderness Guide*

6

Signs of proper hydration include clear and frequent urination, supple skin, good energy level, appetite, and a positive mental state. Signs of dehydration include dark, smelly, and infrequent urination; dizziness; headaches; nausea; dry mouth or tongue; sore muscles or cramps; and feeling thirsty. Thirst is an early sign of dehydration, so never wait until you're thirsty to drink.

Here are some tips on how to stay hydrated while backpacking:

- Prehydrate before staring your hike. Drink plenty of liquids in the morning, including water and hot beverages like caffeine-free tea or decaf coffee, but avoid caffeine, which is a diuretic and increases dehydration. If you depend on coffee to get started in the morning, consider doing a "half-caf" cup, mixing decaf and caffeinated coffee. This will help prevent dehydration later. Be sure to follow your cup of coffee with at least two cups of water.

- Drink small quantities of water often, allowing the body to absorb it more effectively. Chugging a liter of water in one minute is impressive but useless when it comes to hydration.

- Drink more cool water than hot beverages, since your lower intestines absorb cool water more effectively than warm water.

- Avoid drinking liquids with high sugar content, as sugar impedes the absorption of water by your body. This includes fruit juices, energy drinks, sodas, and bottled smoothies.

- Make drinking easy by using a pack hydration system or by placing your water bottle in a location you can reach while hiking.

WATER TREATMENT METHODS

The beautiful, clear streams and remote ponds of the mountains seem as pure as the snows from which they were formed. They look clean and clear and probably taste delicious! But every backcountry traveler should know that drinking this water without treating it brings the risk of ingesting microorganisms that could lead to gastrointestinal discomfort, serious illness, and potential chronic concerns. Protozoan parasites, such as giardia and cryptosporidium, can cause acute gastrointestinal illness (diarrhea, cramping, vomiting), and these parasites can occur in any untreated water. Water sources with heavy human impact can also contain viruses, such as hepatitis, or bacteria, such as E. coli.

For hikers who want to greatly lower the risk to themselves and their fellow travelers, there are several good options for treating water and reducing the likelihood of a protozoan, bacterial, or viral infection. These water treatment options include boiling, filtering, ultraviolet radiation, chlorine-based chemicals, mixed oxidant systems, and iodine.

All of the options below remove or kill giardia and crypto, as well as any additional protozoa or bacteria in the water. Viruses, which are too small to be captured by filter systems, can be eliminated only with chemical treatment, boiling, or UV light.

Boiling

The oldest of water treatment methods, this technique is still a viable option for most Northeastern backcountry travelers and is a reliable method for reducing the number of pathogens. Wilderness medicine experts agree there is no need for lengthy boil times; at the altitudes found in the Northeast, water is adequately treated as soon as it reaches a full, rapid boil. This method relies on kitchen equipment nearly all backpacking groups will be carrying, although it will utilize fuel resources that may have been planned for cooking. Time requirements vary with stove setup, but our practice drills suggest about a five-minute "best time" for boiling a quart (32 ounces) of water. This is a good method to use when the kitchen is already set up, and you're craving hot drinks.

DRINKING WATER TREATMENT METHODS FOR BACKCOUNTRY AND TRAVEL USE

Contaminant	Potential health effects from ingestion of water	Sources of contaminant in drinking water	Boiling[1]	Filtration[2]	Disinfection[3] Iodine* or Chlorine	Disinfection[3] Chlorine Dioxide	Combination of filtration and disinfection[4]
Protozoa Cryptosporidium	Gastrointestinal illness (e.g., diarrhea, vomiting, cramps)	Human and animal fecal waste	very high effectiveness	high effectiveness Absolute ≤ 1.0 micron filter (NSF Standard 53 or 58 rated "cyst reduction/removal" filter)	not effective	low to moderate effectiveness	very high effectiveness Absolute ≤ 1.0 micron filter (NSF Standard 53 or 58 rated "cyst reduction/removal" filter)
Protozoa Giardia intestinalis (a.k.a. Giardia lamblia)	Gastrointestinal illness (e.g., diarrhea, vomiting, cramps)	Human and animal fecal waste	very high effectiveness	high effectiveness Absolute ≤ 1.0 micron filter (NSF Standard 53 or 58 rated "cyst reduction/removal" filter)	low to moderate effectiveness	high effectiveness	very high effectiveness Absolute ≤ 1.0 micron filter (NSF Standard 53 or 58 rated "cyst reduction/removal" filter)
Bacteria (e.g., Campylobacter, Salmonella, Shigella, E. coli)	Gastrointestinal illness (e.g., diarrhea, vomiting, cramps)	Human and animal fecal waste	very high effectiveness	moderate effectiveness Absolute ≤ 0.3 micron filter	high effectiveness	high effectiveness	very high effectiveness Absolute ≤ 0.3 micron filter
Viruses (e.g., enterovirus, hepatitis A, norovirus, rotavirus)	Gastrointestinal illness (e.g., diarrhea, vomiting, cramps)	Human and animal fecal waste	very high effectiveness	not effective	high effectiveness	high effectiveness	very high effectiveness

6

[1]Boiling can be used as a pathogen reduction method that should kill all pathogens. Water should be brought to a rolling boil for 1 minute (at altitudes greater than 6,562 feet [>2,000 m], boil water for 3 minutes).

[2]Filtration can be used as a pathogen reduction method against most microorganisms, depending on the pore size of the filter, amount of the contaminant, particle size of the contaminant, and charge of the contaminant particle. Manufacturer's instructions must be followed. More information on selecting an appropriate water filter can be found at cdc.gov/crypto/factsheets/filters.html. Only filters that contain a chemical disinfectant matrix will be effective against some viruses.

[3]Disinfection can be used as a pathogen reduction method against microorganisms. However, contact time, disinfectant concentration, water temperature, water turbidity (cloudiness), water pH, and many other factors can impact the effectiveness of chemical disinfection. The length of time and concentration of disinfectant varies by manufacturer, and effectiveness of pathogen reduction depends on the product. Depending on these factors, 100% effectiveness may not be achieved. Manufacturer's instructions must be followed.

[4]If boiling water is not possible, **a combination of filtration and chemical disinfection** is the most effective pathogen reduction method in drinking water for backcountry or travel use. Manufacturer's instructions must be followed.

*Important: Water that has been disinfected with Iodine is NOT recommended for pregnant women, people with thyroid problems, those with known hypersensitivity to Iodine, or continuous use for more than a few weeks at a time.

Other treatment methods can be effective against some of the above pathogens:

Ultraviolet Light (UV Light) can be used as a pathogen reduction method against some microorganisms. The technology requires effective prefiltering due to its dependence on low water turbidity (cloudiness), the correct power delivery, and correct contact times to achieve maximum pathogen reduction. UV might be an effective method for pathogen reduction in untreated or poorly treated water; there is a lack of independent testing available on specific systems. Manufacturer's instructions must be followed.

MIOX® systems use a salt solution to create mixed oxidants, primarily chlorine. As a result, refer to the category above for chlorine disinfection. Manufacturer's instructions must be followed.

In addition to using the appropriate drinking water treatment methods listed above, you can also protect yourself and others from waterborne illness by **burying human waste** 8 inches deep and at least 200 feet away from natural waters and **practicing good personal hygiene** (wash hands before handling food, eating, and after using the toilet).

Source: CDC Fact Sheet for Healthy Drinking Water, cdc.gov/healthywater.

FIGURE 29. Backcountry water-treatment methods include: (a) a gravity system, in which untreated water flows from one dromedary, through a filter, and into a lower dromedary; (b) a filter straw, which allows a backpacker to drink directly from a water source; (c) a pump system, which requires some elbow grease to pump water directly from a source and through a filter; (d) a chlorine dioxide solution, also known as a chemical treatment; and (e) ultraviolet radiation, which uses a UV light in the water container to inactivate pathogens.

Gravity

This method is simple and relatively quick. A hose connects two bags, one of which is elevated above the other. Untreated water flows from the upper bag through an attached filter then collects in the lower bag once it's clean. A gravity system is a good choice for large groups, as most treat between 2 and 4 liters per fill at roughly 1 to 1.5 liters per minute with a clean filter. These systems run $80 to $140 and weigh 10 to 16 ounces. One of the best is Platypus GravityWorks (11 ounces; $120 for the 4-liter system). Gravity filters are less than ideal when it comes to collecting water from shallow sources and in open terrain, where there's no easy way to hang one bag higher than the other except for holding them aloft.

Ultraviolet Radiation (UV)

Ultraviolet radiation is a relative newcomer to the backcountry water-treatment scene, but it has been used as a final treatment in municipal and residential systems for a long time. The handheld UV devices are the size of a large felt-tip marker and use a battery-powered UV light to inactivate all of the pathogens in the water, including viruses. It takes about 90 seconds to treat a quart of clear water, and treatment does not change the taste or temperature of the water. Murky water requires at least two doses of light to be effective. These devices are usually easy to operate, but they are prone to the same problems as all high-tech electronics. Batteries can fade or die (especially in cold weather). On any extended trip or with a large group, you must plan for this eventuality, either with a backup supply of batteries or a reliable recharging option. A UV device is also vulnerable to accidental impact. If it stops working, field-repair options are limited, so again, you should have a backup option available.

Insert the UV bulb into the water bottle, turn it on, stir, and your water is ready soon after. Ultralight options include the SteriPEN (3 to 6 ounces; $50 to $100) and the CamelBak All Clear water purifier (17 ounces; $99), which integrates the UV system into the bottle cap.

This method relies on battery power, which means an increased risk of failure, and it doesn't remove sediment or grit. It is also not an effective method for groups due to the amount of batteries needed to power the UV bulb.

6

Chemical Treatment

Chlorine dioxide tablets and drops (very different from chlorine bleach) are currently the most popular choice for hikers wanting chemical treatment options. These products effectively treat all known pathogens in about 30 minutes, with very cold or very murky water requiring a longer treatment period, and the hard cysts of cryptosporidium requiring a wait of up to four hours. These tablets and drops do not change the temperature of the water, they're easy to use, and their taste is very mild. The drops, while slightly more complex to use, are also more economical and are less bulky for large groups or extended travel.

Mixed-oxidant systems (e.g., MSR's MIOX) are less common than they once were, but many individuals and organizations still use them. These electronic devices create a cocktail of chlorine-based chemicals by introducing an electric charge to a salt-based brine solution. Their effectiveness is comparable to the chlorine-dioxide drops and tablets, and they are slightly bulkier than a UV-based device. They require batteries and a small supply of rock salt. Mixed-oxidant devices take some practice to operate correctly, produce a slightly more chemical taste than tablets or drops, and are vulnerable to all the same problems as other technological devices. For hikers who prefer a chlorine-based treatment, chlorine dioxide drops or tablets are usually a better choice.

Iodine is a reliable chemical treatment that is used worldwide and was originally designed for emergency purposes. Once very popular with backpackers, it is now a second-choice chemical treatment behind the chlorine-based products. Following the instructions on the container, iodine effectively treats clear water in 30 minutes. Extremely cold or sediment-laden water may require a double dose of the iodine or an extended period of treatment, and the same four-hour waiting time is recommended against cryptosporidium. Since iodine rapidly binds to sugars, any sugared drink mixes must be added after the full treatment time is complete. Iodine impacts the flavor of the water, although some companies offer a flavor neutralizer. Iodine should not be used by pregnant women, very young hikers, or anyone with thyroid illness. It is unknown how safe it is for extended use by avid backpackers or outdoor professionals.

Straws

Maybe you'd rather drink directly from a source—or from previously untreated water stored in your water bottle—via an ultralight filter. Options include the LifeStraw, which has a long, skinny design ($20), and the Sawyer MINI Water Filter, a squatter option ($25). At a paltry 2 ounces each, both remove sediment but require constant use whenever you drink. Each of these treatment methods has its advantages and disadvantages, summarized in the chart "Efficacy of Water Treatment Methods" on page 136.

Pumps and Filters

Filters force water through a medium that has such microscopically small pores (about 0.4 micron) that it strains out most pathogens. Since viruses (0.1 micron or smaller) can fit through these tiny pores, filters are not effective against them, although a few designs include a chemical aftertreatment. Filters are fairly easy to operate, do not impart a taste, and do not heat the water. It takes only three or four minutes to filter a quart of water. But filters are complex machines. Because the pores in the filter medium are so small, they clog easily. The user must care for the filter by prefiltering any sediment or debris out of the water. If the water is not clean and clear, strain it through a bandana into another container or let the water sit undisturbed until the sediment settles to the bottom. Because water is forced through the medium under pressure, the pressure cylinder, gaskets, or seals can fail. Even with proper care, it is common for filters to require some maintenance in the backcountry. Each brand of filter has its own maintenance and repair requirements, and the user should know how to disassemble it, clean the filter medium, replace the gasket rings, and reassemble it in the field with minimal tools. On any trip longer than a few days, you should carry a repair kit with the key replacement parts or have a backup option readily available.

With this system, repetitive pumping pulls water up an intake hose, through an internal filter, and into your container. Reliable pump models range from 8 to 16 ounces for $75 to $100 and include the MSR SweetWater (11 ounces; $90) and the Katadyn Hiker Pro (11 ounces; $85). These pumps are relatively bulky, somewhat awkward, and require maintenance, but they also provide clear, sediment-free water. Bonus: The small intake hose makes these best for shallow water sources.

CHOOSING THE RIGHT METHOD FOR YOU

The best choice for your trip into the mountains depends on your priorities. For ease of use, chlorine dioxide tablets are the way to go. For optimum taste, a filter or a UV device is probably your best option. Much of the water a camper drinks can be purified through boiling, even in summer. (Water you ingest in meals, soups, and hot drinks counts toward your daily requirement.) In practice, it is wise for every group to bring at least two different devices (e.g., UV light and chlorine dioxide drops; a filter pump and iodine tablets) so there's always a backup plan when the first method breaks, runs out, or gets lost. Of course, boiling is always a backup option for any group that has adequate fuel and a stove.

It is important to note that, of the options above, only boiling completely sterilizes the water. In all other methods, there will be some number of active pathogens remaining after treatment. Since treatment only reduces the numbers of an organism, it is not a case of making the water safe to drink but of reducing the likelihood of contracting illness by limiting the number of infectious agents. Drinking any water from the backcountry is still a matter of calculated risk.

6

BACKCOUNTRY WATER TREATMENT TIPS

- Mold and funk is best not drunk. To prevent the growth of destructive mold and other slime, always completely dry your water-treatment system before storing it at home.

- Sediment kills filters. If possible, avoid treating cloudy or gritty water, which can rapidly clog up a filter and greatly reduce its lifespan.

- If you must treat sediment-laden water, cleaning or back-flushing the filter can help keep things flowing. An even better option is a prefilter, which attaches to the intake hose and strains out sediment early in the process. You can also collect cloudy water in a pot, let it settle, then draw from the cleaner water on top to filter as usual.

- To minimize the taste of chemical treatments, add a small amount of powdered drink mix after you treat the water. Vitamin C, in particular, neutralizes iodine and almost entirely eliminates its flavor.

Source: Matt Heid for *AMC Outdoors* magazine

EFFICACY OF WATER TREATMENT METHODS		
Treatment Method	**Advantages**	**Disadvantages**
Boiling	■ Rapidly treats larger quantities ■ Reliable and inexpensive ■ Works on all known pathogens	■ Makes only hot water so requires ample cooling time for some uses ■ Relies on stove or fire ■ Requires fuel ■ Imparts a taste
Pumping	■ Leaves no taste ■ Great for clean, clear sources	■ Bulkier and heavier than other options ■ Requires maintenance ■ Requires effort and time ■ Does not protect against viruses
Ultraviolet light	■ Fast ■ Easy to operate	■ Battery dependent ■ Must not be dropped or crushed in pack
Chlorine dioxide (chemical)	■ Cost-effective, especially drops ■ Easy to use ■ Requires little trail time ■ Mostly neutral taste impact	■ Must have adequate supply for length of trip and size of group ■ Requires 4 hours for complete confidence against cryptosporidium
Mixed-oxidant systems (chemical)	■ As effective as all chlorine-based treatment options	■ Battery dependent ■ Requires rock salt ■ Some aftertaste ■ Requires 4 hours for complete confidence against cryptosporidium
Iodine (chemical)	■ Small and light ■ Easy to use ■ Inexpensive	■ Strong aftertaste ■ Not safe for certain populations ■ Not recommended for extended use ■ Requires 4 hours for complete confidence against cryptosporidium
Straws	■ Small and light	■ Can take quite a bit of suction to get water through the straw

➜ HYGIENE ON THE TRAIL

Many of us enjoy backcountry trips as an opportunity to get a little scruffy and to focus less on personal appearance than we do at home. But another important form of disease prevention while on the trail is maintaining good personal hygiene. Keeping clean hands and bodies and a clean camp is a great way to avoid all kinds of small infections that lead to gastrointestinal distress, eye and skin problems, and other illnesses and discomforts. Staying clean is not that hard, requiring only a little mindfulness.

HAND WASHING

LEAVE NO TRACE 3 Most acute gastrointestinal illnesses, such as vomiting and diarrhea, occur in the backcountry when germs unwittingly pass through the fecal-oral route. Washing hands is the best strategy for preventing transmission of these germs. As at home, any time you go to the bathroom or are getting ready to prepare food, you should wash your hands. Scrubbing with a small amount of soap (200 feet from any water sources) will reduce the likelihood that germs will get passed on and cause problems. To dispense water for washing your hands, suspend a water bladder or have a friend pour from a bottle. We typically carry a small chunk of antibacterial soap in a tightly closed container with our kitchen gear. That way, when it's time to cook a meal it's easy to remember to start off with clean hands. A 1-inch cube is enough for a week with three to four people.

6

BATHING OUTDOORS

LEAVE NO TRACE 3 When the conditions are ideal, bathing outdoors is not only fun, it's natural and rejuvenating. The degree to which you clean your body is determined by personal preference, but for longer trips, it's helpful to know how to get a full-body cleaning if you want one. In warm weather, a quick dip in a lake or creek or under a waterfall is all you need to clean your body of sweat, salt, and grime. No need to use soap in these freshwater locations. A good scrub and a rinse will do the trick. In populous areas, wear a bathing suit. In remote locations in the backcountry, use your discretion on nude bathing, always being respectful of others.

If you have a kitchen water bladder, such as an MSR Dromedary, it is quite easy to fill it with warm water, hang it in a tree, and give yourself a traditional outdoor shower. Doing this with biodegradable soap 200 feet from any water source is an acceptable practice and can feel great. Even without a water bladder, a full-body cleaning is easy to accomplish with a little planning. All you need is a big pot or two of water and a good water source. The summer method is to get wet all over, then move to your chosen spot 200 feet away from any water source. Soap up and clean yourself, then squeegee all excess soap off your body onto the ground. Once you have done that, pour the pot of water slowly over your head and body, rinsing off the rest of the soap. You might need to refill your pot to finish the job, but once the soap is all cleaned off, you can jump in the pond or river for that final spotless rinse.

Dunking in a pond may sound like a great idea in summer, but cold, wet weather can make getting clean seem daunting. But in winter, when you'll be wearing more layers and getting even less fresh air to your skin, getting clean all over is perhaps even more important. With a warm pot of water and a clean bandana, you can achieve a thorough scrubbing. If it is very cold, you can do one body part at a time, keeping the others covered up. Even in cold weather, getting clean will leave you feeling refreshed and will prevent a range of infections.

PERSONAL HYGIENE

Good personal hygiene is essential for all backcountry travelers who want to avoid urogenital infection and illness. Both men and women can experience infections of their urethra and genitals, although such illnesses are more common in women. These infections can be uncomfortable enough to end a trip, and they can also lead to greater problems, such as bladder and kidney infections. These illnesses are fairly easy to avoid with some basic practices.

6

For Women

Choose cotton underwear rather than synthetic for your against-the-skin layer. Cotton's disadvantage of not wicking perspiration is outweighed by its tendency to harbor fewer bacteria. A fine merino-wool base layer is also naturally antibacterial and will offer more comfort and insulation than cotton when wet.

Maintain clean hands whenever going to the bathroom or changing tampons, sanitary pads, or a menstrual cup. Used menstrual pads and tampons must be packed out of the backcountry. One good strategy is to have a dedicated gallon-size zipper-closure plastic bag or opaque stuff sack. Adding a crushed aspirin or two into the bag minimizes odors. At night it is important to store this bag out of reach of bears and other creatures, the same way you protect food. Another option is to use a menstrual cup: a small silicone cup worn over the cervix that needs to be emptied only once every 12 hours. There is far less packing in and out with this method and it's much more environmentally friendly, as it produces no extra waste. Be sure to dig a small cat hole away from your campsite and dispose of the blood there before filling the hole back up with soil the same as you would for defecation.

Women should also consider the amount of sweat produced while hiking and backpacking. In order to prevent infections, change underwear twice a day whenever possible, particularly if you are prone to infections. It's best to sleep without underwear to encourage airflow and reduce the chances of getting an infection while on a trip.

For Men

Cotton underwear is also a good idea for men, although less important than it is for women. If chafing becomes an issue, consider wearing more supportive undergarments (like briefs) and use a medicated drying powder daily.

For Both Sexes

Maintain air circulation in your groin area by wearing restrictive or waterproof garments only when necessary. If it has been a cool or wet trip, prioritize some "fresh air time" each day or keep some clean cotton undergarments exclusively for sleeping. Bringing a few baby wipes in a zipper-closure plastic bag is a great way to keep your genital area clean, especially if circumstances don't allow for a warm-water wash. Using a wipe every other day is a great way to avoid skin irritations and more serious infections. Just be sure to pack those wipes out with the rest of the trash.

SHARING FOOD

Personal hygiene on the trail is challenging at times, but it is perhaps even more important than when you are at home and is essential to avoiding food contamination. Be diligent when it comes to washing your hands before cooking a meal. The same can be said when it comes to sharing food or water on the trail. It's risky to share a bag of trail mix by allowing everyone to dive into the bag with their bare hands. A better and more hygienic practice would be to pour the trail mix into everyone's hands. Sharing a water bottle is also risky; instead, it's better to pour water into someone's mouth or into their own empty water bottle. To stay heathy on the trail, learn to share with care.

6

LAUNDRY

Yes, it is possible and sometimes advisable to do laundry in the field. If your excursion lasts for several days or weeks, you will eventually need to wash your clothes. Clean clothes feel great, smell better, and last longer. So, if your socks, underwear, and upper and lower layers need to be spruced up, try the following. Fill an empty plastic bladder or gallon zipper-closure bag with very hot water and a bit of soap. Place your dirty laundry in the soapy water and shake and massage the washing bag from the outside for a few minutes. Then walk at least 200 feet from any source of water and empty the soapy water into a sump hole. Make sure you carefully rinse your clothes by adding cold water to your bag. You might need to repeat for two or three rinses. Air-dry your clean clothes for fresh, soft clothing.

TOOTHPASTE DISPOSAL

The importance of dental hygiene should not be underestimated during a camping trip. Tents are small and require close-proximity talking ("inside voices"), so daily dental hygiene is a must. No need to use charcoal from the campfire. You can bring toothpaste on the trail; just take the time to go for a short walk when brushing and spray your watery toothpaste into a mist when you are done, taking care not to leave a glob of toothpaste concentrated on one plant or vegetation area. You can—and should—use dental floss. Actually, dental floss is a great item to have when camping. Not only can it keep your gums and teeth healthy, but it can be used to repair equipment and clothing. We even teach our students to use dental floss when cutting their cinnamon rolls before baking them.

If you choose to bring dental floss, just make sure to pack it out with your trail trash.

HUMAN WASTE DISPOSAL

When nature calls, answer. We must do what needs to be done, but we must also manage our own waste. Unless you are visiting an area that requires you to pack out your own solid waste (see "Wag Bag," below), you will have to properly dispose that which you choose not to pack out. Here are the options you have on the trail and the tips we have for each.

Urine

Liquid waste is the easiest to deal with. Going for a "number one" in the woods does not require much planning. Our urine is mostly composed of water (95 percent) and minerals, which are most likely sterile unless you are suffering from a kidney, bladder, or urethra infection. The LNT way of disposing of liquid waste is to urinate away from your campsite, the trail, or your water source. Be discrete along the trail so other hikers do not spring up on you.

A useful hygiene tip for female hikers: Use a bandana to wipe after urination. You can attach the bandana to the outside of your backpack to dry while hiking, and you can wash out the bandana in the evenings, if desired. This method is simple and effective, freeing female hikers from the burden of having to carry extra toilet paper in and out of the woods. There are also female urination products available, such as the Shewee and GoGirl, which allow women to urinate while standing.

Feces

Human solid waste presents a different set of challenges. Contrary to urine, feces contain myriad microorganisms, including pathogens that can be dangerous for our health if they infect us via the fecal-oral route. Common causes of these infections are improper hand washing after defecating in the woods, insect exposure to human waste then food, and backcountry water contamination. It is imperative to take the task of properly disposing human waste seriously. Here's what to do in various situations.

Latrine

 If latrines are present in your campsite, use them. It is better to concentrate human waste in one area than to create several small waste-deposit spots. Latrines managed by AMC are designed to recycle human waste. If you properly follow the posted instructions when using an established latrine, you can be assured your waste will return to the land without negatively affecting it.

Cat Hole

When latrines are not present, it is best to use the "cat hole" technique. This method has you walk 200 feet away from campsites, established trails, and water sources. Once you have found the ideal site, dig a hole about 6 inches in diameter and at least 8 inches deep. A small garden or camping trowel is great for this task. The goal here is to make sure that the cat hole is big enough for your deposit and that enough organic soil is present to help break down your solid waste.

When it comes to squatting over the hole, you have to find the technique that works for you. If squatting is challenging, you can place a medium-size dead branch at the edge of the hole and position your heels over the branch. This way your squatting position will be more comfortable and easier to maintain.

Once you have completed your business, it is perhaps strange—but appropriate—to take a stick (never your digging trowel) and mix your feces with some of the organic soil. This stirring will speed up the breakdown of your feces through an increase of soil microorganisms intermixed with your waste. Make sure to keep the stick in the hole and cover the hole with the material you dug out in the beginning. Camouflage the area and voilà! You have just disposed of your waste the LNT way.

6

HOW FAR IS 200 FEET?

When it comes to taking a personal walk in the woods, it can be challenging to estimate how far you've walked simply by looking backward. As a rule, for many adults of average height, walking 70 steps or 35 paces will bring you about 200 feet from where you started. It's important to orient yourself before leaving your zone of familiarity as many people become lost when they leave the campsite or trail for a bathroom break.

Pace is often easier to count than steps. Pacing is calculated by counting every other step; in other words, if you start walking with your left foot first then count every time your right foot touches the ground. The number of steps or paces you need to cover 200 feet varies according to your height, of course, so the only truly accurate method is to measure 200 feet on flat ground and calculate how many steps or paces it takes you to cover the distance. You can do this at home before heading into the mountains. Once you have found your personal number, remember it and use it when taking a walk in the woods with your trowel.

Wag Bag

In certain areas (e.g., sensitive alpine zones) or seasons (winter), you may be required to pack out all of your waste, including solid human waste. If this is the case, the best method is to use a commercial waste management bag, also known as a wag bag. These bags are quite easy to use and do not require you to walk 200 feet from campsites, trails, and water. That said, it's always wise to seek some privacy before using one. These bags have detailed instructions printed on them, so have no fear.

POSTWASTE PERSONAL HYGIENE

When it comes to personal hygiene after defecating, you have many options. These include:

1. **Toilet paper.** Excellent to clean oneself properly but could require rationing on long trips and must be carried out of the field.

2. **Moist towelettes**. Excellent to clean oneself properly and avoid possible irritations but could require rationing on long trips and must be carried out of the field.

3. **Natural TP.** Works well, readily available anywhere you go, does not need to be carried out, but offers various levels of performance and comfort. Here are some of the best natural toilet papers you can find in the wild.

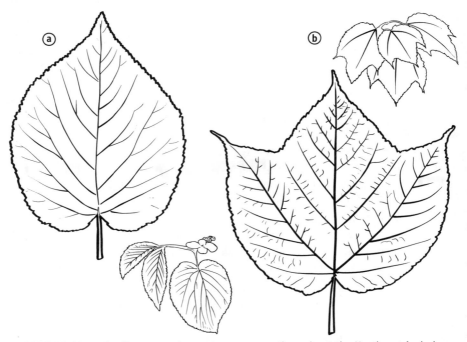

FIGURE 30. Natural toilet-paper alternatives common throughout the Northeast include the leaves of: (a) the hobble-bush, also pictured on the branch (inset); and (b) the striped maple (inset, on the branch).

- **Wet river rock.** Smooth and easy to use.

- **Hobble-bush leaves** *(Viburnum lantanoides)*. Source of smooth, thick, resistant, and large leaves, often abundant at lower altitudes. Sometimes called lumberjack toilet paper for good reason.

- **Striped maple leaves** *(Acer Pensylvanicum)*. Can be very large and found easily at lower altitudes. Thinner than hobble-bush leaves, so may require more.

- **Snowballs.** If you are lucky enough to find some wet snow, snowballs are often the best natural TP you can find. Although they are cold to the touch, they do an excellent job of cleaning. Think of them as a frozen bidet.

Personal Hygiene Kit

Since you will have to answer nature's call on your outdoor adventures, it is a good habit to create a personal hygiene kit specifically for your walk in the woods. This kit should include the following items:

1. Small nylon bag with your name on it

2. Three or four small zipper-closure bags; keep one for storing your supply of unused TP or moist towelettes and another for carrying out used

3. Toilet paper or moist towelettes—or both

4. Small bottle of hand sanitizer, but don't forget that water and soap are better to use before handling food

With your personal hygiene kit kept easily accessible in your pack, you can quickly respond to any emergency by grabbing the kit and a trowel.

6

CHAPTER 7
PREVENTION AND SAFETY

Whenever I talk with someone about our work in the backcountry, one thing I am sure to hear is how adventurous and risky it must be. I often have to explain that traveling in the mountains is generally safer than living a normal life in the city. Of course, even small injuries and illnesses can be a challenge, or possibly end a backcountry trip, so it is wise to stay as safe and healthy as possible. Good judgment and prevention are the keys to achieving this goal. Exercising good judgment means avoiding unnecessary risks and managing or mitigating unavoidable risks with smart choices. A very simple and useful tool for focusing your judgment and prevention efforts is the Dynamics of Accidents theory, by David Hale, below.

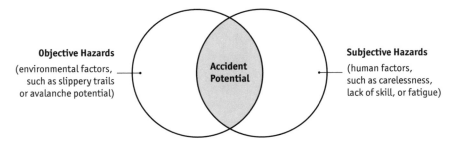

Objective Hazards
(environmental factors, such as slippery trails or avalanche potential)

Accident Potential

Subjective Hazards
(human factors, such as carelessness, lack of skill, or fatigue)

This model shows that accidents always have two contributing components: environmental factors and human factors. Environmental factors are the objective hazards that simply exist in the setting, things such as water on a rock slab, extreme heat, a widowmaker branch in a campsite, a thunderstorm, or a bear. These natural features do not cause an accident simply by existing; they are just there. Human factors are the subjective hazards that come directly from people, such as inexpe-rience, inattention, lack of skill or judgment, fatigue, "summit fever," and many more. Again, by themselves these conditions do not lead to an accident. Both types of factors, however, represent accident potential, and when combined they increase the likelihood of an accident. The inexperienced hiker is much more likely to slip on that wet slab of rock. The hiker with summit fever is more likely to ignore the oppressive heat or thunderstorm. The person who lacks judgment will fail to hang food out of bears' reach. Simply put, accidents are not completely random, chance events. They are the predictable outcome that occurs when two complementary hazards come together.

As outdoor professionals, a huge amount of our time is spent surveying all of the human factors and all of the environmental factors that exist in any given mo-ment, and then trying to keep the two apart. Any backcountry traveler can follow this same process. First, maintain a realistic assessment of yourself and the other individuals in the group, trying to identify any human factors. Are people hun-gry, tired, or cold? Are their travel skills well developed for this terrain? Second, every time you arrive at a new location, enter a different terrain type (e.g., above treeline), or begin a new mode of travel, scan the environment for any objective hazards. Are rocks on the trail loose? Is that river crossing shallow or deep? Are the clouds indicating a change in the weather? How long until sunset? Are we in bear country? (Yes!) Finally, combine the two in a thought experiment. How will *this* tired person respond to *these* sustained, cold winds above treeline? How can I reduce this person's fatigue, or can I avoid these cold winds? By staying attuned to environmental and human hazards, and by acting on opportunities to reduce their intersection, you will help the backcountry trip be a positive experience, with few accidents or emergencies.

7

➜ BEFORE YOU GO

Preparing yourself with knowledge is an excellent step toward preventing acci-dents. Knowing average weather trends for the region and time of year is essential. Also, read as much as you can in trail guides and other authoritative sources about the route or the area in which you intend to travel, and gather the most current information possible about your route and terrain. You may find useful informa-tion on websites, but vet these carefully, as they may not be curated for accuracy or timeliness. Trustworthy resources for information on current conditions include the land management agency that oversees your route or a local hiking club (such as AMC) that is active in that area. A quick phone call before you leave is well worth your time.

Another form of prevention is having a backup plan if things go wrong. A wise group leader will leave a trip itinerary with someone who is staying at home. For an example, see Appendix B, page 290. Having this ally in the frontcountry ensures that, in the event something unexpected happens, there is a person who knows to sound the alarm if you do not return. Because this person should know your route well, he or she will be a ready resource if you unexpectedly need support or transportation. Your trip itinerary document should include the following information, at a minimum:

- Start and end locations
- Start and end dates
- Descriptions of the group's vehicles and expected parking location(s)
- Expected travel route with trail names (if any), campsites, and possible side trips
- Names and contact information of everyone on the trip
- Expected day and time of exit from the trip
- Predetermined "panic" time: when the person at home should contact authorities to report the group missing, if nobody on the trip can be reached

The trip leader should bring this same summary into the field, with a couple of additional pieces of information:

- Emergency evacuation plans for specific locations along the route
- Phone numbers for the agency that manages search and rescue in your travel area
- Contact information and location of critical care facilities, in case of emergency

7

Having all the necessary emergency information, as well as a good backup plan if something goes wrong, can minimize the impact of health and safety emergencies. (Keep reading for more specifics about what to do when things don't go as planned.)

Preparation also means knowing your fellow hikers. General discussions about fitness are likely to be part of the goal-setting phase of trip planning, but a well-prepared group will know further details about one another. It may feel awkward to ask for a full medical history from a fellow hiker, but it is important to freely share some basic medical information. A good health profile of each member of the group will include:

- Specific concerns about joint health or stability
- Daily or as-needed medications
- Relevant chronic health concerns, such as diabetes, heart disease, or Raynaud's syndrome
- Serious allergies to foods, plants, animals, or medications
- Emergency contact information

Share these details well in advance of the trip, so that route and menu planning can take into account any relevant information.

Of course, even with this information a leader will not be prepared without effective first-aid training. The standard for wilderness leaders in North America is the Wilderness First Responder (WFR) certification, available from many different providers. This 80-hour training curriculum assumes that definitive medical care is at least an hour away. With this remoteness in mind, the training provides extra insight into how the human body works, and how to manage injuries and illness for that extra time, leading to the best outcomes for the affected person. If taking a WFR course is not possible before you go, it is still a priority to have some form of medical and first-aid training. There are other options, including Wilderness Advanced First Aid, Wilderness First Aid, or even a basic first-aid course targeting frontcountry emergencies. Another training that is essential for all mountain travelers is cardiopulmonary resuscitation (CPR). This life-prolonging technique is central to rescue efforts after water-based accidents and lightning strikes. CPR courses are widely available from local hospitals, fire departments, community colleges, and other locations.

➔ FIRST-AID KIT

Good preparation means bringing the supplies and equipment necessary for protecting health and safety. First-aid supplies are one of the ten essentials, described on page 7, that should always be in your pack. A good first-aid kit has exactly what you need and nothing else. It is light and small, but plentifully stocked for the length of your trip and the size of your group. Importantly, it should include only equipment and medication that you know how to use. Remember, your first line of defense from injury and illness is exercising good judgment and caution. Much of what you can use to treat injuries in the backcountry—clean water, duct tape, bandanas—will come directly from your backpack, and good training will help a leader improvise effectively. Even so, a few items are must-haves in any backcountry first-aid kit. We tend to think about a first-aid kit's contents according to the category of ailment:

7

BLISTERS AND OTHER FOOT CARE

- Moleskin (3- to 4-inch squares), tincture of benzoin, gel bandages (2 or 3), duct tape, nail clippers

WOUNDS
Small Wounds

- Small and medium adhesive bandages (6 to 8, of various sizes)

More Substantial Wounds

- 4-by-4-inch gauze (3 to 6 strips, including some that are nonadhesive)
- 1-inch-wide adhesive tape
- Irrigation syringe (60cc)
- 2-by-2-inch bio-occlusive dressing (thin, clear film; 2 or 3)
- Sterile wound closure strips, tweezers

STRAINS, SPRAINS, SKELETAL INJURIES

- 3-inch stretch bandage, laminated foam and aluminum splint

OTHER ITEMS

- Common medications: ibuprofen, acetaminophen, diphenhydramine (Benadryl)
- Less common drugs: loperamide (antidiarrheal), bismuth subsalicylate or other antinausea/heartburn drug, triple antibiotic ointment
- Personal protective equipment, including nitrile gloves and a CPR face shield
- Wilderness medicine resource book

OPTIONAL ITEMS (OR FOR LONGER TRIPS):

- Blister-blocking antifriction stick
- Glucose tablets
- Antifungal cream
- Temporary dental filling
- Triangular bandages
- Laminated foam and aluminum finger splint
- Prescription medications, such as epinephrine injectors, pain medications, antibiotics, fluconazole (antifungal), burn cream

This collection of resources does not need to be heavy or bulky, and the amount of supplies recommended above should be modified as necessary. Bring what is reasonable for the size of the group and the length of the trip. Two hikers for a weekend can do quite well with a single sandwich-size, zipper-closure bag. A week-long trip with a group of six will require twice this volume. For bigger groups and longer trips, consider purchasing a dedicated, zippered, first-aid kit container.

EPINEPHRINE INJECTORS AND OTHER PRESCRIPTION MEDICATIONS

Epinephrine is a prescription medication, commonly known as the EpiPen automated injector. It should be carried by all individuals with known severe allergies, and it should be carried by trained outdoor leaders working for organizations with a professional medical control officer. Epinephrine's positive effects may wear off within 15 to 30 minutes, much less time than an evacuation from the backcountry will take, so a second dose may be necessary, and the administration of a steroid like prednisone (or similar medication) is required.

→ COMMON BACKCOUNTRY AILMENTS AND THEIR TREATMENTS

An exhaustive list of possible injuries and illnesses one might encounter in the mountains is more than a separate book. It's a library. There is no substitute for proper training in wilderness medicine, and a wise backpacker will carry a wilderness medicine resource to help in those exceptional situations. That said, in 30 years of trip leading and backcountry travel, we have found a small number of ailments to be relatively common. It is usually easy to manage these in the field.

SOFT-TISSUE INJURIES

Small cuts, burns, and abrasions are all quite common in the woods. Properly managing these little bothers will keep them from disrupting your trip. Basic treatment consists of cleaning the wound, preventing further contamination and injury, and promoting healing.

Cleaning should occur with clean, drinkable water. No other cleaning or antiseptic agent is required for water that has already been treated for drinking, although plain water can cause a stinging sensation when used to treat a wound. You can make a less irritating, isotonic saline solution by adding 2 teaspoons of salt to a liter of clean drinking water. The most effective method of cleaning a wound is to use either a syringe from your first-aid kit or a zipper-closure plastic bag with a tiny hole cut in one corner. If there is any foreign material in the wound, as in the case of a sandy abrasion from a fall, it might be necessary to use tweezers or a small scrub brush to get out the grit.

When the wound is clean (or in the case of a burn, clean and cool), dress it with a light covering that protects it from dirt and sunlight. Once the epidermis has been disrupted, skin has little ability to handle UV radiation, so sunlight will only slow healing. One important recent change in wound care is that most medical professionals now consider the ideal healing environment to be moist, not dry. Dry wounds heal more slowly and have increased opportunity for infection. Wounds that are kept moist heal 20 to 30 percent faster, have a decreased rate of infection, promote greater mobility, and are less likely to scar. To maintain a moist healing environment for a cut or a scrape, keep it covered with a light layer of petroleum jelly or antibiotic ointment under a simple gauze or adhesive dressing. Replenish the layer of jelly whenever the wound feels or appears dry. For cuts of relatively small size, there are also occlusive dressings. These bandages look like adhesive plastic wrap, and they provide a barrier that maintains a clean, moist environment.

During the first few days of healing, it may be necessary to check and redress the wound a couple of times a day. In high-dirt areas, such as shins or ankles, it may be helpful to cover the wound dressing with a barrier made from a clear plastic bag and some tape, sealing out the dirt. In rare instances, if an incision is on a knuckle or another flexible body part, it may be helpful to splint it for a day or two to allow the initial stages of healing to occur without the wound being pulled apart.

BLISTERS AND HOT SPOTS

Really a form of soft-tissue injury, hot spots and blisters deserve their own consideration. A hot spot is an area of skin that is rubbed repeatedly while hiking. Usually it occurs on the heel due to friction from the boot, but a hiker can get a hot spot from contact with a backpack or from trekking poles. Prevention is the first line of defense, so properly fitted boots and packs are essential. Stop and remove grit or sand as soon as you notice it, and consider wearing gaiters to prevent grit from entering your boots in the first place. Stopping regularly for a foot check is essential, especially in the first day or two of a hike. Because the first day of a hike often includes more than the average number of stops to adjust packs and grow accustomed to new gear, activities, and terrain, these are an excellent opportunity to ask the questions: "How are everyone's feet? Does anyone have any hot spots?"

Another preventative treatment that has proved very effective is the use of anti-friction blister-blocking creams. These products come in a stick, similar to antiperspirants, and are rubbed directly on the skin in high-friction areas. They can be purchased in the first-aid sections of most drugstores, as well as in cycling stores, where they are sold to prevent chafing in the chamois area. These can be a proactive way to prevent hot spots, and many hikers will apply them right at the trailhead, at the beginning of the day. If a hiker has feet with unusual shapes (e.g., bunions or heel spurs), covering these features with friction-blocker helps a lot.

Treatment of a hot spot depends on how soon it is caught, but the core concept involves decreasing pressure and eliminating the repetitive rubbing on that area of skin. Sometimes all you need to do is adjust your shoelaces or change your socks. A common culprit is an overly tight boot, so loosening the laces, changing the lace pattern, or wearing a thinner pair of socks can help. Once the hot spot has formed, it will be red and sore, even if there is no actual blister. When this happens, it is necessary to protect the area with some kind of dressing. The best

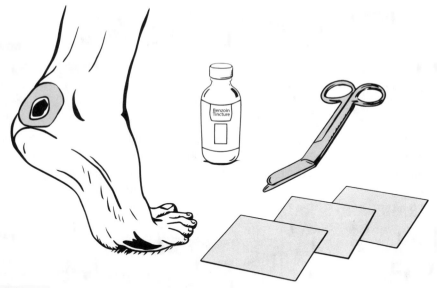

FIGURE 31. To care for hot spots or blisters, apply tincture of benzoin to the affected area then cut a donut of moleskin and adhere it to the skin, leaving the affected area uncovered. Finish by applying a friction-blocker.

treatment is to apply a doughnut of moleskin around the hot spot itself, covering that dressing and the surrounding area with the friction-blocker described above. The moleskin will hold the sock away from the skin, removing the friction and allowing the skin to heal.

If a blister has formed, the center of the hot spot will be a fluid-filled sack of skin or possibly just a red, raw spot where the skin has been worn away. This will be very sensitive to the touch. Treatment starts with gentle cleaning and drying of the area. If the blister is whole, it should be lanced with a sterile needle or blade at the bottom of the skin-blister boundary. Clean the area again, as with any small wound. All the steps that follow are intended to prevent further injury from friction and to promote healing. The classic approach is the moleskin doughnut, described above. Sometimes it is necessary to apply two or three layers of moleskin in order to fully protect the injured area, but too many layers will ultimately create a tighter boot, exacerbating the initial problem. Once the moleskin is in place, follow the steps above for a multilayered dressing. This dressing can be a lot to maintain, so it might be worth the expense and weight to carry a few dedicated blister dressings. These specialized adhesive bandages offer both friction reduction and moist wound care in one package and are easy to apply.

No matter what kind of dressing you apply, keeping it in place will be a challenge, because the sweaty environment of the boot will unstick the adhesives from the skin. For this reason, our first-aid kit always contains tincture of benzoin, an alcohol-based solution made from sticky tree resin. Painting this tincture on the skin before apply-

7

ing the dressing will greatly enhance a bandage's adhesion. It is messy stuff, especially if it leaks into your first-aid kit, so keep it in its own plastic bag.

One final note on blisters: Some experienced hikers advocate the use of duct tape as a treatment for hot spots and blisters, but this has some major drawbacks. It does not breathe, increasing the skin's sensitivity to friction, and it has a tendency to slip and bunch, leading to secondary friction areas. Sometimes it sticks to a blister then rips off the skin when removed. If you have no other options, duct tape might be better than nothing, but try to be prepared with dedicated foot-care supplies. And remember: You will probably be carrying some light camp shoes with you, so if necessary, you can switch your footwear to give those blistered areas a break.

STRAINS AND SPRAINS

Strains are minor injuries to muscles, tendons, or ligaments caused by sudden stresses that are greater than the affected body part can bear. They are often preventable through intentional fitness training for backpacking, using proper lifting and hiking techniques, and getting warm and limber prior to lifting your pack and hitting the trail. For hikers, these injuries most commonly occur to ankles and knees, but they can also happen to hips, wrists, shoulders, the back, and the neck. Although quite painful, they can be distinguished from more serious sprains and fractures by the person's ability to bear weight or otherwise use the extremity without pain. An injury that can be borne with a high degree of tolerance by the hiker is considered a "stable" injury and usually can be treated without evacuation.

Sprains are a more severe form of strain, usually involving the ligaments at a joint such as the ankle or knee. Through a fall or a twist, the joint is forced outside of its normal range of motion, stretching the ligaments to the point of partial or even complete tearing. Mild sprains resemble strains in their presentation and treatment. Severe sprains can sometimes be difficult to distinguish from fractures without an X-ray, but for the typical backcountry traveler, there is no need for a definitive diagnosis. For strains and sprains that can be treated in the field, immediate first aid has three goals: to protect the injury from further damage, to minimize swelling, and to reduce pain. Preventing swelling, in particular, should be a priority, as it causes additional damage and increases pain. The acronym PRICE is useful for putting these goals into action: Protect, Rest, Ice/Ibuprofen, Compress, Elevate. Signs that you should begin planning an evacuation include:

- The person's pain does not lessen after 30 to 45 minutes of PRICE treatment.

- The injury immediately produced an obvious deformity, not just swelling.

- There is a lot of pain at a specific point (point tenderness).

- The person cannot place weight on the injury, even after the acute pain of the initial injury declines.

USING THE PRICE SYSTEM

If you suspect someone has suffered a sprain or strain, follow the steps below to prevent further damage, to minimize swelling, and to reduce pain.

Protect

Protecting the body part from further injury means ensuring that it stays within its normal range of motion but does not necessarily require complete immobilization (as it would for a fracture). A sprained ankle, for example, can get a supportive splint that prevents sideways rolling but still allows for some normal flexion extension, as used in the walking motion. If the activity or the terrain makes it impossible to effectively protect the injury, it is time to go home.

Rest

Resting the injury may mean taking a break for an hour or two, making camp for the day, or continuing to hike with a reduced (or without any) load. Recent physical therapy research suggests that strain and sprain injuries heal fastest when they return to a normal range of motion as quickly as pain-free activity allows. If the injury is effectively protected, as described above, then gentle movement may actually decrease swelling and pain, promoting faster healing. Let the person's pain level guide the speed and extent of his or her return to activity.

Ice

Icing may not be possible on a midsummer hike, but there is no shortage of cold water in the forested mountains of the Northeast. The therapeutic value of icing is not so great that it's worth carrying a chemical cold pack, but icing (or cold-soaking) reduces the person's pain and may help reduce swelling. Apply the cold treatment immediately and then for fifteen minutes every hour or two. Ibuprofen or other nonsteroidal, anti-inflammatory drugs (NSAIDs), such as naproxen sodium or aspirin, will also alleviate pain and, when used at its maximum recommended dose, will reduce inflammation over a period of days.

7

Compress

Compression is one of the easiest treatment strategies to implement, as long as you are carrying a stretch bandage. Compression bandages help to minimize swelling. They also contribute to protection by limiting the joint within a normal range of motion. Wrap the affected area smoothly, starting farthest from the injury and working your way toward the center of the body. The wrap should be snug but should not lead to any numbness or tingling at the injury site or in the extremities. Check the wrap and the area every few hours and loosen it a bit if worn at night.

Elevate

Elevation simply means raising the injured area above the level of the person's heart, using gravity to help minimize swelling. With lower-limb injuries, even after the hiker has returned to activity, it is wise to set aside some time each day to recline with the injured area elevated, allowing any accumulated fluid to disperse.

Following these simple principles for the treatment of strains and sprains will help injured hikers heal more quickly and stay in the backcountry longer.

TENDINITIS

Tendinitis is the irritation and inflammation of the connection between a muscle and a bone. It is helpful to understand a bit about tendons in order to care for them well. Tendons are thin cords that connect muscle to bone, allowing the muscle to create movement. These thin cords slide within a smooth, lubricated sheath, similar to running a string through a slippery straw. If the sheath gets squeezed or kinked, or if it dries out, the cord does not slide easily and will begin to rub and scrape. With any repetitive motion, there soon will be swelling at this point, further reducing the space for the cord to slide and causing pain with movement. This is tendinitis. It is relatively common in the tendons of the foot and ankle (especially the Achilles tendon at the back of the heel), as well as in the hand, wrist, and elbow for hikers who use trekking poles. Tendinitis can be difficult to heal, so prevention is a priority. To do so, maintain good overall hydration to keep the tendon sheaths lubricated and slippery. Wear footwear that fits properly and does not apply undue pressure to any internal parts of the foot. If using trekking poles, try to keep your hands within their usual range of motion and vary your grip when possible.

Once you notice movement-induced pain in a tendon area, you can assume tendinitis is happening. Basic treatment is the PRICE protocol described above. Just as important, though, is to consider the causes of the inflammation. Is the person well hydrated? Can the repetitive motion be eliminated or altered to remain within a more restricted and normal range? Is there something specific that is kinking or compressing the tendon sheath, such as boot laces or a trekking pole strap? Addressing these underlying causes will prevent further injury and begin the healing process. For foot and ankle issues, consider hiking in camp shoes. In remote locations, extreme cases of Achilles tendinitis (sometimes called "heel squeak") might necessitate cutting a hiking boot down the back to alleviate tendon compression. While such drastic measures are not usually necessary, it is a very bad idea to simply press on with a hike, ignoring the underlying causes of tendon pain. Tendinitis can quickly become a chronic, self-sustaining condition or can lead to acute injuries, such as a tendon separating from the bone. With the proper measures, most hikers can continue on the trip—and on the path to recovery—with greater comfort.

➔ ENVIRONMENTAL INJURIES

Consider the following scenarios: A hiker awakes at daybreak, when the temperature is below freezing, and eight hours later is hiking in humid, 90-degree Fahrenheit (32-degree Celsius) heat. A hiker, clothes soaked with sweat, crests a ridge and into a steady gale that's headed for the summit. A hiker travels all day in a light, steady rain with a constant temperature around 50F (10C) and arrives in camp hungry and tired. Each of these scenarios has the potential to produce an environmental injury.

Heat and cold present constant challenges in the mountainous backcountry, in all seasons, and these challenges can sometimes overwhelm the body's natural thermoregulatory capacity. Thermoregulation is the balancing of heat and cold by the body's various systems to maintain optimal temperature. We know the human body functions best in a normal internal-temperature range near 98F (37C), and it has a range of normal responses to generate and conserve heat, as well as to as cool itself. When these normal responses can't meet the environmental challenge, the body will become too cold (leading to hypothermia) or too hot (leading to heat exhaustion or heatstroke). While the symptoms and causes of each of these injuries are obviously different, the basic principles of treatment are the same: Protect the affected hiker from the environmental challenge and support the body's ability to return to normal temperature. First, let's consider cold-related environmental injury and illness.

COLD-RELATED ENVIRONMENTAL INJURIES
Hypothermia
The human body has a range of normal responses whenever it senses a cold challenge. Review the wind chill chart (Figure 6 on page 21) when planning to be out in the cold as cold-related injuries often occur in the context of wind chill rather than just air temperature. These physiological and behavioral strategies work to keep the body's temperature hovering around 98F (37C). If these responses are overwhelmed then hypothermia begins when the body's temperature drops below 96F (35C). There are three stages of hypothermia: mild, moderate, and severe.

Mild hypothermia occurs with a body temperature of roughly 94 to 96F (34 to 35C), and its signs and symptoms usually include the following:

- Shivering, not necessarily violent, but uncontrollable

- Mild lack of coordination (fumbling with zippers, trouble completing complex physical skills)

- Feeling a little withdrawn or confused

- Feeling fatigued

These signs look different than a normal human response to cold. A mildly hypothermic person will often seem distracted or possibly irritable. Although the person is fully aware and conscious, at some level he or she can sense the body is experiencing an existential threat and will seek a way to resolve that challenge. This "mood" is often the best indication a person is entering hypothermia.

7

Moderate hypothermia occurs with a body temperature between 91 and 94F (33 to 34C). It is usually characterized by:

- Violent, uncontrollable shivering (Toward the lower end of the temperature range, shivering may actually stop, as the body has used up all of its energy resources.)

- Confusion and reduced consciousness

- Slurred speech and lack of coordination

- Lethargy

The key difference from mild hypothermia, especially if shivering is not present, is the person's decreased level of consciousness and physical ability. This person will clearly be in difficulty. He or she may seem very anxious and eager to get warm or may seem not to care at all about the cold. This hiker may try to dismiss your concerns and wish to be left alone. It is urgent that you ignore these requests and provide treatment immediately.

Severe hypothermia sets in when the body temperature reaches approximately 91F (33C). This represents an immediate threat to life. A severely hypothermic person is unlikely to be able to stand or walk, will seem sleepy or partially conscious, and will not be shivering. The person will have a reduced pulse and respiration, and below 86F (30C), may appear to be dead, although not. Even if this person is somewhat responsive, it will be obvious he or she is in deep trouble.

The speed at which a person descends through these stages can vary. A hiker with adequate hydration and nutrition but who is facing a severe cold challenge from the environment could take several hours to slowly succumb. A backpacker who has just summited a cold, windy ridge after working very hard for several hours will not have those same energy reserves. If preventative steps are not taken, this person is likely to drop into moderate hypothermia in just a few minutes. Without immediate treatment, severe hypothermia will soon follow. This scenario illustrates a great example of the prevention principle that underlies all health and safety practices. By stopping just below the ridge and out of the wind for a snack and water, and to put on additional clothing layers, the backpacker will avoid hypothermia altogether.

Regardless of the stage, hypothermia has one basic cause: a failure to balance heat produced and retained by the body with heat lost to the environment. The body produces heat only through metabolic activity, or consuming food stores. Environmental heat loss occurs primarily in four ways. Convection is heat being carried away by the warming of cold air. Conduction is heat lost through direct contact with cold materials, such as rock or water. Evaporation is heat lost through perspiration and rain drying on skin. Radiation is heat moving off into the surrounding space, similar to the way a woodstove warms a room. All treatments for hypothermia seek to change this balance, supporting the body's heat generation, capturing that heat more efficiently, and isolating the body from all of pathways to the heat loss.

For mild hypothermia, the key treatment steps are to feed the affected hiker easily digestible foods, to encourage him or her to generate heat through movement, and to isolate him or her from the elements via clothing and additional shelter. Sugary liquids such as lemonade and Jell-O enter the bloodstream quickly, fuel metabolism, and provide needed hydration. Warming these liquids above body temperature may provide a psychological boost but does not contribute significantly to rewarming. Avoid drinks that contain alcohol or caffeine, as these will cause vasodilation (or the dilation of a blood vessel) and exacerbate heat loss. Jumping jacks, toe-touches, sit-ups, or jogging in place are all good ways to get the major muscle groups pumping out heat. Finally, for mildly hypothermic people, putting on multiple layers of dry, insulating, wind-blocking clothing (including hats and gloves) is a good way to trap heat while still encouraging the kind of movement that will produce further warmth. Be sure to remove any wet layers prior to putting on dry ones. In very wet, cold, or windy conditions it may be necessary to set up a tent or tarp to protect the person from the environment, but for most mildly hypothermic people, the greater benefit will come from staying mobile and active.

Once a hiker enters the moderately hypothermic zone, rewarming becomes more challenging for several reasons. For one, the energy required to raise the body temperature 4 to 7 degrees is quite large. It takes up to 24 hours of sustained, well-supported physical effort to fully recover a normal body temperature. After shivering for so long, this person may not be able to endure much more physical activity. People at the low end of the moderate range may find it challenging to eat and drink, or to feel coordinated enough to move briskly at all. With these extra challenges, the treatment goals remain the same, so provide the same treatment for the mildly hypothermic person to the degree that is possible. A couple of newer techniques may be necessary. First, add external heat sources to supplement the natural metabolic production of heat. Apply warm-water bottles, chemical heat packs, or hot stones to the groin, armpit, and carotid area of the neck, ensuring the heat source is not hot enough to burn the skin. This person needs complete isolation from the cold environment. Set up a protective shelter and encase the person in a cocoon of sleeping bags and other insulating items, being sure to prevent conductive heat loss into the ground. When able, the person should exert him- or herself within the confines of the cocoon. If able to drink and swallow warm, high-calorie, sugary liquids and foods, the person should recover effectively in this enhanced, protective environment.

7

The severely hypothermic hiker cannot care for him- or herself, and if unconscious will be unable to eat or drink safely. Treatment goals for this person are to eliminate any further heat loss, add external sources of heat, and plan for evacuation. The medical responder must treat a severely hypothermic person gently, as a cold heart can enter arrhythmia if jostled.

The best way to accomplish total isolation from the environment is with a hypo-thermia wrap. A hypothermia wrap is a device carefully crafted from typical back-packing equipment to eliminate all heat loss due to radiation, conduction, convec-tion, and evaporation. The person is changed into warm, dry clothes; wrapped in a thick cocoon of sleeping bags and a space blanket; and laid on top of a ground pad (preferably multiple pads). This entire creation gets completely encased, like a burrito, in a windproof and waterproof fabric wrap, such as a tarp or tent fly. Only the person's mouth is exposed to facilitate breathing and communication, and when consciousness permits, the feeding of sugary liquids. External heat sources should be placed near the major arteries, as described above, inside the hypother-mia wrap. If possible, the person should be placed inside a tent or another shelter where breathing warmer, more humid air will aid rewarming.

Building a hypothermia wrap is a major undertaking that requires a lot of the group's equipment and human resources. Depending on the level of hypothermia, the person will need at least eight hours in the wrap to reach partial recovery or rescue. During this period, it is important that the layers of the wrap are not opened and do not get wet. Rescuers will have to plan for the person's bodily functions, and it is usually recommended they fashion a homemade diaper made from a plastic trash bag lined with absorptive fabrics, such as fleece. A wrap design should be tidy enough to be transported in a rescue stretcher and be resilient to rain and wind.

Immersion Foot

Also called "trench foot," this is a type of nonfreezing injury in which the feet have been cold and damp so long that the body's normal vasoconstrictive response has deprived the extremity of oxygen. Immersion foot is most common in cold, spring hiking conditions when the feet remain wet for the majority of a day due to walking through slushy trails and crossing cold streams. Boots never dry in these conditions, so a hiker's feet could stay in cold, wet boots for 10 to 12 hours between camps—long enough to cause damage. It is a serious and very painful injury that can cause permanent nerve damage, as well the death of skin and other tissue. Early signs and symptoms include blotchy, itchy, puffy, or painful skin on the feet. Fortunately, im-mersion foot is simple to prevent and treat: The feet must be clean, dry, and warm for at least eight continuous hours out of every 24 hours. If ground conditions per-mit, switching into dry camp shoes immediately upon arriving in camp is a start. (On spring trips when we expect wet camp conditions, we sometimes bring rubber galoshes to wear over camp sneakers.) Even if the camp setting is too slushy or wet to change shoes, it's easy to keep one pair of clean wool socks as dedicated sleeping socks. We usually leave those pairs right inside our sleeping bags. Always dry and inspect your feet before going to bed and change into these socks for the night. If you remember the "8 in 24" rule, your feet will stay out of the trenches.

Raynaud's Syndrome

Raynaud's is not actually an injury. It is a paradoxical constriction of the small blood vessels in a person's hands or feet caused by exposure to cold air or water. Just when the skin would benefit from more warm blood, the capillaries spasm, shutting off the blood supply to fingers, hands, toes, and/or feet. The underlying causes are not well understood, but at least 5 to 10 percent of people are thought to have this condition. It is easily recognized by the sudden onset of blotchy, whitened skin, bluish fingernail or toenail beds, numbness, and tingling. Once blood flow is restored, the person will experience rapidly warmed and reddened skin (and possibly pain). Without blood supply, the affected areas cool very quickly and will be more susceptible to freezing injury. If the impaired circulation lasts for an extended period (more than two hours), a person can experience long-lasting nerve and tissue damage, as well as years of extra sensitivity to the cold. Treatment focuses on quickly warming the affected area, at which point the spasm of the blood vessels relaxes, permitting warm blood to return. The extremity must be isolated from the cold source in dry clothes, dry shoes, or a sleeping bag. Apply chemical heat packs or hold the extremity against the skin of the abdomen inside an insulating layer. Once a person is aware of a tendency toward Raynaud's attacks, he or she should carry chemical heat packs and an extra layer of protective clothing for the affected area. Often a hiker with Raynaud's will benefit from wearing at least thin liner gloves when other hikers are still bare-handed. Preventative measures such as chemical heat packs and extra clothing will ensure a happier trip and healthier extremities on many hikes to come.

Frostbite

7

Frostbite is the freezing of water inside cells of soft tissue, most often caused by extended exposure to below-freezing air temperature. In mild cases, the affected area is the superficial epidermis of the skin; in the most extreme cases, it includes muscle and bone. Frostbite is an environmental injury unlikely to occur in typical Northeastern mountain travel during the spring, summer, and fall. Even so, winter can arrive on the region's higher summits almost any month of the year, so it is wise to know the symptoms and treatments for superficial frostbite.

The most likely places for frostbite to occur are the exposed skin of the hands, face, and ears. Frostbite is especially likely when the skin is wet, the air is near or below freezing, and there is a strong wind chill. Areas affected by freezing injury are usually waxy looking, may be firm to the touch, and will probably feel numb to the person experiencing the frostbite. Treatment for the kind of frostbite injuries likely in the context of three-season backpacking consists of rewarming the injured area and protecting it from further environmental exposure. Rewarm the area in a bath of lukewarm water (102 to 104F; 39 to 40C) or against warm skin. This is likely to be a painful process. Depending on the severity of frostbite, fluid-filled blisters may form over a 24-hour period after rewarming, and some skin may slough off. It is crucial to prevent this area from refreezing while it heals, and infection is a real possibility. If frostbite occurs, the group should plan for an immediate end to the trip.

HEAT-RELATED ENVIRONMENTAL INJURIES

Many of us take to the hills in summer in search of the cool breezes found on ridges and summits. But hot, humid conditions are common in the mountains and forests of the Northeast for several months of the year, and these conditions pose their own health concerns. Some heat injuries and illnesses are minor, but others are very serious and immediately life-threatening. As with cold-related injuries, heat-related injuries represent a failure of the body's natural thermoregulatory balancing system. Review the heat index chart (Figure 3 on page 18) when planning to be active in hot temperatures as humidity levels can increase the likelihood of heat-related disorders.

The body will begin to respond to excess heat as soon as its internal temperature rises above the ideal of 98.6F (37C), working to maintain a balance between heat production and heat loss. The vigorous physical exertion of backpacking inevitably generates a lot of heat. In order to rid itself of this heat, the body activates two primary forms of heat loss. First, it pumps more blood to the extremities so that they can act as radiators. Second, it activates the sweat response, opening up sweat glands on the skin's surface so that evaporative cooling can counter heat production. Both of these involuntary functions require extra fluids. Dilating the blood vessels essentially creates a larger volume container for blood, and sweating uses up the body's water resources. A hiker with an active sweat response who is vigorously exercising in warm weather can lose up to three quarts of fluid every hour.

With all of this demand for bodily fluids, maintaining personal health in hot conditions requires some dedication to intentional hydration and the intake of electrolytes (primarily sodium and potassium, but also magnesium). Drinking water throughout the day is a vital habit to develop. It is also important to take in enough electrolytes to maintain the balance of salts in the body. Salt pills or sports drinks are not necessary, since typical snacks and other foods contain all of the electrolytes you need.

One challenge to remember is that a typical hiker can absorb at most 1 quart (or 1 liter, about 34 ounces) of water in an hour, even though the rate of fluid loss to sweating could be much greater. Hikers should plan to hydrate each morning prior to leaving camp and to rehydrate actively and intentionally each evening after reaching the next camp. If a person is hiking for eight hours a day and losing 1.5 quarts each hour, that's 12 quarts of water (3 gallons!) that will need to be replaced. It's not hard to monitor your sweat rate. If sweat has been soaking your clothes and running off your nose for several hours, it is very likely that you are losing 1 to 1.5 quarts an hour (or more). The easiest way to know your hydration level in the field is to notice the volume and color of your urine. If it is frequent, copious, and mostly clear, you probably are hydrated adequately. If your urine is dark yellow, or if you haven't urinated in more than a couple of hours, you are in need of a major refill.

Keep your water treatment methods easily available while you hike and take the time to refill containers at water sources. This is especially important on hot summer hikes. Avoid drinks that contain caffeine, as these encourage urination, and look for ways to cook your camp food with more water, perhaps making a soup instead of a dry meal. Each time you stop to look at the map or to perform a foot check, encourage your fellow hikers to take a drink. Be aware, though, that drinking a lot more than 1 to 1.5 quarts per hour can inhibit your performance and lead to other problems (such as hyponatremia, a condition in which the blood lacks adequate sodium and the body holds on to too much water), so don't overdo it. (In the Northeast, there is usually an abundant water supply and no need to experience water stress or deprivation. Optimal replacement of fluids and electrolytes will promote optimal hiking performance, reducing the likelihood of a heat-related injury or illness.)

Heatstroke

This is the most serious heat-related environmental injury, and it is immediately life-threatening. Heatstroke occurs when there is a total failure of heat-shedding mechanisms and the body temperature uncontrollably skyrockets. If the core body temperature exceeds 104F (40C) for an extended period, severe and permanent brain damage can occur. Body temperature above 106F (41C) will lead to death within minutes. Heatstroke can occur due to a failure of the sweating mechanism (usually due to a lack of fluids), or it can occur simply because the rate of exertion is producing more heat than can be eliminated in the current environmental conditions. The most likely situation to produce heatstroke is vigorous physical exertion in extremely hot, windless, and humid conditions.

A person with heatstroke looks very different from a person with less serious heat exhaustion. A heat-stroke-affected hiker will have bright red, dry skin and will be disoriented, uncoordinated, and headed toward unconsciousness. The person will feel noticeably hot to the touch, with a body temperature well above normal and rising rapidly. Those with heat stroke often feel panicked over the desire to cool off. Initial treatment is to immediately stop all exertional heat production, to isolate the patient from the hot environment, and to aggressively cool the person. An ideal treatment is to immerse the person in icy-cold, moving water (being sure to prevent any risk of drowning). In the absence of a stream or a large water source, you can achieve cooling by dousing them with large quantities of water and actively fanning. Any shade will increase the effectiveness of the treatment. Once treatment is under way, the person will need to replace both fluids and electrolytes. Heatstroke is a serious injury, and a full recovery can take several days or more. A hiker who has experienced true heatstroke should be evacuated for evaluation.

7

Heat Cramps

Heat cramps result from the widespread, simultaneous cramping of several muscle groups. This is different from a single cramping muscle (e.g., the calf muscle), which is probably related to overuse or strain. Heat cramps occur when the body experiences an electrolyte imbalance. When the body sweats, it also loses electrolytes (sodium, potassium, and magnesium). If these are not replaced along with fluids, the electrolyte imbalance produces muscle cramping. Gentle massage may provide temporary relief, but a hiker with heat cramps needs rehydration with electrolytes as outlined above. Heat cramps are not a very serious condition, but they need to be treated, as they can be painful and halt forward progress on the trail. Also, since heat cramps indicate a low level of electrolytes, they highlight the need for greater intake of salty snack foods and water in order to prevent the occurrence of hyponatremia. (More on this below.)

Heat Exhaustion

Heat exhaustion occurs when the total volume of fluid in the body is too low, and fluid loss through sweating and respiration has not been matched by rehydration. The symptoms of heat exhaustion can include fatigue, weakness, nausea, vomiting, dizziness, and rapid heart rate and breathing. The person's skin will be pale and clammy, and he or she may still be sweating (a big difference from the dry, red heat of heatstroke). It is very possible the person will have fainted or will feel faint. The person's body temperature will not be greatly elevated, another difference from heatstroke. If the fluid needed by the body is not replaced, the sweat response will shut down completely, and heat exhaustion will quickly develop into heatstroke.

Treatment involves rest in a prone position, isolation from the hot environment, and the replenishment of water and electrolytes. This affected person needs to stop moving until the fluid supply has been replenished. At the point of heat exhaustion, he or she probably has at least 3 to 4 quarts of fluid to replace, which will take at least two or three hours. Adding a half-teaspoon of salt and a minimal amount of sweetened drink powder to each quart of drinking water makes a palatable, diluted rehydration solution that will provide optimal replacement of fluids.

Hyponatremia

This complex illness can occur when there is an imbalance between the amount of fluid intake by a person and the rate at which that fluid is excreted by the kidneys. The resulting excess fluid dilutes the salt content of the body, causing swelling in the intracellular spaces of the brain. Eventually, the swelling will compress the brain against the cranium, leading to brain damage and death, so hyponatremia is an urgent condition.

While not as common as heat exhaustion, hyponatremia can occur when a person drinks an overabundance of water while steadily losing electrolytes through sweating. Initially, hyponatremia will produce fatigue and nausea or vomiting.

Symptoms of acute hyponatremia are mostly neurologic, including headache, confusion, blurred vision, lack of coordination, and social withdrawal. If not recognized and treated, hyponatremia can lead to unconsciousness, seizures, coma, or death. Hyponatremia can be distinguished from heatstroke by the presence of a relatively normal body temperature and the absence of hot, dry skin. It can be distinguished from heat exhaustion by a general puffiness of extremities, abundant quantities of clear urine, and the predominance of neurologic symptoms (e.g., blurred vision).

Prevention of acute hyponatremia is essential, as there are no reliable backcountry treatment options. Prevention means drinking no more than 1 to 1.5 quarts of fluid per hour and accompanying this fluid with a small amount of salty snacks. If water is sloshing in the belly as the person hikes, there is no need to drink more. Once you strongly suspect hyponatremia, the best course of action is to support the normal bodily functions while planning for an evacuation. If the person is conscious, drinking a small amount of a high-sodium solution (2 to 3 teaspoons of salt in 4 ounces of water) may be therapeutic. Otherwise, the affected person must not consume any more fluid until symptoms fully resolve. As the kidneys excrete the excess fluid, the electrolyte balance will return to normal and the swelling will recede. Even after symptoms abate, this person should receive a medical evaluation as soon as possible.

Sunburn

Sunburn is one of the most common summer hiking injuries. It is really a soft-tissue radiation burn and should be managed as such. Prevention is obviously the preferred course of action. For full sun protection, a sunscreen with a sun protection factor (SPF) of 30 should be applied to all exposed skin. (SPFs rated higher than 30 are not necessary, even for fair-skinned individuals.) Frequently exposed areas of skin—cheeks, nose, ears, lips—should be protected under a brimmed hat and covered with a zinc-based, total-sunblock cream. Good sunscreen choices will be sweat-resistant, and you should reapply every two to three hours, especially around midday, when the sun's ultraviolet rays are most intense. Ideally, hikers should cover all exposed skin with clothes. On very hot days, wearing loose-fitting, light-colored clothes will actually keep a person cooler than going shirtless (or nearly so). That loose layer of clothing allows air circulation while also reflecting the sun away from the skin.

Once a sunburn has occurred, treatment includes managing the pain, supporting the body's normal healing response, and preventing any further exposure to the sun. First-degree sunburn is recognized by skin redness and pain, and second-degree sunburn will have reddened skin as well as blisters. Both types can be soothed with cool water or wet cloths. Leave any blisters intact, as these protect the underlying skin and promote healing. Ibuprofen or other NSAIDs are appropriate pain treatment. When the skin is burned, it loses much of its ability to retain water, so a person with a large area of sunburn may get dehydrated more quickly. It could take seven days or more before the skin returns to full health, and the skin must be

7

fully protected from all additional UV exposure during that time. If this protection is not achievable, or if the pain of the burn prevents the hiker from carrying a pack, it may be necessary to end the trip. For avid backpackers and outdoor leaders, sun exposure is one of the most significant health and safety hazards, so sun protection must be a long-term personal health practice.

➜ WILDLIFE

Watching wildlife can be one of the most enjoyable elements of a backcountry trip, but wild creatures bring their own safety concerns. And then there are the critters that aren't enjoyable at all. The practices below will help prevent wildlife encounters from becoming a real problem. This section focuses on wildlife common to the Northeastern United States; consult local land management agencies for wildlife in your area.

POISONOUS SPIDERS

In the backcountry of the Northeast, there are two types of venomous spiders you should know: the brown recluse spider (*Loxosceles reclusa*) and spiders of the black widow genus (*Latrodectus*). Medically significant bites from these species are extremely rare, and bites often occur without venom entering the body. Brown recluse spiders live in piles of woody debris and are 0.5 to 0.75 inches in diameter (slightly larger than a penny), including their legs. They are generally brown and nondescript, and their key distinguishing feature is three pairs of eyes instead of four—a difficult characteristic to identify in the field. If a bite introduces venom, pain and swelling will begin to appear in two to eight hours and may continue to worsen over a three-day period. Effects depend on the amount of venom and the person's sensitivity to it. About 30 percent of symptomatic bites will develop a spreading ulcer in which the surrounding skin and underlying tissue slowly die. About 15 percent of symptomatic bites will develop systemic reactions that can include nausea, vomiting, fever, and joint pain. In very rare cases, children, the elderly, and those with suppressed immune function can suffer severe systematic symptoms, such as blood clotting, organ failure, and death.

Spiders of the black widow group in the Northeast are 0.5 to 1.5 inches in diameter (from penny- to quarter-sized). They are dark black and have some red or orange markings on the underside of the abdomen that may resemble an hourglass, and possibly may have red, orange, or white markings on the upper abdomen or legs. Black widows are extremely rare in northern portions of the Northeast, and still uncommon in the Mid-Atlantic and southern New England. As with the recluse, bites may not involve envenomation, and the person's reactions to the venom will vary from small local swelling to systemic problems.

The bites of both of these spiders may not immediately produce painful symptoms, so it may not be obvious that a spider has bitten. Treatment of any bite includes soothing any initial reactions, cleaning the wound, and monitoring the area for infection or delayed reaction. If any insect bite continues to spread and worsen after an initial swelling period of two to four hours, it is time to begin evacuation. Preventative measures against spider bites include shaking out clothing in the morning before putting it on, looking before reaching under logs or other rotten wood, and noting the locations of spiders in lean-tos and outhouses.

SNAKES

Snakes are amazing creatures to observe, and many beautiful species are quite common throughout the backcountry areas of the Northeast, including green, ringneck, brown, black, ribbon, and garter snakes. In addition, there are two species of poisonous snakes to know, particularly if you are hiking in mountainous terrain between Virginia and Massachusetts. These species are the eastern timber rattlesnake (*Crotalus horridus*) and the northern copperhead (*Agkistrodon contortrix*).

The infamous rattlesnake's chunky body can reach 6 feet in length. Its northern range stretches into New York and western Vermont, with tiny, localized populations in Massachusetts and southern New Hampshire. Eastern timber rattlesnakes are identifiable by their large, triangular heads; keeled scales down the middle of the back; brown cross patterns on a dark background; and the telltale blunt tail rattle. The eastern timber rattlesnake is easily confused with the milk snake, the black racer, the black rat snake, and some dark-colored garter snakes. Rattlesnakes rarely bite humans unless harassed or startled, and about 20 percent of bites do not include envenomation. A bite with venom will typically produce symptoms within an hour. Redness, pain, swelling, and bruising will occur around an obvious puncture wound. As the blood toxins in the venom spread through the body, systemic symptoms will occur, including nausea, vomiting, dizziness, and perspiration. In a small number of cases, hemorrhaging and heart failure eventually cause death. Bites to children are far more likely to have serious, systemic impacts, as the ratio of venom to the child's body mass is far greater.

7

The rapid administration of antivenin is the only effective treatment, so evacuation must be the highest priority. During evacuation, field treatment should focus on minimizing the impact of any swelling and slowing the circulation of venom through the body. First, remove any jewelry or constrictive clothing on the

FIGURE 32. The Eastern timber rattlesnake, above, is one of the two species of poisonous snakes all hikers in the Northeast should be able to recognize. Identify it by its triangular head, its brown markings on a black background, and the rattle at the end of its tail.

bitten extremity. Keep the affected body part below the level of the heart and as immobile as possible. If it takes longer than an hour to reach medical care, wrap the limb above the bite with a snug compression bandage. This is not a tourniquet, and it should be easy to slide a finger under the wrap. Try to keep them calm and still, as a lower heart rate will slow venom's spread. But if immobility means an extensive delay in reaching treatment, it is better to focus on traveling toward the trailhead. Use acetaminophen to manage pain.

There are also a few treatment ideas that medical professionals discourage. Alcohol, electric shock, and ice are all ineffective or worse. Similarly, cutting the wound and bleeding it, or attempting to remove venom through suction, are not known to have any beneficial effect. There is no need to kill or capture the snake, although medical professionals will find a good description useful, if you can safely observe the snake. Finally, while the bite is likely to be extremely painful, the affected person must not receive any NSAID pain medication (e.g., ibuprofen or aspirin), as these drugs will exacerbate the blood-thinning effects of the venom.

The northern copperhead is more common than the timber rattlesnake in the mountainous terrain of Virginia and Pennsylvania, but its range does not extend as far north into southern New England. This is also a thick-bodied snake with a large, triangular head, although the northern copperhead is typically less than 2.5 feet long. It has a light brown or salmon-colored skin, with dark reddish-brown hourglass shapes crossing its back. The copperhead is most often confused with the harmless milk snake, but the milk snake has blotchier, less regular markings that include broad bands of white. It also lacks the triangular, pit viper head. Copperheads are so effective at camouflaging themselves that stepping on one is thought to be the most common cause of a bite.

Copperhead bites are reported to be the most common snakebite in the United States. Fortunately, they are also far less deadly, although they still require rapid treatment. Symptoms of a bite with envenomation include immediate pain, bruising, and swelling. Systemic symptoms can include nausea, dizziness, and mild fever. Unlike rattlesnake bites, antivenin treatment is rare for copperhead bites. But because symptoms can vary widely between individuals, rapid evacuation for evaluation by a medical professional is necessary. During evacuation, rescuers should follow similar guidelines as those provided above for rattlesnake bites.

Prevention of snakebites is key to managing risk, and maintaining trail awareness is crucial. Both venomous species prefer rocky, sunny ledges; be extra alert in these habitats. Inspect hand placements when scrambling over rocky trails in snake country and hike mindfully on sunny, warm trails. Whenever you do see a snake, view it as an opportunity to observe backcountry wildlife. If the snake's markings indicate it could be one of the two species above, simply give that snake enough room and space to retreat, or circle widely around it as you make your way down the trail.

BEARS

The American black bear (*Ursus americanus*) is a common resident throughout the Northeastern backcountry. Seeing one from a safe distance can be the highlight of a hiker's trip. Adult black bears average about 250 pounds, but some adult males can grow to 400 pounds or more, especially in northern parts of their range. They are capable of running up to 30 MPH for short distances, can climb trees rapidly, and swim well. They are omnivores, eating a huge range of greens, berries, bark, insects, small mammals, and carrion. A large bear can catch and eat animals as large as a white-tailed deer, although the bears mostly use their sizable claws for digging up roots and ground-dwelling animals or insects. They generally hibernate in the northern part of their range for several months a year but can be active any time of year a food source is present.

Black bears are generally reclusive and avoid human interactions. Even so, given their size and power, they are capable of inflicting severe injury, and a wise backcountry traveler will follow certain preventative practices. These same practices also protect the bear, since a bear that injures a human or becomes habituated to human civilization is likely to be relocated or euthanized. Carefully follow the bear camping practices outlined in Chapter 8, Camping Skills, starting on page 196. In short, food and other items with attractive smells must be hung out of reach, and food and kitchens should always be located apart from sleeping areas. These practices should prevent most unwanted attention, although hikers sometimes encounter bears on the trail, and previously habituated bears sometimes come into camp. In these situations, it is important to know a few strategies to stay safe.

Black bears will almost never attack unless they are protecting a food source or their young, or they feel trapped and threatened. If you encounter a bear that does not immediately bolt into the forest, it is likely due to one of these situations. Bears usually communicate their mood and intent. A bear may turn sideways to look larger and more threatening, and growling or scratching the ground are sure signs of an agitated—and dangerous—bear. In general, standing isn't a sign of aggression, just curiosity, as black bears have relatively poor eyesight. The bear may be trying to get a better sense of what it has encountered. Sometimes bears will "bluff charge" people to try to scare them away from a food source or cub, and this behavior is a clear sign that the bear is capable of greater aggression.

If your group encounters a bear on the trail, immediately form a line in an attempt to look long and large. Stand tall and make some noise while simultaneously backing away slowly. You are trying to show the bear you are not a prey animal. Pick up any small children in the group. Look around carefully for cubs and yearlings (perhaps in a nearby tree), and take care never to get between the adult bear and its young. If the bear does not leave the vicinity then you must assume it is protecting a food source or its young, and you must choose a new route that avoids the bear, giving it a berth of at least 100 yards or more. Finding a bear in your camp means

7

the bear was attracted by a food source or another smell. Again, join forces with the whole group and stand in the most impressive configuration you can. Attempt to scare off the bear by making noise, yelling, and banging pots and pans. In all of these scenarios, be sure the bear has an exit route.

There are a few strategies we don't recommend. It is unwise to throw rocks or other objects at the bear, as hitting the bear could trigger an immediate charge. Do not turn and run from a bear or try to squeeze past it on the trail before running along. Running will trigger the bear's natural response to chase, similar to many dogs, and you will not be able to outrun it. Climbing a tree is not recommended, since black bears can climb better than humans. Finally, remember that traveling solo means a greater risk from black bears, as a solo hiker cannot rely on the safety of a large group.

A bear that appears to stalk you or that attacks while you are in your tent is attempting to eat you. This kind of black bear encounter is extremely rare but has occurred in North America. In these situations—again, extremely rare—you need to fight for your survival. Do not play dead, as is recommended in grizzly attacks. If you can retreat, it may help to drop your pack, as the bear might stop to investigate

rat, mouse, etc.   bat   chipmunk   rabbit   squirrel   woodchuck

otter   mink   fisher   skunk

possum   racoon   fox   bobcat

coyote   beaver   deer   moose

bear

FIGURE 33. Animals leave scat as one sign of their whereabouts. Above are some of the most common types of mammal scat you'll come across in the Northeast.

the pack, but the pack can also add protection to your back. If you are caught, fight back with the strongest blows you can manage to the bear's face, mouth, and snout.

Any threatening encounter with a bear should be reported to the land management agency responsible for the travel area. This is especially true of bears that have shown an interest in camp smells. Often a bear can be relocated before it becomes fully habituated, saving it from euthanasia. Bears are one of the most amazing creatures of the backcountry. Seeing one is cause for caution, not fear, and with care you can observe them from a safe distance.

OTHER MAMMALS

Many other mammal species live in the backcountry of the Northeast. Usually these animals disappear into the forest before a hiker notices them. While wildlife encounters can be a highlight of a trip to the mountains, it's wise to remember that most of these animals can inflict injuries if threatened. For example, the majestic moose is the largest land animal in the region and quite common in northern New England. Moose will usually run from human interaction, but a cow (female) can be a threat if she is with a young calf, and a bull (male) can be a threat during

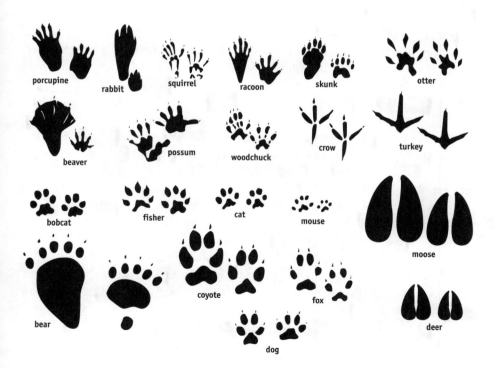

FIGURE 34. You can also identify animals by their tracks. Above are some of the most common tracks you'll see in the Northeast.

breeding season (the "rut," generally late September through early October). A single kick from one of those powerful legs can be deadly. Similarly, white-tailed deer are common throughout most of the Northeast. While much smaller than a moose, a kick from a forefoot can inflict a major injury. White-tailed deer can also become habituated to camp food.

For all wildlife, some basic rules of interaction apply. Use good judgment and remain at a distance that should be nonthreatening to the animal. Keep your food, toiletries, and other camp smells isolated and out of reach. While this practice is often referred to as "bear camping," it is effective at discouraging a wide range of critters: mice, squirrels, raccoons, skunks, and more. If an animal is aware of your presence but does not move away, you must assume it has a major incentive for holding its ground, usually a food source, offspring, or lack of an escape route. This animal should be given a wide berth and a greater opportunity to move on. Some off-trail travel is a small price to pay for the privilege of seeing the regular residents of an area where we humans are merely visitors.

INSECTS
Bees and Wasps

Wasp and bee stings are relatively common in the woods and occur most frequently in late summer and early fall, when ground-nesting bees can be found circulating near trails. For hikers with a medical history of severe reactions to bee stings (anaphylaxis), a sting is immediately life-threatening. (More on this below.) In normal circumstances, while the sting or stings can be painful, treatment is not difficult.

7

After removing the person and all others from the immediate area of the bees, identify the exact site of the sting. Inspect closely to see if any portion of the stinger remains. If so, it should be removed as soon as possible, as the stingers of some species can continue to pump venom into them even after the bee has detached. The best removal strategy is to scrape across the site, flicking upward with the edge of a credit card or similar object. It's not ideal to grasp at the stinger with fingers or tweezers, as doing so can squeeze more venom into the skin, but rapid removal is your highest priority. Once you're sure you've removed the stinger, your treatment goals are to reduce pain and swelling, monitor them for any signs of systemic reaction, and treat the area as you would any small soft-tissue injury.

Localized reactions to stings will include redness and swelling at and around the site. Placing cold water and cold compresses on the sting will alleviate some of the pain, as will ibuprofen or other NSAIDs. If the sting is on an extremity, it is a good idea to remove rings, bracelets, and other items that could constrict swelling. For a mild local reaction, this is adequate treatment. For larger local reactions, you may wish to apply a topical hydrocortisone cream. If the itching is bothersome, you can also offer an oral antihistamine, such has diphenhydramine or chlorpheniramine. It's a good idea to help the person remain still and calm for the first 20 to 30

ANAPHYLAXIS

Anaphylaxis is a life-threatening allergic reaction to a substance the body perceives as a threat. Usually a protein, common substances that cause anaphylaxis are bee venom, nuts, peanuts, shellfish, and certain drugs. In response to the foreign substance, the body overreacts, releasing a torrent of chemicals, including histamine. Multiple body systems respond to this flood of chemicals, triggering an array of symptoms. Depending on the situation, anaphylaxis symptoms will include:

Respiratory System

- Wheezing, coughing, choking, squeaky voice

- Inability to get air in or out of the lungs

- Swelling and itching of the lips, gums, tongue, and palate

Digestive System

- Nausea, cramping, vomiting, and diarrhea

- Inability to swallow

- Abdominal bloating

Circulatory system

- Rapid, weak heartbeat

- Extremely low blood pressure

- Feeling of faintness

Other

- Red, itchy skin

- Hives

- Dizziness

- Metallic smells or tastes

- Feeling of impending doom

7

People having an anaphylactic reaction can die from a failure to breathe adequately or from a failure to circulate blood adequately (due to a complete loss of vascular tension). The only medical treatment that will prevent this outcome is the rapid administration of an epinephrine injection. Administration of the epinephrine should be followed by a maximum dose of diphenhydramine or another fast-acting antihistamine. Additional prescription medications include prednisone, for a long-term suppression of the allergic reaction, and albuterol (or another beta-agonist inhaler), for dilating breathing passages. Without these medications, treatment can only support the respiratory and circulatory systems until help arrives or the person dies.

minutes. Heart rates elevated by vigorous activity will rapidly circulate the venom through the body, increasing the likelihood of a systemic reaction.

Systemic reactions occur when the venom impacts sites other than the immediate area of the sting. The severity of these reactions can range from mild to immediately life-threatening. The extent of the reaction will depend on the person's level of sensitivity and activity, the amount of venom, the number and location of stings, and the species of bee. The challenge is that these reactions can be difficult to distinguish at first. Hives (red, raised skin welts) are an example of a relatively mild systemic reaction. As soon as any systemic reaction begins to occur, give them a maximum dose of a quick-acting antihistamine, such as diphenhydramine. This early treatment with antihistamines will slow or halt the systemic reaction and may prevent the development of more severe symptoms. Monitor them closely. Once a systemic reaction occurs, consider the patient a high risk for anaphylaxis (a life-threatening systemic reaction to a bee sting) for the next 30 minutes. Continue maximum dosages of antihistamines according to label directions for at least 24 hours.

Anaphylaxis (see page 171) occurs in approximately 0.8 percent of the general population, or 8 in 1,000. Signs and symptoms of anaphylaxis include wheezing; swelling of the mouth, lips, and throat; widespread hives; a feeling of faintness; and a generalized feeling of panic. Rapid dosage of appropriate medication is the only treatment that will halt this systemic reaction. Specific treatments for anaphylaxis are discussed separately.

Mosquitoes, Blackflies, and Other Flying Insects

The Northeast is generally blessed with an abundance of water, and this water is the breeding ground of numerous biting insects, especially mosquitoes, blackflies, and midges (a.k.a. "no-see-ums"). Peak population hits in mid-May through mid-June, but we can experience these pests any time in the late spring or summer. Hordes of biting insects greatly decrease the enjoyment of a mountain trip, especially for novices. Plus, if someone receives an excessive number of bites, severe reactions can occur or infection can set in. Fortunately, it isn't hard to keep the little biters at bay. The first line of defense should be a physical barrier. Covering the body with clothing is nearly 100 percent effective. Cover your face by draping a simple bug net over any brimmed hat and tucking the net into the collar of your shirt. If it's too hot for a clothing barrier or the bug density is really high, it's time to seek chemical help. Effective, conventional insect repellents include DEET and picaridin, in no more than a 30 percent concentration. Used according to directions, these repellents are effective and safe, according to government studies. Herbal options are also available, although with varying efficacy. Apply repellents first to clothing and then, if necessary, directly to the skin.

Sometimes a person receives so many bites that the itching seems like it could drive them crazy. Soothing specific areas with cool, wet cloths will reduce itching and swelling. Also, diphenhydramine (Benadryl or Dramamine, for example) at night will reduce the reaction and help encourage sleep. Watch out for younger or inexperienced hikers who are itching a lot. If their scratching turns the welts into small open wounds, it's easy for skin infections to take hold. Be sure to clean these areas as you would any soft-tissue injury and do what you can to reduce the itching.

Over years of exposure, a person can develop a physiological tolerance to these insects, with smaller, localized reactions. They can also develop "bug Zen," the ability to remain calm while in the midst of a swarm of flying bloodsuckers. Even without these developments, though, it is worth trying to appreciate all these biting flies. Their abundance is why birds travel from the tropics to summer in the North-east, and they support fish populations in streams throughout the region. If nothing else, if you're in the woods when they're out and about, it's likely you will enjoy the backcountry with fewer human companions.

PERMETHRIN SPRAYS AND CLOTHING

One preventative treatment for insects is not applied to the skin at all: perme-thrin. Permethrin is applied directly to clothing or shoes and allowed to dry, after which it becomes colorless and odorless. When dry, it is an insecticide, killing in-sects that come into contact with it, and one application is said to last through six to ten washes. There are several brands of outdoor clothing with a more durable form of permethrin built into the fabric, with a purported durability of up to 70 washes. Permethrin is considered quite safe for humans when used according to directions. For individuals seeking maximum protection from ticks and other bit-ing flies, permethrin spray and fabric is an excellent choice.

7

Ticks

The rapid increase in occurrence of tick-borne illnesses, particularly Lyme disease, in the Northeast has been an important development for backcountry travelers over the past ten years. Lyme disease is a complex of symptoms produced by the infec-tion of a specific bacteria, and that bacteria is passed along to humans through the bite of one species of tick, *Ixodes scapularis*, the black-legged (or "deer") tick. The bacteria is present in deer ticks in all backcountry areas of the Northeast. While widespread, this relatively new environmental hazard doesn't mean we should all stay out of the woods. With some knowledge and good practices, you likely can enjoy a backcountry trip without bringing home an unwanted illness.

The deer tick is relatively easy to differentiate from other species of ticks, which, while perhaps a nuisance, are not implicated in the transmission of any human dis-eases. Current research suggests that the Lyme pathogen is not transmitted unless the tick has been embedded in the skin and feeding for a period of eight hours or

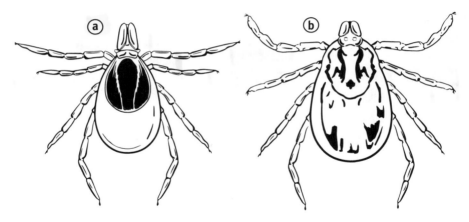

FIGURE 35. The deer tick (a) is the notorious carrier of Lyme disease, while the dog tick (b) is far less hazardous to humans. Deer ticks can be as small as a pinhead, while dog ticks are much larger and easier to spot.

more. Finally, a tick moves slowly and methodically, and physical and chemical barriers can be very effective at preventing their access to skin. To manage risk related to tick-borne illnesses, take the following interdependent measures:

- Ticks are attracted to dark objects, so wear light-colored clothing that fully covers the legs and tuck it into socks or gaiters.

- Use insect repellents, such as DEET or picaridin, and permethrin on clothing worn on the lower body, as instructed on the label.

- Conduct thorough tick checks at intervals shorter than eight hours (morning, midday, and bedtime) with a partner and immediately remove any tick found on the skin.

- Unattached ticks are easily washed off, so swim and bathe as often as is reasonable, daily if possible. Immature ticks (nymphs) are so small that they can be difficult to spot, so a quick rinse is an excellent defense.

- For accurate identification, you may need to carry a small magnifying glass.

- Grassy fields and open areas are prime tick habitat. If your route takes you through this kind of area, take the time immediately afterward to inspect clothing and skin.

- Remove and identify any deer tick that has become embedded and engorged. Mark the bite area with a pen and observe it for 72 hours for signs of a target-shaped rash with concentric rings, similar to a bull's-eye. Most medical practitioners will want to see the tick for themselves, so try to save it and transport it out of the backcountry. (One good method is to stick the tick to duct tape then put it in a clear plastic bag.)

Lyme disease itself usually starts with flulike symptoms about 72 hours after a bite. The bull's-eye rash noted above occurs in 70 to 80 percent of patients. Some people don't experience symptoms for 30 days or more, and others never see a rash. Because untreated Lyme disease leads to severe, chronic health concerns, many medical experts recommend an immediate course of antibiotics for any person with a confirmed deer-tick bite. Early administration of certain antibiotics is thought to reduce the likelihood and severity of infection. Any person who has had a confirmed bite from an engorged deer tick, or any person who has shown a targetlike rash, should seek medical attention as soon as possible.

In the Northeastern United States, bites from other species of tick (such as the "dog tick," *Dermacentor variabilis*) are far less hazardous. Remove any embedded ticks as completely as possible, and wash and treat the bite area as you would any wound. Tick mouthparts often remain embedded, and these can become inflamed and itchy. While this is a nuisance, there is no reason for alarm. As with any small infection, this area will resolve with normal care and time to heal.

➜ PLANT HAZARDS

Several plants in the Northeast can cause discomfort or injury if they come into contact with skin. The best known is the group that includes poison ivy, poison oak, and poison sumac. All are members of the same plant family, and all contain a potent allergen called urushiol. Each has glossy leaves in clusters of three that grow on a vine or a small bush. Hikers should be able to identify these species; carrying a small plant guide is a good idea.

7

Skin reaction to urushiol differs among hikers. Some will develop only a few minor, itchy bumps, while others can develop severe, systemic reactions. Since skin rash and other symptoms are thought to be an allergic reaction, your treatment goals are to remove the allergen and to suppress the allergic reaction with topical and oral medications. As soon as a hiker has confirmed physical contact with one these three plants, he or she should scrub the area with soap and water. Specialized poison ivy and abrasive hand-cleaning scrubs are more effective than soapy water. These are worth their weight if traveling in areas where these plants are common. Even if a skin irritation has already developed, the skin should be cleaned, as should any clothing that may have been in contact with that area of the skin. After cleaning, you can aim to relieve itching with hydrocortisone or antihistamine creams and cool, wet cloths. Oral antihistamines (such as diphenhydramine) will help systemically. The affected area should be protected from the sun, as the disrupted skin will easily burn. Similarly, the hiker will need to prevent any rubbing of the area by clothing, backpack, or shoes.

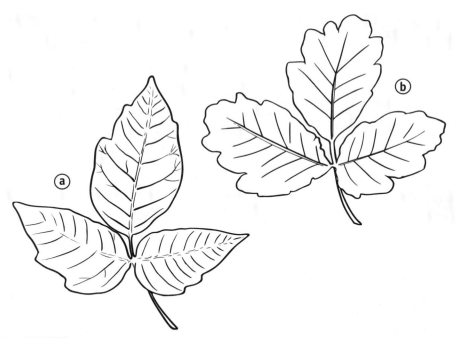

FIGURE 36. Poison ivy (a) and poison oak (b) are recognizable by their distinct groupings of three leaves. Remember the colloquialisms: "Leaves of three, let them be," and "Longer middle stem, don't touch them."

7

Some individuals are highly allergic to urushiol, and these people may experience an anaphylactic reaction. Even a "regular" reaction becomes serious when it involves the eyes or the mouth, especially if urushiol has been ingested. In these cases, prescription medications can be lifesaving, and urgent professional care is necessary. Even when the severity of a reaction seems manageable, it may be best to leave the backcountry for professional treatment. In these situations, a medical professional will follow additional protocols to protect the skin and prevent infection.

- If the rash involves the genitals or the face
- If it is pervasive through the joints of the hand or toes, or across other major joints of the body
- If the rash covers a very large area (equivalent to approximately 90 percent of the patient's hands)

➜ WHEN THINGS GO WRONG

No matter how well we prepare, and no matter how good our accident and illness prevention practices are, chances are that all regular backcountry travelers will eventually encounter some kind of accident, illness, or other emergency. Good wilderness medical courses, such as the Wilderness First Responder, will include basic emergency-response practices, and training with search-and-rescue teams will provide even more skill development. Remember that preventative practices always include creating a detailed itinerary with evacuation routes and emergency services numbers. In all emergency cases, it is important to know some basic principles and practices that can lead to the best possible outcomes for everyone involved.

UNIVERSAL EMERGENCY MANAGEMENT

With the following principles, backcountry travelers can respond most effectively to all emergencies, from lost or injured hikers to extreme weather:

1.   **Assess the situation.** Rapidly identify true hazards and their possible outcomes as accurately and completely as you can in the shortest possible time. This list should be broad enough to include not just any injured individuals but the entire group, and should include foreseeable events in the near future.

2.   **Identify leadership.** Emergencies are not a time for democratic decision-making processes that take extra time. The person with the most experience and knowledge—and the coolest head—should be in charge of the emergency response, although this person should not be isolated and autocratic. The best emergency leader will quickly seek insights and ideas from all members of a travel group and work the relevant ideas into the response plan.

3.   **Develop and implement a response plan.** Every emergency is different. An injury will require first aid and possibly evacuation, while a lost person will require systematic search strategies and, possibly, activation of a search-and-rescue effort. Using the situational assessment and information gathered from group members, make a plan and act. Each plan must include these elements:

     ▪ Protect all group members. Do not allow current or future hazards, or a dangerous response plan, to create more victims. Be especially mindful of how emergency responders are caring for their bodily needs and protecting themselves against the environmental hazards of heat and cold.

     ▪ Help the victim or victims. Make them more comfortable when possible and provide the greatest level of first-aid care possible. Keep one person with the victim at all times to monitor the victim's health signs while providing a calm, reassuring presence.

     ▪ Promote a positive group attitude. Help others in the group stay calm and focused by providing realistic reassurance and assigning meaningful jobs that

7

allow each person to contribute to the emergency effort. For example, heating water on a cookstove for rescuers to have hot drinks is a valuable auxiliary task.

- Develop a plan for the extended outlook. Does the hiker require immediate transport to get advanced medical care? If so, activate professional emergency personnel and/or plan for a self-supported evacuation. Is travel going to be impossible due to nightfall or a storm? In these situations, designate group members to set up camp, feed rescuers, and support the ongoing effort.

- Monitor and adapt. As time passes, maintain your situational assessment and make changes as required. For example, if the weather appears to be turning cold and wet, you may need to move the group, set up shelters, or provide additional warm food and drink.

EVACUATION PLANNING AND IMPLEMENTATION

Sometimes a group member requires evacuation. This can be for nonmedical reasons, but usually it will be due to a medical condition that requires evaluation and treatment by a medical professional. Evacuations can happen in three ways: The person can walk out unassisted, walk out with assistance, or be transported out by others. The hiker can walk out assisted or unassisted if the condition isn't aggravated by movement. If protecting them is impossible, they must be transported by others. Most groups do not have the physical or equipment resources to safely carry one of their own out of the woods, especially over a rugged, steep, or narrow trail. Improvised litters (stretchers) are rarely secure enough to transport an adult for an extended distance in backcountry terrain. To carry out a 160-pound person in this terrain, search-and-rescue teams use a professional litter at an estimated maximum pace of 0.5 to 0.75 MPH, with an ideal team of eighteen litter carriers. If evacuation is necessary and the person cannot travel under his or her own power, nearly all groups should send a request for assistance.

SENDING FOR HELP

Part of many emergency response plans is how to send a request for help. This request might go to a public agency (e.g., U.S. Forest Service, a state fish and game department, local or state police), a nonprofit group (e.g. AMC), or to the person identified on the trip itinerary as the emergency contact back home. If cell phone or satellite phone service is available, prepare to call the emergency contacts on your itinerary list. If no communication technology is available, the group will need to send a subgroup out to a trailhead. In either scenario, rescuers will need the same information, so write out the following information prior to making the call or sending off the subgroup:

- Location of the group, in the greatest detail and accuracy possible. Provide UTM or latitude-longitude coordinates, as this information eliminates any guesswork or interpretation. With or without coordinates, provide a detailed description of the group's location in relation to known landmarks, such as trail intersections, water features, designated campsites, or lean-tos. If a subgroup is carrying out this information, include a marked map.

- Description of the problem requiring urgent assistance.

- Victim description, including name, age, sex, weight, height, and relevant medical history.

- Group profile, including number of people, organizational affiliation, relevant characteristics (e.g., youth, elderly), and current health status.

- Requested assistance. Does the victim need an assisted evacuation (a shoulder to lean on), or a full litter carry? Does the victim require specific lifesaving medications (e.g., insulin, oxygen) or specific first-aid equipment (e.g., backboard or traction splint)?

- Resources available. Resources can be material, such as first-aid supplies, or they can be human resources, such as twelve strong group members ready to assist with a carryout.

- Current plan. Is the group intending to remain stationary or to travel toward the trailhead? If traveling, exactly which trail will the group follow and on what expected timetable?

- Any known hazards to the rescuers.

7

If the only way to request assistance or to activate emergency service is to send out a subgroup, the following principles will help everyone stay as safe as possible.

1. The subgroup should have at least three members in it and as many as five members if this number will not slow the group's progress. One of these members should be designated as group leader.

2. Always travel with the ten essentials and plan to be self-sufficient, if necessary. That usually means a subgroup will have, at least, some food, a stove, a pot, and a tarp or tent, as well as other essentials.

3. Make sure the emergency response leader and the subgroup leader have a clear travel plan. The subgroup must adhere to that plan, if at all possible.

4. Travel as rapidly as the situation requires but not so fast that it endangers anyone. Do not take chances on technical terrain, and jog or run only if the trail conditions are ideal.

BE A SURVIVOR

When everything seems to be going wrong, some people will crumble and others will adapt and prevail. While everyone has different personal resources of resiliency, if you and your travel companions find yourselves in an emergency situation, it should be everyone's priority to adapt and prevail. These five qualities are commonly found in experienced leaders, and they will help you be as resilient as possible in any challenging situation, from sudden storms to medical evacuations:

1. **Use your powers of reason.** Do all you can to set aside your emotions, analyze the situation, and rationally develop a plan of action.

2. **Be focused.** Accept that the problem is happening and be in the present moment with it, not in the past or the future.

3. **Keep your sense of humor.** Finding humor in difficult situations, while perhaps irreverent, is a source of strength and perspective.

4. **See the event in context.** This emergency is one event in your long life, one bad day out of many other days. Don't let the event dominate your life story. You are bigger than it.

5. **Stay positive.** The adversity is real, but you can choose to gain from it. Life experience, wisdom, courage, and confidence are all possible outcomes of prevailing in the face of adversity. An emergency is an opportunity to learn valuable lessons.

7

Experienced campers feel at home in the wild. They have ways of finding the best campsites, and of being organized, efficient, safe, and comfortable around camp. When you know how to set up a great campsite, it's possible to relax and enjoy the rejuvenating experience of living in the great outdoors. And with enough practice and knowledge, anyone can become this "good" camper. All it takes is enough information to set up your camp and the will to practice your learned skills in the real world. Read on to pick up the tips and tricks we have been teaching for more than 25 years of outdoor camping instruction.

➜ FINDING A SITE

Finding a good campsite is the product of effective planning. The first things you need to consider before making your own campsite are the land regulations where you are setting up camp and the Leave No Trace (LNT) principles. Guidebooks, recreational maps, and information shared among campers can lead you to discover a beautiful spot, but if you are diverging from established campsites to seek these quiet and secluded locations, you'll need to look at a topographic map.

REGULATIONS

Make sure you know the local camping regulations before you set out. Popular or fragile areas often have regulations that will require you to camp away from certain locations. For instance, in the White Mountain National Forest, the U.S. Forest Service has established Forest Protected Areas (FPA) where no camping or campfires are permitted except in official and designated camping areas. FPAs often extend a quarter-mile around or along a popular natural feature.

LNT CONSIDERATIONS

Avoid selecting a campsite near obvious animal dens, beddings, or trails. For many reasons, it is best to camp away from areas that are frequented by wildlife. Although pristine sites are often tempting, a better LNT practice is to use an existing site. Impacted sites have already been trampled and sacrificed, so they should be used before creating a newly impacted site. Keep your campsite small when using an existing site and avoid places where impacts are just beginning. Make sure not to increase the size of the existing site by trampling its edges. Avoid dropping your pack against trees at the edge of the campsite or you will trample more vegetation.

FINDING A CAMPSITE FROM A TOPOGRAPHIC MAP

You can predict some potentially good campsite locations from a quick glance at your topographic map—before you even drive to the trailhead. Using a topographic map will allow you to find areas with reliable water sources and flatter terrain. Remember, wide distances between contour lines indicate gentle slopes or even flat areas. The map will not tell you how dense the forest floor might be at a specific location, but knowing that deciduous forests often provide a more open floor will help you guess where a better campsite at lower elevations might be. (Tip: Deciduous forests are often found at lower elevations.)

Obvious points of interest—such as a lake, waterfall, or the junction of two important trails with gentle contour lines—will yield a higher probability of an unmarked but well-established campsite. Campers are often more alike than we think. We all want flat terrain that's near water and not too far from the trail.

SELECTING A CAMPSITE ON THE TRAIL

While you're hiking, keep an eye out for small, unmarked trails that leave the main trail, especially near junctions and other points of interest. When traveling on flat terrain, look on both sides of the trail and seek out obvious clearings and sun wells, where the sun reaches the forest floor due to a hole in the canopy. These areas can yield great campsites. Another way to find potential pristine campsites in the Northeast is to look for signs of old, abandoned logging roads. These forest roads from the past often give you access to flat terrain, even on the slope of a mountain.

Now that you know some of the best ways to find a potential area for a campsite, note that great campsites are found—not made. Forget the temptation to remove living plants, dig trenches, or build dirt platforms. It is appropriate and acceptable to move dead branches or rocks when setting up your tent as long as you take the time to replace anything you moved when you leave, in keeping with LNT principles.

Finally, when you are looking for the ideal site, remember that we often make better decisions when we don't have heavy backpacks on our backs. Take the time to put down your pack and search for the ideal site free of your trail burden.

WHAT TO LOOK FOR IN A CAMPSITE

- **Surface.** The ground surface should be large enough to accommodate the footprint of your shelter, durable or already impacted, and free of fragile flowering plants. Avoid surfaces that are concave, as they might pool water if it rains.

- **Weather.** Anticipate the direction of the prevailing wind and where surface water might run during a torrential rainfall.

- **Safety.** Make sure to look above the site and keep an eye out for potential widowmakers: dead, hanging branches or leaning dead trees. If the wind picks up, these hazards can come down on your site and shelter. When you find potential widowmakers, look for a new site.

- **Water source.** You don't have to set up your shelter near a water source, but doing so is convenient. Note that when camping, the greatest amount of impact will occur at your cooking site. Both your shelter and your kitchen should be at least 200 feet from any source of water.

- **Vista.** Don't forget why you are out in the mountains and forests: Seek out camping sites with great vistas, but make sure not to place your shelter or cooking site in an obviously visible location where other hikers will see you. It is good hiker etiquette for your campsite to keep a low profile.

➜ KNOT TYING

Once you have found the perfect site for your camp, you have the task of putting together your tent or sleeping shelter. Before you set up, it is essential to know a few knot-tying skills that will help you when you're getting your camp ready. Ropes are perhaps the most versatile piece of gear you carry in your backpack. They can help you build a shelter, negotiate difficult terrain, protect your food against opportunistic wildlife, repair equipment, or be used in a first-aid situation. But a rope alone is not useful if you don't know how to use it.

First of all, it is essential to understand that not all knots are the same, although all knots belong to a few families. These families are:

- **Stopper.** A knot designed to prevent the end of a rope from slipping through a hole.

- **Loop.** A knot designed to secure part of a rope to an object.

- **Hitch.** A knot designed to secure part of a rope to an object by cinching the rope around that object.

- **Bend.** A knot designed to join two ends of a rope to each other. The ends can be from the same rope or from two different ropes.

8

You might not realize it, but ropes have different parts with specific names. There are even names for the way the rope is folded. For instance, the part of a rope held in your hand is referred to as the running end, while the rest of the rope is known as the standing end. When a rope's running end is folded along the standing end, this part of the rope is known as the bight. Finally, when the running end crosses the standing end, the rope is said to be a loop.

An overhand knot is perhaps the easiest knot to tie and to remember. Simply take the running end of the rope, make a loop, and pass the running end through the backside of the loop. There you have it! You just made a stopper knot called an overhand. This classic pretzel-shaped knot is one of the first most people learn, and it would be the first knot a beginner would tie if someone handed them a rope and said, "Tie a knot." We'll look at three families in this chapter, loop, hitch, and bend.

LOOP FAMILY
Overhand on a Bight
Similar to the overhand knot, this knot is performed with a bight. Begin by creating a bight, which will be known as the running end. Use the running end bight to make a loop, then pass the running end through the backside of the loop, and pull until the knot is taut. You now have a loop known as an overhand on a bight.

This knot does not have to be tied at the end of a rope so it is useful in many different situations. You can clip a carabiner to it to quickly connect it to another object—such as a food bag in a bearproof food system.

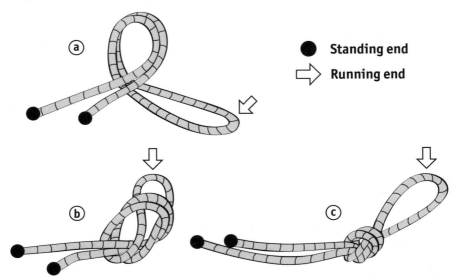

FIGURE 37. To tie an overhand on a bight: (a) Begin by forming a bight, or doubling the rope back on itself so you have a bend at one end (the running end) and two tails at the other (the standing end). Next make a loop with the standing end. (b) Pass the running end through the loop. (c) Pull the rope taut.

Bowline

The bowline is perhaps the most popular camping knot, as well as the most difficult to learn. Do not try to tie this knot without using an anchor point to tie the knot to—tying this knot to an imaginary object will only confuse you. Second, unless you want to learn to tie this knot to yourself, always face the object you want to tie the bowline to. Knot-tying is hands-on learning and must be done in the exact context you'll use the skill. To tie a bowline:

1. Facing an anchor point such as a small tree, pass the running end of the rope around the tree from right to left.

2. Make a loop on the standing end of the rope; this will be the rope that is on the right side of the tree. The loop you make must have two characteristics: It should be pointing toward the running end, which is on the left side of the tree; and the long, standing end of the rope should be on the bottom of the loop, meaning that when you make the loop, the rope should loop itself as if it were spiraling down to the ground.

3. While holding the loop with your right hand, feed the running end through the loop coming upward through the loop. (Note in this setup, going through the loop in a downward path with the running end will lead to failure and frustration.)

4. Feed the running end of the rope along the left side of the standing end, go under the standing end, and return inside the loop in a downward motion.

5. Pull the running end and the standing end away from each other, and you will see the knot form.

The bowline is a popular knot because it creates a loop knot around an object, thus securing one end of the rope to that object. The most important characteristic of the bowline is that it can be put under a lot of tension and still be easy to undo by flipping its loop—very useful when setting up a shelter, such as the ridgeline of a tarp.

8

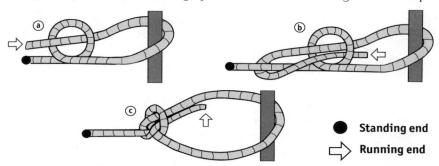

FIGURE 38. To tie a bowline: Pass the running end of the rope around an anchor point, such as a small tree or a hook. (a) Using the standing end, form a loop in the rope then form a second loop in the running end and feed it back through the first loop. (b) With a downward motion, use the running end to grab the standing end and pull the running end back through the first loop. (c) Pull the rope taut.

HITCH FAMILY
Trucker's Hitch

The trucker's hitch is a compound knot that functions as a kind of pulley, giving you a 3 to 1 mechanical advantage (meaning the puller can pull three times his or her weight), although rope-on-rope friction might reduce this to 1.5 to 1. Nevertheless, the trucker's hitch is quite effective at creating tension on a rope, such as when setting up a shelter.

Note: Make sure that one end of the rope is already secured to an anchor point, or attached to a tarp or tent fly, and that tension can be created when completing the trucker's hitch.

1.   While facing a small tree, begin this knot by passing the running end of the rope around a tree, feeding the rope from right to left.

2.   On the standing end of the rope, make a loop through which you pass a bight of rope taken from the rope between the loop and the tree. Pull on the bight until the slip knot is formed. The knot you just created is known as a marlin spike hitch.

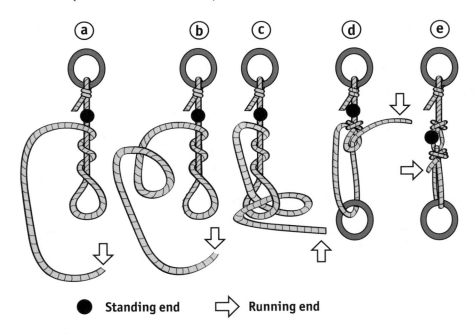

● **Standing end**   ⇨ **Running end**

FIGURE 39. In this variation of the trucker's hitch, we use a ring as our anchor point. Begin by tying a knot to secure the standing end to the anchor point. (a) Now wrap the running end twice around the standing end. (b) Leave a loop in the standing end. (c) With the running end in your left hand, form a second loop. Pass the loop in your left hand through the loop in the standing end, in your right hand. (d) Pull taut. (e) You will now be able to apply tension to the rope and secure it to a second anchor point.

3. Pass the running end of the rope that went around the tree through the bight and pull the running end toward the tree. You can now apply a lot of tension to the rope.

4. Complete the knot by forming a slippery half hitch (see Figure 39 on page 186) in the running end against the tip of the bight.

Clove Hitch

The clove hitch is another very useful knot that can be created anywhere along the middle part of the rope. Like any other good hitch, the knot will need to be cinched around an object to keep its form. Use a trekking pole to practice this knot.

1. Pass the running end around an anchor point (your trekking pole).

2. Pull the running end up, over the anchor point, to form an X across the standing end and the anchor point, pulling the running end down so that it's parallel to the standing end.

3. Lift the X part of the knot and slip the running end under this X vertically.

4. Pull the knot tight.

Now, you have two strands of rope that are firmly secured to an object. This knot is very useful when setting up a lean-to-style tarp.

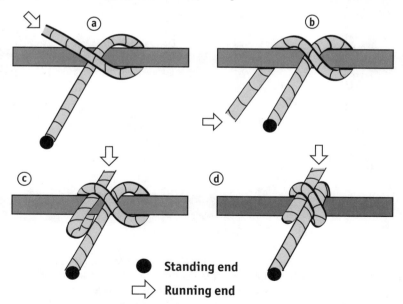

Standing end

Running end

FIGURE 40. To tie a clove hitch: (a) Pass the running end around an anchor point. (b) Using the running end, feed the rope down over the top of the anchor point so the running and standing ends are parallel. (c) Create an X then lift the X, passing the running end underneath it. (d) Pull the rope taut.

8

Taut Line Hitch

The taut line hitch is another very popular knot for setting up a shelter. A bit like the trucker's hitch, the taut line can create and sustain tension on a rope. Note that this hitch can loosen if tension is not maintained. To make the taut line hitch:

1. Pass the running end of the rope around an anchor point, such as a tent stake.

2. Coil the running end twice around the standing line, working back toward the tent stake.

3. Make one additional coil around the standing line on the outside of the coils you just made.

4. Pass the running end through the loop created on the outside of the coils. Tighten the knot and slide it on the standing line to adjust tension.

5. A great variation to this knot is to place a bight instead of the running end on the last coil. This gives you a slippery knot, allowing you to quickly undo the taut line hitch if needed.

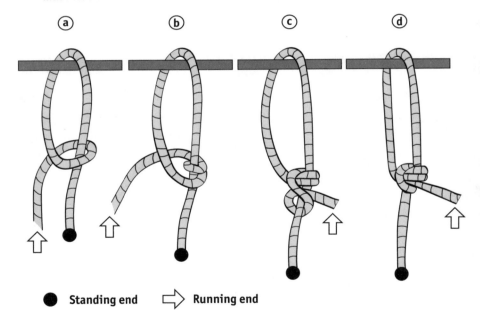

● **Standing end**   ⇨ **Running end**

FIGURE 41. To tie a taut line hitch: (a) Pass the running end around an anchor point and make a half hitch in the standing end. (b) Using the running end, make two coils around the standing end. (c) Now make an additional coil around the outside of the two previous coils and pass the running end through that outer coil. (d) Pull the running end taut.

BEND FAMILY
Square Knot

The square knot is the easiest knot to screw up. Many people trying to tie a square knot end up with a granny knot, which is quite different and quite useless. While the square will hold two ends of rope together, the granny knot will roll on itself and most likely come undone. The square is often used to tie cravats in first aid or to join two ropes or cords, such as when extending a rope for a shelter.

1. Hold the running ends of the same rope or the running ends of two different ropes, one in each hand, then cross them by placing the running end in your left hand over the running end in your right hand.

2. By doing the above, you will end up having to hold each running end with the opposite hand. Cross the running ends again, this time by placing the strand in your right hand over the strand in your left hand.

3. Pull the running ends away from each other. You have now tied a square knot. You will know your knot is correct when you see that both running ends are parallel to their respective standing ends.

To remember this knot, memorize this catch phrase: "Left over right and right over left."

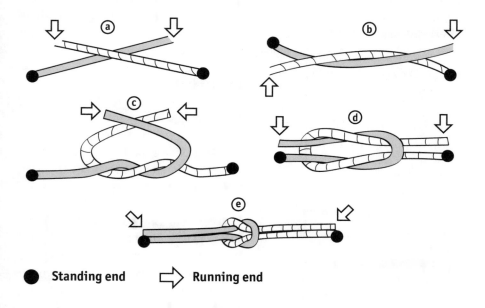

● **Standing end**   ⇨ **Running end**

FIGURE 42. You can use a square knot to join two ropes together. To tie a square knot: (a) Make an X with the two ropes. (b) Then cross them again. (c) Pull the running ends upward. (d) Feed the running ends back through each other. (e) Pull the ropes taut.

→ PITCHING A TENT

Setting up your home away from home is always exciting, but don't get distracted. Any poorly constructed shelter might not be so enjoyable when rain, wind, or snow comes hurtling down on you in the middle of the night. Today's self-standing tents come in many shapes, sizes, and options and are great—if set up properly. Use the following tips to set up your tent without damaging its parts.

- **Zippers.** Zippers are perhaps the most fragile components of a tent. Be careful with them. Always take the time to close all door zippers before pitching your tent so that you don't overstretch the tent walls when anchoring its corners. Over-stretching puts a lot of stress the door zippers in particular, leading to damage. Take the time to follow the zipper path when opening or closing a tent door or a tent screen. Pulling the zipper toggle sideways will damage the zipper's teeth. Finally, keep the zipper clean and lubricated. Avoid exposing your zippers to sand and dust, if possible. Adding a few drops of mineral oil to a zipper toggle will reduce the effects of natural wear and tear.

- **Poles.** Modern tent poles come in various configurations, but all brands now equip their poles with self-holding bungee cord systems. The only problem with these types of poles is that it's tempting to let them snap by themselves. This technique can damage the pole's joints, so avoid snapping the poles together under the force of the bungee cord. Instead, take the time to insert each pole carefully into the adjacent pole. This way you will set up your tent while avoiding potential chips, cracks, or breaks at the pole's joints.

- **Pegs.** Pegs or stakes are essential to pitching a tent. Even if the tent is self-standing, the pegs will anchor the tent floor, the fly, and the vestibule(s), if your tent has such a feature. Pegs come in various sizes, shapes, and weights. Regardless of these differences, all tent pegs must be installed the same way. Carefully push them into the ground at a 45-degree angle, with the top of the peg pointing away from the shelter. A final note: Always make sure the peg is placed with its hooks, or at least one of its hooks, facing away from the shelter. This way, the cordelette (paracord) or loop from the tent will be solidly anchored to the peg.

→ **PRO TIP** To avoid bending a peg when encountering tough soil, never kick the peg with your boot. Instead, use a medium-size rock to gently hammer the peg into the ground. Another trick we've been teaching for years is to use the sole of your boot to apply a gentle pressure on the end of the peg. By keeping the heel of your boot on the ground and aligning your foot and body in the direction you want the peg to travel, you will be able to push the peg into tough soil without damaging it. To retrieve a peg that is stubbornly anchored in the ground, use a piece of paracord to pull the peg out by slipping the cord around the peg's hook and pulling.

8

- **Floor.** The floor is perhaps the best part of any tent. A well set up tarp can serve you as well as any good tent, except when it comes to the floor. It is important to keep your tent's floor in top condition, so avoid sharp objects, such as twigs and rocks, while setting up your tent. We once had a student who placed a tent over a rock just by the entrance of the door. The rock had an edge-like top that sliced the tent floor like a pair a scissors. If needed, remove rocks, branches, pinecones, and any other removable object before setting up your tent floor. You can replace all of these objects upon your departure.

  You can also purchase a tent "footprint"—a piece of nylon that serves as a second layer for your tent floor—or you can make one yourself with a heavy-duty plastic sheet. This isn't a necessity; your tent will work fine without one. A footprint does add an additional layer of protection against sharp objects and water between your tent and the ground. If you use one to protect your tent from rain, make sure all corners of the footprint are tucked under the footprint itself. This will prevent water from pooling between the footprint and the tent body.

- **Fly.** The fly is often the most misunderstood and misused component of a camping tent. Too often inexperienced campers set up a tent, buckle down the fly before going to sleep, and then wake up in the morning wondering why their sleeping bags are wet. The issue here is that the fly trapped all of that warm air (sleepers' breathing, body heat) and moisture from the tent and turned it into condensation. Air warmed up inside the tent will not escape as easily with a fly. But the bigger problem is that people think that a tent must have a fly to work. Actually, a tent only needs a fly when it is raining, snowing, very windy, or on cold evenings as an insulation.

  If the night sky is clear and the weather forecast is good, it is appropriate to set up only the body of the tent and enjoy a great night under the stars while still protected from hungry mosquitoes. If the sky is uncertain, attach two corners of the fly and roll it only halfway over the tent body. This way you can enjoy the night sky while being ready for a quick adjustment if the fair weather changes on you. If the weather is obviously leaning toward rain, hail, or lightning, you will need to anchor the tent fly down. Here are a few tips to make sure your fly keeps you dry:

1. Make sure the fly zippers are closed before attaching the fly to your tent poles. This will avoid potential problems with your fly's door zippers.

2. If the fly anchor points have adjustable straps, make sure that all the straps are loosened before installing the fly. By doing this, you will be able to properly center the fly over the tent body. Once this is done, you can tighten each adjustable strap.

3. Tighten the adjustable straps until the fly is covering all sides and corners of the tent floor.

8

4.   Use guide ropes to pull the fly away from the tent wall. This will increase the air flow between the tent and the fly, which will keep your tent drier.

5.   If possible, keep part of the tent vestibule door open to increase air flow and avoid tent condensation. Once a storm has passed, fully open the vestibule door or doors to allow better air flow.

TARPS

Tarps are one of the most versatile and useful pieces of equipment you can carry in your pack. Even if you have a tent as a shelter, a small, light tarp can significantly improve your camping experience in good or bad weather. A 9-by-6-foot tarp made of silicone-impregnated nylon (Silnylon) weighs only 1 pound and is easy to pack away.

You can use a small tarp to build a sheltered area for cooking or a dry garage for your equipment. You can even use it to extend the vestibule of your tent, giving you a dry, shaded area to relax in or to enter and exit without immediately being exposed to the elements. Some hikers will even use a tarp as a shelter before or after bug season. This option allows them to shelter themselves comfortably while drastically reducing their pack weight. Many wilderness expeditions we have led have included a few group-size tarps (9 by 12 feet) and bivies for all. This equipment combination can be used even in the worst weather conditions.

Tarp kits should come with their own set of pegs (stakes) and light cord. They can be set up in various configurations for different purposes. Here are a few of the most popular tarp setups:

- **A-frame.** The A-frame is a useful design for a sleeping tarp. Make sure you tie the ridgeline high enough so that you don't end up with a tarp so low it becomes difficult to crawl in or out of.

- **Lean-to.** The lean-to tarp is ideal for a kitchen. The back wall can reach the ground if you need to create a windless shelter. To do this, simply set up the back wall of the lean-to facing the dominant wind direction. Use clove hitches to tie the corner cords to trekking poles or wooden poles. This way the cord will stay firmly attached to the tops of the poles.

- **Flat top.** This setup provides excellent shade and dry space. If it's raining, just make sure you set up the tarp at a slanted angle to channel the rain.

- **Pyramid**. Some tarps come with an anchor point at the middle of the ridgeline. If your tarp has this feature, setting up the tarp in a pyramid shape will provide maximum shade and rain protection.

Whichever tarp design you choose to pitch, remember to use the bowline to anchor one side of the ridgeline and the trucker's hitch to create tension on the ridgeline and corners. One last tip about tarp setup: Make sure you extend the anchor cord at a 45-degree angle at the corners of the tarp. This way the tension you apply to the corner will be evenly distributed along the tarp wall.

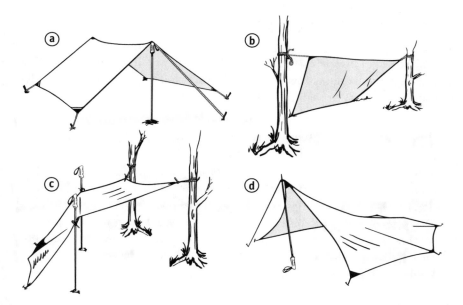

FIGURE 43. Methods of pitching tarps include: (a) the A-frame, useful for sleeping; (b) the lean-to, handy for camp kitchens; (c) the flat top, for shade and dryness; and (d) the pyramid, which uses an anchor point for even better shade and rain protection.

SLEEPING UNDER THE STARS

When the night is clear, the bugs are absent, and the constellations are shining, there is nothing better than sleeping under the stars. If you select the perfect spot to lie down in your bivy, you can sleep under the stars any night when the weather forecast is favorable.

To avoid an excessive amount of morning dew on your bivouac, avoid laying your bedding in grassy meadows. The best option is to select a dry forest floor, such as pine needles or dry leaves. You can also stay dryer if you lie on flat bedrock or—strangely enough—under a thin canopy of trees. You might not see the stars but you will wake up with a dry sleeping bag in the morning. If you use a bivy, you can sleep in a flowering meadow, as long as you are fine with having to dry your bivy in the morning. Here are a few tips on how to best use your bivy.

1. If your bivy has a waterproof bottom layer, place your sleeping pad and sleeping bag inside your bivy. This way you won't risk sliding off your sleeping pad.

2. Similar to with a tent, you'll want to increase air flow in your bivy, so do not zip it shut, if possible. Most importantly, do not tuck your head inside and breathe in your bivy all night long. Doing so is a sure way to get your sleeping bag wet.

8

SETTING UP A TENT IN THE RAIN

If you spend any amount of time camping in the mountains you will encounter rain, from a light drizzle to a heavy downpour. When setting up camp in these conditions, it is important to avoid getting the walls and floor or your tent wet. Here are some tips on how to deal with camp setup when it is raining.

1. First, don't set up your tent in the rain if it can be avoided; wait for the weather to get better before exposing your tent to the elements. A better choice would be to set up a tarp, if you have one, or to tuck yourself under a natural shelter, such as a large tree or a rock overhang, and wait out the rain. These are safe, dry spots if there is no chance of lightning. If there is lightning, avoid standing under large, tall trees or shallow rock overhangs. Any large structure, manufactured or natural, will attract lightning, so look for low, dry areas. Stay away from water and remember that mountaintops also attract lightning strikes, so if you are on a ridge, get to lower elevation immediately. The safest place to be during a lightning storm (if you can make it there) is in a car with the windows rolled up. For more information on lightning safety see "Lightning" in Chapter 1, page 24.

2. If you do have a tarp, you can set it up over the site where you'll set up your tent. Once the tarp is up, you can set up your tent under the tarp and avoid getting the walls and the floor of the tent wet.

3. If you do not have a tarp and must set up your tent in a downpour, it is wise to first set up your tent fly. Most modern, freestanding tents will allow you to set up the tent fly without having set up the tent body. Once you have the fly up, you'll be able to crawl under the fly and set up your tent from the inside. Note: This technique works only with tents that have clip-on attachment points to the poles. Tents with long sleeves for the poles won't allow you to set up the tent once the poles are holding up the tent fly.

8

SLEEPING WARMLY AND COMFORTABLY

Having a great shelter is the first step toward ensuring a good night's sleep on the trail, but the shelter alone is not enough. There are a few important concepts to understand to help you sleep warmly and comfortably.

The first concept is that sleeping bags are like thermoses: they insulate what is inside them from changing temperature. If a cold liquid is placed inside a thermos, it will remain cold, even on a hot summer day; similarly, if a hot liquid is placed inside a thermos, it will remain hot, even on a cold winter day. Sleeping bags operate the same way. If you go to bed cold, you will have a hard time getting warm in your sleep. It is very important that you feel warm and toasty before slipping inside your sleeping bag. If you need to, elevate your body temperature through exercise. A few jumping jacks or sit-ups should do the trick.

The second concept is that your body can create its own heat—we are warm-blooded mammals, after all—if it has fuel to burn. It is important to eat some food just before going to bed. This way your body will burn calories and produce heat. Being well hydrated is also essential to effective caloric burn.

The third concept in the science of sleeping warm is thermodynamics. If your sleeping bag is too large for your body, you will lose body heat (entropy) until the inside of the sleeping bag is as warm as your body (thermodynamic equilibrium). The problem is that sleeping bags are not a fully closed system. They also lose heat to their surrounding environment, so if you spend a lot of energy warming up a large empty space in your sleeping

→ **PRO TIP** Since we rarely have the luxury of bringing a dozen pairs of socks on our wilderness outings, it is essential to keep the few socks we have dry and clean. But you can use your body heat to dry your socks at night. Place the socks you've been wearing during the day (they will most likely be a little moist) inside your pants or long underwear, on each side of your groin. This way your femoral arteries and the warm blood they carry will slowly dry your socks while you sleep. If you do this, you will effectively turn your body into a human dryer. You can also try drying clothing items, such as socks and underwear you may have washed, by sandwiching them between your sleeping bag and sleeping pad while you sleep on top of them.

bag, you risk the chance of heat leaving you at a faster rate than your body can produce it. You will sleep warmer if you are in a snug and tight sleeping bag—hence the importance of selecting the right sleeping bag size. If you feel your sleeping bag is too big for you, you can always stuff the free space around your body with spare, dry clothing. You will find personal tricks to help you sleep warmly and comfortably, but here are a few that always work:

1. Open your sleeping bag only when you are ready to go to bed. There's no need to open your bag as soon as you arrive in camp. Opening your bag too soon could expose it to moisture if the conditions are damp.

2. Wear a warm hat—or better, a balaclava—to sleep but make sure your nostrils and mouth are uncovered.

3. Wrap your feet in the sleeves of your warmest jacket and tuck the whole bundle at the bottom of your sleeping bag.

4. Empty your bladder just before going to bed.

5. Put some warm water in a water bottle and place it at your feet or between your legs in your sleeping bag.

8

6. To avoid frozen or cold boots in the morning, place your hiking boots inside your sleeping bag stuff sack and place that inside your sleeping bag, under your knees.

7. Keep water near you so you can hydrate during the night as needed.

8. Finally, if you are cold and cannot warm up by yourself, wake up your camping partners and ask them to help. They could make you food or get you water. Getting out of your sleeping bag will lose any heat you've managed to build up.

→ BEST BEAR CAMPING PRACTICES

Although we have a combined 50 years of camping experience, we have never encountered a problematic bear in all of our outdoor excursions. We like to attribute our success to simple but effective bear camping practices—and a great deal of luck. We can't help you with the latter, but we can share the former. First, you have to understand that bears are not interested in human activities. They are great opportunists, however, and if food is easily accessible, like Yogi Bear, they will go for the easy meal (e.g., your picnic basket).

Second, we need to make a paradigm shift and understand that we do not use bearproof techniques to protect our food from bears but instead to protect the bears from our food. Bears that feed on campers' food become habituated bears, and habituated bears often become problem bears. Unfortunately, problem bears can be dangerous for campers, which ultimately leads to a bear's relocation or euthanasia.

Here are a few of the best bear camping practices:

1. Keep your camp kitchen free of food waste, including microwaste.

2. Never keep any food or food packaging in your pack, pockets, or tent at night.

3. Put away all attractive "smellables" (all food and any scented items) in your bearproof system.

4. Keep food storage and your camp kitchen away from your sleeping area.

CAMPSITE SETUP

A good camping practice in bear country is to set up your camp kitchen about 100 yards from your sleeping area and then set up your bearproof system another 100 yards away from your camp kitchen and your sleeping area. Ideally, these three locations should be configured in a triangle, with the food storage area placed downwind so any smells caught by a bear will not lead it to travel through your sleeping area when following its hypersensitive nose. The reality is that you will often have to do the best with what you have. So keep the triangle in mind but do not lose time or sleep over it. What is crucial is that your camp kitchen and your food storage areas are far from your shelter.

BEARPROOF SYSTEMS

There are a few options when it comes to selecting a bearproof system. One is the classic bear hang: using a rope to hang a food bag away from a potentially curious bear. Increasingly popular and sometimes required by public land agencies is the bear canister, a bin in which all food items are placed. A new system to protect your food and the bear is the portable, electric antibear fence.

Bear Hangs

Bear hangs are fun to build but can also be frustrating and time-consuming. Too often we find old bear-hang ropes stuck in trees. We've also encountered flying rocks in the forest when campers tie a stone to a rope and attempt to toss their contraption over a tree branch, only to see it fly off the improvised knot and come crashing dangerously into the least expected locations. One solution we have found to avoid these problems is to use a system we call the bison ball.

Bison Ball (used for bear hangs)

The bison ball is a rope system that allows you to build a bearproof food-hang system without the inconvenience of throwing ropes over branches or exposing yourself to flying rocks. Here's how to build and use your own.

Materials
- 25 feet of 3mm (1/8-inch) cordelette (a.k.a. parachute cord or p-cord)
- 1 tennis ball
- 1 flat washer (1/4-inch hole)

Assembly
1. Cut a 1-inch slice in the wall of the tennis ball with a utility knife.

2. Cut a second 1-inch slice in the ball, perpendicular to the first cut, to make two crossed cuts.

3. Tie two overhand knots near the end of the rope, feed the tip of the cordelette through the flat washer, and tie two other overhand knots. The goal here is to have the washer held in place by the knots at the end of the cordelette.

4. Insert the washer and knots into the tennis ball through the slices you made.

5. Test the bison ball by pulling on the cordelette while firmly holding the tennis ball. If it is built properly, the washer and knots should pop out after you apply a moderate amount of tension on the cordelette.

How to Use Your Bison Ball
1. Find a tree with a strong branch reaching out. With experience, you will discover that mature trees on the edge of a sun well (a clearing in the forest canopy) provide many strong extending branches.

8

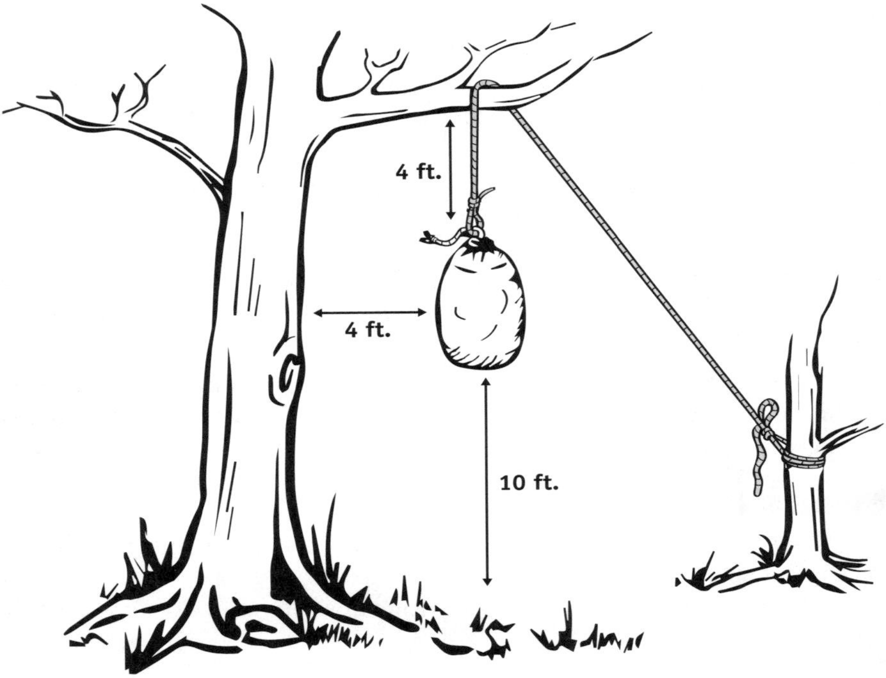

FIGURE 44. A traditional bear hang keeps food at least 10 feet off the ground and at least 4 feet in all directions from any trunks or branches

2. Make sure the branch you select will allow you to place your food bag at least 10 feet away from the ground, 4 feet away from the trunk of any trees, and 4 feet below the branch supporting the food bag.

3. Before throwing the bison ball over the branch, take the time to weigh the ball by removing the cordelette and filling the ball with ready materials, such as sand, small pebbles, or even water. A heavier bison ball will be easier to throw and easier to lower down via flicking the cordelette. Empty the ball afterward to reduce your pack weight—there's no need to carry a tennis ball full of sand when you can find more sand to weigh your bison ball at the next campsite.

4. Throw the bison ball over the branch. You can use an underhand or overhand throw but just make sure you have the rope coiled properly in your other hand, allowing a smooth delivery of the cordelette once you've thrown the ball. Be patient, as it might take you more than one throw to be successful.

5. Once you've successfully thrown the ball over the branch at the right position, flick the rope to slowly bring down the weighted bison ball.

6. Once the ball is reachable, pull the cordelette over the branch until the other end is just above the ground.

7. Now you can attach your food bag with all of your smellables. Hoist the bag up until the bottom of the bag is at least 10 feet above the ground and the top of the bag is 4 feet below the branch. Tie off the rope to the trunk of the tree or sturdy branch.

Bear Canisters

Bear-resistant canisters are becoming widely available throughout the Northeast for purchase and rental. They are very effective against all kinds of marauders, even for habituated bears. They are so effective, in fact, that they are required equipment for backcountry camping in large sections of New York's Adirondack State Park. The canister is typically a hard plastic cylinder, 8 inches wide and 12 inches high, with a locking lid that bears have yet to master. It weighs about 3 to 5 pounds empty and can hold up to five days' worth of food. You simply fill it up, close it securely, and place it 100 yards from your camp kitchen and sleeping area. No need to spend time looking for the ideal tree, wishing you had learned to play outfield or to manage ropes on a sailboat. It takes some practice to pack one well and fit it comfortably into your pack, but they are effective. They're especially useful in areas where bears have been habituated or where large trees with suitable branches are rare or nonexistent. Approved canisters cost about $70, but they are usually available for rental in towns adjacent to common backcountry areas. If you know you are heading to a location that requires or recommends canister use, be sure to research the availability of rentals before heading out.

Electric Antibear Fence

Although this option is not for everyone as it does involve a small shock to the bear (though nothing harmful), it is an effective deterrent for even the most habituated bears. While not yet prevalent in the camping community, its advantages over the other bearproof systems are noteworthy. Electric antibear fences are basic livestock electric fences that use a portable, battery-operated energizer to deliver a significant electrical shock. The system we have been using at New Hampshire's Plymouth State University (PSU) works with two D-cell batteries that deliver 0.04 joule, or about 2.5 electron volts. If these numbers do not mean anything to you, you should be aware that the shock experienced when touching the fence with only one finger when grounded to the soil is great enough to make you jump. Electric systems are not in conflict with state or federal wilderness regulations, but they will not be acceptable in locations where a bear-resistant canister is required.

8

Studies with grizzly bears at the National Outdoor Leadership School have proven not only that these antibear fences are effective at protecting the food placed inside their perimeters, but that they also provide a negative reinforcement for bears. Sooner or later, a bear will associate these contraptions with a discomfort not worth experiencing, even if the smell of nearby food is tantalizing. You can purchase premade kits for antibear fences, and you can also put them together yourself. Most of the equipment you will need (poles, insulation, fence, connectors) can be found at any good farm supply store. Battery-operated energizers are available online. The energizer we have been using at PSU for years is the Speedrite AN20 Battery Fence Energizer. Note: Set up correctly, an electric fence will deter even the most habituated bears, but they are not at all effective against smaller creatures such as mice, squirrels, or birds.

PROTECTING FOOD FROM SMALLER ANIMALS

The food we bring with us into the backcountry is just as delicious for many animals as it is for us. Bears, raccoons, squirrels, and mice will all show an interest in our food bags, as will birds, such as gray jays and ravens. Other scented items, such as toothpaste and sunscreen, also attract animals, as will any garbage we generate while camping. If we want to keep our food for ourselves, and also keep wildlife healthy, we have to find a way to prevent these animals from eating it up. Fortunately, this usually isn't hard to accomplish, depending on how much food weight a group has to manage.

Lightweight Toss-Rope

For smaller groups on shorter trips, the food weight will not be large. Let's imagine each person has 2 pounds of food per day (generous), with two people out for three days. That's 12 pounds of food that needs to be protected (plus additional scented toiletries and garbage). This amount of weight can be managed with the simplest of approaches: a lightweight length of cord tossed over a tree branch. Parachute cord (p-cord) is adequate for this task. Since the lowest acceptable branch is at least 10 feet high, the p-cord must be double that, plus some extra length to reach a tie-off. Forty feet of p-cord won't add much weight to your pack and will do the job.

Advanced Rope System

Once the food weight reaches 25 pounds or more (not uncommon with larger groups or longer trips), it is time to develop a better rope-based haul system. An advanced version of a haul system uses the same 40-foot section of p-cord for the simple toss-rope, then adds two stouter 30-foot ropes (8mm is fine) and a pair of carabiners. With this equipment you can create a haul system that gives you a mechanical lifting advantage, and saves wear and tear on the branch's bark. For the heaviest expedition loads (more than 50 pounds), it is a real advantage to add a couple of lightweight rescue pulleys. This total package may add a little weight, but if you are carrying that much food, it's likely you have several people to share the load, and you might even find additional uses for the ropes (e.g., using them as fixed lines for short roping on a steep and slippery section of trail).

8

➜ LIGHTING A CAMPFIRE

5 One of the essential outdoor skills to master is the ability to easily light and maintain a campfire. Although many people manage to produce flames, this does not mean that they can build and start an effective campfire. But as we'll discuss in Chapter 9, stoves are the most LNT-friendly method of cooking in the backcountry and should be used wherever possible. Lighting a campfire should be done only in areas that permit fires or as a last resort in the wilderness. There are some essential principles you should understand and apply before you can build a good campfire.

FIRE PRINCIPLES

To create fire, you will need three essential elements: a heat source, appropriate fuel, and oxygen. The mix of these three elements in the appropriate ratio will create an effective campfire.

Your initial source of heat could range from a windproof lighter to waterproof matches to a simple ferrocerium rod (a.k.a. a "fire striker"). Obviously, the easiest tool in this category is the lighter, and especially the windproof lighter, which is basically a little torch. Matches, even the waterproof types, require skill. You might want to practice refining your striking technique before going out on the trail. Fire strikers are very reliable and impervious to moisture, but they are the most challenging to use. If you adopt this method as your primary source of heat, make sure you have plenty of practice time before attempting to use one on your next trip.

FUEL

When we talk about "fuel" in the context of a campfire, we are talking about natural tinder, kindling, and wood—not charcoal briquettes. Proper fuel selection accounts for perhaps 80 percent of a campfire's success, so take the time to gather good material for your tinder, your kindling, and your wood.

8

- **Tinder.** For your tinder, you have many choices. You can bring special tinder from home, such as waxed cotton balls, but a long piece of jute string or rope is a more eco-friendly choice. Jute is a natural fiber and, if prepared properly, it will easily ignite when exposed to flame or even a spark. To turn your jute into highly flammable tinder, simply cut a short piece, 2 to 3 inches, then separate the three strands of the fiber and pull the center of each strand sideways to loosen the microfibers. Your goal is to make a fluffy ball of jute. You can use this as tinder to start your fire.

  Other natural forms of tinder are paper birch bark, as well as the thinner bark of the yellow birch. Bark from the paper birch is waterproof, and many American Indian tribes use it to build canoes. Even if the paper birch bark you find on the ground is wet, you can peel off the outer layers to reach dryer layers underneath.

FIGURE 45. Don't be lazy when it comes to preparing tinder. For good tinder: (a) Repeatedly shave one end of a downed twig; (b) thereby creating lots of curls that will easily ignite. Examples of poor tinder include: (c) thicker, less delicate shavings; and (d) short, stumpy shavings that won't ignite as easily or burn as long.

- **Kindling.** Kindling is far more important than the larger pieces of wood you will gather to make your fire. Properly electing and preparing your kindling will often determine the success or failure of your fire. Some of the best kindling in the Northeast comes from the small, dry branches of the eastern hemlock tree. You can find these trees at lower altitudes, where it will be safe to make a fire. The dry branches of the eastern hemlock provide perfect kindling because they are very small in diameter and are often found dry at the bases of hemlock trees. If wet, they are easy to dry by placing them inside a jacket, where they will dry from your body heat.

  If you collect a large quantity of these tiny branches, enough to create a bundle the size of a small saucer, you will have excellent kindling. If eastern hemlock is not present in your hiking region, you can substitute balsam fir, or red or black spruce branches. Make sure any branches you collect for tinder are without needles. If they have needles, you will mostly make smoke when lighting your tinder.

- **Wood**. When it comes to gathering wood, all you have to remember are the five D's: down, dead, dry, digit, and distant.

  1. **Down.** Collect only wood on the ground. Do not break branches from standing or downed trees.

2. **Dead.** Use dead wood for your fire. It will burn much better than any green, punk, or rotting wood. To know if a piece of wood is dry enough for burning, simply bend the wood until it breaks. If it breaks with a snap, it is dry; if it bends and does not break easily, it is too green to be used in your fire.

3. **Dry.** Dry, dead, downed wood is better than any wet wood. If it has been raining, look near the bases of large trees with full foliage, as you will have a greater chance of finding dry wood there. If all of the wood on the ground is wet, you might need to prepare your wood before burning it. Shaving wet wood with a knife will allow you to expose a wet branch's dry interior.

4. **Digit.** "Digit" means that, as an LNT practice, you should only collect and use firewood that's about the size of your largest finger—in other words, no branches thicker than your thumb.

5. **Distance.** The final D reminds you to always collect firewood away from your campsite or cooking site. This is especially true when you are staying at a popular campsite. You will soon discover that the firewood supply on the ground at popular campsites is very low due to heavy use. Take a walk when collecting wood. It will reduce the impact on your campsite.

■ **Oxygen.** Just as oxygen is necessary for you, it's necessary for a fire. No fire could exist without oxygen. You need to plan for the oxygenation of your fire, either through proper construction or by adding supplemental oxygen (fanning; details below) when needed.

LEAN-TO FIRE

One effective way to build your fire is to use the lean-to shelter method. The lean-to method will provide proper oxygenation to your fire and will easily ignite your kindling. To build a lean-to fire, follow these steps:

1. Place two pieces of wood (each the size of your thumb) parallel to each other at the center of the fire ring.

2. Use another thumb-size piece of wood to bridge the first two pieces. This bridge should connect the ends of the first two pieces.

3. Take your bundle of kindling and fold it in half to increase its density, then lean it on top of the piece of wood bridging the first two pieces.

4. Cover the sides of the bundle with pinky-finger-size pieces of wood.

5. Place your tinder under the entrance of the lean-to. Locate it so that you can easily access it to light it.

6. Light the tinder with your source of heat: a lighter, match, or fire striker.

8

FIGURE 46. To create a lean-to fire: (a) Plant a large, downed branch in the soil to stabilize your fire; (b) build a frame using thumb-size downed branches, fold your bundle of kindling in half to increase its density, and cover your frame with pinky-size downed twigs; (c) continue adding twigs until the kindling is protected on three sides, leaving one side accessible.

If you have built a good lean-to fire, your tinder should easily catch on fire and quickly ignite your kindling. Once your kindling is burning, the larger pieces of wood will begin to catch fire. If you keep adding larger pieces of wood on top of your lean-to, you will soon have an effective and enjoyable campfire.

As the fire burns, you'll occasionally add new pieces of wood, which might require you to increase the oxygen intake. A good way to do this is to use a pot lid. Fan the lid near the fire at a fast pace to start, then when the flames have increased in size, reduce the cadence of your fanning motion. You'll know your fire is getting the right amount of oxygen when the flames jump from the coals to larger pieces of wood. This technique is often safer than the classic "put your face near the fire and blow hard." We have seen too many campers who blow on fire to reoxygenate the flames end up with smoke in their eyes, or lightheaded from huffing and puffing too much for too long. Try fanning instead.

MAKING A FIRE IN WET CONDITIONS

Making a campfire in the rain or after a long, rainy day is a challenge—even for the experienced camper. Don't get frustrated and give up. There are ways to make a fire in the rain or when the forest is soaking wet. If it is raining, first build a lean-to shelter with a tarp. If you can site the tarp or the fire near the edge of the lean-to, you'll be able to protect yourself and the material you've collected from getting wet.

Since the wood you've collected is not dry, you will have to find ways to dry it. Look for material under trees with large and dense canopies. Remember, you can place small hemlock branches inside your rain jacket, near your inner layers, and use your body as a kiln. It's good to collect your kindling first and let it dry in your jacket while you are collecting and preparing the rest of your wood. If you have a good knife, use it to split open the small braches you have found. You can also use your knife to create deep notches along the pieces of wet wood. Again, paper birch bark is great if you take the time to peel off the outer layers.

Finally, making a fire in wet conditions will require more work and maintenance. You will have to spend more time preparing your wood before lighting it. You will have to constantly dry bigger pieces of wood by placing them around the fire, where the heat from the flames will slowly dry them. Maintaining your fire in wet conditions will also require you to keep adding small, kindling-size wood to your fire, so make sure you have a large amount of kindling before starting your fire. Last, plan ahead and put away dry wood in a dry location before it rains. Preparing for the worst will save you a lot of work.

LNT FIRE TECHNIQUES

Obviously, the best way to minimize the impact of campfires is not to build them in the first place. There are times and situations, however, when a fire is essential. If a legal fire ring is already present at a campsite and there is a large amount of firewood in the area, making a fire is just part of the human experience. Enjoy what our ancestors have enjoyed for thousands of years. If you are camping in a pristine campsite, or if your campsite does not have a campfire ring but it is legal for you to make a fire, using what we call an LNT technique to make your fire is the best option. There are two LNT fire techniques: the mound fire and the fire pan.

Mound Fire

The mound fire technique requires you to build a mound—or really, more like a mesa, with a flat top—of mineral soil over a blanket. This technique is simple but time-consuming to set up, so again, plan ahead. The steps for building a mound fire are as follows:

1. Because you planned ahead, you will have a piece of cloth measuring 3 feet by 3 feet. The best material we have found for this layer is a camp-kitchen fire blanket, which is made of fire-resistant fibers.

2. Lay this cloth on the flat surface where you want to build your fire. This brings up one advantage of the mound fire: You can build it almost anywhere.

3. Collect mineral soil—sand, gravel, dirt—that has no organic material (earthworms, roots, leaves). You will need a large quantity, so get ready to work. Your stuff sack turned inside out makes a good container for this material. You will find exposed mineral soil on river and stream banks, in the holes of uprooted fallen trees, or in the banks of trails cutting a slope.

4. Build a mesa on top of the cloth using your mineral soil. You will need to build up this flat-top mound until it's about 2.5 feet in diameter with a minimum

FIGURE 47. The LNT-friendly mound fire consists of three components, from bottom to top: fire-resistant cloth; mineral soil shaped into a mesa; and a lean-to or other fire-starting method.

height of 6 inches. If you build a thinner mesa, the heat from the fire will impact your cloth and the soil underneath it.

5.   Build your fire on top, in the center of your mesa.

To clean up after your mound fire, make sure you burn all wood and coals to ash, put out the campfire completely by dousing the ashes with water, and scatter the damp ashes in the woods. Return the mineral soil to where you collected it and clean up the area where you laid the ground cloth.

Fire Pan

This method is much easier than building a mound fire. All you have to do is plan to carry with you a deep and lightweight metal pan. Oil pans or barn animal feed pans are great; just be sure to bring a cloth envelope, such as an old pillowcase, to avoid dirtying your backpack with charcoal smudge. (Don't use a plastic bag, which dirty or hot pans can stick to or melt.)

To be safe and effective, the pan should measure between 15 and 20 inches in diameter with a side wall of at least 3 inches. Use your fire pan as follows.

1.   Find a desirable and flat surface for the fire pan.

2.   Lay the fire pan on medium-size rocks so the pan does not touch the ground. The bottom of the pan should be at least 4 inches above the ground. If your pan is closer to the ground or is lying flat on dirt, the heat of the fire will travel though the floor of the pan and burn the ground.

3.   Build your fire at the center of the pan.

FIGURE 48. Also LNT-friendly, the fire-pan method (above) is easier to build than the mound fire but requires you to carry a pan.

To clean your fire pan, make sure you burn all wood and coals to ash, put out the campfire completely by dousing the ashes with water, and scatter the damp ashes in the woods. Return the rocks to where you found them and put away your pan when it is cold and safe to touch.

→ BEING A GOOD NEIGHBOR

If you choose to visit a popular location in the wild, you're bound to encounter other nature lovers. You'll notice hikers and backpackers are often friendlier than strangers in an urban environment. It seems less out of place to say hello and strike up a short conversation with strangers when we encounter them on a trail or in a campsite. This seems to be even truer the farther away you are from the trailhead. Perhaps it's unspoken mutual respect among hikers who have experienced similar challenges to get so far away from civilization and comfort—a kind of camaraderie genuinely shared among outdoors people.

Even so, we must remember that many of us go to the forests, mountains, and lakes to escape our daily routine, to avoid overcrowded streets and highways, and to get away from everyone else. Seeking solitude or a few quiet days with close friends or family is often one of the main reasons to go camping. With this in mind, it's not surprising that the Leave No Trace principles include recommendations for interacting with other visitors we encounter in the wild. "Respect other users," our LNT code of ethics tells us—a good rule to live by.

How do we respect our neighbors on the trail and at our campsite? Here are a few dos and don'ts for camping etiquette:

1. Be polite and offer a friendly greeting when encountering fellow hikers on the trail, when you arrive in camp, or when someone is moving in next to your campsite.

2. If appropriate, introduce yourself and exchange any valuable data about the trail or the area. Don't force a conversation when your fellow campers are obviously tired or give you the impression they wish they were alone in this area.

3. Keep your noise level to a minimum on the trail and in camp. Although it's tempting to play music through a smartphone or lightweight speakers, it's more appropriate to use headphones to listen to music in the wild.

4. Avoid having a big bonfire with loud sing-alongs unless everyone in camp is up for it. If you are camping over the Fourth of July, do not give in to the temptation to bring fireworks or sparklers. Look at the stars, the biggest fireworks in the galaxy.

5. If you're camping at a shelter and yours is the first party to arrive in camp, make sure you do not take up the entire shelter. Leave some floor space for potential sheltermates. Most important, do not set up your tent inside a shelter. It will send all of the wrong messages to your fellow hikers.

6. Public latrines are just that—public. Don't hog them in the morning. Take the time you need but don't bring reading material with you to the outhouse. Use the latrine according to the posted instructions—for example, close the lid before leaving—and clean up after yourself.

8

CHAPTER 9
COOKING SKILLS

Food can make or break an outdoor expedition. Fail to bring enough, and people will go hungry, lack energy, and be very moody. Bring too much, and your companions will suffer and complain about the weight of their packs. Bring the wrong type of food, and the two previous scenarios will both occur. Taking the time to carefully plan your expedition meals is essential.

In this chapter, you'll learn how to set up a camp kitchen, as well as ways to preserve and transport your food, and we'll review the basic principles of good nutrition. You will also learn how energy intake affects hikers, who torch more calories than the average person. You'll explore two approaches to food planning, learn how to package your food, and glean some ideas about the types of foods that are ideal for breakfast, lunch, snacks, and dinners on the trail.

→ SETTING UP YOUR CAMP KITCHEN FOR SAFETY AND EFFICIENCY

Unless you are camping at an improved campsite with the luxury of a picnic table, you will most likely be setting up your camp kitchen directly on the ground. This presents many challenges, from hygiene to safety, but planning and knowledge will help you meet those obstacles.

CAMP KITCHEN SITE SELECTION

Selecting the proper kitchen area is perhaps one of the most important decisions you will make when choosing a campsite. The kitchen area will experience the greatest amount of trampling, much more than your shelter area. To that end, it is a good LNT practice to seek flat and durable surfaces for your kitchen. Examples of durable surfaces for outdoor kitchens include exposed, flat bedrock; a grassy patch; a sandy beach; a gravel bar; or a forest floor with pine needles. Remember that your outdoor kitchen should not be next to your shelter. It should be at least 200 feet from naturally occurring water sources, and it should be far enough from any trails that it's not intrusive to other hikers.

ORGANIZATION

To keep your kitchen clean and effective, an organized system is essential. You'll realize quickly that as soon as you're sitting on the ground near your stove, you'll want to remain there and not spend your time retrieving items you've left in your pack. Take the time to pull out all of your kitchen-related items and organize them around your stove so they're within reach. Before you start cooking, retrieve all of the food items you'll need for that meal from your bearproof system. You'll also want access to plenty of water—hence the use of a water carrier, such as a collapsible water bladder.

Being organized also means having in mind the sequence of steps you'll take to prepare a meal. If you are only rehydrating a meal, the first step will be to boil some water. But if you are cooking something more involved, you'll want to account for the number of pots you'll need and the sequence in which the foods will be cooked. Experience is your best teacher for developing this skill, but we do have some tips on how to stay organized around an outdoor kitchen.

1.   Never put a lid on the ground that had been covering a cooking pot without taking the time to flip it over. Rest it on the dry side of the lid and not the wet side.

2.   Never place your cooking utensils on the ground; always put them in a clean bowl or on a clean lid.

3.   If you open a food bag to pour an ingredient, take the time to roll back the edge of the bag; that way, you will not get the top of the bag dirty.

4.   If you open a food bag to use an ingredient, close it as soon as possible. Don't leave it open, waiting to be spilled or get wet. The same can be said for all spice bottles: recap them after use.

5.   When chopping food, place the cutting board on the ground to reduce the possibility of cutting yourself.

6.   Never let someone walk over your kitchen. You will avoid many unpleasant events, such as spilling a pot of food or kicking dirt onto your dishes.

SAFETY

Outdoor kitchens are areas with high injury potential. We're often more concerned about our students' safety in the kitchen than on the trail. For instance, when using a camping stove on the ground, never straddle the stove with your legs. The last thing you want is to spread your legs on either side of a hot stove with a boiling pot of water on top. Instead, get in the habit of sitting parallel to the stove or, better, kneeling down or squatting on a small insulated pad. That way you can be more comfortable while also staying ready to move away quickly, if needed. Try to avoid sitting cross-legged in front of the stove, since this position is harder to move out of quickly if a pot spills. And, when handling hot pots or pans, always use a pot grip to avoid burning your fingers.

If you are using a white-gas stove with a priming phase, make sure not to spill liquid fuel on the ground when you open the valve to fill the priming cup. If you have to refuel during the course of a meal, take the time to shut down your stove and refuel away from your kitchen site. That way, you'll avoid any fuel-to-food contamination or a potential ground fire if you spill any fuel. And we want to emphasize that there should be no walking, stepping, or jumping over the kitchen area. Ask your group members to walk around it for their and your own safety.

CAMPFIRE

Again, we stress that cooking over campfires should be avoided in any area where fires are not permitted or where fire rings are absent. Below are LNT and U.S. Forest Service recommendations for how to make fires with the least amount of environmental impact:

- Do not build a campfire in hazardous or dry conditions. Campfires can cause a lasting impact on the environment. Where fires are permitted, use existing fire rings and keep them small.

- Use only sticks from the ground that can be broken by hand. Burn all wood and coals to ash, put out campfires completely and douse the ashes with water, and scatter the damp ashes.

- If there is no existing fire pit but pits are allowed, choose a site at least 15 feet from tent walls, shrubs, trees, or other flammable objects. Beware of low-hanging branches. Choose an open, level location away from heavy fuels, such as logs, brush, or decaying leaves.

- Take wind, and its direction, into account when choosing the site. Find a spot that's protected from gusts.

- Clear a 10-foot-diameter area around the site. Remove any grass, twigs, leaves, and firewood. Dig a pit in the dirt about a foot deep. Circle the pit with rocks. If it is not possible to dig a pit, build a fire ring of rocks on the ground surface.

9

If you choose to cook over an open campfire, you can apply many of these recommendations toward keeping your kitchen organized and safe. For specific details on building different types of fires, see Chapter 8, Camping Skills, page 201–207.

You will have to keep feeding the fire while cooking, so again, make sure your firewood supply is organized, prepared, and readily available. It's often useful to prepare all of your firewood ahead of time or to assign someone to maintain the flames.

When it comes to efficiency, make sure you place the right grill or grate over the fire. If a grate has been provided by a managing land agency, make sure it is stable and sits at the proper height for your needs. If the fire ring needs to be rebuilt, take the time to do so. Empty the ring of all excessive coals by scattering them in the forest, far away from the campsite. Rebuild the wall of the fire ring but do not increase its original size and do not use new, unscorched rocks. Finally, install a stable grill over your new and improved fire ring.

For safety, make sure you always use thick leather gloves when cooking over an open fire. Also make sure you have plenty of water readily available to manage any situation in which the fire gets out of hand and for use at the end of the day, when you extinguish your fire. (This doesn't need to be treated, drinkable water; you can collect and use it directly from a nearby water source.) If you can still feel heat from the ashes, even after drowning your fire ring with water, you will need more water to fully put out your fire. At that point, it's a good idea to stir the water in the bed of ashes with a stick, not just to pour more water in the fire ring.

USING A WATER BLADDER TO WASH YOUR HANDS

Using a water bladder with a valve is an easy way to wash your hands in the backcountry. Once a water bladder is filled with water (which doesn't need to be treated if you're not drinking it), place it on the ground, open the small spigot valve, place one knee on the bladder, and push gently to create your own running water. You can also hang the dromedary from a branch and open the small spigot valve to let out a stream of water fed by gravity. These techniques allow you to wash your hands without assistance, so no excuses!

9

KITCHEN HYGIENE

Hygiene is an overall challenge in outdoor expeditions, especially in the kitchen. Without running water means, it's easy to let our guards down and skip good hygiene practices. But it's essential, perhaps even more so outdoors, to practice excellent hygiene and careful and thorough hand washing. Be aware that alcohol-based hand sanitizers are not sufficient. While practical, these options do not match the effectiveness of a bar of soap, vigorous hand rubbing, and plenty of water. (Antibacterial products carry all kinds of public-health concerns of their own, but that is another book.) The Centers for Disease Control and Prevention (CDC) still recommends "hand washing with soap and water as the best way to reduce the number of microbes." The CDC also recommends that "if soap and water are not available, use an alcohol-based hand sanitizer that contains at least 60 percent alcohol." So, bring a small bar of biodegradable soap or some liquid all-natural soap (look for a kind without phosphate) in a plastic container with a lid, such as a small peanut butter jar (we use a 4-ounce Nalgene jar on our academic program), and a water bladder (the 6L MSR DromLite works great for our program).

If you are well equipped to promote and practice good hygiene around camp, and especially the kitchen, it will be easier to keep your hands clean, your food uncontaminated, and everyone healthy.

KITCHEN CLEANUP AND WASTE DISPOSAL

Unless you are using an MRE (meals ready to eat) menu, you will have to face the aftermath of cooking in the outdoors. Dishes are dishes: they get dirty at home and on the trail, so don't try to avoid them. Keeping your pots, frypans, personal bowls, and all other cooking utensils clean not only will keep you healthier, it will greatly reduce your chance of attracting opportunistic wildlife. A clean kitchen is part of the LNT principle on respecting wildlife.

The best way to do dishes in the outdoors, as at home, is with hot water. Always put a pot of water on your stove when you're done cooking. This way, you can enjoy your meal while the dishwashing water gets ready. Make sure the water comes to a boil before letting it cool enough that it's safe to handle, then use plenty of it to clean your cookware and dishes. You can scrub with fingers, pinecones, or a small plastic or rubber food scraper. Most of the time, you won't need soap to wash your camping dishes. Use biodegradable soap only when your cookware is very greasy. If you do use soap, remember to thoroughly rinse your dishes afterward. Trust us: You do not want to ingest soap residue at your next meal.

Gray water, or dirty dishwater without soap, can be scattered (or "broadcast") on the forest floor a few feet away from your kitchen site. When you use soap, remember to scatter the soapy water 200 feet away from any source of fresh water. If the gray water contains lots of food particles, we recommend using a food strainer to strain the water before scattering it. Add any food particles to your garbage bag. A metal kitchen sink strainer or a small square of window screen with duct-taped edges works best.

If you're backpacking with a large group that produces a high quantity of gray water, or if you're staying at the same campsite for several days, you may choose to dig an 8- to 10-inch-deep sump hole in which you can pour your gray water. Don't forget to refill the sump hole with dirt before going to bed. Digging a new sump hole is not a best practice, however, as it leads to unnecessary impact on the environment.

9

The last task to perform when cleaning your kitchen is to look for micro food particles. If you've been organized and careful while cooking, this task should go fast, but if you had an accidental food spill, you will need to be patient and take the time to pick up all of the particles and bag them to carry out. The same goes for any burned food or leftover meal scraps. Unless you are willing to eat them, you will need to carry them out to the nearest trash can or back home. Like Woodsy Owl said in his 1970s public service announcements: "Give a hoot. Don't pollute."

NO FOOD WASTE IN THE LATRINE OR FIRE RING!

Although food waste is biodegradable, do not dump it in established latrines designed to handle human waste only. Again, the best practice here is to carry out any food waste. We have also seen campers unsuccessfully attempting to burn leftover food—and even aluminum foil—in a fire pit, but it simply does not work. Unless you are ready to build an industrial incinerator, your best LNT option is to carry out food waste.

➜ NUTRITION BASICS

The basic elements of good nutrition in the outdoors are mostly the same as those for your daily life. Let's begin by dividing your nutritional intake into three major categories: macronutrients, micronutrients, and water. All are essential for providing energy and keeping you warm and happy on the trail.

MACRONUTRIENTS

Macronutrients are the nutrients you need to consume in large quantities: carbohydrates, proteins, and fats.

Carbohydrates

These are a major source of energy production in your body. When hiking for long hours, your body needs to metabolize glucose—the technical word for blood sugar. It's easier for your body to metabolize glucose from carbohydrates than from the two other macronutrients, proteins and fats. So, it's important to include carbohydrates in your diet when exercising outdoors. Carbohydrates (or carbs) come in two forms, simple and complex. A simple carb is a sugar molecule, while a complex carb is a starch that combines more than one molecule of sugar. Examples of simple carbs you might find in your rations are dry fruits (fructose), dehydrated milk (lactose), and chocolate chips (sucrose). What's important to remember here is that simple carbs can be absorbed by your body more quickly, so while on the trail, it's appropriate to eat the simple sugars often found in trail mixes: dry fruits, yogurt-covered pretzels, chocolate chips.

Complex carbs are your longer-term source of energy; these are metabolized slower but will last longer. Examples of complex carbs are bread, pasta, and rice. But be careful here: If these complex carbs are from refined sources, meaning they've already been processed (i.e., anything made from white flour), you will end up with simpler carbs. So if you want real complex carbohydrates, choose whole-grain bread, pasta, and brown rice. You can also add quinoa to this list, as it is a great source of complex sugar.

In addition to providing you with a short burst of energy on the trail and a longer source of energy throughout the evening and night, carbohydrates are a great source of fiber, especially when they come from oats and beans. As you probably know, a high-fiber diet is essential for the proper operation of your digestive system. Include fiber-rich food in your menu, since no one wants to deal with constipation on the trail.

Proteins

The building blocks for your muscles, proteins are essential during any long or short outdoor excursion. Proteins help repair your muscles after exercising, boost your immune system, and deliver oxygen and other nutrients to your active muscles.

Composed of twenty amino acids, proteins are found in many sources, from meat to plants. The issue with proteins is that only some types of food include all twenty amino acids in sufficient quantities. Of the twenty amino acids, nine are known as the essential amino acids. This is because we cannot produce them ourselves, so we need to acquire them through balanced nutrition. Animal-sourced proteins, such as meats, fish, poultry, eggs, and dairy products, are known to contain the most complete proteins. The same can be said for certain plant-based foods, such as soybeans, quinoa, and many legumes and nuts. Although some of these nonanimal-based sources of protein might have lower amounts of the nine essential amino acids, mixing them into your outdoor diet will help you get all of the complete proteins you need. Note that for a long time it was believed that mixing dairy products (cheese and milk), grains (rice, wheat, barley), legumes (beans, peas, lentils, peanuts), and seeds (sesame, sunflower, pumpkin) in specific pairs in the same meal was essential to create complete proteins. Today we know that simply eating these varied sources of proteins during the day will be sufficient to meet the nutritional needs associated with protein intake. See Figure 49 on page 216 for all of the possible combinations you can use to create complete proteins in your outdoor diet.

Although it would be difficult and risky to bring along steaks and chicken breasts in the backcountry, there are some animal-based foods that you can easily carry on an outdoor trip. Cheese, powdered eggs, and dry or cured meats (such as summer sausage, salami, and pepperoni) are easy and safe to bring. You can also find sterile pouches of chicken, tuna, and salmon at the grocery store. But if you are a meat lover, be careful: Carrying a block of cheese, a foot-long sausage, and a half-dozen tuna pouches can add considerable weight to your pack. Even when you eat meat, it's still important to supplement your trail menu with a variety of plant-based proteins, which are often lighter in weight.

9

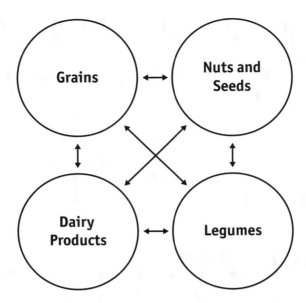

FIGURE 49. Any of the above combinations will yield the complete proteins necessary for a healthy outdoor diet.

Fats

When exercising at a low-intensity level for a long period of time, such as a multiday backpacking expedition, fats are your friend. Why? Because they are a good source of muscle glycogen (i.e., sugar), which your muscles can store in greater amounts than carbohydrates. So, to keep your energy up and stay warm on long outings, adding some fat to your daily menu will help your body meet the challenges of long days of exercise and cold weather.

As we know, not all fats are created equal. The recommendations regarding fat consumption in our daily diets still apply to our outdoor menus. Keep the consumption of saturated fats (butter, lard, animal fat) to no more than 10 percent of your daily caloric intake. You should favor unsaturated fats (plant-based oils, seed oils, and nut oils). Consider opting for vegetable oil, such as canola or olive oil. If you want to bring a spread, avoid any margarine that has trans-fatty acid. An even better choice would be a vegetable oil blend that combines butter and vegetable oil without the trans fat and has lower percentages of saturated fat and cholesterol.

In the end, we recommend not shying away from including fat in your outdoor ration. Even if you are used to a low-fat diet, the physical demands placed on your body will require you to add long-lasting sources of energy, and healthy fats are the best way to do this. The human brain is nearly 60 percent fat. Consuming essential fatty acids can greatly improve brain function and should be considered an important aspect of outdoors eating.

MICRONUTRIENTS
Vitamins and Minerals

Although vitamins and minerals aren't a source of calories and therefore do not produce any energy on their own, they are essential to energy production. They assist the metabolic and physiological functions that are essential for your body's survival. To make sure you have an adequate intake (a.k.a. the recommended daily allowance) of vitamins and minerals in your outdoor diet, bring a diverse range of foods. There's no need to bring along supplemental minerals and multivitamin pills. A diverse diet will do just as well.

Water

As discussed in Chapter 6, Health and Hygiene, water is life. The most important nutrient of all is the one in your water bottle. Hydration is essential for the proper functioning and survival of the human body. Think about this fact: You can survive weeks without food but only a few days without water.

In our wilderness expedition courses, we often treat any initial malaise our students might experience by asking them to increase their water intake. Hydration is a daily topic when traveling in the mountains with new hikers and backpackers. We sometimes have daily check-ins on the essential goal of "clear and copious" urination output.

As with micronutrients, water is not a source of energy in your diet, but it is necessary for the proper operation of all your metabolic functions. Drinking the often recommended 8 cups of water per day might be fine for a sedentary lifestyle, but when exercising and living in the outdoors, your body will soon be dehydrated if you do not increase your water intake. The agreed-upon recommendation by outdoor professionals is to drink 3 to 5 quarts or liters (approximately 20 cups) of water per day. In the outdoors, you either hydrate or die. Your water bottle is your best friend.

➜ PLANNING

Food planning should be fun. It allows you to think about what you really like to eat and to daydream about savoring that comfort food in a beautiful and peaceful place. Embrace the planning; Do not throw something in your pack at the last minute. Instead, take the time to confer with your group and to come up with a menu that will truly enhance your experience. When planning with your hiking partners, you will have to cover some or all of these topics:

- Appetite
- Allergies
- Dietary choice
- Food preference

9

Not all of us have the same metabolism; some of us need to consume many more calories just to exist, while others have lower calorie thresholds. In our wilderness courses, we often have students who eat like bears coming out of their dens after a long winter and others who eat like goldfish. Estimate whether your party has either of these extremes or if most of the members of your group have an average appetite. Discussing allergies is also essential. You can make a mistake about the quantity of food you bring, but bringing food that endangers the health of your party is a much bigger risk. Cover your bases and ask about nuts and tree nut allergies, as well as egg, shellfish, milk, and gluten allergies or intolerance. There are ways to avoid all of these types of foods and still ensure that everyone in your group is well fed and healthy. As for dietary choices, find out if anyone follows a vegetarian, vegan, kosher, or any other form of religious or special diet. Finally, take the time to ask what people like to eat. It's pointless to carry food on your back that you or other people in your party do not enjoy eating. For instance, Christian, does not care for oatmeal at breakfast, but Jamie loves it, so we might bring oatmeal in our ration, wth Christian knowing that he needs to plan for an alternative. Perhaps an extra 0.5 pound of dehydrated hash browns will keep both of us happy. Take into consideration all these factors and plan a menu that will please and keep all members of your party healthy. Remember, on an outdoor expedition, what you carry is what you have.

THE FIVE FOOD VIRTUES

You may be surprised to learn how many forms of food you can bring on an out-door trip. Select foods that are:

1. Lightweight
2. Easy to cook
3. Calorie-dense
4. Tasty
5. Healthy

Lightweight

These virtues are true if you are going out for more than two or three days, when every ounce on your back counts. If, however, you're planning an overnight or a long-weekend expedition, you can afford to bring heavier foods, such as oranges or apples, that travel well. But avoid soft fruits, such as bananas, strawberries, and kiwi. You can also bring fresh vegetables, such as carrots, onions, garlic, and even potatoes. These fresh ingredients can really enhance a dinner at the end of a long hike. (If dry food was so great, we would eat it every day.) Instead of completely neglecting fruits and veggies on long trips, think about ways you can incorporate lightweight rations of these foods, such as freeze-drying and dehydrating. And don't forget whole grains such as rice, pasta, or quinoa.

Easy to Cook

While modern camping stoves are great, their best function is boiling water outdoors. For this reason, you might consider selecting foods that are easy to prepare in the field, meaning they don't require long periods of time to cook. Longer cooking means more fuel, and more fuel means more weight. By promoting this virtue, we are not telling you to plan for one-pot meals only—rather, to be thoughtful about preparation. Sometimes that will be extremely simple, such as heating premade soup, and other times it will be more complex: think pizza, bean burritos, or tuna casserole.

Calorie-Dense

If you are lugging food on your back, you want to make sure it is calorie-dense. Hiking with an average pack weight—up to 40 percent of a hiker's body weight—can easily burn 400 to 600 calories per hour. On more difficult terrain or with a heavier pack, you will burn even more calories. To replace what you burn, avoid processed foods that are high in calories but low in nutrients—commonly called "empty calories." Examples of these types of foods are cookies, chips, candy, and soda. Also avoid what Tim Jones calls "The Rice Cake Conundrum." Although rice cakes might appear to be the ideal lightweight food to bring on a trip, they hold very few calories: about 35 each. You would need at least fourteen rice cakes to replenish your body from only one hour of moderate hiking. A better choice would be to bring an energy bar, which often exceeds 250 calories per bar.

Tasty

Again, if you are going to carry it, make sure you'll eat it. It's worthless to bring food you or others don't like. It doesn't matter how many calories a food has or how nutritious it is if it's not going to make it into your mouth. Know that physical exertion affects appetites. Some might find their appetite increases, but for others, it might decrease. If you find the latter happening, it's vital to have fuel handy that you think of as comfort food. Bring food that tastes good to you and is good for your body.

9

Heathy

Take care of your engine, especially when you are using it on a daily basis for long periods of time. Hiking and backpacking will tax your engine, so it's best to refill with premium fuel. Again, avoid highly processed foods such as white pasta, instant rice, or white flour–based products. Instead, take the time to select food that is rich in fiber and nutrients, and low in saturated fats or trans fats. For ideas, look to the health section of your grocery store.

INSTANT COFFEE

As discussed in Chapter 6, avoid caffeine before and during long hikes, as it's a diuretic that can quickly dehydrate hikers. If we're realistic, though, we know that many people cannot get started in the morning without their coffee. Even if you don't care much for coffee, there may be people in your group who truly need it—and you'll have to deal with them if they don't get their morning fix. In this case, instant coffee is worth its weight to keep the coffee addicts civilized. Consider carrying packets for yourself and to share, should anyone forget. If you prefer add-ins like sugar and powdered creamer, take those as well.

TYPES OF FOOD YOU CAN BRING

There are many types of food you can bring on your next outing. Some are lighter weight and easier to prepare; others are tastier and healthier. Let's look at the choices available to you.

Freeze-Dried Food

Commercially available freeze-dried meal packages are quite popular in the outdoor recreation industry. These provide easy meal planning and packaging, since each bag represents a single meal. Some packages contain one or two servings, but be aware that a single serving might leave you feeling hungry—especially if you have a large appetite or after a particularly hard day on the trail. There are many brands on the market, and these easy meals can be found in outdoor equipment retail stores (and on their websites) and in the camping departments of big-box stores.

Freeze-dried meals are easy to prepare: just add hot water to the mix and wait for the food to rehydrate. You can even rehydrate the meals in their respective pouches, which saves on washing dishes later. In addition, their shelf life is long, so you can easily stockpile them at home for months or years before using them, a definite plus when you find them on sale.

About the taste: Some hikers love these premade meals while others might see them as emergency food only. You will have to try them yourself to find out which camp you're in.

The main disadvantage of ready-made freeze-dried food is that it tends to be more costly than other options. Plus, freeze-drying is one of the most energy-intensive ways to preserve food. The food has to be precooked then frozen before being exposed to a lower-pressure environment so that the crystalized water molecules in the frozen food can be removed via sublimation. And that's before you ever turn on your camp stove.

Instant Food

All major grocery stores carry instant food products that are easy to use and prepare. Think dry soup packages, seasoned rice meals, and couscous dishes. These products require only a short cooking period and perhaps a few additional ingredients to spice them up. Imagine picking up a brown rice jambalaya mix at the grocery store and repackaging it in a plastic bag for easy transport in your pack. Once in the field you can boil water, add the jambalaya mix with some olive oil and a few chunks of summer sausage, and bam: *Bon appétit!*

There are many types of these ready-to-cook meals in the grocery store. Just make sure you don't buy only ramen noodle packages. Though inexpensive, these are very unhealthy and provide little nutrition for the weight. Look for healthy options with low sodium content and the least amount of processing. You can find great soups, sauces, rice, couscous, quinoa mixes, and even desserts, such as cheesecake mix, that only require some milk or dehydrated milk.

Note that you might need to repackage most of these meals. Don't forget to cut the cooking instructions from the box and include them in the bag holding the corresponding mix. Find more on repackaging your outdoor food below.

Premixed Food

This option means cutting out the middleman and creating your own premixed meal at home. You can take one of your favorite meals and combine all of the dry, uncooked, or dehydrated ingredients, plus spices or flavors, such as a veggie, chicken, or beef broth cube. Recipe-test these meals at home beforehand and make sure to write down the right amounts of each ingredient and spice. Once it is time to prepare your outdoor menu, premix the ingredients in a single plastic bag and add a note about the amount of water needed. Don't forget to write down the name of the meal on the bag with a permanent marker.

With this method, you can create your own gourmet dishes and save some money. If you have a dehydrator at home, you can add dehydrated vegetables, mushrooms, tofu, meat, or even tomato sauce in the form of a leather. (Think Fruit Roll-Ups: Much like a fruit leather, you can make tomato leather by using a dehydrator, then rehydrate it by adding warm water.)

FOOD DEHYDRATORS   9

Dehydrators can be worth the investment if you travel in the backcountry often or if you prefer to be in control of all your meals' ingredients. Store-bought dehydrated meals can be costly and often come with chemical preservatives to extend the shelf life. With an at-home food dehydrator, you can make all kinds of dishes to transport into the field, without the additives and preservatives. Soups, vegetables, meat, pasta—almost any meal you can think of can be made right in your kitchen using a food dehydrator. *AMC's Real Trail Meals,* by Ethan and Sarah Hipple, provides in-depth information on do-it-yourself backpacking meals. You can also find step-by-step instructions from *AMC Outdoors* magazine at outdoors.org/dehydratedfood.

Fresh Food

As mentioned, if your outing is an overnight or a long weekend, you can afford to carry some fresh food. High-flavor produce, such as onions, garlic, and green onions, is a great treat in the field. A few carrots, a potato, or even some tempeh are delicious possibilities on a short trip. The same can be said about fresh fruits with hard skins, such as apples, oranges, and pomegranates.

You can also think about bringing chicken, tuna, and salmon, which now come in easy-to-use pouches. These aluminum-foil-coated plastic pouches, called re-tort pouches, are easy to carry and to pack away once empty. You could also think about bringing peanut butter and hard cheeses (sharp cheddar, colby, Monterey Jack, Swiss, Jarlsberg), which are great sources of proteins and fats. With the right packaging and some careful handling of your pack, you can also bring fresh (or hard boiled) eggs.

Finally, if you cannot go out without your daily bread, pick among the following, which have been proven to travel well on our backpacking trips: bagels, pita bread, and flour tortillas. You can also add pretzel sticks to this list.

Spice Kit (Optional)

A diverse spice kit, also known as a "food repair kit," enhances any backpacking experience. Dry spices, iodized salt, and a few essential liquids are easy to pack and will pay for their weight a thousand-fold. Of course, the content of your spice kit depends on your palate, as well as the length of your expedition. Even if you are bringing freeze-dried meals only, we recommend bringing a good spice kit (see "Suggested Spices" on page 223). Nations have sent explorers and merchants across oceans and continents to find salts and spices. That's how important they are to your food.

MENU PLANNING

The length of your outdoor adventure may determine your approach to food plan-ning. If your trip is six or fewer days, you might want to use a menu-planning method, but if your outing will last longer than six days, you should consider using a bulk ration plan.

From an overnight to a nearly weeklong trip (i.e., six days and five nights), the menu-planning method is often best. This involves meal-per-meal planning. For instance, if you are going out for four days and three nights and planning to be at the trailhead by 10 A.M. and to return to the parking lot by 4 P.M., you will have to plan for three breakfasts, four lunches, and three dinners.

You'll plan these meals per all of the advice above, taking into account group members' appetites, preferences, diets, and allergies. For every meal, you'll create a list of each item and its quantity. Once you've created a list for all meals, you can generate a master grocery list. The table "Menu Plan Sample for Four People" on page 224 will give you a good idea of how to follow this form of menu planning.

SUGGESTED SPICES

Small, wide-mouthed polyethylene (HDPE) bottles made by Nalgene and other companies are very effective for carrying and conserving dry spices, as well as essential liquids. They are safe to use with food, and they are leak-proof, water resistant, long lasting, and easy to clean. Note: Unless you have a fine nose for identifying spices, labeling them is a good idea.

DRY SPICE	BOTTLE SIZE
Salt	60 ml
Black Pepper	60 ml
Oregano	60 ml
Basil	60 ml
Garlic Powder	60 ml
Curry	30 ml
Dill	30 ml
Cinnamon	30 ml
Cayenne	30 ml
Cumin	30 ml
Garlic Salt	30 ml
Baking Powder	30 ml
Yeast	30 ml
Chili Powder	30 ml

LIQUIDS	BOTTLE SIZE
Hot Sauce	125 ml
Soy Sauce	60 ml
Vanilla	30 ml
Vinegar	60 ml
Oil	250 ml

When following a menu plan, it's best practice to pack all of the items related to a specific meal in the same plastic bag, then label these meal bags according to their contents. Your first lunch on the trail will be in a bag labeled "Lunch 1," while your first dinner will be labeled "Dinner 1," and so forth. One exception to minimize packaging: Pack all staple items—brown sugar, drink mixes, spice kits—separately from the individual meal bags.

9

The advantages of using this form of menu planning include:

- Ease of planning multiple meals
- No puzzlement on what to eat
- Little to no waste
- No food shortage
- No surprises

MENU PLAN SAMPLE FOR FOUR PEOPLE			
	Breakfast	**Lunch**	**Dinner**
Day 1	At home	**Pita Bread and Summer Sausage** • Pita Bread • Summer Sausage • Marbled Cheese • Mustard • Fig Newton	**Lentil Shepherd's Pie** • Red Lentils • Vegetable Broth Cube • Instant Potatoes • Mozzarella Cheese • Dehydrated Milk • Butter • Dry Corn • Onions • Tea
Day 2	**Hash browns, Cheese, and Bagels** • Hash browns • Butter • Marbled Cheese • Bagels • Chai	**Bagels PB&J** • Bagels • Peanut Butter • Jam • Energy Bar	**Noodles, Tomato Sauce, and Falafel** • Rotini Noodles • Dry Tomato Sauce • Falafel Mix • Onion • Garlic • Brown Sugar • Dry Carrots • Dry Green Pepper • Tea
Day 3	**Oatmeal and Dry Fruits** • Brown Sugar • Dehydrated Milk • Dry Apricot • Dry Apple • Hot Chocolate	**Pita Bread and Tuna** • Pita Bread • Tuna • Marbled Cheese • Fig Newton	**Black Bean Burrito and Rice** • Dehydrated Black Beans • Rice • Tortillas • Mozzarella Cheese • Salsa • Tea
Day 4	**Honeybunch and Toasted Bagels** • Cereal • Dehydrated Milk • Bagels • Peanut Butter • Jam • Chai	**Bagels PB&J** • Bagels • Peanut Butter • Jam • Energy Bar	At home

9

Also, note that planning can be shared among the group. Just make sure to share the plan beforehand to avoid unfortunate repeats. You can also have one person in the group write down who is carrying which meals in their packs so that everyone in the group doesn't have to rummage through their packs at mealtime.

BULK RATION PLANNING (very complex)

If your trip lasts more than six days, you might want to consider another approach to food planning. The bulk ration plan has been used by thousands of students at the National Outdoor Leadership School (NOLS), Outward Bound, and other outdoor wilderness schools. This system is comparable to a well-garnished pantry at home. When carrying diverse items in your backpacks, your meal planning is based on the current energy needs of the hikers, the environmental conditions at the time of the meal, and the food available. This is similar to how some people cook at home: planning a meal based on what we feel like eating, the time we want to spend cooking, and what is in our pantry.

Although this form of food planning can seem loosey-goosey at first, careful preparation before your trip allows for proper calorie intake and the consumption of appropriate macro- and micronutrients. The steps used to plan a bulk ration are as follows.

1. **Determine the expected amount of daily calorie intake.** The first step in this process is to determine the amount (in dry weight) of food per person—or pound per person per day (PPD)—that will be needed according to the expected amount of calories you'll burn per day of hiking. In simple terms, the more calories you expect to burn, the larger the amount of food (calories) you should plan to bring. We all know that hiking in different terrains, environmental conditions, or with different pack weights requires different amounts of physical exertion—hence the need to match your physical effort with your food intake. Determining the correct PPD seems a bit complex, but the flexibility in this system is enough that you can accurately estimate values using the table "Calorie Intake and Food Weight Based on Physical Activity" on page 227.

2. **Determine the total amount of food weight for the trip.** This is the easy math you've been preparing for. The equation is simple: Multiply the PPD you selected by the number of people in your party and the number of days for the trip you are planning.

   (PPD x Number of Participants x Number of Days)

   For instance, if you are planning a moderately strenuous overnight hike along the Appalachian Trail in mid-autumn, you might select a PPD of 1.75. If your party size is five participants and you intend to be out for eight days, the total amount of food you will need to prepare and carry is 70 pounds:

   1.75 x 5 x 8 = 70

9

This means that if you separate the food load equally among all participants, each should start the hike with about 14 pounds. With a little extra attention and thoughtfulness, group members will continuously redistribute the weight equally throughout the trip. By the end of the trip, everyone should carry much smaller amounts of food, between 1 and 2 pounds depending on the appetites of your group members.

3. **Distribute the total weight among various food categories.** The math gets a bit harder in this step, but don't worry. We'll walk you through it. Now that you've calculated the total amount of food you need to bring, you'll subdivide it into various categories: breakfast (16 percent); dinner (18 percent); trail snacks (21 percent); cheese (13 percent); staples (14 percent); baking (7 percent); sugar and drinks (7 percent); and soups, bases, and desserts (4 percent). Refer to the table "Food Weight to Type Ratio" on page 227 for examples of types of food in each of these categories.

   If we take the example we used above for the eight-day trip, all we have to do is subdivide the total amount of food among these food categories. The table "Total Food Weight Breakdown" below illustrates this simple process. Note that rounding to the nearest half-pound will simplify your planning.

TOTAL FOOD WEIGHT BREAKDOWN				
	Categories	**Percentage**	**Equation**	**Round-up**
	Breakfast	16 percent	70 x 0.16 = 11.2	11.0 lbs.
	Dinner	18 percent	70 x 0.18 = 12.6	12.5 lbs.
	Trail Snacks	21 percent	70 x 0.21 = 14.7	14.5 lbs.
Total Food	Cheese	13 percent	70 x 0.13 = 9.1	9.0 lbs.
70 lbs.	Staples	14 percent	70 x 0.14 = 9.8	10.0 lbs.
	Baking	7 percent	70 x 0.07 = 4.9	5.0 lbs.
	Drinks	7 percent	70 x 0.07 = 4.9	5.0 lbs.
	Soups, Bases and Desserts	4 percent	70 x 0.04 = 2.8	3.0 lbs.

4. **Select food among various food categories.** This last step is the best: Now you get to select specific foods in each of the categories. This selection is based on food preferences, diets, and food allergies among the group members. Select and package your food in weights of 0.25 pound, 0.5 pound, 0.75 pound, or 1 pound to make packing easy. The table "Sample Bulk Ration for an 8-Day Trip" on pages 228 and 229 provides a sample of what this selection could look like for an eight-day trip for five people at 1.75 PPD.

CALORIE INTAKE AND FOOD WEIGHT BASED ON PHYSICAL ACTIVITY		
Pound per Person per Day (PPD)	**Approximate Calories (calories per day)**	**Appropriate Activity and Conditions**
1.25 PPD	2,000	Base camping and easy strolls around camp, no pack or a hip pack, warm weather, low altitude
1.50 PPD	2,500 to 3,000	Easy hiking day, light pack, good weather, warm, low altitude
1.75 PPD	3,000 to 3,250	Moderate hiking day, average pack, good weather, warm/cool, moderate altitude
2.00 PPD	3,250 to 3,500	Long/moderate hiking day, heavy pack, various weather, cold, moderate altitude
2.25 PPD	3,500 to 3,750	Difficult hiking day, heavy pack, bad weather, cold, high altitude
2.50 PPD	3,750 to 4,000	Hard and long hiking day, heavy pack, bad weather, very cold, high altitude

FOOD WEIGHT TO TYPE RATIO		
Categories	**Types of Food**	**Percentage of Total Ration**
Breakfast	Oatmeal, granola, cereals, hash browns, etc.	16 percent
Dinner	Pasta, rice, beans, grains, instant potatoes, etc.	18 percent
Trail Snacks	Nuts, dry fruits, trail mix, energy bars, etc.	21 percent
Cheese	Hard varieties such as cheddar, Swiss, etc.	13 percent
Staples	Milk, butter, eggs, brown sugar	14 percent
Baking	White flour, wheat flour, cornbread mix	7 percent
Drinks	Tea, fruit drink, chai mix	7 percent
Soups, Bases, and Desserts	Instant soup, broth, sauce mix, cake mix, etc.	4 percent
TOTAL		**100 percent**

9

SAMPLE BULK RATION FOR AN 8-DAY TRIP FOR 5 PEOPLE AT 1.75 PPD (70 POUNDS TOTAL FOOD RATION)		
Food Categories	**Food Items**	**Quantity**
Breakfast (16 percent) 11 lbs.	Granola	3.00 lbs.
	Oatmeal	2.00 lbs.
	Cereal	2.00 lbs.
	Hash browns	4.00 lbs.
	SUBTOTAL	**11 lbs.**
Dinner (18 percent) 12.5 lbs.	Orzo	1.00 lb.
	Elbow Noodles	2.00 lbs.
	Rotini Noodles	2.00 lbs.
	Couscous	1.00 lb.
	Red Lentils	1.00 lb.
	Textured Vegetable Protein (TVP)	0.50 lb.
	Dehydrated Humus	0.50 lb.
	Dehydrated Refried Beans	1.00 lb.
	Dehydrated Black Beans	1.00 lb.
	Falafel	0.50 lb.
	Basmati Rice	1.00 lb.
	Quinoa	1.00 lb.
	SUBTOTAL	**12.5 lbs.**
Trail Snacks (21 percent) 14.5 lbs.	Roasted Almonds	1.00 lb.
	Salted Cashews	1.00 lb.
	Roasted Peanuts	1.00 lb.
	Dried Bananas	1.00 lb.
	Peanut M&M's	1.00 lb.
	Fig Newtons	1.00 lb.
	Wheat Crackers	1.00 lb.
	Spicy Trail Mix	1.00 lb.
	Fruit and Nut Trail Mix	1.00 lb.
	Pretzels	1.00 lb.
	Snack Mix	1.00 lb.
	Cajun Sesame Sticks	1.00 lb.
	Beef Jerky	1.00 lb.
	Energy Bars	10 bars or 1.5 lb.
	SUBTOTAL	**14.5 lb.**

9

SAMPLE BULK RATION FOR AN 8-DAY TRIP FOR 5 PEOPLE (CONTINUED)		
Food Categories	**Food Items**	**Quantity**
Cheese **(13 percent)** **9.0 lbs.**	Colby	2.00 lbs.
	Cheddar	3.00 lbs.
	Pepper Jack	2.00 lbs.
	Mozzarella	2.00 lbs.
	SUBTOTAL	**9.00 lbs.**
Staples **(14 percent)** **10.00 lbs.**	Instant Milk	2.00 lbs.
	Instant Potatoes	3.00 lbs.
	Butter	3.00 lbs.
	Egg Powder	1.00 lb.
	Brown Sugar	1.00 lb.
	SUBTOTAL	**10.00 lbs.**
Baking **(7 percent)** **5.00 lbs.**	Cornbread Mix	1.00 lb.
	White Flour	2.00 lbs.
	Wheat Flour	2.00 lbs.
	SUBTOTAL	**5.00 lbs.**
Drinks **(7 percent)** **5.00 lbs.**	Fruit Drink Mix	1.00 lb.
	Apple Cider Mix	1.00 lb.
	Chai Mix	2.00 lbs.
	Hot Chocolate	1.00 lb.
	Herbal Tea	20 items or 0.2 lb.
	SUBTOTAL	**5.20 lbs.**
Soups, Bases **and Desserts** **(4 percent)** **3.00 lbs.**	Tomato Powder	0.75 lb.
	Instant Chicken Noodle Soup	0.50 lb.
	Vegetable Broth	4 items or 0.12 lb.
	Chicken Broth	4 items or 0.12 lb.
	Brownie Mix	1.5 lb.
	SUBTOTAL	**3.00 lbs.**
	TOTAL	**70.20 lbs.**

9

Although the bulk ration system looks complex to plan, it is quite easy to use in the field. We have taught and used this ration system with thousands of students for hundreds of wilderness expeditions, and we can assure you it's a great way to cook in the outdoors on long expeditions. Advantages include:

- Organized planning: A few calculations lets you select food items from a master list.

- Easy packing: Food items are bagged in quantities of 0.25 pound, 0.5 pound, 0.75 pound, or 1 pound.

- Easy purchasing list created by your planning (see the quantity column in the sample bulk ration table on pages 228–229).

- Offers greater cooking freedom in the field

You can add bread products (bagels, pita bread, etc.) or heavier items (peanut butter, jam, tuna, summer sausage, onions, fresh garlic) to use within the first few days of your trip. If you do so, just make sure not to add too much weight to your overall ration weight. If fresh food is a must, consider reducing the PPD to allow more weight from fresh items.

➔ PACKAGING

Properly packaging food is an important step in your planning. No one likes to open a backpack after a deep river crossing only to find a bag of wet and soggy noodles or an explosion of pancake mix. To avoid these problems, it's essential to repackage food in trustworthy containers or plastic bags. Here are a few tricks we have developed during many years of backpacking.

- **Zipper-closure plastic bags.** Freezer zipper-closure bags are a great option. They are water resistant, and their zipper seals make them easy to use. If packed properly (meaning if you remove most of the air in the bag before closing it), the bag shouldn't explode in your pack, even if you sit on your pack or throw it on the ground. (Low-air bags also take up less room in your pack than puffy, air-filled bags.) To easily remove air from a zipper-closure bag, zip the bag almost shut then insert a straw in the opening and suck out the remaining air before fully sealing the bag.

FIGURE 50. Using a straw to suck the excess air out of a zippered food bag before sealing means the bag will take up less space and is less likely to explode in your pack.

9

- **Vacuum-seal bags.** These work well with the menu planning system. You can vacuum-seal premixed soups or meals at home. Your food will remain secure, waterproof, and smell-proof, which can be useful in habituated-bear country. Once you open a vacuum-sealed bag, however, you cannot vacuum-reseal it in the field, so plan on using the entire contents when you open it.

- **Gusset plastic bags.** A low-cost solution to food packaging is to purchase 2-mm-thick gusset plastic bags. You can purchase these online from specialized plastic retailers. For years, we have used the 6-by-3-by-18-inch 2-mm-thick clear plastic gusset bags with great results. We purchase the bags in boxes of 1,000, which brings the cost to about 8 cents per bag. These bags are great for bulk rationing, and you can secure their contents by tying an overhand knot in the long neck. If you're looking for tough and affordable bags, these are the best. Avoid using the light and thin produce bags you get from your grocery store; they won't withstand the abuse of an outdoor expedition.

CONTAINERS

Items such as peanut butter, jam, salsa, and other types of spreads or liquids are best transported in solid plastic containers. Again, the best in class are Nalgene containers. Their 4-ounce, 8-ounce, and 16-ounce straight-sided, wide-mouth jars are shock-resistant, leak-proof, and reusable. They're also a bit pricy, but they will last for many years of outdoor adventure. If you go with this option, try to use the polypropylene type; they are more shock-resistant than polymethylpentene or the polycarbonate (brands such as Lexan or Merlon).

REPACKAGING

Many food items come in their own packaging, so why bother repackaging your food? Repackaging is often a good way to minimize your micro trash in the field. Plus, it can save you a few ounces of weight on long expeditions. It's also part of the first LNT principle, "Plan Ahead and Prepare," so take the time to minimize your impact by repackaging your food. For instance, a cracker box can be recycled and its contents repackaged in a zipper-closure bag. This way you will greatly reduce the volume of your ration while minimizing your micro trash. Do not burn any leftover trash in the field. All trash needs to be carried out with you. Avoid bringing tin cans and glass containers. While glass is an eco-friendly material, it's lighter and safer (think breakage) to transfer the contents of a glass jam jar into a Nalgene jar. Note that all of your plastic bags can be washed and reused, or at the very least recycled. There is always a way to minimize your hiking footprint—even at home.

9

CHAPTER 10
WINTER SKILLS

For those who already heed the call of the backcountry, the siren song of winter can be particularly loud and persistent. Winter adventures offer solitude, challenge, and beauty. New-fallen snow transforms the common hiking trail into a highway for snowshoes or skis, covering the land in an untouched canvas of white. The special ecology of winter is exciting in the way animals and plants adapt to thrive in its unforgiving cold. The nights are long and skies clear, offering amazing stargazing. And the crowds of summer backcountry travelers are reduced to a smaller band of passionate, hardy souls. Winter, though sometimes harsh and unforgiving, has an inviting beauty all its own.

Winter backcountry travel is adventurous and joyful, but it requires skills to enjoy it safely and well. These winter-specific skills are added on to foundational skills built in the warmer seasons. Aspiring winter travelers should plan to learn these skills from experienced hikers, from the multitude of professional workshops available, and from the many excellent books on winter camping and travel. This chapter does not cover every aspect of winter-skill development. Instead, it introduces the basics of adapting a summer system to the requirements of winter travel. Use it as a guide to identify the additional learning experiences and gear purchases that will enhance your safety and enjoyment of the winter backcountry. For a more in-depth book on winter, look for the next book in AMC's skills series, *AMC's Winter Skills Manual*, coming in 2017.

→ PLANNING A ROUTE

Winter travel routes in the Northeast tend to follow river valleys; forest floors; and relatively protected, low-elevation ridges. For the typical winter hiker, adventures above treeline are usually reserved for side trips, not overnights, unless the group is intentionally pursuing winter mountaineering activities. An ideal winter route will be level enough for travel with snowshoes or skis, with sheltered campsites along the way. Because backpacks are heavier, snow travel is slower, and days are shorter, a typical winter travel route will cover much less ground than a three-season route. A single day of travel might cover 3 to 5 miles and rarely more than 10.

➜ WINTER NUTRITION

In winter more than ever, packing nutritious and satisfying food is essential to trip success. The nutrition principles and food preparation practices covered in Chapter 9 apply equally to winter food planning, with a few additions and modifications. First, the cold temperatures and demanding activity level of winter backpacking and camping require an additional 2,000 to 4,000 calories above the hiker's basal metabolic rate, depending on the specifics of the individual hiker and the route. Second, dry winter air removes water from the breath and body at a much higher rate than summer conditions. Winter hikers need to consume roughly 25 percent more water than on a comparable summer hike. Much of the winter menu revolves around these two principles, along with some special preparation techniques to cope with the freezing temperatures.

MIX OF NUTRIENTS

The best way to achieve the increased calorie intake without a proportional increase in bulk and weight is to increase the percentage of calories that come from fats. A reasonable winter camping menu will deliver about 60 percent of calories through fats, 30 percent through carbohydrates, and only 10 percent through proteins. Due to their high caloric density, fats provide much more fuel at a lower weight penalty. To illustrate, one pound of pasta offers about 575 calories, while one pound of olive oil offers about 3,950. Also, fats are a slower metabolizing, extended energy source, ideal for the consistent demands of the winter environment. Obviously, it is not desirable to eat sticks of butter or drink straight olive oil, but when adding calories to winter menus, focus on sources of healthy fats. Chapter 12, Ultralight Backpacking, offers many suggestions for foods that have a greater number of calories per ounce.

As you've learned, different nutrients work together to keep us warm and energized. Carbohydrates are quicker burning, like the kindling and small logs of a campfire. Fats are like the big logs that burn through the day or night. We need carbohydrates for quick energy, especially during high-output activity times. Adequate fat intake balances the energetic peaks and valleys, providing fuel for a metabolic foundation that can resist the cold temperatures. Hikers sometimes express concern about protein availability in their backcountry diet, but there is no need

10

for extra protein, especially in winter. The protein sources already found in pasta, nuts, and other common camping foods provide at least the 10 percent suggested. For example, 15 percent of the calories found in whole wheat pasta come from naturally occurring plant proteins. If your winter menu also includes small portions of eggs, tinned fish, sausage, or textured vegetable protein, you will have more than enough protein for healthy performance in the backcountry.

WATER

If your route provides access to liquid water in streams or ponds, you can consume it exactly as you would in summer. If, however, there is no liquid water, you will be forced to melt snow for your hydration needs. If you'll be melting snow for most of your water, bring three times as much stove fuel as you would otherwise. In other words, if a summer hiker can subsist on one-third of a quart of fuel per day, in winter, plan for almost a full quart per day. In order to get adequate hydration, most winter hikers consume a large portion of their water in food. For example, soups and hot drinks are satisfying foods in cold conditions and also have a high water content. Sometimes after cooking pasta, a winter hiker will simply add soup mix or tomato powder instead of draining it and consume it, water and all.

WINTER FOOD PREPARATION

Winter backcountry travelers will find that the season's below-freezing temperatures offer some challenges and opportunities for outdoor food preparation. Any food with a high enough water content will freeze, and many oily foods will solidify. It's a good idea to experiment with foods at home by placing them in the freezer overnight. If a food is unusable once frozen, maybe you can prepare it at home, cut it up, and then freeze it. At the same time, if the temperature is expected to stay below freezing, enjoy the opportunity to bring frozen foods! Many hikers will bring cubed frozen meats and frozen vegetables from home.

WINTER MENU TIPS

- Frozen cheese crumbles and is hard to cut. Cheese is easier to cube, shred, or slice at home.

- Fatty meats, such as salami or pepperoni, offer a lot nutritionally but can be difficult to prepare when frozen. These are easier to cube or slice at home as well.

- Olive oil or other liquid oils will turn solid in freezing temperatures. Pack them in a wide-mouthed container so they can be spooned or spread like butter.

- Bring small frozen cubes of tomato sauce, pesto, or other sauces. Some sauces with a high salt content, such as fish sauce or sriracha, stay liquid until well below 32 degrees Fahrenheit (0 degrees Celsius), sometimes as low as 0F (-18C).

10

- Frozen mixed vegetables can be added to any meal for better nutrition and appeal.

- Small tins of oily fish, like sardines or herring, are nutritious and go well with multigrain crackers, which are durable in their pack.

- Nut butters get much harder in freezing temperatures, about the consistency of ice cream, and become difficult to spread. You may need to thaw them in your jacket before spreading them on bread or crackers—or just eat them by the spoonful.

- Eggs in the shell will be useless once they freeze solid. Instead, scramble them at home and freeze them in zipper-closure freezer bags in single-meal portions. You can even add ingredients, such as spices, cheese, or vegetables. These frozen eggs can be cooked right in the bag by boiling (omelet-in-a-bag), or you can add them to other meals.

- For a treat, chocolate and hard candies keep well, but consider bringing presliced cookie dough (easily fried in a pan) or even ice cream.

➜ SHELTER

Generally, a winter hiker has the same range of sheltering choices as a summer hiker. Tents, tarps, and lean-tos provide the most reliable options, while a few hikers will choose hammocks. Snow shelters (several versions are described below) are a fun and traditional winter-only option worth the experimentation for avid winter campers.

WORK-HARDENING SNOW

No matter which option you choose, you will need to adapt your methods when pitching your shelter in the deep snow of winter. Fortunately, snow can be a wonderful medium for creating platforms, windbreaks, and many other structures. When shoveled, packed, or otherwise "worked," the sharp points of individual snow crystals break off, densifying the snowpack. Simultaneously, the friction of the crystals against each other causes a melt-freeze process at the molecular level, bonding the crystals together. This work-hardening (also called "sintering") is familiar to anyone who has ever formed a snowball, and it allows a hiker to turn the snow into nearly any shape imaginable. The sintering process takes some effort and time. The colder and moister the snow and the sharper the snow crystals, the more responsive it will be to work-hardening. New, high-moisture snow in 15 to 20F (-9 to -7C) temperatures will take about twenty minutes to harden after being worked, while old, sugary snow and wet, corn snow may not respond to work-hardening at all.

The most fundamental use of work-hardening is to create a flat space for sleeping in deep snow. When arriving in camp, the first task for any winter camper using a bivy, tent, tarp, or snow shelter will be to tramp out a level surface slightly

10

larger than the shelter. Using skis, snowshoes, or just boots, stomp the area thoroughly. Imagine that you are trying to drive the air out of the snow. When you have stomped it for a few minutes, smooth it out as level as possible and pack the surface one last time. Let it sit without disturbance for at least fifteen to twenty minutes then test it. In good snow conditions, it will feel firm enough to lie flat on without any subsidence, although it may not be able to withstand the weight of a standing hiker. If it is still soft, allow it to sit longer, up to an hour.

Once you have mastered the process of work-hardening your sleeping surface, you are well on your way to one of the most entertaining aspects of winter camping. In good snow conditions you will find it easy to customize your campsite. Need a wall for a wind break? No problem. Want a little trench next to your sleeping bag so you can sit up more comfortably to don your boots? Simple. What about a shelf in the camp kitchen to serve food? Got it covered.

TENTS

Four-season or mountaineering tents replace much of three-season tents' bug-mesh inner wall with nylon fabric, minimizing the effect of wintry winds. The fly on winter tents typically drops down to ground level, and there may be zippers or other mechanical vents to minimize condensation. Pole construction in four-season tents is very strong, designed to withstand high winds and significant snow loads. Tents provide a relatively warm sleeping environment, but they are much heavier than other options, and water vapor from breathing will accumulate inside the fly and tent body.

If using a tent in winter, shake out the fly and the inverted tent body each morning to remove as much of the accumulated frost as possible. Staking tents in winter requires some thought. If there are trees nearby, use guylines (long pieces of paracord used to hold the tent in place) instead of stakes. If stakes are necessary, try to use a dead man anchor: Dig a small trough lengthwise in the snow, about 8 inches deep and perpendicular to the direction of pull from the guyline. Lay the guyline across the trough and then place a long stick in the base of the trough. (Skis and poles work well, too.) Wrap the guyline around and back toward the tent then bury the stick, packing and work-hardening the snow on top and all around the anchor. You should be able to adjust this guyline as you would around any other anchor.

10

TARPS

Free from the scourge of biting insects, the winter environment is a place where the versatile, lightweight tarp really shines. A tarp can be pitched over any flat place, just as in summer, but the snow allows for more creativity. Dig a deep hole and work-harden the bottom, then pitch the tarp over it so you can stand up beneath the tarp. You can even work-harden the snow near the entry and build a set of durable stairs. If there's not quite enough snow for that design, pitch the tarp at your desired height and then pile snow walls up the sides and along one or both ends. In slightly warmer weather or just for a great view, pitch the tarp in a lean-to shape, providing a windbreak on one side but an open feeling on the other. If heavy snow falls, pitch the tarp at more of an angle. Good tarp designs for winter will have guy-out points in the middle of the fabric, providing support and reinforcing against winter winds. Tarps are light, versatile, can be just as warm as a tent, and reward creativity. They don't suffer from the same issues of condensation as tents do. Since tarps don't have a bottom, most hikers will want to use a bivy or have a sleeping bag with a water-proof-breathable shell.

PERMANENT STRUCTURES

Lean-tos can be a simple option for winter travelers looking to lighten their packs. There is no need to worry about bulky, heavy tents or time-consuming snow shel-ters. But permanent structures do have some disadvantages in winter. The hard wooden floors conduct away body heat much more quickly than the snow. Also, it can feel as though the forest's entire population of mice is hiding beneath those floors, fed all summer on hikers' rations and hungry now to ravage winter food packs. Finally, even for hikers confident in the location of their intended lean-to, it is not wise to travel without an emergency shelter. A backpack for a winter over-night should include a tarp, at least, and probably a bivy as well. With these items already in your backpack, the ease of setting up a warm and comfortable tarp will quickly overwhelm the disadvantages of lean-tos.

SNOW SHELTERS

The work-hardening process described above is central to the primary snow shelter of the Northeast, the quinzee, as well as an emergency option, the dug-out. The dugout is a trench that's just long, wide, and deep enough to sleep in. Branches or extra gear (such as skis or poles) are laid across the top to support a tarp, which is then insulated with a top layer of snow. To build a dugout, you will first need to work-harden an area about twice as long and twice as wide as your body. When it has sintered, excavate the dugout with smooth, straight walls and a level bottom. If it is 3 feet deep, you will be able to sit up beneath your roof. Descend a ramp or stairs into the sleeping area and use your pack to close off the doorway. A dugout is a very quick shelter to construct compared to a quinzee, can be durable in stormy weather, and will be quite warm.

Building a quinzee shelter is a fun project and one of the legendary traditions of winter camping. While the igloo is famous as a shelter of the coastal Inuit of the polar regions, the quinzee was a favored winter sleeping structure of native people living in the northern interior of the continent, away from the ocean. An igloo requires large amounts of wind-packed slab snow, while a quinzee does not. It can

10

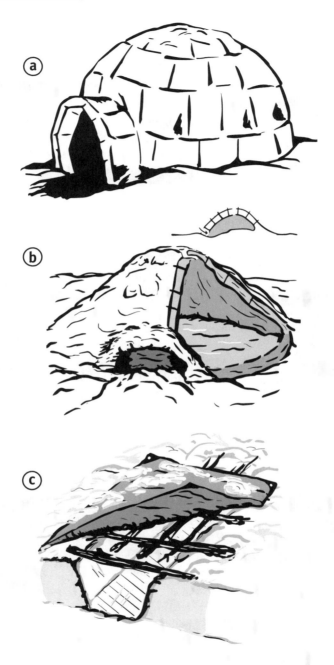

10

FIGURE 51. Common types of snow shelters include: (a) the igloo, which requires a large amount of wind-packed slab snow; (b) the quinzee, which needs a pile of snow at least 15 feet across and 4 feet tall; and (c) the dugout, a long, wide trench just deep enough to sleep in. The dugout is quick to build and durable in stormy weather, making it a great emergency option.

be built wherever there's enough snow to create a pile at least 15 feet across and 4 to 6 feet tall.

To build a quinzee that accommodates four backpackers, first work-harden a platform about 15 feet in diameter. When it is solid, begin to shovel snow on top, packing and pounding the snow as you pile it, until your mound is a smooth, steep-sided dome 5 to 6 feet tall. If the snow in the area is deep, this process will take about an hour. If you must haul snow on sleds or on tarps from a long distance, it will take much longer. Eventually you will have a solid pile, which you must allow to sinter for at least an hour, perhaps more. While it solidifies, insert small sticks or ski poles about 12 inches through the outer shell; these will mark the thickness of your walls when the pile is hollowed out from inside.

Once you are confident the snow pile has solidified, choose a door location away from the prevailing winds and begin to excavate. Keep the door small, as this will promote the best heat retention. Initially the digging will seem easy, but before long a person will need to get inside the structure and send the snow out the door. This job is very wet, so be sure to wear your waterproof jacket and pants. Carve away at the walls until you encounter the inner end of the sticks that you inserted through the shell. Each stick indicates you should excavate no farther in that direction. Once the full interior is excavated, smooth the walls and floor and consider custom options, such as small wall shelves for water bottles or lanterns. Always complete the project by poking a 3- to 4-inch hole in the ceiling of the dome to ensure ventilation.

The foot-thick walls of snow have tremendous insulation capacity. Once you're inside for the night, you can close the door with a pack, and a single candle will elevate the temperature to freezing or higher, regardless of outside temperatures. In fact, for campers with a very warm winter sleeping bag, quinzee sleeping can feel almost too warm and damp. Quinzee construction is labor intensive and is well suited to a group of three or more who are base camping in one location for a few nights. The quinzee relies on a large supply of deep snow that will respond to work-hardening. If the snow is shallow and sugary, do not bother to attempt a quinzee, as the snow will never bond well enough to excavate. Despite these challenges, successfully building and sleeping in a quinzee provides a real sense of satisfaction and self-reliance, and is one of the rites of passage for winter backpackers in the Northeast.

10

➜ EQUIPMENT

Besides shelters, there are other equipment considerations for the winter hiker and camper. You must add to your summer selections of clothing, footwear, kitchen gear, and sleeping gear, and your winter pack must be able to swallow it all, plus any added food weight. For a person skilled enough to spend a few nights backpacking in summer, pulling together a kit for winter doesn't have to be difficult.

CLOTHING

Even more than in summer and warmer seasons, using the WISE system to dress in layers is essential to comfort and safety in winter. Below are our winter recommendations for each of these layers.

Wicking

- Two complete layers of wicking clothing for torso and legs; depending on the person, these layers can be midweight or heavyweight polypropylene or merino wool.

- Thin, wicking layers for head, hands, and feet.

Insulating

- A thick wool or fleece layer for both top and bottom.

- A warm, hooded parka, insulated with down or synthetic fill; for overnights or in temperatures approaching 0F (-18C), add insulated pants as well.

- Insulated gloves or mittens. Modular versions work best, with an insulated liner that can be removed and dried in the sleeping bag at night.

- Warm hat.

Shell

- Most breathable-waterproof summer shells will work in winter as long as they are sized to accommodate all of the winter layers, including the parka.

- Because of the inevitable wetness of breaking trail, as well as sitting or kneeling on snow, waterproof shell pants are a must. Many experienced winter campers and hikers prefer a high-rise or bib-style pant for its warmth and extra protection.

- "Soft" shells block the wind and vent perspiration extremely well. They are not waterproof, but they are a winter favorite when the weather is reliably cold and dry. Unfortunately, there is always a chance of wet snow or even rain in the Northeast in winter, so it's a gamble to head into the mountains without a waterproof layer. If you use a soft shell as your primary outer layer, then be sure to carry a backup. An ultralight cycling shell or even a disposable poncho weighs almost nothing but will provide a margin of safety in unexpected rain or sleet.

10

Extra

- Goggles and sunglasses

- Gaiters (Be sure they fit over those winter boots!)

- Second pair of warm gloves or mittens

- Second warm hat

- Lighter weight hat and/or sun hat
- Balaclava or face mask
- 2 to 3 pairs of wool socks
- Insulated booties (for overnights)

FOOTWEAR

It is dangerous to hike during winter in summer boots. They are not insulated and fit too snugly, leading to frostbite or other cold injuries. But it can be difficult to find winter boots that do everything well. Winter footwear must be waterproof and insulating, and must have extra room to promote maximum circulation in the feet and toes. Some winter boots must also work for skiing, crampons, or snowshoeing. The search for your ideal winter footwear may take a while, but it is worth the effort.

Look for boots with an insulating layer and a breathable shell. If you are focused on overnight camping, opt for boots with a removable liner that can be dried inside your parka and sleeping bag. Felt-pack boots have such a liner and are usually very warm, but they can be clunky to hike long distances in and may not be fully waterproof. Single-layer, winter-specific hiking boots are often great on the trail. These boots shine on winter day hikes, but for overnights you must sleep with the entire boot to keep it from freezing. Double mountaineering boots offer removable liners and decent performance on the trail, but they can feel quite heavy and aren't compatible with many snowshoes or skis.

Some winter hikers, especially those on snowshoes, find that a mukluk is very warm and comfortable. These moccasin-style boots have a removable liner inside a knee-high shaft with a soft sole. They are warm enough to provide comfort in the coldest temperatures because they promote excellent blood circulation and breathability. With such soft construction, however, they do not perform well on technical terrain, and don't withstand wet conditions well, either. Consider each of the options above and choose whichever is right for your type of winter needs. Regardless of boot type, try them on with all of the sock layers you intend to wear on the trail. There should be no pressure points, and the boots should feel roomy and comfortable.

REMAINING EQUIPMENT

With your clothing, footwear, and shelter all set, it is fairly simple to gather your remaining winter equipment. The other pieces to consider are sleeping bags and pads, kitchen gear, and your backpack, as well as a few very useful specialized items.

Sleeping Bags

Sleeping bags should be rated for at least 10 degrees colder than expected temperatures. For most of the Northeast, a bag rated for -20F (-29C) should cover you, even

10

in mid-January. If, however, you are a cold sleeper or are planning on sleeping high in the alpine, consider getting a bag rated for even colder temperatures. Using a bivy will keep your sleeping bag drier in any temperature, and will add about 10 degrees of warmth to its rating. Down bags will compress more and will be lighter, but you have to keep them dry to maintain the down's loft. A winter bag is a specialized, single-purpose piece of equipment, and a high-quality model could cost in excess of $700. Some hikers avoid this purchase by using a normal three-season bag (20F, -7C) with a summer-weight bag (40F, 5C) over it. As long as both bags can fully loft up, this will be a warm and versatile system, although it will take up a huge amount of space in a backpack. Be sure to experiment near home to understand any solution's true comfort level for you.

Sleeping Pads

A sleeping pad is just as important as the bag itself. A person in a top-end winter sleeping bag will still be dangerously cold if he or she is not protected from conductive heat loss through the snow or cold ground. Nearly all winter camping situations call for two sleeping pads. A very common system is an air mattress or self-inflating mattress layered on top of a closed-cell foam pad. For only a few ounces of weight, the foam pad offers excellent insulation value and can act as a backup if the inflatable pad gets a leak. The insulation value of a sleeping pad is called its "R-value" and is a number between 1 and 10 provided by the manufacturer. The higher the R-value, the more the insulation, and the values of two pads are additive. For winter camping, create a sleeping pad system (either one or multiple pads) that has an R-value of at least 5, and aim for an R-value of 7 or more if you are a cold sleeper.

Kitchen Gear

Kitchen gear for winter differs in a few ways to accommodate the colder temperatures. When a natural gas canister gets cold (below freezing), the propane blend inside will not have enough pressure to push itself out. There are improvised fixes to this problem, but you shouldn't plan on them working. Instead, nearly all winter backpackers choose to use a liquid-gas (white gas) stove. This type of stove can be pressurized in any temperature and has an output capable of quickly melting snow. Groups of more than two people should consider bringing a second stove, which will let you boil water at the same time as you're cooking. Certain stove models really excel at producing a powerful flame. These stoves are usually louder than the average, but the trade-off for that fighter-jet power is exceptional speed for boiling high volumes of water or melting snow. They make a great choice as the second stove for winter travel. If you do bring a dedicated snow-melting stove, be sure to carry a dedicated melting pot with a lid.

Another important item for the winter kitchen is a stove pad. In cold, wintry environments, any stove will sink into the snow as the stove heats up. This situation quickly becomes dangerous when the pot of hot water sitting on top of the stove

10

falls off. A stove pad provides a firm surface and some insulation, keeping the stove level. There are premade models on the market, but you can easily make one at home. A simple approach is to duct-tape a square of closed-cell foam to a wooden clipboard with the clip removed. Drill a couple of holes for a loop of elasticized cord to grip the fuel bottle, and your stove pad is complete. Bring one pad for each stove; stoves are worthless in deep snow without one.

Cold and windy conditions can rob heat from your cooking and melting pots, but you can keep some of that heat from escaping. A windscreen for the stove will promote efficiency by funneling heat upward, toward the pot. Putting a lid on a pot is the simplest efficiency trick, reducing boil times by 10 percent or more. For extended trips, consider carrying a heat exchanger, which you can buy or make. These devices wrap around the cooking pot and channel heat from the stove up beside the pot. They can increase efficiency by another 10 percent or more, but they do come with a weight penalty. If your winter trip is longer than three days, consider bringing one, as the weight of fuel you save could exceed the weight of the heat exchanger.

Backpacks

Packs for winter travel simply need to be bigger to swallow your sleeping gear, extra clothes, increased fuel rations, and added food. If your pack for a summer weekend trip is 60 liters, you will want 80 to 90 liters of capacity in your winter backpack. You will find that the weight burden adds up, so the pack should have all of the comfort features possible for an expedition-size load: padded hip belt and shoulder straps, adjustable suspension, and more.

If this load sounds unreasonable, if your trip will extend beyond five or six days, or if you'll be traveling in snow deeper than 3 feet, it is time to consider using a sled to transport your food and equipment. An expedition sled (sometimes called a "pulk") removes the load from your back and connects to your waist via a backpack hip belt. Often a winter traveler with a sled will carry a small day pack as well, and the sled may attach directly to that. Not only do sleds ease the weight on your shoulders, they are fun to have in the backcountry and can be very useful for a winter evacuation. Expedition sleds can be purchased, but most sled aficionados will tell you that the best pulk is homemade from a conventional sled (e.g., the Paris Expedition model, made in Maine). Plans and ideas are readily available on the internet, and making your own backcountry sled can be an easy, fun project. For control on the trail, be sure your design includes rigid poles for connecting the traveler to the load.

10

Regardless of the method of construction, there are a few common concepts when it comes to using sleds. Instead of getting packed in a backpack, your gear can go into a single, large zip-duffel or a collection of smaller duffels, all secured onto the sled. Since this baggage will be sliding along against the snow, it needs to be weather-tight, so most will have an integrated tarp of some sort. Sometimes a travel group will bring fewer sleds than there are people in the group, and members will take turns pulling a sled. Sleds are great for fairly open, level winter routes. If, however, the terrain becomes very hilly, slopes sideways, or has tightly spaced vegetation, a sled will become unmanageable. Sometimes it takes two hikers to wrangle one sled through thick brush or down a steep hill. Know your route before committing to traveling with a sled.

And the Rest

There are a few other essential items for safe and fun winter camping. The most important not mentioned yet is a shovel. You will need a shovel for all the work-hardening, shelter building, and kitchen shaping, as well as to dig down to water sources. Folding models for backcountry skiing work well as long as they have a full, deep blade. Regular, small-size home snow shovels also work well and are available for just a few dollars. Also be sure to pack plenty of batteries. Cold temperatures sap the power from most batteries, and winter nights are twice as long as in summer. Be sure to keep any critical electronics warm inside your jacket and sleep with your headlamp in your bag. Chemical heat packs do not weigh much but can be literally lifesaving. It is reasonable to expect every person in a group to carry four packs to ensure a ready supply in an emergency.

Because the days are short, many winter campers enjoy bringing a lantern as a luxury item. There are portable lanterns powered by white gas, isobutane, batteries, or candles, each with its own set of advantages and disadvantages. Finally, if your route takes you into the high mountains, you will need to consider a whole new list of mountaineering equipment, such as crampons, ice axes, avalanche beacons, climbing ropes, and more. If this is the case, you must pursue specific training in these skills.

➜ TRANSPORTATION

When the snow depth reaches mid-shin, it begins to hamper a hiker's forward prog-ress. When the snow gets to be 2 feet or more deep (over the knee), the increased energy demand is so high that it is time to choose a way to transport yourself and your gear over the snow rather than through it. You can choose between snowshoes and skis, and each shines in certain conditions.

10   Skis can be energy-efficient travel tools. They feel graceful and fluid, almost magical, to the experienced skier. They can also be a tremendous hassle when the terrain gets vertical (at least in the Northeast) or is congested with trees. Steep uphills require various specialized techniques and equipment. Downhills are fun only when the runout is clear and there are few trees. Skiing usually requires spe-cialized boots that may not work well for winter overnights in truly cold weather.

If you are an experienced skier who is traveling on a gently rolling route, skis may be a great choice. For camping in the backcountry of the Northeast, look for skis with a waxless base that are fairly wide (120 millimeters underfoot) and short (140 to 160 centimeters), possibly with a Berwin binding to accommodate regular felt-pack boots or mukluks. If you must use specialized boots, they should be made with a double construction and fit much looser than boots intended for ski-resort recreation.

For the average winter backcountry traveler, snowshoes are a much more versatile and accessible transportation choice. They handle a wide range of terrain, including movement through thick vegetation or up steep slopes. There is a learning curve when using snowshoes, but novices can quickly master the basics, especially when using ski poles, too. Snowshoes do not provide the blissful gliding experience of skis, and they can feel awkward and clunky on your feet. But they do save a great deal of energy by floating the hiker above the snowpack, preventing "post-holing," and plowing as they move forward. Most contemporary winter campers use snowshoe models with aluminum frames, plastic decks, and some teeth on the bottom for better traction on sloping terrain. Be sure that the binding will work with your winter boots. Snowshoes come in various sizes based on weight, so choose a model that will handle both you and your pack together.

➜ WINTER SAFETY

Winter's cold temperatures bring extra hazards, but with extra preparation and know-how, you do not need to view winter travel as a survival experience. Of course, the cold greatly increases the opportunity for environmental injuries, such as frostbite, immersion foot, and hypothermia. Be sure that you are fully informed about the symptoms and treatment of each of these maladies, as well as the best techniques for packaging and transporting an injured winter traveler. Good training in wilderness medicine, as well as self-study, will give you the tools you need. Beyond these medical situations, there are a few other important winter-specific safety concerns.

The first step toward winter safety begins at the trailhead. Know your route well and be sure that you have left your itinerary with a reliable person at home (as well as under your car seat). The car itself will be an important resource, so be sure it will start reliably when you return to the trailhead. Stock it with the usual automotive emergency equipment, such as jumper cables, blankets, tire chains if you don't have snow tires, and chemical heat packs. If you are not hiking with a shovel, be sure your car has one so that when you return after a week of snowstorms you can get out of the lot. Many parts of the Northeast contain forest access roads that are not maintained during winter. The snow may be shallow when you arrive, but if

10

it snows heavily while you're in the mountains, you may end up finding yourself stranded many miles inside the forest boundaries. Before you drive in, check that your road will be plowed after it snows. Local land management agencies and hiking clubs should be able to provide this information.

Another simple but important winter hazard is slipping on ice. While this may sound fairly innocuous, it becomes much more serious if the slip leads to a fall into a creek or off of a cliff, or if the victim breaks a limb. For safe traction, it is a good idea to carry some kind of microcrampon, often called microspikes. For trails that involve steep ascents or alpine terrain, these are absolutely required. There are many models available, most of which have some kind of stretchy material that secures a set of metal spikes or coils to your boots. Be sure to practice with these at home so you know how to attach them to your boots and that they will stay on as you walk. For a lighter option, some winter hikers stud each boot with ten to twelve small, hex-head sheet-metal screws. Weighing only an ounce, this handful of studs is completely effective in rolling terrain and moderate ascents, and you never have to think about putting them on or taking them off. Whatever method you choose, be sure you have a strategy to keep your footing secure when the trail turns icy.

Bodies of water in winter present a special kind of hazard. On one hand, it can be very efficient to traverse the iced-over surface of a pond or river. And camping on a pond, while unsheltered, offers an amazing view of the winter sky. Falling through ice, however, is a desperate scenario that you must avoid at all costs. The first and most basic safety principle is to never go out on ice when alone. The second is to never take chances with ice if you're uncertain. Hikers who know they will be on ice regularly should bring an ice chisel to help evaluate ice thickness and soundness. Look for a model that has a removable handle, as these will be lighter to carry into the backcountry. Another item to consider is a pair of ice rescue picks (available at hunting and fishing stores), which are worn around the neck and can be used for self-rescue. Institutional groups may also bring a length of floating rescue rope. As in many situations, this rescue gear is only a backup to knowledge and skill. The best plan is to avoid an incident entirely.

Winter campers must develop a body of experience and observations on which to base judgments about the safety of ice sheets on lakes, ponds, and moving water. Fortunately, there is credible research into ice strength conducted by the U.S. military and by northern countries, such as Canada and Sweden. Based on this research, a winter backcountry traveler can rely on the following principles:

- Clear blue ice is the strongest ice.
- Opaque white ice includes air bubbles. It was formed from snow and is considered half as strong as clear blue ice. For all strength-safety guidelines, double the recommended safe thicknesses below if the ice is opaque and white.

- On stationary water bodies, 8 inches of clear, blue, nonfractured ice is safe for foot travel. This thickness is approximately the same as the width across a human hand, including the thumb.

- On stationary water bodies, 4 inches of clear, blue, nonfractured ice is safe for static activities, such as camping. This thickness is approximately the same as the length of a human hand, from the tip of the longest finger to the wrist crease.

- Because ice expands and contracts with temperature changes, large and sudden temperature drops stress the ice sheet, creating stress cracks. Exercise extra caution for at least the subsequent 24 hours following rapid temperature drops of more than 20 degrees.

- When air temperature is above freezing for six of the previous 24 hours, the ice will start to lose strength; exercise extra caution for at least 24 hours. If the air temperature has been above freezing for 24 hours or longer, *stay off the ice.*

- Stress cracks in lake ice are a normal feature and are not hazardous when dry. If water is seeping upward through the crack, avoid it or cross it at a perpendicular angle.

- Recent changes in water level, either up or down, decrease the reliability of ice.

- Listen for hollow-sounding ice, especially near the shorelines of lakes and ponds. This ice is not safe. The ice-thickness recommendations above are valid only when the ice is supported by floating on water.

- Deep snow will depress the ice sheet, forcing water onto its surface through stress cracks and along edges. The slushy overflow water may not freeze for a long time, as it will be insulated by the snowpack. Be careful in these conditions: the slush will instantly freeze to boots, ski poles, and other items.

- River ice is thinnest where the current is fastest, usually in the center of a straight channel or at the outside of bends. For river crossings, double the ice thickness guidelines above and follow all the warm-weather principles provided in Chapter 8 except for group-crossing techniques.

- Ice over marshy terrain or vegetation is unpredictable and should be avoided.

- Avoid areas where snow is darkened by water underneath or areas where hoar frost ("frost feathers") forms on the surface of clear ice at night. Both of these conditions indicate thin, unsafe ice.

Ice travel is one more opportunity to use observation to develop your judgment. Mindful attention to the weather, the ice conditions, and your senses will provide you with the clues you need to make safe decisions. With time, winter backcountry travelers can understand ice travel as well as they understand a hiking trail. As you develop these skills, stay off the ice when in doubt and find a new way to accomplish your route.

10

CHAPTER 11
GROUPS

Sharing nature with other outdoor enthusiasts is one thing, but when it comes to sharing the trail with children, a beginner, or a pet, you should expect your experiences to be quite different. This chapter will address the various ways you can adapt your outdoor outings to ensure a fun, safe, and rewarding experience for all. We will also look at the impact of group dynamics, as well as how individual behavior can affect the group experience. Because the success of an outing depends on member interaction, it's essential for everyone to be prepared to observe, understand, and help manage these dynamics.

➜ TRAVELING WITH CHILDREN

Before getting into the details of hiking with kids, it's important to understand that most infants and children can go just about anywhere you'd like to take them in the great outdoors. Obviously, it's wise to avoid bringing your young one into extreme environments, such as very high altitudes (i.e., 11,500 to 18,000 feet), hot desert regions, and bitterly cold arctic weather. When it comes to other regions you'd like to explore—forests, lakes, rivers, oceans, mild deserts, and low- to moderate-altitude mountains—you can enjoy all of these places with your family while introducing your children to the beauty of our planet. You just need to plan accordingly.

Don't wait for the kids to be teenagers before you take them outdoors. A love of the wilderness is cultivated in childhood. Camping and hiking with kids will help you rediscover the beauty of nature through their ever-curious eyes.

AGE RANGES

For the purpose of this chapter, we'll define age groups as follows:

- Infants: Birth to 15 months
- Toddlers: 16 months to 3 years
- Preschoolers: 4 to 5 years
- Children: 6 to 10 years
- Preteens: 11 to 13 years
- Teens: 14 to 17 years

→ ADJUSTING EXPECTATIONS FOR RECREATING WITH CHILDREN

The first step toward ensuring a successful trip with children is to adjust your expectations—most importantly, your mileage goal. An appropriate purpose for your outing is to help connect your children with nature; doing so means focusing on their experiences and to adopt this Montessori mantra: "Follow the child." This means you should be flexible in your travel plans and be ready to rearrange your day if your young trail partner suddenly chooses to spend 30 minutes observing frogs or building a dam in a small creek.

Adjusting your expectations also means adjusting your destination. Remember that peakbagging is an adult goal and, generally, not on a child's bucket list. Hiking with kids means traveling shorter distances, respective to their ages and personalities. Here are some suggestions for appropriate hiking distances with children.

Anyone who has hiked with children will tell you that it is a fun but "heavy" endeavor, meaning you can expect your pack to be heavier than usual. Therefore, it is essential to know what to bring and what to leave behind. It's a good idea to start with what your kid will need on the trail or in camp and then add what is truly essential for you and for the type of outing you're planning. When selecting these items, consider their weight and the total weight to be carried for each family member. Read our recommendations on page 250 for day-hiking or backpacking with the various age groups.

11

CHILD AGES AND RECOMMENDED HIKING DISTANCES		
Age Group	Recommended Distance per Day	Note
Infant and Toddlers	1 to 5 miles	This distance depends greatly on your ability to carry the necessary hiking/camping gear and the infant or toddler on your back.
Preschoolers	1 to 3 miles	This distance depends greatly on the ability and attitude of your preschooler to hike on a trail with a very light pack. This distance is intentionally shorter than the infant/toddler range, as preschoolers might be walking on their own the entire way, as opposed to being carried. For preschoolers who spend some time being carried, the distance can be increased based on your own stamina and interest.
Children	3 to 5 miles	This distance depends greatly on your child's fitness and attitude toward hiking with a small day pack.
Preteens	5 to 8 miles	This distance depends on your preteen's ambition and experience hiking with a medium-size pack.
Teens	7 to 10+ miles	Incorporate your teen into your planning, including distance.

HIKING WITH INFANTS AND TODDLERS
Day-Hiking

Day-hiking with infants and toddlers is a bit like going anywhere with them: You need to bring your "New Parents Kit," the large diaper bag you lug around anytime you're away from home. This bag includes essentials such as diapers, a soiled-diaper bag, diaper rash cream, baby wipes, a changing pad (which could be as simple as a bandana), a change of baby clothes, a bottle kit and formula if you are not breastfeeding (which would be the easiest option on the trail), a teething toy or pacifier, a burp cloth (possibly another bandana), baby/toddler food, a baby spoon, hand sanitizer, baby sunscreen, and a play/napping blanket and small toy. When on the trail, you will also be tasked with including the ten esssentials for day-hiking. (See Chapter 1, page 7, for a refresher on these.)

Backpacking

For a backpacking trip involving one overnight or more, the list of baby items you need is the same as above, with additional diapers, changes of clothes, and food. Sharing a sleeping bag with an older child might be the best option for a lighter trip. For babies, however, the CDC warns against co-sleeping. Remember, when backpacking, already-tired parents will become exhausted parents. Consider bringing a small, portable co-sleeper crib for babies. This closeness might help your baby

11

or toddler feel comforted when in the wilderness, which, for them, will be an entirely new (and potentially frightening) experience. Note that for an overnight trip, you will need to bring some toys or baby books. See below for more tips on what to bring to entertain your young campers.

DEALING WITH DIAPERS ON THE TRAIL

Disposable or reusable cotton diapers need to be brought back home to be disposed of properly or washed. You can bury the baby's feces just as you would do for your own by digging a cat hole or using an official outhouse. Wet diapers can be dried at camp to reduce their weight before packing them out. While cleaning soiled cotton diapers in the wild—or anywhere else, for that matter—isn't pleasant, you can do so if you are using the LNT laundry technique covered on page 139 in Chapter 6.

HIKING WITH PRESCHOOLERS
Day-Hiking

When it comes to day-hiking with 4- to 5-year-olds, it's all about bringing the right snacks in the right amounts. Some cool exploration tools, such as a child's magnifying glass or a pretend (or real) kid's camera, can also make a difference in motivating your preschool hiker. Most importantly, think about bringing a treasure bag for your kid. Teach kids what they can collect along the trail (twigs, rocks, dead leaves, etc.) and what trail treasures they should leave where they found them (such as flowers, bugs, slugs, and green leaves). This is when having a camera becomes useful, as they can take photos of trail treasures they cannot put in their treasure bag. Don't forget to pack all of this in a small and very light backpack, which can also include a snack, a bug net, sunscreen, and a lightweight 6- to 8-ounce water pouch. The kids will love to feel independent; for them, the hike will be like a great expedition role-play.

Again, extra clothing and a raincoat would be good for young explorers, as well as rubber boots or wet shoes, so they can explore water and mud holes without parental disapproval. This is a basic instinct for them.

Backpacking

When backpacking with preschoolers, bring all of the suggested items for a day hike, plus some additional items. We've field-tested the following in our own families. If your preschooler has a preferred plush or blanket, bring it! Forgetting this essential item could easily ruin an overnight in the woods. Think about getting your children their own headlamps. They'll love playing and exploring with their very own light source. Unless you prefer otherwise, preschoolers can sleep in their own child-sized sleeping bag, with a light and a kid-size closed-cell sleeping pad.

11

HIKING WITH CHILDREN, PRETEENS, AND TEENS
Day-Hiking and Backpacking

When day-hiking or backpacking with children, preteens, and teens, often the best "item" you can bring on the trail is a friend or a cousin. If you have siblings that get along, great! But most likely your children, preteens, and especially teens would love to bring along a best friend with whom to share their outdoor adventures—and perhaps misadventures. If you can find another family that also enjoys hiking or backpacking, combining two families with children of the same or similar ages can be a real advantage.

Children, preteens, and obviously adolescents can carry some of the weight. See the recommended load table, below, from the American Occupational Therapy Association. Remember that children, preteens, and teens have developing bodies, which means they have immature skeletons and musculatures. It is very important for their health (and enjoyment) to ensure their backpacks fit them and are not too heavy.

CHILD AGES AND RECOMMENDED PACK WEIGHT		
Age Group	**Recommended Pack Weight**	**Sample Pack Contents**
Preschoolers	1 to 2 pounds	Small water pouch, snack, magnifying glass, kid's camera (toy or real), trail treasure bag, bug net, small tube of sunscreen for sensitive skin
Children	10 percent of child's body weight	Small water pouch or bottle, snack, favorite plush animal or small blanket, headlamp, sunscreen and lip balm, rain layer, extra socks, gloves, and warm hat
Preteens	10 percent to 15 percent of preteen's body weight	Water bottle, snack, lunch, headlamp, sunscreen and lip balm, sunglasses, map, fire starter, knife, personal tableware, small book, rain gear, warm upper layer, extra socks, gloves, warm hat, sleeping pad
Teens	20 percent to 30 percent of teen's body weight	Water bottle, snack, lunch, headlamp, sunscreen and lip balm, sunglasses, map, fire starter, knife, personal tableware, small book, rain gear, warm upper and lower layer, extra socks, gloves, warm hat, sleeping pad, sleeping bag, one piece of group camping gear (e.g., cooking pot, tent fly, or fuel bottle)

11

The load amount will vary for each young hiker based not only on weight but also on athletic ability and hiking experience. For instance, we have seen many experienced, mature, and athletic 17-year-olds carry a full adult load. As a reminder, healthy adult hikers should usually be able to carry 35 to 40 percent of their body weight, while experienced and seasoned hikers can carry 40 to 50 percent of their body weight, when needed.

EXPECT WORK FOR EXTRA REWARDS

Another adjustment you should be prepared for when traveling the backcountry with kids is that you will have to do extra work on the trail as well as around camp. Not only will you have to take care of your own needs, you will have to take care of your kids' needs, and as a rule of thumb, the younger they are, the more needs they will have. It's like being at home, but with the outdoor setting as an extra challenge.

For that reason, we recommend you become an experienced hiker and camper before you decide to bring along members of the next generation. Once you have all of your basic outdoor skills mastered, from shelter setup and cooking to navigation and first aid, it will be easier for you to bring the kids along. That said, regardless of your experience, plan for short hiking days to save time for work and play in camp.

Although there are many challenges to camping with kids, there are many rewards as well. Not only will camping create family memories, it will help your children connect with nature. In this age of screen addiction, time spent in nature is often seen as a remedy for—some would say an antidote to—what the founder of Outward Bound, Kurt Hahn, called the "spectatorism syndrome" in youth. Hahn's message was simple: Don't let your child be a spectator in the game of life; help your child be a player.

> **→ PRO TIP:** A good way to reduce the challenges of backpacking for youngest kids is to plan to stay at a base camp for a few days. Choosing to hike 1 to 3 miles to a great campsite will allow you and your kids to explore a larger area by conducting short, daily excursions without having to carry all of your camping gear. This way you can combine the adventurous experience of camping with the ease of day-hiking.

Multiple Scandinavian studies, including those conducted by Ingunn Fjørtoft, have concluded that child play in outdoor settings helps with the development of physical abilities and agilities. One can easily imagine that letting kids play on uneven terrain will promote a far greater sense of balance than time spent only on uniformly flat playgrounds.

Other research has also indicated that young children are able to better develop what biologists and environmental education researchers call "biophilia." Edward O. Wilson defined the term in his 1984 book by that title as "the urge to affiliate with other forms of life." Connecting your children to nature is perhaps one of the greatest gifts you can give them. With a deep and personal connection to the natural world, they may well grow into environmentally conscious adults with a greater sense of the role humans play in nature. Go out with your kids and save the planet, one child at the time.

11

→ TOYS AND GAMES FOR THE TRAIL

Camping with young kids should be fun for you and for them. Although kids can easily find a lot of play in nature, it's always good to have one or two surprises in your back pocket. Rainy days are always a possibility, so having something fun to play with under a tarp or in the tent can make the difference between good and bad camping memories. Here are a few toys and table games that have been field-tested by many hiking families.

TOYS AND TABLE GAMES

Toys and table games, especially ones that are new to your brood, are a great way to entertain and engage your kids while on a camping trip. The most successful toys are those that require interaction though cooperation or playful competition:

- Mini figures (Lego, Playmobil, My Little Pony, etc.)
- Animal figures (dinosaurs, farm animals, wild animals)
- Frisbee, beach balls (the kind you can deflate), marbles
- Playing cards, Uno, checkers, chess (with a canvas board)
- Trivia card games, puzzles, action card games (Spot It!, Slamwich, SET, etc.)
- Play-Doh, paper and crayons, craft materials for making bracelets and necklaces, etc.

Often the best strategy when it comes to packing toys and games is to involve your children in selecting their favorites while respecting two simple rules: Anything they choose must be small and lightweight.

OUTDOOR GAMES

Playing games with your kids around camp or along trails can enhance their experience in nature. Here are a few that are always popular.

Camp Games

- **Camouflage** (three players or more). Establish a central area for someone who assumes the role of the "photographer," about 6 feet by 6 feet. We call this the photographer's box. While the photographer has his or her eyes closed, the rest of the players hide in the forest but must keep the photographer in their line of sight. After the countdown is over, the photographer has five minutes to spot and identify people while remaining inside the photographer's box. When the photographer spots a player, the photographer can try to identify the location and name the player. If correct, the player comes to the photographer's box. Once the photographer runs out of time, the closest player to the photographer who was not found or identified correctly wins the round and becomes the next photographer.

11

- **Hug-a-tree** (two players or more). One player is blindfolded and gently spun around three times, losing his or her bearings. Another player then leads the blindfolded player through the woods, taking a wandering route so the blindfolded player grows even more confused. The players should stay within sight of the starting place. The leader picks a tree and leads the blindfolded person up to it, saying, "This is your tree," and putting the blindfolded player's hands on the trunk.

  The blindfolded player can take as much time as desired getting to know the tree, feeling its trunk, learning where its branches are, and checking out roots or other distinctive features. Once finished, the leader guides the blindfolded player back to the starting place and removes the blindfold. The player then tries to find his or her tree. Reversing roles is the natural next step for this nature sensory game.

- **Silent walk** (three players or more). One player sits on the ground with eyes closed. The other players begin walking toward the central player, moving as quietly as possible. If the player at the center of the game hears someone walking, he or she can point a finger in the direction of the noise. If a walking player is in the path of the pointed finger, that player must return to his or her starting place. The goal of the game is to walk silently, without being detected, and gently touch the head of the player at the center of the game. Whoever accomplishes the perfect silent walk will be the next player at the center of the game.

Trail Games

- **Trail blazer** (any number of players). This is a very easy game to play along the trail while encouraging your kids to hike. Simply challenge your children to find the next trail blaze on trees or rocks. Whoever sees and calls a blaze first gets a point. The player with the most points at the end of the hike is named King or Queen of the Trail.

- **Who am I?** (two players or more). This is another fun game to play while hiking. One player thinks of a very well-known person or an animal and invites the other players to guess who that person is or what the animal is. The players can only ask questions that can be answered with "Yes" or "No." The game goes on until someone guesses correctly.

- **Twenty-one** (two players). This game is great for a pair of older kids, such as preteens, hiking alongside each other. One player starts the game by saying one number or two consecutive numbers, such as "one" or "one, two." The second player then also says one or two numbers in a row. For instance, if the first player says "one," the second player can say "two" or "two, three." The goal of the game is for the players to count from one to 21 by taking turns saying one or two consecutive numbers. The player who ends up saying the number 21 loses the game.

11

→ HIKING GEAR AND CLOTHING FOR INFANTS AND YOUNG KIDS

INFANT CARRIERS

Infant carriers are backpacks specifically designed for carrying an infant or a toddler, plus some extra supplies (but not much more). If you choose to take an infant or toddler camping, make sure at least one other adult is accompanying who can carry most of the required camping gear, since you'll be carrying the little one. If carrying all of this equipment is too much for you and your partner or companion, consider car camping and using the infant carrier for day hikes.

Infant carriers have a child weight limit, usually 40 to 45 pounds, so if your precious cargo is near this limit, you might want to carry only your child in the carrier and no other gear. If your child is 20 to 25 pounds, you can add some weight, assuming the carrier has additional gear storage.

When a child's weight surpasses 45 pounds—typically around 6 years of age—you might want to focus on having the child walk most of the trail. If, however, you want another option between the full-size infant carrier and the autonomous child hike, you might consider carrying your preschooler on your shoulders with a specialized child-carrying yoke, such as the SaddleBaby. This type of child carrier will keep your preschooler safe and comfortable while keeping your hands free.

In addition to a maximum weight, all infant carriers also have a recommended minimum age of development. To transport an infant in a backpacklike carrier, the infant needs to be able to hold his or her own head up, a developmental skill that typically occurs around six months of age. Newborns and babies without this core ability should be carried in a front pack or sling carrier.

There are lots of good infant carriers on the market, and you can often find them used, since families will grow out of them within a few years. Before you buy this specialized piece of gear, new or used, consider the following recommended features.

11

- **Integrated kickstand.** Make sure your carrier has a kickstand, which makes the loading and unloading of an infant much safer and easier.

> → **PRO TIP:** When using a loaded infant carrier, never bend at the waist and lean over. This could create a scary and dangerous situation for your infant or toddler, not to mention a potential back injury for you. Instead, always bend at the knees. If possible, having someone else help load and unload an infant carrier from your back is a good and safe habit. If you're hiking alone, ask a passerby near the trailhead for assistance. This is not an instance where you should politely refuse help or try to accomplish the task on your own if assistance is available. Sometimes two pairs of hands are needed, and you wouldn't want to risk dropping your child or unintentionally tipping him or her out of the carrier.

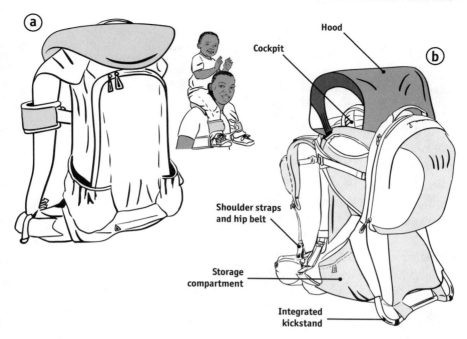

FIGURE 52. The best backcountry options for toting small children are: (a) for toddlers, a child-carrying yoke; and (b) for infants who can sit on their own, a baby-carrier backpack.

Remember, though, that a child carrier standing upright by itself with a kickstand is not an approved infant high chair. Never leave an infant sitting in a carrier without holding on to, or at least being very close to, the carrier. Some carriers have kickstands that self-deploy when you put the carrier on the ground. This is a cool feature, but what's most important is that the kickstand can be locked in place once open.

- **Cockpit.** The cockpit is the seat where the infant sits in the carrier. Make sure the cockpit is well padded, especially on the bottom, and that the leg openings can be adjusted to fit your infant's legs. Some cockpits come with a removable, washable inner layer (handy for baby drool), which can be useful. Some also come with stirrups that allow infants to shift weight from their bottoms to their legs, adding to their comfort.

- **Five-point harness.** Your infant should be well anchored inside the cockpit. Carriers with adjustable five-point harnesses are best. An infant fidgeting within the cockpit could throw you off balance and to the ground with your precious load.

- **Shoulder straps and hip belt.** Like any good backpack, you want an infant carrier that has well-designed and properly padded shoulder straps and hip belt for you. Make sure the straps and belt are fully adjustable and can conform to both your and your partner's body types if you intend on sharing the infant load. The car-

11

rier harness should also have adjustment straps, allowing you to properly anchor the carrier to the harness. These load adjustment straps are usually attached to the shoulder straps and the hip belt.

- **Hood**. The infant carrier should have a removable hood that can protect your child from sun, rain, and blood-sucking insects.

- **Storage compartment.** Choosing a carrier with extra storage is helpful. Just make sure you don't overload the carrier. The weight limit on most carriers is for the child's body weight and any gear carried on or in the pack.

- **Mirror.** Some parents and infants like to have eye contact while hiking. Using a small pocket mirror or the mirror on your sighting compass will allow you to keep an eye on your child and share a smile.

RECOMMENDED CLOTHING FOR CHILDREN

As with adult campers, there is no bad weather for kids, just poor clothing selection. Don't be surprised that we recommend you apply the same principles of proper outdoor clothing to kids as we did for adults on pages 28 and 29 in Chapter 2. Dressing WISE applies to kids, from infants to adolescents. Unfortunately, most outdoor companies don't make many specialized garments for infants and toddlers, so you might need to get a bit creative using the tips below.

Dressing Infants and Toddlers for Cold and Wet Weather

Because infants and toddlers will mostly be transported via carrier, they won't be able to generate their own body heat through movement. Since they often cannot tell you if they are too hot or too cold, avoid assessing their body temperature by simply touching their hands or cheeks. Instead, sneak your hands into their armpits to check their skin temperature. If kids are sweaty, remove a layer. If kids are cool and dry, that's great, but if they feel cold, add a layer and make them move or feed them to generate some body heat. If kids are very cold, make sure to warm them up by first removing them from any cold sources, such as wind and moisture, and use the skin-to-skin warming method. To do so, remove some of the child's layers and place him or her inside your own jacket to generate as much skin-to-skin contact as possible. If needed, set up camp and place the child in a shelter, such as a tent, and have the child bundle up with you in your sleeping bag.

As for specific clothing selections, avoid cottons as much as possible during cold and wet seasons. If you

> **➔ PRO TIP:** Although it's possible to find one-piece warm outer layers, synthetic or wool inner layers for infants can be trickier. Consider repurposing your old base-layer shirt by cutting and sewing a snug-fitting one-piece base layer for your infant. An infant bathing suit can also work as a backcountry base layer.

11

are using cotton diapers, add a layer of synthetic cloth between the child and the diapers This will help kids stay dryer after urination. Select wool, synthetic, or silk fabric for the base layer. You could even use a "rash guard" swim top if you have one on hand. Outdoor retailers, such as L.L. Bean and REI, typically carry children's clothing specific to outdoor recreation. If you aren't looking to spend a lot of money, you can use clothing you already have, as long as it's a polyester blend.

- **Insulation layer.** Using fleece or wool for these upper and lower inner layers will give you more flexibility. For the outer insulation layer, we recommend a one-piece suit or bib overalls to keep your child clean and dry.

- **Shell layer.** The rain layer should be excellent, so this is where you should spend some extra money. If the waterproof layer keeps kids dry, they will be free to enjoy the great outdoors in all conditions.

- **Footwear.** Consider bringing rubber boots. These will keep your kids' feet dry, especially if you purchase a pair with a drawstring at the top, allowing you to cinch the boots around kids' legs. For cold days, consider putting a pair of your own socks over infants' or toddlers' feet and legs while they ride in a carrier.

- **Cold-weather accessories.** A hat with flaps, a neck gaiter or scarf, and a couple of pairs of mittens are essential to ensuring your infants and toddlers stay comfortable and warm. Don't forget to attach the hat and mittens to the coat. Otherwise, these items (or you) could end up becoming your little one's primary source of entertainment, as he or she sees you repeatedly squatting down to pick up the items flying (or thrown) from the carrier cockpit.

Dressing Infants and Toddlers for Hot and Sunny Weather

Infant and toddler skin is very sensitive to sunlight, so beyond the obvious need to use infant-appropriate sunblock, it's equally important to dress them properly for sunny and warm days. This is when it's preferable to use some tightly woven, high–Ultraviolet Protection Factor garments that fit loosely to encourage airflow and the cooling effect of convection. Long, loose pants with elastic at the ankles and short gaiters for children to keep away biting insects are both useful. If you don't have these, long socks above the pants will do the trick. You might have to remind your child that in the great outdoors, function always trumps fashion, so be a role model and roll your socks over your pants. And in hot and sunny weather, a hat with a large brim is simply the best.

11

→ HEALTH AND SAFETY FOR INFANTS AND CHILDREN

When it comes to safety on the trail and around camp, children are an additional source of potential risk. Take the time to adapt your traveling and camping habits to include the following kid-related safety recommendations.

- **Whistle.** Everyone from toddlers to adults should have a whistle around their necks. Young kids should be taught how to use an emergency whistle and should practice a few times before taking to the woods. Take the time to simulate an incident and show them how to blow three loud blasts at regular intervals. We've practiced this skill with our kids, and they all loved pretending to look for us and bring us help. Make it a game that can be applied in the real world, if needed.

- **Staying found.** Also take the time to teach your kids what to do if they get disoriented. Tell them to sit down, stay calm, and simply blow their whistle. Emphasize, "Do not run." Teach them how to make themselves visible by hanging unneeded clothing layers or a bandana in the tree branches around them. Teach them to be patient and remind them that you will be looking for them, so that all they have to do is sit, blow their whistle, and be visible.

- **Mushrooms, wild plants, and fruits.** Here's a simple rule for on the trail: Tell your kids they should always ask a grownup before eating any mushroom, wild plant, or fruit they find. Tell them that many of the fruits along the trail or around camp might look like familiar ones from the garden or the grocery store, but to be sure, they should always check with an adult.

- **Insects.** Use proper clothing as a barrier for insects rather than soaking your kids in N, N-diethyl-meta-toluamide (a.k.a. DEET). When used as directed, products containing between 10 percent and 30 percent DEET have been found by the American Academy of Pediatrics (AAP) to be safe to use on children, as well as on adults. The AAP, however, recommends that DEET not be used on infants less than 2 months old (aap.org). There are now many other synthetic and natural alternatives to DEET, such as picaridin (a.k.a. Natrapel), synthesized oil of lemon, eucalyptus, and natural oil of lemongrass (a.k.a. citronella), but again, it is best to apply any insect repellent to the outside of a child's clothing rather than directly on the skin. A good option

> **→ PRO TIP:** If your young hiker is still too short to reach your assisting finger or hand, consider attaching a loop of fat rope around your wrist. The rope can be as short as a foot, with an overhand knot at the end. This way, your child can grab on to the rope to maintain his or her balance while avoiding having you "just so slightly bend" at the waist, which we all know is the cause of many backaches. Kids older than 4 might find it cool to have their own pair of trekking poles, just like their parents.

is to apply some insect repellent to a bandana and to tie the bandana around the child's neck. The same can be done for a hat. When the bugs are especially bad, kids may find sprays more fun to apply, but lotions are typically milder on their skin. Finally, it's essential to take the time to check for ticks before going to bed

- **Heat.** Young infants and toddlers are quite susceptible to heat, so avoiding direct sunlight is often the best plan. This is why using an infant carrier with a hood is so important. In camp, using a tent as a crib for nap- or playtime can work, but make sure there's good air flow through the tent on hot, sunny days. If it is sunny, don't put the fly down. A tent with a fly can get as hot as a car with the windows rolled up. Instead, use the fly or a tarp to create shade on the tent if there's no natural shade in your campsite. Lastly, while traveling, think about cooling young kids by placing wet bandanas around their necks.

- **Water.** Direct adult supervision of your kids is a must when they are playing in or near water, whether that's in lakes, ponds, or pools in a creek or river. A small personal floatation device (PFD) is always an option and should get packed if you plan on swimming in deep water with kids or taking them on a boat. PFDs are lightweight and ensure safe swimming.

- **Slippery terrain.** Have Kids, Will Travel . . . and Fall: Yes, it is inevitable: Your young ones will take some spills on the trail, but they will bounce back. Unless your child has a motor-skills disorder, it might not be necessary to have them wear a helmet on difficult terrain, but it still could be a good option. Otherwise, the best way to prevent slips, trips, and spills is to spot your child or to give them an assisting finger or hand for balance. Pay attention to the trail and anticipate problem areas to avoid the big and painful crashes.

- **Cliff edges.** Cliff edges are what we call "attractive nuisances." Although many kids will have an instinctive fear of heights, it can be hard to resist the amazing vista a cliff's edge provides. Again, do not take chances. Always have an adult supervise children when walking or resting near the edge of a cliff. Take the time to establish a safe zone along the cliff: Lay a rope on the rock to provide a visual reminder and explain that kids should not cross this line without a grownup.

➜ BRINGING A NOVICE ON THE TRAIL

Planning a trip with novice hikers is a little like going out with a young child. They might share the same excitement and anxiety about sleeping in the woods. Contrary to a child, they will be able to carry their share of weight. It might be wise to encourage newbies to go light for their first backpacking trips. Packing only what is essential is a challenging task but a good lesson to learn. We have all tried, at least once, to carry every piece of gear or clothing we could stuff into our packs. Remember the excitement of your first shopping trip for cool little carabiners and nifty gadgets? All experienced backpackers were once novices, too.

11

The key thing to remember about novice hikers is that they need to acquire outdoor skills and knowledge. Unless they have taken a backpacking course in college or through AMC or another outdoor skill school, they may come to the field with many misconceptions about what they need to bring. The first rule of hiking with novices is: "Don't assume that they know." The second rule is: "Don't expect them to ask for help." You will need to put your instructor's hat on and help them learn how to hike and camp in the backcountry.

This does not give you license to show off your skills or to be patronizing. It simply means you'll need to anticipate their needs and be patient with them. For instance, you could invite them over before your trip's departure and ask them to bring all of the gear they're planning to pack for the trip. You can go through their haul together and help them make sound decisions about what to bring, buy, rent, or borrow from you or other hikers. You can also demonstrate how to properly pack lift, and adjust a pack. The time you take to help friends make good choices and acquire basic skills will help you and them on the trail.

Around camp, ask them what they would like to learn on this trip: lighting a camp stove, LNT principles and their application, map and compass skills. The more you empower your novice friends, the less they'll feel like a burden and the more they'll enjoy going out with you. (Plus, it will free you from some camp chores.)

Don't assume, and don't expect a call for help. Instead, be a caring leader, anticipate first-timers' needs, and invite them to learn.

→ BRINGING YOUR CANINE COMPANION

Most dogs like to go for a walk—that is, a 20- to 30-minute walk around the neighborhood or park. Hiking on a rocky ridge trail for 5 to 8 miles with no water sources in sight is a challenging endeavor not only for you but for your dog as well. Bringing a dog on a trail or a backpacking trip can be fun, but it requires some planning. Don't assume your dog will love it or even that your dog is fit for hiking. Like anyone else, your dog will have to learn new skills. Start your dog trail training slowly, beginning with short and then longer day hikes before moving on to an overnight trip on easy trails. Only after these expeditions should you progress to steeper and longer hikes. Your dog will thank you for it. Below are some factors to consider when taking your dog on an extended hike or backpacking trip.

- **Paws.** Unlike you, dogs hike with bare paws, so rocky trails can become painful. Take the time to check paws for cuts before and after a long hiking day, including between the claws. If the trail is very rocky or icy, you might be able to talk your dog into wearing some special hiking booties. There are many brands of paw wear, and these could be a good investment if you take your dog onto trails often. A good pair of paw covers is certainly less expensive than a trip to the vet for infected cuts or other paw-related injuries.

11

- **Food.** If your dog will be hiking and running most of the day, he or she will need high-calorie food. Consider bringing more food than you usually would and make sure it's appealing to your pup. Your dog will be hungry!

- **Water.** You might have forgotten, but dogs don't sweat the way we do. They have to cool down through their mouths, which can get very dry if they don't drink enough during a hike. Plan a route along a creek or a brook so your dog can drink clean, running water whenever desired. On a ridge, make sure you plan to carry—or have the dog carry—enough water for you both. And remember, dogs can catch a bad case of leptospirosis or giardia, just like you, so it's best to treat standing water before giving it to your pooch to drink. If you see a stagnant pool of water that looks suspicious, especially after a heavy rainfall, don't let your dog drink from it.

- **Naps.** You know your dog. When you're gone, Fido is not at home writing the Great American Novel. Fido is napping. So, plan for a nap or two during a long day of hiking. It will be a good rest for both human and hound.

- **Load.** Yes, your dog can carry a load, but remember, dogs aren't pack animals, like horses or mules. Dogs can typically carry no more than 25 percent of their own weight, although some larger breeds can carry 10 to 15 percent more than an average-size dog. And, of course, other breeds aren't cut out to carry much at all. Don't saddle your dachshund with enough provisions for an Alaskan malamute. Always keep an eye on your dogs, and if they look too tired to continue, lighten their loads.

- **Leash.** Yes, dogs like to run free, but there are often rules about dogs on trails, and these rules differ from place to place. Don't get you and Spot kicked out of a park because you don't know the rules on the trails you traverse. Many state and federal areas require dogs be leashed, and it's your legal obligation to follow these rules. In some places, dogs are not allowed to hike with you at all. Know before you go.

- **Extra mileage.** When you're planning your mileage for a day of hiking, remember that your dog will often hike back and forth in front of you along the trail, especially if not on leash. Don't be surprised if your dog is too tired to play fetch when you get to camp. On long trips, dogs will need a day of rest (a "zero day"), just like you.

- **Health.** Also like humans, dogs can get sick or injured on the trail. So keep an eye out and make sure your dog is happy. If it's cold or your dog gets wet, he or she can get hypothermia. On hot days, dogs can get dehydrated or have hyperthermia. If you are going to bring a dog hiking, take the time to learn how to read these signs. There are books solely about first aid for dogs.

11

- **Ticks.** Check your dog for ticks daily, just as you do for yourself. Many dogs acquire Lyme disease and other tick-borne illnesses solely because it's so hard to see where the ticks are lodged under all that fur. Feel their skin with your hands and inspect any bumps or ridges you encounter. A tick key is a useful tool in the backcountry, but you can also be proactive. Ask your vet about pretreating your dog with a medication that prevents ticks from hitching a ride on your dog's back.

- **Social life.** Dogs love people . . . well, most people. Most of the time. For whatever reason, dogs can dislike or be frightened by strangers, leading to unexpected growling, even from a typically friendly dog. You will encounter many other hikers on the trail. Some will be dog lovers and some won't be, so don't let your pup get in trouble. Anticipate encounters with other hikers (and other dogs) and make sure your dog responds to voice commands when not on leash.

- **Instinct.** Dogs may have become humans' best friends, but they still share a common ancestor with the modern wolf. They are, at heart, somewhat wild. This is why they like to run after small animals, including squirrels, chipmunks, bunnies, and birds. They also like to explore and get to know new animals, such as skunks and porcupines, which is good for neither those animals nor your dog. Please, try to keep your dog's wolflike instincts in check and control their urges. The other animals will thank you. Be sure your dog's vaccinations are up-to-date (in particular for rabies, which is legally mandated in almost all states) before venturing into the woods, and carry a copy of your dog's shot records. The last bit of advice for you and your dog: Ask your vet about any concerns you might have regarding your dog's health before and after a long backpacking trip.

→ GROUP DYNAMICS

Unless you are planning a solo hike, you will most likely experience the great outdoors in a group. This group could include your immediate family, your extended family, friends, work colleagues, or even people you just met at the trailhead and agreed to join in a common adventure. Or it could be a combination of the above. Groups sometimes are composed of members who have a lot in common, and other times, very little. Nevertheless, any group will always have one thing in common: the outdoor adventure they choose to share together.

It's important, however, to first define what we mean by a group. For the purpose of this chapter, we will define a "group" as two to ten individuals sharing an outdoor experience, all aware of their interdependence for achieving common or individual goals for a certain period of time. A small group must have a shared identity; in other words, individuals must identify themselves as members of the group. For instance, if you and three of your closest friends decide to go backpacking, you will be considered a group. If your group shares a shelter with two other hikers, your group will remain the same four individuals, even if you spend a night sharing common space, a meal, and a few good stories with the other hikers. Your group number doesn't increase to six, but remains the four friends who set out together on an adventure.

We choose a maximum group size of ten because most wilderness areas have a limit of ten individuals per group. The group dynamics we describe below can occur in a group of two or of twelve. With more than twelve members, most social scientists believe small-group dynamics are not as predictable. In large groups, fractioning into subgroups is common because it's difficult for each individual to have meaningful interactions with all of the other members of the group.

ALL GROUPS HAVE DYNAMICS

All groups venturing into the outdoors will experience some form of social dynamics due to three principal reasons. First, groups are composed of individuals, and these individuals have their own personalities that affect their behaviors and relationships with other individuals and with the group at large. Although our species is gregarious and has learned to survive through mutual cooperation, we still haven't mastered the essential social behaviors that always assure group cohesion and harmony. That makes learning how to be a positive member of a group essential. This is especially true on an outdoor expedition, which by its nature will create a social environment of mutual interdependence.

Second, outdoor experiences require group members to become part of a self-sufficient social group with interdependent group members. If a hiking group is out for a few days, sharing equipment and food, the members of the group agree to be codependent. For example, if a group member with proper wilderness first-aid training volunteers to put together a field first-aid kit and carries it during the trip, other group members will rely on that person for assessing first-aid supplies and care. The same can be said of sharing a shelter, a kitchen set, a map, and food. This is why it's very important during the planning phase of a trip to have full disclosure of who is bringing what. If there's no logistical coordination among group members, individuals may feel they can bring whatever they need to be autonomous (i.e., their own shelter, food, stove, etc.), which might lead to more dissension than cooperation.

In addition to logistical interdependence, group members depend on one another for safety and well-being. If one member of a backpacking group gets injured, the rest will feel responsible for offering assistance. It is a simple, unwritten rule of the trail: "I help you if you are injured. You help me if I am injured."

Third, groups will experience social dynamics because intrinsic and extrinsic factors stress individual members, forcing them to display new or hidden aspects of their personalities through positive or negative behaviors. Some examples of the intrinsic or internal factors that could affect group members are food, fatigue, and social

11

ADAPTIVE OUTDOOR ADVENTURES

Outdoor adventures are for everyone. Regardless of ability, all people can experience the joys and challenges of mountain travel. It's possible to create adaptive experiences to suit the needs and goals of outdoor travelers with a wide range of abilities. Adaptation modifies the outdoor activity just enough to compensate for a person's impairments without robbing that person of the opportunities for challenge, risk-taking, accomplishment, and meaningful participation.

Adaptation starts with a full understanding of a person's impairments and abilities. Common impairments could affect a person's mobility, cognitive function, visual or auditory senses, or social-emotional connection. The next step is to identify which activities are absolutely essential for success in a given outdoor adventure. A backpacking trip obviously includes traveling through the woods, but it also includes living outdoors in a remote location. Once an impairment is understood and the person's goals clarified, adaptation addresses the impairment while preserving as much of the original experience as possible. Helpers and other companions do the least amount possible to enable a positive and rewarding experience. Some examples:

- A person with a visual impairment may be able to proceed with verbal guidance or may want a hands-on guide, especially in difficult terrain.

- A person with moderate limits to lower-body mobility may be able to proceed independently on the trail, as long as some or all of the person's gear is carried by a partner. Others may wish to travel with pack stock like horses, to use a wheeled device for assistance, or to choose terrain that is more level. Mobility impairments often require planning for a slower pace on the trail.

- A person with a sensory/communication impairment (e.g., an autism spectrum disorder) might need to travel in a small group with a trusted one-on-one companion, with careful attention paid to all aspects of the person's sensory experience.

At the core of the adaptive-adventure process is the understanding that all people grow from the opportunity to experience independence, accomplishment, and the joy of the natural world. In fact, the rewards can be even greater when someone surpasses the limits others have laid out for them. Successfully adapting a backcountry outdoor adventure for a person with extensive physical, social, or cognitive impairments requires expertise and careful planning. There are numerous organizations throughout the Northeast, especially in mountain country, that specialize in adapting outdoor sports for all individuals. A few are Adaptive Sports New England, Inc. (adaptivesportsne.org), Adaptive Sports Partners of the North Country (adaptivesportspartners.org), and Maine Adaptive Sports & Recreation (maineadaptive.org). It's a good idea to consult with these organizations as you plan your adaptive outdoor experiences.

11

proximity. Food and fatigue are easy to understand. Hiking for a few days with a backpack will fatigue muscles we do not use every day. Sleeping on the ground, even with the best sleeping pad, can stress the body. Food stress can come from a shortage or a dislike of certain camp foods, or a combination of both. Although you can take steps to limit food and fatigue stress, the possibility is always there.

Physical proximity is a bit more complex. It includes social proximity, which simply means that if you choose to go out on the trail for a few days with friends, you are committing yourself to spending most of that time with them. On a short outing this factor is negligible, but if you are out for a longer period of time, this intrinsic factor will have a major effect on your social experience, positive or negative. You might have heard of AT thru-hiking couples who voluntarily choose to hike separately for a few days or weeks before coming back together. This is a prime example of intrinsic stress caused by social proximity.

Extrinsic or external factors can be caused by stressors such as weather, altitude, and isolation. Weather, in particular, can have a strong effect. A day of rain is one thing, but seven days of rain and cold can stress the most avid camper. The same can be true for higher altitudes. Lower pressure and less oxygen at high altitude can have a significant impact on the brain. Some hikers who travel at high altitude may even notice their personalities changing due to this external stressor. Traveling in remote areas can also reveal a hidden stress for some backpackers. Consciously or unconsciously, knowing you're many hours or days away from help can make you uncomfortable, nervous, or irritable.

Because groups comprise individuals with various social skills who are placed in a situation that creates interdependence while facing various intrinsic and extrinsic factors, group dynamics will come to bear. These can be positive dynamics, reinforcing friendship, compassion, and mutual respect. If going camping was a universally bad social experience, no groups would go. Even so, stressors exist, and the few steps you can take to promote positive social interaction—and to enjoy the outdoors with your family, friends, or strangers who share the same passion as you—will enrich your adventures. Just remember that unless you travel solo, your experience will be social and therefore will involve group dynamics.

THE PERILS OF A LEADERLESS GROUP

A common practice among friends embarking on an outdoor trip is to share leadership—in other words, no one is the official leader of the group. No one has the final say if a serious decision needs to be made, and no one is responsible for the group members' relationships or tasks. We call this type of group leaderless. Although a member of the group may eventually emerge as the leader, vagaries of group roles can be a source of tension or worse.

11

The dangers associated with a leaderless group are numerous and consequential. For example, a group without a leader will have difficulty clarifying the goal or goals of the trip, which can lead to conflict and difficult decision-making once on the trail. A group without a leader might see its members splinter into sub-groups with opposing agendas without a unifying voice. Members of a leaderless group have a tendency to be more self-centered and less committed to a common goal. Finally, without a leader to facilitate decision-making, a group of friends can fall victim to what social psychologists call "groupthink." Groupthink can occur when no individual wants to challenge a controversial action or decision made by the group. This happens when no one feels responsible to ask, "Is this a good idea?" or "Should we do this?" When everyone wants to please each other and to avoid causing ripples, members begin to make poor or dysfunctional deci-sions based on maintaining harmony rather than on rational, critical evaluation of the situation at hand. Groupthink is not the same as group consensus, where a group has evaluated and discussed the various options in front of them and come to an agreed-upon decision.

For all of these reasons, it's important to avoid traveling outdoors as a leaderless group. Sharing leadership is a viable option, as long as everyone knows one person among the group is the de facto leader if a situation requiring leadership emerges. The best option is for a group of friends to openly elect a leader before reaching the trailhead and have members of the group actively support the leader by expressing their likes, dislikes, and concerns when appropriate.

BASIC GROUP STAGES

In social psychology, the development of group dynamics has been an area of study since the mid-1960s. Especially relevant is the work of Bruce Tuckman, who pro-posed a sequential stage theory for the development of small-group interaction. The five stages proposed by Tuckman are known as forming, storming, norming, performing, and adjourning. Note that these stages of development are most com-mon when a group is formed by individuals who are acquainted with each other but do not know each other very well—or who are strangers.

- **Forming.** This stage is characterized by group members who are learning about one another and trying to identify what role(s) people in the group will play. Peo-ple in this social stage usually are showing the best sides of their personality and trying to avoid entering into conflict. This is when group members like to con-verse, seek commonalities, share personal stories, and observe others' behaviors.

- **Storming.** This stage is often present once the members of the group are ques-tioning group goals, behavioral norms, and the decision-making process. Some-times groups experience this stage when there is no identified or accepted leader, or when a few members are vying for leadership. As these questions are resolved, the group begins to agree on accepted norms of behavior and on a common goal. This stage is often essential to allow the group to move forward without having members hold on to feelings of resentment. Once the "storm" has passed, the group can enter the next phase.

- **Norming.** This stage of development is marked by the stabilization of interpersonal relationships among group members. Rules of behavior have been accepted, a focus on effective communication has been established, and decision-making is shared democratically when appropriate. Although conflict among members can still arise, the group now has agreed-upon ways to solve conflicts, as everyone is now committed to the group functioning efficiently. With the relationship side of group life improved, the group can focus on the task at hand.

- **Performing.** In this stage, the group is functioning effectively and efficiently. Members have found their roles, know the tasks that need to be accomplished, and have forged harmonious relationships. This is when members often recognize they can accomplish more by working together than alone. The group may experience a sense of cohesion.

- **Adjourning.** The final stage of Tuckman's group development model is illustrated by groups that are very effective at working and living with one another. The better "performing" a group is, the more important the adjourning stage will be.

11

FIGURE 53. Good planning, leadership, and group dynamics support what should be a given: that the outdoors is for everyone.

In this stage, group members might feel anxiety and sadness as they see the end of the group experience approach. This is also when unresolved conflicts swept away during the norming and performing stages might erupt.

Each stage can last for a range of time periods. Some stages might last only a few hours, while others can last for days or weeks. Chances are a group will experience all of these stages (or most of them) if they spend long enough together. For shorter experiences, a group might not have enough time to experience all of the stages.

STRATEGIES FOR SHORT TRIPS

If you are planning a short trip with friends or family, you may not go through the stages of small group development theorized by Tuckman. Remember that these stages are more common among individuals with little or no history as a group. What's more, weekend trips usually don't provide enough time for a group to experience all the stages.

But if you are planning or participating in an outdoor trip, short or long, with people you know little about, consider the following recommendations:

1. Discuss leadership roles so that you can appoint, elect, or have someone volunteer to be a leader. Often this is the person with the most outdoor experience, but knowledge and skills are not always enough to be a good leader.

2. Discuss and agree on common goals. Individuals should share their goals so that logistics, time, hiking pace, and route can be adjusted accordingly.

3. Commit to being on your best behavior. Your time together will be short, so make it fun, safe, and pleasant for all group members.

If you follow these recommendations, you are more likely to have a pleasant and enjoyable outdoor experience. If you don't, you might still have fun with your hiking partners, but you might choose never to hike with them again—or they with you.

EXPEDITION BEHAVIOR

The term "expedition behavior" was coined by the legendary American mountaineer Paul Petzoldt, who founded the National Outdoor Leadership School and the Wilderness Education Association. Petzoldt's experience as a member of an early mountaineering expedition on K2 in the Himalaya led him to observe that one of the most fundamental elements of a successful outdoor expedition was the social interaction among its members. He argued that having skilled climbers, navigators, outdoor cooks, and even experienced outdoor leaders was not enough to guarantee the success of an expedition. He felt, rightfully, that the social behavior of each expedition member and the way members interacted with one another was as important, if not more, than the raw technical skill or combined experience of a group of outdoor adventurers.

11

So Petzoldt used the term "expedition behavior" to underline the differences between the behaviors one should employ during an outdoor expedition and the behaviors one might express back home. Petzoldt understood that the social context we experience on an outdoor expedition differs from those in our daily lives. Because of this difference, Petzoldt suggested we behave differently on an outing trip because our behavior will have a ripple effect on the social fabric of the group.

But what is expedition behavior—or EB, for short? EB can be classified as either "good" or "poor." Obviously, good EB is favored, while poor EB is discouraged. There are many concrete examples of good and bad EB that can occur during a backpacking trip. Let's look at the two lists below for examples of what we mean by bad, good, or poor EB.

Good EB

- Smiling when appropriate.
- Being positive—even if the weather or trail is less than ideal.
- Always being polite and respectful with other expedition members.
- Doing your share of the chores around camp.
- Carrying your load and helping others carry their loads when needed.
- Taking care of your own health: staying hydrated, taking care of hot spots on your feet, and brushing your teeth.
- Sharing food in a fair and equitable way.
- Keeping your equipment organized so you can be prepared to hike as planned.
- Encouraging others when needed.
- Anticipating the needs of your fellow members.
- Always communicating with others by being honest and respectful.
- Supporting a leader's decisions but also asking questions or expressing concern when appropriate.
- Being accepting of other members' habits and not taking offense easily.
- Being selfless in your actions and words.

As you can see, good EB is simply being on your best and most mindful behavior during the entire expedition. Please note that the list above represents only a short sample of good EB. There are many other ways to be a good expedition member. There are also many ways to display poor EB. Here are a few examples.

11

Poor EB

- Not washing your hands before cooking for the group.

- Not getting up in the morning at the agreed-upon time.

- Washing your personal laundry in a group cooking pot.

- Taking unnecessary risks.

- Talking, singing, or being loud around the campfire when others are trying to sleep.

- Not picking up your trash and leaving it for others to carry out.

- Losing equipment due to poor personal organization.

- Not committing to and supporting the goal(s) of the group.

- Being careless about spreading a cold when you're sick.

- Talking or complaining about others in their absence.

- Disrespecting others' needs for peace and solitude.

- Being sarcastic when it is not appropriate.

Although this list of poor EB seems obvious from the comfort of home, these behaviors can occur without the person displaying them being aware of his or her actions. It's important for all members of a group to be conscious of their own behavior. It can be appropriate for a group to gather at end the of the day and ask how people are doing in terms of health, level of energy, equipment, and EB. Remember, poor EB left unaddressed can ruin an expedition.

To learn more about EB and group dynamics on outdoor expeditions, we invite you to read AMC's *Guide to Outdoor Leadership,* by Alex Kosseff. The following vignettes are examples of the different ways group dynamics play out in the field.

SITUATION A: A HUT TOO FAR

Jenny invites her friends Nara, Lin, and Esther on a hike to Galehead Hut. It's Jenny's birthday, and she wants to celebrate it on the trail with her friends. The four friends have never hiked together but are excited about the opportunity. Jenny plans the hike and chooses a challenging and long route to Galehead. She decides to start hiking from Lincoln Woods and travel to the hut via Mount Bond and South Twin Mountains—about 15 miles, with considerable elevation gain. Of the four friends, Esther has little to no hiking experience and brings heavy and unnecessary gear in her backpack. Since their destination is a full-service hut, none of them brings a shelter or sleeping equipment except for Nara. Nara is an experienced outdoor educator with many years of leading NOLS expeditions under her belt. Because Nara plans to sleep under a tarp away from the

(continued)

11

hut for the night, she brings her sleeping gear. Although Nara is the most experienced outdoor traveler, Jenny is the leader, since she organized this event to celebrate her birthday.

Not long into the hike, the friends notice that Esther lacks the necessary physical fitness for this long route. As Esther hikes up Bondcliff, her knees give out and she becomes exhausted, with no chance of reaching the hut without help. Lin and Jenny are too tired to help Esther, so Nara takes the initiative and volunteers to take Esther's pack so that Esther can hike without the weight. Nara hopes they can readjust their goal and proposes that the group considers spending the night at Guyot Campsite, which is about 1.75 miles from the summit of Bondcliff. But because no one has brought sleeping gear except Nara, and the leader, Jenny, reallywants to reach the hut, the group—including a reluctant Nara—decides to push on to the hut, more than 6 miles away. The group reaches the hut late in the afternoon with every member exhausted and unhappy with their hiking experience.

This story illustrates a problem that often occurs when not all group members are involved in selecting a goal for a hiking experience. It also shows how resentment can build up among members when poor logistical planning reduces a group's ability to shift gears when needed. It also shows how delegating leadership to a less experienced hiker can lead to miscalculation in goal setting, equipment selection, and decision-making.

SITUATION B: BEST TRIP EVER

In early November, a group of eight college students is planning a three-day backpacking trip in the Pemigewasset Wilderness. The students are all experienced hikers and campers, and this hike is their final challenge for a course in outdoor leadership and wilderness skills. Their instructor has appointed each of them a specific role for the expedition. One will be the leader; another the assistant leader; one will be in charge of logistics and gear repair; one will be the medical officer; two will be in charge of nutrition and cooking; and one will be responsible for filming all of the important decisions made by the group or the leader(s).

The goal for the hike is to start at an unknown location and to reach a destination via two pre-established caches. The group organized their food and logistics the day before their departure, and on the morning of their last hike, the instructor blindfolded them and drove them to an unmarked location along a forest road. Once they arrive at their starting point, the group is given a set of maps and one GPS with a location for their pickup in two days.

Everyone in the group agrees to this goal and is excited by the challenge. The hike involves long days of hiking, off-trail travel, multiple river crossings, traversing a mountain notch, and finding two hidden food caches.

11

(continued)

274 CHAPTER 11: GROUPS

Although the group encounters cold and wet days of hiking, at the end of the hike, they arrive at their pickup location in great spirits, with big smiles on their faces and a lot of pride. What led this group to have such a successful experience? During the post-trip discussion and review of the expedition video, itbecomes evident the group functioned cohesively because they all shared the same goal; their leadership structure and roles were accepted and understood by all members; the members were polite, cordial, and respectful of one another; they all chose to display their best expedition behavior; they had daily check-ins to assess how everyone was feeling; and they communicated effectively.

This story highlights the fact that good social dynamics are possible on outdoor trips and that, with some planning, good EB, and effective leadership, everyone can exit the trailhead with a big smile.

11

CHAPTER 12
ULTRALIGHT BACKPACKING

Ultralight (UL) backpacking is simply backpacking with an extremely light load of gear and food. As mentioned on page 69 in Chapter 3, a standard backpack with modern gear for a two-night, three-day trip would weigh a bit more than 30 pounds. With extra fresh food and some camp luxuries, it might get up to 40 pounds. An ultralight approach to the same-length trip would aim for a pack that weighed 20 to 22 pounds. Expert ultralight hikers, dedicated to a minimalist ethic, might even have a pack of 12 to 15 pounds (or less). These goals are possible with careful selection and modification of equipment, as well as the intentional development of a simple and lightweight menu.

→ ULTRALIGHT GEAR

When looking to shave weight from your equipment kit, focus first on the four heaviest and bulkiest items: shelter, sleeping bag, sleeping pad, and pack. For each of these items, the key questions are: What do I absolutely need? What can I currently afford? With careful choosing, it is possible to develop a collection of these four items that weighs less than 8 pounds, and will function well for a summer trip of two to four nights.

SHELTERS   • aim for 1.5 lbs a person

Shelters for ultralight hiking should be no more than 2 pounds, and many weigh far less. Most common UL shelters are some version of a tarp or pyramid shelter. They are typically pitched without poles or use trekking poles for support. Their material is not the usual heavy, coated nylon but is instead made of thinner nylon or exotic materials such as sailcloth. One such fabric is a laminate polyester-film hybrid called Cuben fiber that weighs 0.5 ounces per square yard. That means that an 8-by-10-foot tarp weighs 4.5 ounces, tarp lines and all, about one-quarter the weight of a traditional tarp. Cuben fiber illustrates another principle (and possible pitfall) of an ultralight approach. Items made from Cuben fiber are likely to cost two to three times as much as comparable items made from more conventional fabrics. You do not have to spend a lot of money to go ultralight, but some desirable gear will cost quite a bit more.

Even when traveling ultralight, most backpackers will still want to use a bivy to protect their sleeping bag under a tarp. While a standard backpacker's bivy might weigh 24 ounces, there are several affordable choices of less than 12 ounces. A bivy's integrated bug netting will also come in handy in conditions where biting insects are a bother. For better bug protection, several manufacturers make small "bug houses" that hang beneath a tarp, creating a luxuriously bug-free space that is removable when not needed. If biting flies are not a concern, and you are confident in your ability to pitch a weather-tight tarp, you can replace the bivy with a small ground sheet made of Tyvek. A piece the size of your sleeping bag's outline weighs less than an ounce.

Just because tarps and pyramid shelters are the norm doesn't mean tents are useless to the ultralighter. If you are traveling in a group, it is possible to split the load of a traditional three-season tent among everyone sharing the sleeping space. There are also some impressively light single-wall, poleless tents constructed from light materials. Some spacious, two-person models weigh less than 2 pounds and are available at a reasonable price. These tents eliminate the need for separate bug screens and bivies, so in very wet or buggy weather they compare favorably with the tarp systems. In drier, bug-free conditions, however, they represent a pound or so of excess weight, and they do not offer the multifunctionality of a tarp.

The final consideration for shelter is size itself. An 8-by-10-foot tarp can easily sleep four hikers, so if you are going solo, why not choose a 6-by-8-foot version? This will save nearly half the weight of the larger tarp and will be less expensive, too.

•8x10 best for 1 or 2 people

SLEEPING BAGS

These are the most personal pieces of gear, so the most important factor is to figure out what helps you sleep best at night. Ultralight hikers often do not use bags at all, instead sleeping under open-backed quilts. Quilt designs eliminate the typical sleeping bag's insulation under a sleeper, which, because it is compressed, does not provide warmth; it is nonfunctional weight. Quilts attach directly to sleeping pads, or wrap around them, and rely on the insulation offered by the pad. They also save weight by omitting the zippers, hoods, and other features of a full sleeping bag. It takes a little skill to prevent cool drafts from slipping in the open back, but experienced quilt users rave about the sleeper's freedom of movement and, of course, the weight. A 40-degree Fahrenheit (4-degree Celsius) quilt with 800-fill power down can weigh as little as 14 ounces, although a more typical quilt weight is in the 24-ounce range.

Before you curl up in a quilt, consider upgrading your sleeping bag. While a traditional 20F (-7C) bag with synthetic insulation can weigh as much as 3.5 pounds, a trim-cut, 32F (0C), down-filled version can weigh 1.25 pounds. The bag may be more versatile and feel more comfortable to those used to the hug of their mummy cut. It will also have traditional features such as a zipper, a hood, and a drawstring, and it will not suffer any of the cold gaps along the quilt-pad interface.

Finally, whether choosing a bag or a quilt, consider its temperature rating. Do you really want to carry a winter-worthy bag in July? Is a spring snowstorm really going to strike in August? When purchasing a product for summer hiking in the Northeast, you can rely on a 40F (4C) bag or quilt. On rare unexpectedly cold nights, that rating can be stretched a long way with smart camping practices, such as choosing a site out of the wind and above cold hollows, as well as sleeping in a puffy jacket, wearing a hat and cozy socks, or snuggling a hot water bottle. The 40F summer bag could weigh as much as a pound less than a comparable 20F (-7C) version and could be less expensive. Most important, though, is to sleep well, so if a few ounces of insulation will help you gain a sound night's sleep, go for it.

SLEEPING PADS

Sleeping pad choices for ultralight travel depend on the comfort threshold of the hiker and on the hiker's skill in choosing flat, comfortable campsites. Many ultralight hikers use the same pads as a modern, traditional backpacker—self-inflating mattresses or pool-raft-style air mattresses. Lightweight versions of these can weigh as little as 14 ounces and provide plenty of comfort. But the lightest sleeping pad, by far, is made from closed-cell foam. It will be lighter still if it is cut short to pad only the shoulders to the hips. A pad like this will weigh only 4 or 5 ounces, is warm, will never spring a leak, and can be used all around camp as a seat and a kneeling pad. The remaining parts of the body can be padded with leaf litter, an empty backpack and other gear, or extra clothes. For many ultralighters, the sleeping pad is integral to the structure of the backpack, so the pack system you develop will inform your choice of pad. More on this below.

PACKS

Packs for ultralight backcountry travel do not need to be as structured or as full-featured as a traditional pack. A traditional pack intended to carry 40-plus pounds will weigh 5 to 6 pounds or more empty. Lighter, in-between models that still offer many traditional features and are still capable of carrying 25 to 35 pounds might weigh only 2.5 pounds. At the lightest end of the spectrum are packs that weigh just under a pound, with a target total pack weight of less than 20 pounds. As the total load weight decreases, the need for some pack features decreases as well. Com-

12

FIGURE 54. Thinking about going ultralight? A traditional backpacking backpack (left) can weigh up to 40 pounds, while an ultralight pack (right) reduces that load to 20 to 22 pounds for the same trip.

plex suspensions, pivoting hip belts, extreme padding, and heavy internal frames become less relevant and at the lower end are no longer necessary. The lightest functional ultralight packs are 25 to 30 liters in volume, still enough for several days of backcountry travel. They typically have very few pockets, attachment points, or other weight-adding features. Sometimes they do not have a lid, instead using a roll-top closure, similar to a dry bag. They typically don't come with adjustable suspensions but do come in a variety of sizes.

One of the most interesting design elements of the lightest packs is the minimization of the pack frame. A traditional pack has aluminum bars or some other mechanical structure to support the load and transfer it to the pack's suspension. These pieces are heavy, so ultralight packs (designed to carry a light load) do not include them. Instead, manufacturers use plastic sheets (light) or foam pads (lighter), and the lightest packs have no frame at all. In these models, the hiker uses a sleeping pad to create pack structure. This system will work with any kind of sleeping pad. The pad can be inserted as a cylinder in the pack bag, with all gear stuffed inside it, or it can be folded flat against the back of the bag, where the bag contacts the hiker. These packs often will have a dedicated sleeve for this purpose.

Good ultralight packs should still offer some critical features. A hip belt may not be required for load transfer to the hips but it is still useful for preventing unwanted pack movement as you travel down the trail. Most hikers will want at least one external pocket that allows for easy access to important day-use items, such as a map, water treatment, and sunscreen. The pack's exterior may have several stretchy mesh pockets that can expand to swallow water bladders, wet tarps, a rain poncho, or dirty socks. The pack's internal load should be compressible somehow, although this may be with thin elasticized cords rather than the traditional straps and buckles. Load-lifter straps that extend from the top of the shoulder strap up to the pack bag will provide some relief over the course of the day, and an adjustable sternum strap will ensure a good fit of the shoulder straps. Fit, in general, should still be excellent. No matter how light the load, an uncomfortable pack will lead to an unenjoyable trip. Only choose a pack with the correct torso length and adequate shoulder padding. Durability of the fabric, the straps, and the attachment points should also be priorities. A light load will put much less strain on a pack, but the pack will take a lot of use and abuse in the backcountry. Expect it to stand up to the test.

The ultralight pack should be the last big item a hiker purchases or replaces when moving into the ultralight realm. You will not be ready to use a 20-liter pack until you have downsized all of your other pieces of gear and have refined your lightweight kitchen. Developing the equipment kit and the skills for ultralight backcountry travel is usually a lengthy process that involves trial and error, and often the prioritization of a limited budget. Individuals may work their way downward in pack volume over several trips or years as they refine their wants and needs, swapping out pieces of gear. If your current pack is not a monster, focus first on reducing what you put inside it. You can reward yourself with a flyweight load-hauler when you have all of your systems figured out.

➜ LIGHTWEIGHT KITCHEN

As you begin to reduce your pack weight, you can also begin to refine your food, cooking practices, and kitchen gear. Your efforts here will complement the gains you make in the big four items above. The kitchen is an excellent place to practice the emphasis on needs versus wants. While a little comfort food is certainly OK, bringing that bag of apples, extra log of salami, whole fresh onion, or block of cheese will quickly add weight.

When it comes to ultralight food planning, your focus will shift from pounds per person per day to calories per ounce of food. In other words, you will choose food items that are nutrient- and calorie-dense, such as nuts and nut butters, chocolate, or olive oil. To these high-calorie ingredients you will add spices and complemen-

12

tary foods, such as dried whole milk, granola, meal bars, meat jerky, quick oats, couscous, and instant potatoes. Other typical ingredients are dried fruits, cheese-sauce powder, and dried vegetables. Since fresh breads take up a lot of space and often crumble in the pack, many ultralight hikers prefer tortillas. With foods such as these, aim for an average caloric value of at least 125 calories per ounce or more, if you can.

How much of these rations should a person actually bring? The answer depends on your caloric needs. The U.S. government estimates that the average U.S. male should consume 2,500 calories per day. Add an extra 500 calories to account for hiking and that adds up to 3,000 calories per day. (This amount will be too much for many hikers but could be too little if the hiking is very strenuous or the days very long.) If you have succeeded in averaging 125 calories per ounce of food in your pack, the 3,000 calories will equal 1.5 pounds per person per day. If you achieve a 150-calorie-per-ounce average, you will carry only 1.25 pounds per person per day, far less than the traditional backpacking load, but you will still have the required nutrition.

"Cooking" for most ultralight hikers will mean boiling water and adding it to something or perhaps boiling a quick-cooking rice or pasta for two or three minutes. Longer cook times require more fuel, and that fuel weighs a lot. Foods that are not ready to eat should be dehydrated for quick-cooking. Does this mean all of your food will be bland instant oatmeal or soup mix? Definitely not! Using the few ingredients mentioned above, and with only boiled water, it would be very easy to create a daily menu with hot muesli granola for breakfast, Nutella on a tortilla for lunch, and spicy-sweet almond couscous for dinner. Nutritious, delicious trail snacks, such as jerky and dried fruit, round out the day, providing additional nutrients and boosting energy as you hike.

Premade dehydrated backpackers' meals are designed to meet these exact needs. A hiker simply tears open the top, pours in the right amount of boiling water, seals it up, and waits the prescribed amount of time. This approach works for some hikers. Others may find that prepackaged meals have some drawbacks. They are not always filling enough, produce a lot of trash that must be packed out, and are typically quite expensive (as much as $10 per meal). It is much more economical to create your own meals from your own dehydrated ingredients. For particularly long trips, you might carry the ingredients in bulk-ration form, but most ultralight trips are fairly short and will use a menu-planning approach. A common technique is "freezer-bag cooking." After designing a menu at home, the hiker will prepackage each meal in its own labeled, zippered-closure freezer bag, including all of the dry ingredients (spices, too). When it's time to eat, the hiker picks a bag, adds boiling water, and zips the bag shut until the contents are "cooked." Open the bag, add a little olive oil or Parmesan cheese, and eat. An advantage of this technique is that you'll pack only what will be eaten and no more, and it is certainly very easy to pre-pare each meal. The major disadvantage is that each meal produces a plastic bag that will become trash at home, not an Earth-friendly practice for a backcountry traveler. Look for innovative ways to combine the ease and weight of dehydrated cooking with the reusability of a covered, insulated eating bowl.

With exploration and experimentation, you will find many foods you can thrive on when traveling in ultralight style. A few favorites of long-distance and ultralight hikers are:

- Instant mashed potatoes. We especially like the type with dehydrated butter.

- Instant soup and gravy mixes. These can transform a bland meal into a real delight.

- Dry cheese sauce (the kind that would come in au gratin potatoes). It's flavorful, calorie-dense, and far lighter than actual cheese. Another option is dry, grated "shaker" cheese.

- Peanut butter and hazelnut-chocolate spread or other nut butters. Transfer these into zippered plastic bags.

- Salted mixed nuts. Excellent as trail foods.

- Chocolate. It offers about 140 calories per ounce, is delicious, and is mood-lifting on those rainy, long-mileage days.

- Dehydrated milk. A great source of protein and flavor. Look for whole milk rather than skim, as this will offer greater calorie density.

- Granola. Most granolas are fairly high-calorie foods, about 130 per ounce, with lots of flavor and texture.

- Meal bars. Different from simple granola bars, meal bars use whole foods and focus on well-rounded nutrition. Some weigh only an ounce but pack 225 calories. Slightly costly, these are excellent on-trail foods during the day.

- Couscous. This small, bead-shaped pasta cooks quickly in boiling water. For the quickest-cooking "real" pasta, choose angel hair, which often takes only two to three minutes of boiling. Another fast starch option is instant rice.

- Lentils. These nutritious legumes are not the highest in caloric value, but they are tasty and add excellent protein and soluble fiber to meals. Red lentils cook fastest, requiring about two minutes of boiling after a few minutes of soaking.

- Tortillas. These are the best premade bread option. They are durable, stay fresh, double as a plate or bowl, and can even clean the pot when the meal is over.

- Olive oil. At about 240 calories per ounce, olive oil is highly efficient and a nutritious source of healthy fats.

The final note about food is similar to that on shelters and sleeping bags. Consider how much you really need. Do you need to bring "emergency" food on that weekend trip? Nearly all routes will have bail-out options if food scarcity becomes dangerous, but how likely is that? How bad would it be to be slightly hungry in the

12

backcountry? A dedicated ultralight hiker will think very critically about all aspects of food preparation and bring just enough to arrive back at the trailhead healthy and hungry.

ULTRALIGHT KITCHEN GEAR

The rest of an ultralight kitchen outfit is quite small, usually just a stove, a spork, and a single large mug for both meals and hot drinks. Based on the food principles outlined above, most ultralight hikers will not be sautéing, grilling, or simmering for extended periods. They will prioritize a heat source that is extremely light, portable, and fuel-efficient. For these three reasons, liquid-fuel (white gas) stoves are less desirable for ultralight travel than are canister stoves or other options. The integrated pot-stove canister systems have the greatest fuel efficiency, but they also force the user to tote extra weight in the integrated heat exchanger and insulated bowl. These systems do not allow much heat adjustment, either. A lighter and more versatile option is a tiny canister stove. One of these (about 3 ounces), with one full, short can of liquefied natural gas (enough fuel for about 10 to 12 quarts of hot water), weighs a total of 10 or 11 ounces.

Other stove options that are less desirable for traditional backpacking are often the choice for ultralight hikers. For example, it's easy to build a homemade alcohol stove from a soda can. These weigh essentially nothing (less than 0.5 ounce) and are fueled by inexpensive denatured alcohol (see Figure 13 on page 62 for an example of an alcohol stove). Their major drawbacks are that the fuel, a liquid, is weighty, and the boil time for a quart is quite long. Another superlight option is a tiny foldup stove that burns solid fuel tablets. Originally designed for emergencies, these stoves are inexpensive and light. The fuel, however, is quite expensive per use, has an unpleasant odor when burning, and suffers from some of the same inefficiencies as alcohol stoves.

In the right weather and environment, ultralight hiking is where a biomass burning stove really shines. Wood burners eliminate the fuel load completely, except for perhaps a little plastic bag of tinder or sticks. Some models weigh 5 or 6 ounces and have boil times of six to eight minutes. These stoves can be used only where they do not violate regulations, and they require skill to operate effectively while leaving no trace. For longer ultralight trips in a suitable environment, though, these stoves can be the best choice for the dedicated long-distance minimalist.

➜ OTHER TIPS AND TRICKS FOR GOING LIGHT

There are many other ways to shave ounces from your pack, and you will slowly sort out which are worth the effort for you. Once you address the major items above, consider the assorted principles and ideas below:

- Repackage everything into the tiniest quantity and lightest container possible. For example, rather than bring an entire bottle of camping soap for a weekend, bring only a half-ounce in an appropriately sized container.

- Cook less for less fuel consumption. Once you get a feeling for how you eat on an ultralight trip, consider saving fuel by planning non-cooked meals. You can even experiment with an overnight that has an entirely cold menu.

- Carry less water (or none). If you know that your route will cross small streams every twenty minutes, don't carry 2 quarts of water. A partially filled 16-ounce water bottle will provide plenty of hydration for that distance.

- Use the lightest water-treatment option possible for the length of your trip. For many, this is chlorine dioxide drops, although a filter straw is another good option.

- Leave the stainless steel and polycarbonate water bottles at home. The lightest water bottle is the kind spring water comes in at the grocery store. The more durable ones will easily endure two weeks of constant use on the trail. Water bladders are also a lighter choice; roll them up when not in use, and they can even do double duty as a pillow, if you're careful!

- Minimize or eliminate the sleeping pad. Use a half-pad that reaches from the shoulders to the hip, and then use your other gear as a substitute for the bottom half. Some hikers will stuff their backpack with leaf litter for padding, and very skillful minimalists will simply pick durable surfaces that are also soft enough on which to sleep comfortably.

- Make every item serve multiple purposes, such as using your sleeping pad as the pack frame and leaving your bivy at home. You can use your backpack as a half-bivy if rain creeps into your tarp.

- Leave your hiking boots at home. When your load reaches the sub-20-pound range, low-cut day-hikers and even trail-running sneakers provide more than adequate support. Since these are comfortable, have smaller tread, and ventilate well, leave your camp shoes at home, too.

- Rainwear is negotiable. In warmer weather, consider leaving your rain pants at home. Lightweight hiking pants will feel more comfortable and dry very quickly. For the top, try out a poncho instead of a jacket and then someday try to make your poncho your sleeping shelter!

- Ounces add up. This is the truism of ultralighting. So, if you feel like it, cut off every one of those tags, flaps, and zipper pulls. Remove the strap from your fly-weight headlamp. Saw off that toothbrush handle (or switch to a fingertip brush) and dry your toothpaste into single-serving dots. Cut your comb in half—or just shave your head! Any of these steps will earn you a tiny fraction of an ounce in

12

weight saved, but together they could add up to half a pound or more. Once you begin to see your gear through the lightweight lens, there's no telling how far you will go.

Who should try an ultralight approach? Any hiker can pick and choose from all of these tips to reduce the weight that they carry without embracing ultralightism. Pursuing the goal of a minimalist pack, though, requires some specific qualities and skills. A successful ultralight mountain traveler will have experience-based knowledge to use in place of the things he or she leaves behind. Skills and judgment must grow as your pack shrinks. Rather than feeling like a burden, relying on fewer things can enhance your connection to nature. The best candidates for ultralighting will have a fairly high tolerance for the occasional discomfort. There are some ethical qualities, too. An ultralight approach requires a total commitment to the practice of Leave No Trace camping. In those instances where the ultralight approach leads to discomfort, you must resist the temptation to sleep on that sphagnum moss mound or to build a fire for extra heat. The ultralight traveler must also have a commitment to self-reliance. Again, with a thin margin of error, it is possible to get into an unexpected tight spot. Committing to an ultralight approach means managing the problems that might arise due to that approach without unnecessarily involving rescue personnel.

It is best to get started slowly with ultralight packing, one piece at a time. There are many great ideas to be found in books, on the internet, and by connecting with others passionate about this niche sport. While you develop your skills, knowledge, and gear, be patient with the process of whittling down your pack weight. Even with just a pound or two shaved, there is satisfaction in knowing you are saving wear and tear on your body while enjoying the journey even more.

➜ TRAIL ULTRARUNNING

Trail running is exactly what it sounds like: taking the practice of jogging onto hiking trails in forests and on mountains. It blends the fitness rewards of running with the experience of remote, natural places. Many define ultrarunning as running any distance longer than a traditional road marathon, 26.2 miles. For the purposes of this chapter, though, let's consider trail ultrarunning as covering any distance in the backcountry that a person might typically complete in longer than a day or two. For example, a reasonable weekend route might cover 24 miles, long enough to cross most of the large backcountry areas of the Northeast. Depending on the terrain, an ultrarunner might cover this distance with a small hydration pack over the course of four to eight hours, traveling between 3 and 8 MPH. This distance may sound extremely long to run, but most ultrarunners use a very slow running pace, preventing the accumulation of lactic acid in their muscles.

12

Trail ultrarunners carry only a small hydration pack with the lightest possible version of the ten essentials and just enough food for their route. Real trail ultrarunners are highly aware of what it would mean to twist an ankle, get caught out at night or in a storm, run out of food, or face other serious problems. They actively work to manage these risks throughout their runs. The margin for error is extremely thin—part of the sport's appeal—so mistakes and injuries are avoided at all cost. It is not an activity where the runner gambles on safety; it is the opposite. To succeed safely in this sport, a trail ultrarunner will be armed with knowledge.

1. **Know the route.** Before leaving, the runner must have a clear understanding of the distance, elevation gain and loss, areas of good and bad footing for running, escape routes, water spots, areas of exposure to potential bad weather, remote locations, and much more. The careful study of maps and trip reports prior to your departure is essential.

2. **Know yourself.** Runners should avoid unplanned problems by ensuring that they have the endurance to complete their route. They should know what food works for them, how much water they will need, and how likely it is they will cramp up halfway through a run.

3. **Know the weather.** The weather can make or break an ultrarun, so it is essential to make a careful study of the forecast and to be skilled at reading the weather. Difficult weather does not necessarily mean aborting a run, but it does mean bringing the required gear and mental attitude to continue to make forward progress in bad weather without injury.

4. **Know your partners.** Whoever you choose to run with in the backcountry, you should have a clear understanding of their fitness levels and trail-running experience. Novice or expert, elite runner or everyday Joe, it will help you have realistic expectations for the journey. Just as important, partners should know if they're a good interpersonal match. Many expeditions fail, get into danger, or are just plain miserable because the members do not mesh well. Keep the same from happening to your trail ultrarun.

For those who practice it, trail running is a joyful and satisfying activity, bringing physical health, connection to nature, and many adventures. Beyond these benefits, many hikers find that trail running gives them a smaller dose of the backcountry when they cannot spend an entire week on the trail. Trail runs are also practice opportunities for many of the same skills required for all backcountry travel. Every mile offers practice in map reading and route finding, keeping your footing, pace estimation, river crossing, weather reading, hydration, nutrition, foot care, and natural history. When ultrarunners return to the slower pace of a weeklong journey, they may find they have a new trove of backcountry knowledge to inform their slower mountain travels.

12

➜ FASTPACKING

Fastpacking is simply overnighting in the backcountry while traveling like an ultrarunner. It is the marriage of a minimalist packing approach and a focused effort on covering long miles at a running pace. Certainly a niche sport, fastpacking appeals to backcountry enthusiasts with a high level of overall fitness, high competency in skills such as navigation and judgment, and a dedication to monastic asceticism. Experienced fastpackers have completed nearly unbelievable journeys in minimal times.

Gear for fastpacking is similar to that used for the most minimal ultralight hiking. Footwear is always some version of a purpose-built running shoe. The most significant difference is in the pack. Contemporary fastpackers usually use vestlike packs that have substantial storage on the front of the body as well as the back. This even weight distribution minimizes pack sway and bounce, which rewards the runner with greater energy conservation and less abrasion. In addition to weight reduction, fastpackers also choose techniques that do not require much time on the trail. For example, rather than use a filter for water treatment, a fastpacker will choose chlorine dioxide tablets (or drops) that can be added to a water bladder so that purification takes place while the fastpacker is running. Fastpacking is high adventure. It carries the ideals of ultralight travel and the goals of trail ultrarunning to their extremes.

All of these variations of going light share the same core: challenging our beliefs about our needs and wants, and re-envisioning what is possible in backcountry travel. Even if going ultralight is not for you, there may be nuggets of wisdom you can borrow from these practices. Backpacking is not about enduring suffering. It is about celebrating being alive in the backcountry. Instead of asking, "Why go ultralight?" a better perspective might be to ask, "Why not lighten up?"

12

APPENDIX A

PERSONAL GEAR CHECKLIST

ITEM	NUMBER RECOMMENDED	HAVE	NEED
Personal Equipment			
Backpack	1		
Sleeping Bag	1		
Sleeping Bag Stuff Sack	1		
Sleeping Pad	1		
Small Stuff Sacks	as needed		
Garbage Bags	as needed		
Water Bottles	1 or 2		
Water Treatment Method	1		
Bowl	1		
Cup	1		
Spoon	1		
Headlamp	1		
Small Knife	1		
Compass	1		
Whistle	1		
Lighter	1		
Sunglasses	1		
Lip Balm	1		
Sunscreen	1		
Toothbrush	1		
Toothpaste	1		
Moist Towelettes	1		
Hand Sanitizer	1		
Prescribed Medications	as needed		
Personal Clothing			
Hiking Boots	1 pair		
Camp Shoes	1 pair		
Socks	2 to 3 pairs		

Note: Items in italics are part of the recommended ten essentials.

ITEM	NUMBER RECOMMENDED	HAVE	NEED
Personal Clothing continued			
Underwear	1 to 2 pair(s)		
Bras	1 to 2		
Shorts	1		
Long Pants (windproof, lightweight pile/fleece)	1		
Long Underwear Bottoms (medium weight)	1		
Long Underwear Top (lightweight)	1		
Long Underwear Top (expedition weight)	1		
Warm Jacket	1		
T-shirt	1		
Sun Hat	1		
Warm Hat	1		
Gloves	1		
Bandanas	2		
Rain Jacket	1		
Rain Pants	1		
Optional Personal Equipment and Clothing			
Waterproof Backpack Cover	1		
Bug Net	1		
Bivy	1		
Hydration Bag	1		
Cell Phone	1		
Emergency Device (Spot, InReach, etc.)	1		
Liner Socks	2 pairs		
Gaiters (short or long)	1		
Vest	1		
Wind Shirt	1		
Wind Pants	1		
Camera	1		
Camp Chair	1		
Small Camping Towel	1		

Note: Items in italics are part of the recommended ten essentials.

ITEM	NUMBER RECOMMENDED	HAVE	NEED
Camping Equipment			
Shelter (tent, tarp, or hammock system)	as needed		
Camping Stove	1		
Fuel Bottle/Canister	as needed		
Cooking Pot Kit	1		
Cooking Pot Grip	1		
Cooking Frypan	1		
Cooking Spoon	1		
Cooking Spatula	1		
Cooking Ladle or Small Measuring Cup	1		
Gray Water Strainer	1		
Liquid or Creamy Food Containers	1		
Food Stuff Sack	as needed		
Kitchen Hand Soap	1		
Water Bladder	1		
Bearproof Rope System	1		
Camping Trowel	1		
First-Aid Kit	1		
Gear Repair Kit	1		
Map	1		
Optional Camping Equipment			
Binoculars	1		
GPS	1		
Bear Canister	1		
Bearproof Electric Fence	1		
Fire Pan	1		
Camp Lantern	1		
Camping Saw	1		
Water Treatment: Pump	1		
Water Treatment: UV Light Pen	1		
Water Treatment: Gravity Feed	1		
Camping Shower Bag	1		

Note: Items in italics are part of the recommended ten essentials.

APPENDIX B

TRIP INFORMATION FORM

HIKING PARTY	
Name	Cell Phone #
Name	Cell Phone #
Name	Cell Phone #
Name	Cell Phone #
Name	Cell Phone #
Name	Cell Phone #

EXPEDITION DATES	
Departure Date	Estimated Departure Time from Trailhead
Return Date	Estimated Return Time to Trailhead
Late Party Emergency Call Time	

ROUTE	
Departure Trailhead	
Return Trailhead	
Route Description (indicate names of trails to take, from beginning to end)	
Campsite 1 Location	Date
Campsite 2 Location	Date
Campsite 3 Location	Date
Campsite 4 Location	Date
Campsite 5 Location	Date

ROUTE EVACUATION POINT(S)
Evac Point 1
Evac Point 2
Evac Point 3
Evac Point 4

VEHICLE(S) AT TRAILHEAD(S)		
Departure Trailhead		
Vehicle 1 – Type	Color	Plate #
Vehicle 2 – Type	Color	Plate #
Return Trailhead		
Vehicle 1 – Type	Color	Plate #
Vehicle 2 – Type	Color	Plate #

EMERGENCY
Search and Rescue Phone #:

APPENDIX C

EXPEDITION PREPARATION CHECKLIST

	ROUTE PLANNING
	Plan a route.
	Check public or private land regulations for this area.
	If needed: Contact public or private agencies to inquire about camping, parking, or other fees.
	If needed: Make campsite reservation.
	If needed: Get fire permit.
	If needed: Plan and organize vehicle shuttle or dropoff and pickup.
	If needed: Create waypoints for the route, campsites, trail heads, and evacuation points on your GPS.
	Check most recent weather forecast for your hiking area.
	Leave pertinent information (names and contact information for all group members; trailheads, campsites, evacuation points; phone number(s) of the cell phone(s) you will carry with you; vehicle type, color, and license plate; day/time of departure, day/time of return; phone number of the local search-and-rescue [SAR] agency) with someone reliable and ready to contact SAR authorities if you are not back or have not checked in according to your plan. See sample "Trip Information Form" in Appendix B.
	MENU PLANNING
	Prepare a questionnaire/survey to inquire about food allergies, dietary choices, preferences, and caloric needs for members of your group.
	Inventory your current food supplies and make a shopping list for the missing items.
	Repackage food for expedition.
	Plan and prepare dry and wet spice kits.
	EQUIPMENT AND TRANSPORTATION PLANNING
	Check camping stoves.
	Calculate stove fuel need.
	Fill stove fuel bottles.
	Check each shelter for damage or missing parts.
	Check batteries for each electronic device and headlamp.
	If needed: Waterproof boots, rain gear.
	Check first-aid kit(s).
	Check repair kit.
	Check to make sure you have the ten essentials.
	Organize meeting location and departure time for the trailhead.
	Plan driving route.
	Check road map or enter GPS coordinates for the trail

APPENDIX D
LIST OF CHARTS, TABLES, AND FIGURES

CHARTS AND TABLES

FIGURES

NOTES

INDEX

F

fastpacking, 286
fats, 216
field bearings, 96–97
find-me cross, 126–127
fire pans, 206–207
first-aid, 44, 147–154
 blisters, 150–152
 PRICE treatment, 153–154
 soft-tissue injuries, 149–150
 strains and sprains, 152–154
first-aid kit, 147–149
floods, 25
food hanging, 197–200
food (re)packaging, 230–231
food sharing, 139
foot placement, 111
footwear, 35–40, 44
fitting of, 38
 winter footwear, 241, 246
freeze-dried food, 220
fresh food, 222
frontcountry land ethic, 16
frostbite, 159–160

G

gaiters, 35, 40
gear. *See also* clothing
 backpacks, 68–74, 278–279
 child carriers, 256–258
 for cooking, 58–68, 242–243,
  279–282
 electronic devices, 48
 essential gear checklists, 7–8, 42–44,
  287–289
 first-aid kits, 147–149
 optional items, 46–48
 personal hygiene kit, 143
 repair kits, 44–46
 safety essentials, 42–43
 shelter, 49–52, 275–277

sleeping gear, 53–58, 277–278
 trekking poles, 112–113
 ultralight backpacking and, 275–279
 winter considerations, 239–244
getting lost, 124–127
gloves, 35
GPS units, 48, 97–102
group dynamics, 264–274
 basic stages of, 268–270
 expedition behavior, 270–272
 strategies for short trips, 270
 trip leadership and, 267–268
group sizes, 124

H

hammocks, 58
hand straps, 110
hand washing, 137
hats, 35
headlamps, 43
heat index, 18
heat-related injuries, 160–164
heatstroke/cramps/exhaustion, 161–162
heavyweight boots, 37
help requests, 178–179
hiker responsibility code, 1–2
hikeSafe card, 8
hiking. *See* trail skills
horses, 123
hot spots, 150–152
human waste disposal, 140–143
humidity, 19
hydration, 128–136, 160, 217
hygiene, 43, 137–143
 bathing, 137–138
 food sharing, 139
 hand washing, 137, 212
 human waste disposal, 140–143
 kitchen hygiene, 212–214
 personal hygiene, 138–139
 personal hygiene kit, 143
 toothpaste, 139–140

ABOUT THE AUTHORS

CHRISTIAN BISSON (Ed.D.) teaches Adventure Education at Plymouth State University. He has taught backpacking in higher education for the past twenty years and instructed in the outdoors for the past 30 years. He has been a NOLS instructor since 1990—specializing in wilderness backpacking expeditions for outdoor educators. Personally, he has hiked all over the United States, Canada, Australia, New Zealand, and Nepal. He lives in New Hampshire where he regularly hikes with his wife and children.

JAMIE HANNON (Ed.D.) lives with his family in the Baker River valley of New Hampshire. An Associate Professor of Adventure Education at Plymouth State University, he teaches a range of practical skills and theory courses. He has been leading outdoor experiential programming since 1981, and loves to run, hike and ski throughout the mountains of the Northeast

APPALACHIAN MOUNTAIN CLUB

At AMC, connecting you to the freedom and exhilaration of the outdoors is our calling. We help people of all ages and abilities to explore and develop a deep appreciation of the natural world.

AMC helps you get outdoors on your own, with family and friends, and through activities close to home and beyond. With chapters from Maine to Washington, D.C., including groups in Boston, New York City, and Philadelphia, you can enjoy activities like hiking, paddling, cycling, and skiing, and learn new outdoor skills. We offer advice, guidebooks, maps, and unique lodges and huts to inspire your next outing. You will also have the opportunity to support conservation advocacy and research, youth programming, and caring for 1,800 miles of trails.

We invite you to join us in the outdoors.

YOUR CONNECTION TO THE OUTDOORS

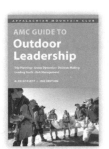

Guide to Outdoor Leadership, 2nd Edition

Edited by Alex Kosseff

Master the critical skills and concepts that every outdoor leader—professional or volunteer—needs to know: effective decision-making, group dynamics, and backcountry ethics; plus leading youth, risk management, and crisis management.

$19.95 • ISBN: 978-1-934028-41-4

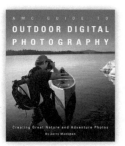

Guide to Outdoor Digital Photography

Jerry Monkman

Explore the process of outdoor photography—from packing and taking care of gear, to setting up and taking great shots, to processing photos in the digital darkroom. Full-color photographs pair with seasoned tips and advice to comprise a must-have guide for anyone interested in outdoor nature and adventure photography.

$19.95 • ISBN: 978-1-934028-50-6

Real Trail Meals

Ethan and Sarah Hipple

Coming in Spring 2017! Kick your backpacking menu up a notch with trail-tested recipes that give readers a buffet of lightweight and nutritious meals. Adopting a practical, easy-to-follow approach, the book features handy icons noting which recipes are vegetarian, vegan, gluten-free, kid-friendly, or require kitchen prep ahead of time. *AMC's Real Trail Meals* offers a diverse range of wholesome fare for outdoors adventurers of all levels.

$18.95 • ISBN: 978-1-62842-060-9

AMC's Winter Skills Manual

Michael Ackerman

Coming in Fall 2017! Outdoor lovers of any skill level can experience the thrill of winter, with the right tools and skills. This comprehensive guide will help you plan outdoor adventures of all kinds—hiking, camping, backpacking, and beyond—with practical advice emphasizing preparation, safety, outdoor stewardship, and fun. You'll learn when to go, what gear and clothing to bring, the essentials of staying warm and dry, how to navigate, and what to eat to stay energized in winter weather.

$18.95 • ISBN: 978-1-62842-051-7